YPSILANTI UNION SCHOOL.

Ground Plans at pp. 366 and 367.

SCHOOL FUNDS

AND

SCHOOL LAWS OF MICHIGAN:

WITH

NOTES AND FORMS.

TO WHICH ARE ADDED

ELEMENTS OF SCHOOL ARCHITECTURE,

AND THOUGHTS ON

WARMING AND VENTILATION, SCHOOL FURNITURE APPARATUS, ETC.

IRA MAYHEW,
SUPERINTENDENT OF PUBLIC INSTRUCTION.

LANSING:
Hosmer & Kerr, Printers to the State.
1858.

STATE OF MICHIGAN:

OFFICE OF PUBLIC INSTRUCTION,
Lansing, *Nov. 6th*, 1858.

Both the Constitution and the Statutes provide that the Superintendent shall have general supervision of Public Instruction in the State. It is especially provided that he shall prepare plans for the improvement and management of all Educational Funds, and for the better organization of our Educational System, when in his opinion the same are required.

The Statutes further provide for the publication of the School Laws, with Forms, Regulations, and Instructions, with a proper index. It is made by law the duty of the Superintendent to print with the volume of Laws and Instructions, a list of such books as he shall think best adapted to the use of Primary Schools, and a list of books suitable for Township Libraries, with such rules as he may think proper for the government of such Libraries.

The performance of these duties was undertaken by the undersigned, in the publication of a volume of Laws, Forms and Instructions, in the year 1847.

Five years later, in 1852, the Hon. F. W. Shearman, then Superintendent, published a volume on the "System of Public Instruction and Primary School Law of Michigan." Although a large edition of this volume was printed, it is now more than a year since we have been able to supply a single order for it, such as we have been accustomed to receive almost every week, from all parts of the State, but more especially from the new and more recently settled Counties and Townships of the northern portion of the State, that have never been furnished with it.

Numerous evils resulted from this state of things. The District and Township School Officers, anxious to discharge their duty, found it necessary, in seeking to comply with the requirements of the Statutes, to address to this Department more questions than the Superintendent was able to answer, even with assistance of a clerk. So pressing, however, was the necessity , and so great were the advantages anticipated from its circulation, that he resolved to undertake the preparation of the present volume.

With the amount of work which had accumulated upon his hands, the Superintendent found himself unable vigorously to prosecute this enterprise without calling to his aid additional assistance. But such were the necessities of the case, that he hesitated not as to the propriety of undertaking to meet them.

The greater part of the labor of preparing this volume, from the necessities of the case, has devolved upon the Superintendent, in person. In its performance, in connection with other labors that have necessarily engaged a portion of his time, he has, for months together, labored from fourteen to sixteen hours a day. Many times has he left the office after 10 o'clock in the evening, and returned to labor again by 5 o'clock the next morning.

From the magnitude of the interests involved, both Educational and Pecuniary, in the subject of our School Funds, and from the fact, that the history of these Funds, filling a space of over twenty years, has never been written, the Superintendent believes he could render the public no more acceptable service than to give, in a brief form, a statement of the manner in which our Educational Funds have been managed and applied, from the beginning. The facts, as ascertained by a most careful and laborious search of the Public Records, and from such other sources as were available, will be found, in part, as unexpected to the reader, as the whole will be interesting. Many important details are here placed upon record—

facts which in a few years would probably have been forever lost. It is believed that all the articles comprising Part I. of the volume, embracing a brief history of the several Institutions, will prove of permanent public interest and benefit, by preserving to future generations, important facts concerning the origin and early history of these Educational, Reformatory, and Humane Institutions, which, by the provisions of the Constitution, are included in the Educational Department of the State.

In collecting and collating the valuable information contained in the several articles on our School Funds, essential service has been performed by Mr. C. B. Stebbins, who has been employed in the Office for several months, and to whom the credit of their preparation is due.

The Statutes provide for the publication of the "School Laws." The Superintendent, therefore, in the publication of this volume has embraced all the Statutes relating to Primary Schools, the Normal School, the University, and the Agricultural College, together with the general provisions of law for the Incorporation of Institutions of Learning.

In the preparation of Notes on the School Law, in 1847, the undersigned consulted the extensive correspondence of the Office at that time, and answered in them, essentially, the several thousand questions that had been addressed to the Office during the three years he had then been connected with it. From the satisfaction which the publication of that volume produced, he has been led to pursue a similar course in the execution of the present undertaking. In the Notes to the School Law, as now published, more than ten thousand questions which have been addressed to this Office during the eight years of his connection with the administration of its affairs, are carefully answered, and referred to in the copious Index given.

These opinions are, many of them, upon subjects of great importance. School Inspectors, District Officers, and others who are charged with duties under the School Law, will find more than four-fifths—probably nine-tenths—of the questions most commonly asked, clearly and fully answered in the following pages. They will also find their attention called to many violations of the Laws, and of justice, which can be accounted for only from a lack of the information here given. The preparation and publication of this volume, it is hence believed, will greatly abridge the necessary correspondence of the Office in future, by enabling the officers and citizens of Townships and School Districts amicably to settle such questions as ordinarily arise, without the vexation, trouble and delay incident to what is often an *ex parte* correspondence.

The Supervisors of the State are charged with the assessment of a Mill Tax on the property of their respective Townships, which is collected by the Township Treasurers, and apportioned to the Districts by the Township Clerks. From a very extensive correspondence on this subject, the Superintendent has long been aware that great injustice has been done in the distribution of these moneys, and especially in the case of Fractional Districts. And he has recently been confirmed in this belief by communications from several intelligent Supervisors from different Counties of the State, who confidently express the opinion that the requirements of the statutes have not been understood, and have not hence been complied with, in the case of Fractional Districts, in one-tenth of the Townships in the State. The mode of correcting these abuses, and of answering the requirements of both law and justice, are clearly set forth under their appropriate heads in this volume.

The Superintendent has often been called upon to furnish Plans for Schoolhouses. In order to do this it has been necessary to refer to the edition of the School Law published in 1847, to the writer's work on Education, or to works not much circulated in the State. In this edition of the School Laws, several excellent plans of Schoolhouses have therefore been given. The drawings of three of these plans have been furnished by Messrs. Jordan & Anderson, of Detroit, without charge. The only expense that has been incurred for these plans, has been for wood engravings of a part of them. The cuts of the Ypsilanti Union Schoolhouse, one of which appears as a Frontispiece to this volume, were kindly loaned by the Officers of the District for the use here made of them.

Among the Plans for Schoolhouses here given, are three of the best ones in the State,* to wit: the Union Schoolhouse of Monroe, the Bishop Union Schoolhouse of Detroit, and the Ypsilanti Union Schoolhouse. These houses were erected, severally, at a cost of about $10,000 00, $20,000 00, and $40,000 00.

This volume has been richly illustrated with Cuts of the most approved School Furniture. But the use of the Engravings employed has been obtained without charge to the State. The same is likewise true of the illustrations of School Apparatus here given, although both have been obtained at considerable sacrifice on the part of the Superintendent.

As small an edition of this volume has been published as seemed compatible with its design, with the great amount of labor that has been bestowed upon its preparation, the permanent value of the information herein contained, and the length of time before another edition will probably be required. Every precaution has been taken to render the edition published most serviceable to the interests of Education in the State. It will be furnished only to officers requiring its use, and will be held by them officially and delivered to their successors in office.

IRA MAYHEW,

Superintendent of Public Instruction.

---

* For the purpose of furnishing the variety desirable in the Plans of Schoolhouses given in this volume, some of the finest School edifices in the State have not been embraced in the illustrations here given. These will generally be found referred to in connection with the Union School Reports in the Superintendent's Report for 1857.

CONTENTS.

PART I.

PART II.

PART III.

PART I.

THE PRIMARY SCHOOLS OF MICHIGAN, AND THEIR FUNDS;
THE STATE NORMAL SCHOOL, AND ITS FUNDS;
THE UNIVERSITY OF MICHIGAN, AND ITS FUNDS;
THE STATE AGRICULTURAL College;
HOUSE OF CORRECTION FOR JUVENILE OFFENDERS;
ASYLUM FOR THE DEAF AND DUMB, AND THE BLIND;
ASYLUM FOR THE INSANE.

THE PRIMARY SCHOOLS OF MICHIGAN, AND THEIR FUNDS.

The lands set apart for the support of Public Schools in Michigan, comprise one thirty-sixth part of the entire territory of the State. Each township is divided into thirty-six sections of one mile square; and section 16 (a central section) was by an ordinance of the old Congress, in 1785, sequestered "for the support of public schools."

The ordinance of 1787, for the government of the Northwestern Territory, declared that "SCHOOLS AND THE MEANS OF EDUCATION SHALL FOREVER BE ENCOURAGED."

An act of 1804, making provision for the sale of lands in the Indiana Territory, comprising the present States of Indiana, Illinois, Michigan and Wisconsin, expressly reserved from sale section 16 in every township, "for the support of Schools."

In 1805, the Territory of Michigan was organized, comprising the Lower Peninsula of the present State, and including what is now two tiers of towns on the north border of Indiana, and one tier on the north border of Ohio. In this act, all the rights secured by the above acts were confirmed.

In 1828, Congress placed the School lands under the supervision of the Territorial Governor and Council, to protect and lease, so as to make them productive. Nowhere, and at no time, was any disposition shown by the General Government to annul these grants; and the Ordinance of 1836, admitting the State of Michigan into the Union, declares:

"That section numbered 16 in every township of the public lands, and where such section has been sold, or otherwise disposed of, other lands equivalent thereto, and as contiguous as may be, shall be granted to the State for the use of Schools."

The first Territorial School Law was enacted in 1827; the year previous to the above action of Congress giving the Territorial authorities power to make use of the School lands. That law ordained that the citizens of any township having fifty householders, should provide themselves with a Schoolmaster of good morals, to teach the children to read and write. Any township with two hundred householders was required to have a Schoolmaster who could teach Latin, French and English. For any neglect, the towns were liable to a fine of $50 to $150. This law was repealed in 1833, and another enacted, providing for three Commissioners and *ten* Inspectors; and the management of the School lands was transferred from the Governor and Council, to them. This act also created an office of "Superintendent of Common Schools."

The original Constitution of the State declared that the proceeds of all lands granted by Congress for the support of Schools, should "remain a perpetual fund for that object." The same specifications are found in our present Constitution.

All the grants from Congress, and our first Constitution, speak of section 16 as sequestered for the support of "Schools," or "Public Schools." But by common consent, this has been construed to mean Common or Primary Schools; and upon this construction all our legislation has been based, for more than twenty years; and it is understood that no portion of the avails of section 16 can ever be used for any other purpose.

The original design of Congress seems to have been, to make the avails of section 16 accrue to the exclusive benefit of the township in which each section was situated. It is believed, however, that no act forbade the State to place the whole in a general fund for the benefit of all. By thus consolidating the fund, it can be managed with greater economy and safety, and made much more effectual in securing the greatest good to the greatest number. The wisdom of the act can hardly be doubted.

After these lands came under the control of the State Government, (not ownership, for the State holds them really only as a trustee,) it was a subject of debate whether they should be leased or sold. Discussion and reflection soon convinced most, if not all, that the State could not practicably make itself a landlord to thousands of tenants: and it was decided that the lands should be sold, and the avails invested in a common fund, the interest of which only, could be used.

The total amount of the sections numbered 16, in the State, was estimated at a little more than a million of acres; and the Legislature of 1837 passed a law for the sale of the school lands, under the direction of the Superintendent of Public Instruction—which office had been created by the Constitution. The Land Office, as a distinct department of the State Government, had not then been established.

By this law the Superintendent was authorized to sell University lands to the amount of half a million of dollars, and School lands to the amount of one and a half millions; the minimum price of the former being $20, and of the latter, $8 per acre. The reason of this difference in the price, was—the University lands were all *selected*, and supposed to be of the choicest quality and most eligible location; while the School lands, with slight exceptions, consisted of section 16 in each township, and of such quality as it might chance to be. The terms of payment were, one-fourth at the time of sale, and the remainder in annual instalments of five per cent., commencing in five years after the purchase, at seven per cent. interest. The sales were to be at auction, and the lands were subject to forfeiture for non-payment according to the terms.

The first sales were held on the 5th of July, 1837; and as might be supposed from the apparently easy terms of payment, and the extravagant ideas of the times, the sales were extensive, and at high prices. In a few months the sales amounted to over four hundred thousand dollars, at an average of about $12 per acre; one fourth of which was paid down. The result, if not anticipated, was natural; and of all the sales for the first four years, amounting to more than six hundred thousand dollars, about one-third of the lands were forfeited for non-payment of interest; notwithstanding the Legislature granted an extension of time in 1838, and again in 1839. Many of the purchasers found that their land was worth less than the amount yet unpaid, and preferred to lose the one-fourth already paid, to paying the balance; while others (and these had in many cases made improvements on the lands) found themselves without the *ability* to pay the interest when due.

In 1841 the minimum price of School lands was reduced to five dollars per acre. Relief to the previous purchasers was anticipated from an amendment to the law, which released them from payment of the principal at their pleasure; still subject to forfeiture for non-payment of interest. This applied also to future purchasers, after having paid one-fourth. But this did not meet the necessities of the case, or stop the forfeitures. Men had agreed to pay for their land more than it was worth; and they were hardly more willing, even when able, to pay interest on its fictitious value, than to pay the principal itself. Men who were in Michigan in 1838, '39 and '40, when it was often said, that the more land a man owned, the poorer he was, through inability to pay the increased taxes, will fully appreciate the embarrassment of that class of men.

In 1842 practical relief was granted them by a law for the appraisal of all School lands that had been sold for eight dollars or more, per acre, and all University lands that had been sold for $20 or more—the former to be appraised at not less than five dollars per acre, and the latter at not less than twelve; the difference between the appraised value and the original contract, to be credited upon the principal. Within ten months after the passage of the act, over twenty-six thousand acres, which originally sold for $287,930 87, had been appraised by the Associate Judge and Surveyor of the respective counties; and the aggregate price of the same was thereby reduced $101,-770 47. The reduction was from an average of eleven dollars per acre to about seven dollars—not far from thirty-six per cent. At the close of 1842, the account stood thus:

Sales to Dec. 1st, 1842,		$711,404 85
Forfeited,	$240,004 35	
Reduction by appraisal,	101,770 47	
Total reduction,		341,774 82
		$369,630 03
Forfeited lands re-sold, 10,202 acres,		76,769 54
Paid on lands previous to forfeiture,		28,233 16
Total supposed fund, Dec. 1st, 1842,		$474,632 73
The reductions on the above original sum, subsequently amounted to		114,823 32
Showing the reliable fund, Dec. 1st, 1842, to have been only		$359,809 41

Upon the situation of affairs as they appeared at the close of 1842, the Superintendent of Public Instruction, Hon. Franklin Sawyer, jr., said in his next Report: "The magnificent air-castles once supposed to be immovably founded upon the valuation standards of 1837, have proved baseless, and floated off like much of the capital of that day, to parts unknown." The reduction that afterward occurred, showed that the fund continued to "float off," till but about fifty per cent. remained.

Mr. Sawyer thought the law for reducing the price of the lands previously sold, unwise. It may have been so, taking into consideration only the question of raising the greatest amount of money; for even had the forfeitures, without the law, exceeded the reduction with it, the land would still have been "on hand" for future sale. But some would contend that a question was involved of higher moment than that of dollars and cents.

It had become evident that hundreds had contracted with the State to pay considerably more for their land than it was then worth, or would be, for many years. If an individual consents to a hard bargain with his fellow, public policy forbids the law to step in to shield him from the consequences of his folly. But in its own dealings, the State is under no such constraint; and when it found a hard bargain had been driven with its citizens, (and thus in a measure with itself,) though no wrong was intended, it was deemed by its legislative Representatives to be no more than just to remit a portion of the claim. Though the law cannot rectify a bad trade between individuals, the individuals themselves may, if they see fit; and both they and the State should be governed by equity, without the necessity of law. If a man sells his son a piece of property for twelve dollars—both supposing it to be worth that sum—upon which one-fourth is paid at the time of sale, and it afterward appears to the satisfaction of both that it was worth but six dollars and eighty-four cents, and beside this, that the son is unable to pay the full amount, what would be said of the father who should exact the full price, or the entire forfeiture of the property, with all that had been paid?

The State, in its legislative capacity, stands somewhat in the position of a father to its citizens; and though it were well to create as large a School Fund as was practicable, should it be done by legal extortion from its sons? There would have been more reason for so doing—or room for more apology—had the School lands been of comparatively a small amount, like the University lands; but, with more than a million of acres upon which to raise a fund, was it at all needful, or would it redound to the honor of the State, to have exacted the pound of flesh, because it was written in the bond?

The years 1841 and 1842 constitute a sort of crisis in educational affairs. The commencement of 1841 found the School lands that had been sold, being fast forfeited to the State, with the prospect of a large part of the noble fund, supposed to be accumulated, becoming thus extinct. By the law above referred to, the forfeitures were measurably stopped, and by the close of 1842, new foundations were laid, if not as broad as the former, at least more secure.

The Reports for 1842 showed—

The number of school districts,..................	2,312
Children between 5 and 17 years of age,.........	64,800
Apportionment of interest of the Primary School Fund,................................	$15,000 00
Raised by towns and districts,...............	71,655 87
Total amount expended for Schools in 1842,.	$86,655 87

At that time, the towns could vote annually such tax as they pleased, not exceeding one dollar per scholar, and the Supervisors were *required* to assess to each town an additional sum equal to its apportionment of the public money.

In 1843 the State Land Office was established, and the control of the University and School lands was transferred from the Superintendent of Public Instruction to that department. Thus had the custody of these lands been seeking a home, and till now, finding none. First, it was given to the Governor and Council of the Territory; by them transferred to Commissioners; then assigned to the Superintendent of Public Instruction; but now—where it should have been, on the organization of the State government—to a State Land Office.

The early Legislation of our State shows that the men who laid the foundations of our institutions entertained enlarged views—often so broad as to appear extravagant—and yet, time has shown them to be so, only in their expecting too speedy results. But this error, while it was the cause of many failures with individuals, and much embarrassment to the State, had a tendency to hasten the results they had expected too soon.

Five years after the complete organization of our State government—five years of defeated hopes, and dissipation of air built castles—when bankruptcy had prostrated thousands who thought themselves rich—when total failure as a State enterprise, was stamped upon our magnificent plan of Internal Improvements, and partial failure and great embarrassment were attendant upon our Educational Institutions, we see in imagination, a prophet standing up in the midst of a disappointed and discouraged people, proclaiming that:

In fifteen years our strap railroads shall be completed by private enterprise, with heavy rail, and yield to the State an annual income of over $100,000;

A canal shall be built without expense to the State, by which large vessels may sail into Lake Superior, and a mining business commenced, the ultimate magnitude of which, a prophet's vision may not safely limit;

The taxable property of the State, from $29,000,000, shall be assessed at $150,000,000; our annual specific taxes, from $4,200, shall increase to $133,000; our population, from 250,000, shall become nearly 800,000; our School children, from 65,000, shall number over 200,000; the amount raised annually from all sources, for Primary Schools, from $86,000, shall swell to more than $600,000; our School Fund, from $359,820, shall be, $1,613,000; our University Fund, from $137,000, shall be $503,000; there shall be a Normal School with 500 pupils and a fund of $73,000; our University, with 25 students and 4 Professors, shall have 450 students and 18 Professors;

Nearly one hundred thousand dollars shall have been expended in establishing an Agricultural College, whose one hundred students would be doubled, but for want of accommodations;

There shall be a House of Correction for juvenile offenders, which united humanity will regard as the school of schools for the prevention of crime, and the salvation of youthful offenders;

There shall be an Asylum for the deaf and dumb, and the blind, whose eminent success will bear witness to the liberal humanity of the State; and—

An Asylum for the insane shall be founded, on a scale commensurate with the woes of that unfortunate class of our fellow-beings.

Had such a prophecy been made in 1842, the prophet would hardly have found more believers—inclined though the people were, to expect great things—than did the prophets of ancient days; yet, in half of one generation of time, has all come to pass!

Advancing another period of five years—from 1842 to 1847—we find that the entire sum expended in the latter year for Common Schools, was, ... $130,531 75
Interest on the School Fund, ... 31,250 54
Mill-tax, ... 7,368 75
Total School Fund, ... $573,931 49
Children between the ages of 4 and 18, ... 108,130
Volumes in township libraries, ... 43,926

The legal sources of the means for the support of Schools at that time, were as follows:

1st. The interest of the School Fund.

2nd. A tax of one mill upon the dollar of all taxable property in the State.

3rd. The voters in any township might, at their annual meeting, vote a tax not exceeding fifty cents for every scholar between four and eighteen years of age.

4th. Districts might vote a district tax for building school-houses, not exceeding two hundred dollars in one year, where there were not more than thirty scholars; and not exceeding three hundred dollars, where there were not more than fifty scholars. Districts might vote any "necessary" tax for repairs and furnishing the house, and for the payment of legal debts. Districts with more than fifty scholars, could vote a tax of twenty dollars for the purchase of globes, maps, &c.

5th. The rate-bill.

6th. The proceeds of all fines for any breach of the penal laws in the several counties, were to be distributed to the townships therein, for the benefit of libraries.

It was found that in many instances the laws were not complied with by township officers. The proceeds of fines did not always find their way into the fund for libraries, and in many cases Supervisors refused to assess the "mill-tax." The Superintendent of Public Instruction, Hon. Ira Mayhew, in 1845, procured the publication of the law, and these defects were in general remedied. Of 90,000 children in 1845, 20,756 did not attend school.

During the previous years, a want of well qualified teachers was greatly felt; not so much that there were not enough who were qualified according to former standards, but the necessity was perceived of raising the standard of qualification; and by none more so, probably, than by the teachers themselves. Several local Educational Societies were formed; but these, while they served to awaken in the minds of the people an interest on the subject of education, were little adapted to the purpose of qualifying teachers. The Superintendent of Public Instruction devoted a large portion of the year, 1846, to personal effort with the people. He visited every organized county in the State, save four, organizing societies, and arousing the minds of the masses, as a necessary preliminary to a successful effort for organizations of the teachers for their own improvement.

The first society of this kind was the "Lenawee County Teachers' Association." This Society is still in existence.

The first "Teachers' Institute," organized under that name, was in Jackson County.

The Superintendent hoped much from the organization of Teachers' Institutes; and strongly recommended aid from the Legislature in their behalf, as being better adapted to the immediate wants of education than a State Normal School would be; though (to quote from his Report,) he "deemed a Normal School indispensable to the perfection of any system of National Education." The State Legislatures, however, saw fit to leave the enterprise to the teachers themselves, to bear the expense, till after the Normal School was established.

The Superintendent also, in 1845, '46 and '47, devoted much time to the subject of Union Schools, and in persuading the people of the great advantage which might be derived therefrom. It required much persuasion, argument, and information, at first, to interest the people in the plan of Union Schools, which has since become so prominent a feature in our Primary School System.

Making another advance of five years from the period last considered, to 1852, we find the legal provisions for the support of Schools slightly changed, as follows:

1st. The interest of the School Fund.

2d. A tax of *two* mills on the dollar. (This was changed from *one* to *two* mills in 1851, and changed back again to one mill in 1853.)

3d. The districts (not the towns, as before,) might vote a tax of one dollar per scholar.

4th. The same as in 1847, above.

5th. The rate bill.

6th. The proceeds of fines, &c.

The whole amount raised in the State for the support of Schools, in 1852, was about.................. $200,000 00
Interest of the School Fund,................. 53,881 92
Two mill tax,............................ 30,009 91
Number of Children,................150,531
Volumes in Libraries,........... 100,161
School Fund,............................ 864,476 10
Sales in 1852,............................ 52,709 89

The sales in this year were about five thousand dollars less than the average for the previous eight years; but in 1853 they increased four fold; and in 1854 nearly six fold; amounting in the two years to $519,801 88.

This was about equal to all the sales of previous years since the lands were offered, excepting the first year; and the sales from 1853 to 1857, inclusive, were nearly equal to all previous sales from the beginning.

From these extensive sales, the amount of interest rapidly increased, till from thirty-four cents per scholar, in 1851, it reached fifty-three cents in 1857; but in the latter year the sales amounted to but a little more than forty thousand dollars—not keeping pace with the increase of population—and the amount, the present year, 1858, is but fifty cents per scholar. The sale of the lands depends much upon the financial prosperity of the State; and must of necessity show a wide difference between years of commercial activity, like 1853 and '54, and a year of revulsion, like 1857. The increase of population is more uniform, and less affected by these causes.

The entire amount expended in support of Primary Schools in 1857, was $636,000 00. This shows a gratifying increase of interest in the public mind in behalf of Public Education; and the more so, inasmuch as about two-thirds of the whole amount was raised by the voluntary self-taxation of the people, in addition to more than one hundred thousand dollars they were required to raise by law. Yet, large as this sum seems in the aggregate, it is probably not more than *ninety cents* for each inhabitant of the State. But it presents, nevertheless, a gratifying contrast with 1842, when the entire amount was but about *thirty-five* cents to each one of our population.

The money so liberally expended in the erection of School-houses by voluntary taxation, speaks well for the intelligence and broad views of the people of Michigan. More than one hundred and forty thousand dollars was raised for that object alone, in 1857. A most gratifying feature of this subject is the fact, that men of wealth are generally quite as ready to tax their own property for the erection of commodious and elegant School-houses, and for the support of the ablest teachers who can be obtained, as are the men of moderate means; or as those who have no property, are to tax those who have. Indeed, it is probably true generally, that the poor, whose tax would be very little or nothing, have been the strongest opposers of Union Schools, on the ground of anticipated expense. While we thus behold our rich men taxing themselves to build School houses, at an expense of five thousand to forty thousand dollars, with the interest that must consequently be felt in making the schools all they should be, for the proper development of the intellectual and moral faculties of the rising generation, we need not greatly fear for the perpetuity of our free institutions. We may reasonably hope that such a people can never be made the dupes of political demagogues, or social empirics.

The following table exhibits the sales of land, and interest, for the several years since 1843, after deducting forfeitures:

Year.	Acres.	Amount.	Interest.
To Nov. 30, 1843...	58,552.78	$401,425 39	
" " 1844...	7,454.66	38,860 60	$28,099 77
" " 1845...	3,009.93	6,974 17	30,820 01
" " 1846...	6,879.63	35,169 70	31,308 20
" " 1847...	18,350.32	91,501 63	33,770 08
" " 1848...	15,026.84	68,763 83	40,175 19
" " 1849...	8,846.66	38,509 74	44,988 65
" " 1850...	10,978.79	47,111 26	47,684 33
" " 1851...	19,189.95	83,449 89	50,982 11
" " 1852,..	12,602.59	52,709 89	56,823 60
" " 1853...	48,850.04	225,160 16	60,513 29
" " 1854...	68,520.46	294,641 72	76,274 50
" " 1855...	27,194.92	109,366 99	96,899 42
" " 1856...	19,192.96	79,192 34	104,555 11
" " 1857...	9,122.59	40,597 27	110,098 57
	333,773.12	$1,613,434 63	

The capitol at Lansing was located on the School section; no part of which had at that time been sold. The section was divided into lots, reserving about forty-five acres for State, Church, and local School purposes.

The remainder has all been sold—principally prior to 1855—for the aggregate sum of $90,640 75, averaging $152 33 per acre. It is safe to estimate the present value of these lots, as now held by their owners—and about one-half of which were sold no longer ago than in 1852 and 1853—at half a million dollars.

The following table shows the comparative progress of Primary Schools, at periods of five years from November 30, 1837:

	1842.	1847.	1852.	1857.
Primary School Fund,....................	$359,810 00	$573,931 49	$864,476 10	$1,613,434 63
Total amount expended,..................	86,000 00	130,531 75	200,000 00	636,071 49
Number of Children,.....................	65,000	108,130	150,531	215,928
Volumes in Libraries,...................		43,926	100,161	168,179

An act was passed in 1849, establishing a State Normal

School, for the specific purpose of qualifying teachers. This institution is now producing most gratifying results.*

In 1855, the Legislature appropriated funds not exceeding eighteen hundred dollars per annum, for sustaining Teachers' Institutes; to be held at the discretion, and under the direction of the Superintendent of Public Instruction. These have been held from time to time, as circumstances and other duties of the Superintendent would admit, with highly beneficial results.†

An examination of the records of the management of the School Funds, for the first four years, shows the greatest confusion, contradiction, and deficiency. The Reports appear ambiguous and imperfect; and the School and University Funds are at times so united that it is impossible to separate them. Until the establishment of the Land Office in 1843, there appears to have been but little system in keeping the accounts, or it was so imperfect that the Reports conveyed no intelligent understanding of the situation of the Funds. The first Report from the Commissioner of the Land Office, at the close of the fiscal year 1843, says:

"Upon an examination of the books transferred to this office, it was soon perceived that their keeping was deficient in system, and incapable of affording exact and perfect information of the business transactions of the department."

This "exact information" must probably be reckoned with the lost arts; though the latter may be recovered, while the former never will. It is, therefore, impossible to go back to the commencement, and make a table of the receipts and expenditures of the Funds. The *details* of the first four or five years cannot be obtained and arranged so as to give a clear exhibit of the subject. The earliest

* See article under head of "State Normal School," following.

† See Report of Superintendent of Public Instruction, recently published, page 479, and on.

specific statement of affairs is found in a Report of the Superintendent of Public Instruction, December 1st, 1842. From the most thorough examination he was able to make, of the subject, he arrived at the following aggregate result, as it appeared at that date:

Receipts on account of principal,............		$121,332 73
Amount loaned,..................	$84,820 00	
Amount in the treasury,...........	30,533 50	
		115,353 59
Deficiency unaccounted for,...........		$5,979 14
Received on account of interest,..............		$92,127 05
School moneys apportioned,.........	$69,141 80	
Expenses,........................	10,502 74	
In hands of agents,................	1,777 72	
Uncurrent funds,...................	958 00	
		82,380 26
Deficiency unaccounted for,............		$9,746 79
" on principal, above,.........		5,979 14
Total deficiency in principal and interest,......		$15,725 93

The deficiency was really more than this; as the "expenses" (and perhaps the "uncurrent funds") were partly on account of the University Fund, (probably one-fourth,) but the Report does not state how much; and we here let the deficiency in the School Fund stand as above, instead of $20,000 00, as it probably was.

The following tables have been prepared with some days of labor in searching and comparing the official Reports and records, and are believed to be as correct an exhibit of receipts and expenditures as can be obtained. If any person wishes to search for further information, he will truly find it a "search for knowledge under difficulties."

Previous to 1843, the confusion and contradictions in the

records are such, that an attempt to go back of that time for details was given up in despair. The tables therefore, commence with the accounts as reported in the aggregate by the Superintendent of Public Instruction, up to November 30th, 1842. The first table shows the receipts to the School fund, as reported by the Superintendent of Public Instruction and the Commissioner of the Land Office, and the receipts and amount of fund loaned to the State, according to the reports of the Treasurer. The amount loaned to the State, is given from 1839. The amount loaned to counties and to individuals, up to 1842, (and nothing has been thus loaned since that time,) was $84,-820 00. This deducted from the amount received, according to the Treasurer's Reports, leaves $868 43 more in the hands of the State than is reported by the Treasurer.

Year.	Receipts for principal per Land office Reports.	Receipts for principal, per Treasurer's Reports.	Amount in the hands of the State.	Expenses.
1839			$ 4,756 40	
1840			3,315 64	
1841			12,076 27	
1842	$121,332 73	$115,353 59	29,665 16	
1843	14,898 63	14,125 60	41,245 23	$2,545 53
1844	19,766 04	19,784 44	54,799 00	6,230 89
1845	20,130 63	20,028 20	71,827 20	3,000 00
1846	19,863 35	20,226 43	92,053 63	
1847	37,933 19	37,826 98	129,880 61	
1848	27,651 19	27,450 73	157,331 34	
1849	17,959 72	17,918 72	175,250 06	
1850	22,499 90	22,462 90	197,711 96	
1851	41,166 77	40,540 22	238,252 18	
1852	32,623 76	32,399 81	270,611 57	40 42
1853	107,417 20	107,417 20	378,028 77	
1854	116,991 85	116,991 85	494,525 04	495 58
1855	62,228 45	62,228 45	555,994 82	758 67
1756	49,060 61	49,060 61	604,855 43	200 00
1857	26,203 82	26,203 82	630,742 94	316 31
	$737,721 84	$730,019 55		$13,587 40

Thus, according to the Land Office Reports, the receipts have been,.................................$737,721 84

Of which there was loaned,....	$84,820 00	
Expenses paid,................	13,587 40	
Now in the Treasury,.........	630,742 94	
		729,150 34
Apparent deficiency,.................		$8,571 50

Of the $84,820 00 loaned, $30,820 00 has been paid, and that amount is consequently reckoned twice in the accounts, and makes the aggregate footings so much more than the actual proceeds from the lands.

Of the $54,000 00 still on loan, $11,900 00, which was loaned to individuals, is considered worthless—the securities being insufficient, and no interest having been paid for many years. The remainder is in the hands of several counties and is considered safe.

The present entire Primary School Fund is situated as follows:

Loaned to the State,........................	$630,742 94
" to Counties,........................	42,100 00
" to individuals, (worthless,)...........	11,900 00
Due from about 7,000 purchasers, payable at their pleasure,.........................	928,691 69
Total Primary School Funds,...........	$1,613,434 63

The following table shows the receipts for interest, according to the Land Office Reports, and the expenditures, exclusive of the interest upon the funds loaned to the State, commencing with the aggregates at the close of 1842. The first aggregate of expenditures includes, as near as can be estimated, some $4,000, which should be in the University Fund account:

Year.	Receipts.	Expenditures.
To Dec. 1st, 1842.	$ 92,127 05	$ 82,380 26
" " 1843.	19,567 33	20,878 26
" " 1844.	21,218 06	28,617 40
" " 1845.	26,831 39	22,810 97
" " 1846.	23,543 33	23,209 52
" " 1847.	25,653 91	31,274 74
" " 1848.	27,147 84	12,133 42
" " 1849.	31,500 20	28,831 03
" " 1850.	33,990 31	30,903 37
" " 1851.	36,301 53	33,987 18
" " 1852.	55,785 19	42,340 00
" " 1853.	43,664 65	32,984 43
" " 1854.	44,320 13	43,394 32
" " 1855.	57,281 87	47,237 18
" " 1856.	62,310 56	59,999 61
" " 1857.	66,667 65	64,855 38
	$667,931 00	$605,837 07

In the Treasury, Nov. 30, 1857,.............	$ 36,430 78
	$642,267 85
	667,931 00
Apparent Deficiency in Interest,...........	$25,663 15
" " in Principal, above,....	8,571 50
Total Deficiency in Principal and Interest,.	$34,234 65

The School lands in the State are estimated at 1,148,160 acres. Of this amount, 704,000 acres are in the lower peninsula, and 444,160 in the upper. Of all this, 334,413 acres were disposed of, to Nov. 30th, 1857. Estimating the part yet unsold, at four dollars per acre, (and it is believed it will average that sum,) or one dollar less than the present minimum price, we have a fund of $4,868,022. But call it $4,000,000; which must, in the worst possible event, be below the ultimate result, and it gives a yearly fund for distribution, of $280,000. This will be a rich fund, to be realized in the future; but ere one-half of the present lands are sold, Michigan will have a population of two millions, with five to six hundred thousand scholars; and it is probable that the population will ever hereafter increase quite as rapidly as the School Fund. This being the case, it cannot be expected that the Primary School Fund apportionment will ever be much, if any, greater per scholar than at the present time. Something may be gained, however, in an economical view, as the population becomes more dense, by the increased size of schools; thus reducing the expense of teaching per scholar.

But the School lands are not the only source of revenue upon which our Schools, are expected ultimately to rely. The State has some five and a half million acres of "Swamp land," the present minimum price of which is $1 25 per acre. By the law of 1858, one-half of the proceeds of these lands goes into the Primary School Fund. If we estimate one-half of these lands as valueless—which is probably not the case—the other half, at $1 25 per acre, will amount to about three and a half millions; a moiety of which, added to the School Fund, will be equal to the entire Fund at the present time. But this is a matter subject to the uncertainty of legislation; and some future Legislature may repeal or amend the present law, and prevent any further additions to the School Fund from this source; though the proceeds accruing up to the time of such change, cannot be constitutionally diverted therefrom.

Another important prospective source of revenue to Primary Schools, is found in the Constitutional provision that all specific taxes, (except those from the Mining Companies of the Upper Peninsula,) which are now applied to the State indebtedness, shall, when those debts are extinguished, be appropiated to the support of Primary Schools. These taxes (paid by the railroad companies, banks, &c.,) already amount to about $130,000 per annum, and are constantly increasing. Were it not for the State indebtedness, the apportionment of the public money per scholar, would now be over one dollar, instead of fifty cents.

Thus it appears that the yearly income of the Primary School Fund—should there be no change in the disposition of the proceeds of the Swamp lands—will eventually reach five or six hundred thousand dollars. This result is remote, but toward it, time is tending.

But whatever the actual amount of the School Fund may hereafter be, it is certain that it will be sufficient at all times, to afford essential aid in the education of the young.

But it might be asked, what is the real benefit of a School Fund, great or small? Money of whatever amount, can never by its own power, teach a child its letters, erect a School-house, or employ a teacher. Its efficacy is not in itself, but in the hearts of the people; as the power of the axe is in the muscles of the woodman. A thousand axes can never bring down the towering oak until their possessor wills that the tree shall fall, and puts his own hand to the work as the active power. So will a School Fund, however large, be valueless for any great results, unless the people *will* that it shall do its appropriate work. And they cannot thus WILL, unless they have a deep sense of the importance of the subject, that shall create a *personal interest.* A large fund of money will prove of little use, unless, underlying it, is found a great fund of warm human hearts, throbbing with patriotism and virtue, and an active desire to prepare the youth of the land worthily to fill their places when they shall have shuffled off this mortal coil. Then, indeed, a large fund becomes a great blessing; endowed with moral power; and money in changed into knowledge—sordid gold into living thought!

That a large School Fund *begets* indifference in the minds of the people, is an assumption sometimes made, but which is yet to be proved. It is not proved by the fact that such indifference may somewhere have existed. Such a state of the public mind must be sought for, in some cause back of this. Men who are at all impressed with a sense of their responsibilities as rational, immortal beings, cannot under any circumstances be indifferent to the intellectual and moral training of the young. Ignorance, moral depravity, and blind selfishness in the man, alone can render him uninterested in a work so important, so essential to the prosperity of our country and the good of our race. Find a community where no interest in education is felt, and a corresponding indifference will be found to all subjects which rise above mere physical considerations. If such a community is furnished with an educational fund, and there is not found moral sense enough to make any good use of it, what tendency would the withdrawal of it have to awaken an interest? If these things are done in the green tree, what shall be done in the dry?

On the other hand, the citizens of a community where exists a high moral tone, where the newspaper of established character is found in almost every house, and the claims of a Supreme Being are recognized, will not fail to educate their youth, with the same or a higher standard of excellence in view, though they enjoy the aid of no public funds. This is illustrated in no small degree, in the State of Michigan at the present time, in the fact that during the past year, with a public fund of about one hundred thousand dollars, the people have taxed themselves over *five hundred thousand* dollars more! The same spirit, amounting almost to enthusiasm, is shown in the regard felt by the people for all our institutions of learning—in the numerous private schools and seminaries, the Normal School, the State University, the Agricultural College, as well as the Asylums for the Deaf and Dumb, and the Blind, and the Insane, and that no less noble Asylum, the House of Correction for Juvenile Offenders. To build up these institutions, the people are liberally taxing themselves to a large amonnt—regarding them, both as the loftiest monuments they can erect of commendable State pride, and as the highest demands of an enlightened humanity, true patriotism and social good.

Our School Fund should be prized as a rich inheritance to ourselves and our posterity; but still more ought we to appreciate and rejoice in that high-toned public sentiment which determines that Education shall be universal—that this Fund shall never be perverted from its original design and greatest possible influence, and that the noble sentiment of our fathers, whose hands gave form to our institutions, that "Religion, Morality, and Knowledge, being necessary to good government and the happiness of mankind, SCHOOLS and the means of EDUCATION shall *forever* be encouraged," shall never be repealed or disregarded.

THE STATE NORMAL SCHOOL, AND ITS FUNDS.

All the legislation of our State, from the commencement, upon educational affairs, seems to have contemplated, not only the necessary pecuniary aid for Primary Schools, but the highest grade of talent and aptitude in their vocation, that could be secured in teachers. This in our legislation was but the reflection of sentiment manifested by the active friends of Popular Education, among whom the teachers themselves stood foremost. Instead of leaving the district officers, who are usually elected more with reference to their business activity and financial skill, than to their education, to judge of the qualifications of the teachers they employ, as has been, and perhaps still is done in some States, our State has made provision for the election of officers who are expected to be chosen for their ability to judge of a teacher's qualifications, to examine every person proposing to teach a Primary School, and without whose certificate of fitness, no teacher can be employed, on pain of the district's being deprived of its proportion of the public funds.

This was well calculated to stimulate teachers to a desire to excel, and Associations and Institutes were organized in many places by them, for the purpose of improvement in their profession. With these organizations the Superintendent of Public Instruction gave a hearty co-operation, and recommended legislative aid in their behalf; which, however, was not granted until a recent date. These Associations were, perhaps, more than any other cause, the means of concentrating public opinion upon the subject of a State Normal School; showing as they did, the necessity of such an institution, and to some extent, what might be expected from it.

The State Normal School was established by the Legislature in 1849; and its main design is to be a School for Teachers; where they may receive instruction peculiarly adapted to their profession; though the law contains some rhetorical flourishes about giving "instruction in the mechanic arts, and in the arts of husbandry, and agricultural chemistry, in the fundamental laws of the United States, and in what regards the rights and duties of citizens." The Normal School is to the Primary Schools, what Theological Seminaries are to the Churches—it is simply the Teacher's College, and a school *for professional training.*

The law creating the Normal School of Michigan placed it under the direction of a Board of Education, consisting of three persons, to be appointed by the Governor, and approved by the Senate; one of which was to retire from office each year, by one new appointment being made in each year. The Legislature of 1850, made the Lieutenant Governor, the State Treasurer, and the Superintendent of Public Instruction, *ex-officio* members of the Board. The Superintendent was made the Secretary of the Board, the Treasurer its Treasurer, and it was to elect its own President.

All this, however, was changed by the Constitution of the same year, which provides for a Board of three members, elected by the people, to hold their office for six years—one being elected at each biennial election. The Superintendent is *ex-officio* a member, and Secretary of the Board.

Ten sections of Salt Spring lands were appropriated to meet the expense of buildings, apparatus, &c., to be denominated the "Normal School Building Fund."

The Salt Spring lands consisted of seventy-two sections,

granted by Congress to the State, in connection with the salt springs, which it was then hoped would become a source of wealth to the State in the production of salt.

In appropriating the ten sections for the necessary improvements to put the Normal School in operation, they were not offered for sale for cash. But all labor and materials were to be paid for in warrants on the Commissioner of the Land Office—which warrants alone could be received for the land.

In addition to the above, fifteen sections of Salt Spring lands were appropriated, subject to sale, for an Endowment, which was made inalienable for the support of the School. The proceeds were to be placed in the State treasury, like the other Trust Funds, and upon which the State was to pay six per cent., annually. This interest, with that received on unpaid balances from purchasers, was to constitute the "Normal School Endowment Fund."

The Board of Education held its first meeting in May, 1849. The location of the School became a subject of interest to the citizens of different localities, and at the next meeting of the Board in September, propositions were received from the citizens of Ypsilanti, Jackson, Marshall, Gull Prairie, and Niles; each tendering to the State a site for the buildings, together with large subscriptions in money. Upon a full comparison of these liberal offers, and upon a general view of the subject, the Board decided to locate the institution at Ypsilanti, upon the following proposition of the citizens of that place:

They were to give a suitable plat of ground for a site for the buildings, a cash subscription of $13,500 to be paid, one-third in September, 1850, and the remainder in one and two years thereafter, the use of temporary buildings for the Normal and Model Schools until suitable buildings could be erected, and the payment of the salary of the teacher of the Model School for five years.

The site consisted of four acres, beautifully situated

upon the high grounds on the west border of the village—now city—of Ypsilanti.

By an act of the Legislature of 1850, the ten sections of land appropriated for a building fund were consolidated with the other fifteen sections, to be denominated the Normal School Endowment Fund, and made inalienable, except so much of the same, not exceeding ten thousand dollars, as might be required to complete the buildings, purchase necessary books, apparatus, &c., after exhausting the amount of donations.

The minimum price of the lands was fixed at four dollars per acre; but the Commissioner of the Land Office was required to procure an appraisal, below which none could be sold. An appraisal was made in 1850. A large portion was appraised below the minimum price. Some were valued as low as $1 50 per acre. These, of course, must remain unsold until they rose in value, or till the minimum price should be reduced.

In the same year, the Board added four acres more of land to the site for the buildings, and contracted for their erection for the sum of $15,200—of which $12,000 was to be paid by the citizens of Ypsilanti.

An act was passed by the Legislature of 1853, appropriating to the Endowment Fund the moneys arising from the Swamp Lands previously sold by the General Government, not exceeding $30,000. From this the School received no benefit.

After the grant of the Swamp Lands to the State, it was supposed that the General Government had disposed of enough to reach the above amount; and that, as the lands had been granted to the State, the money would be refunded. The amount of lands thus sold was afterward found to be comparatively small, and no money has ever been received by the State on their account.

The Legislature of 1853 also appropriated $2,000, annually, for two years, from the State treasury, to the Endowment Fund, and $3,000 to the same, to be applied to the purchase of books, apparatus, and improvements upon the grounds.

But the income of the Normal School Fund, notwithstanding these appropriations, was inadequate to the wants of the institution. At the beginning of the year, 1855, it had exhausted its funds, and had contracted a debt of $2,000. In this embarrassment, it encountered the evils that have attended the first years of every State institution, of whatever kind, from the organization of the State. It was found that the School must have further aid, or its usefulness would be so circumscribed that it could not accomplish half its work.

The Legislature of 1855, appropriated $7,700 for that year, and $6,000 for 1856. This gave relief for those two years; and in 1857, upon the recommendation of the Superintendent of Public Instruction, the same sums were appropriated for 1857 and 1858.

The following table exhibits the amount of sales and receipts of the Normal School lands, and the expenditures for the several years named. The expenditures include the appropriations from the State :

Year.	No. of Acres sold.	Am't of Sales.	RECEIPTS.		EXPENDITURES.	
			On ac't of Prin.	On ac't of Int.	End'm't Fund.	Interest Fund.
1850	920.	$ 8,600 00	$ 2,150 00	$ 15 26	$ 611 60	221 77
1851	3,215.98	13,524 19	3,601 05	206 28	2,380 31	717 03
1852	1,055.95	4,195 70	1,613 33	980 75	3,556 80	275 00
1853	2,227.98	9,870 42	3,909 79	1,319 04	1,479 57	3,731 38
1854	3,063.35	21 033 40	4,591 37	1,783 79		8,132 56
1855	1,609.62	7,718 48	3,814 51	2,590 55	67 56	6,568 08
1856	2,309.31	9,557 24	4,463 47	2,715 07		11,367 74
1857	1,081.77	4,327 08	1,525 67	3,000 55	80	10,063 18
	15,433.96	$78,826 51	$25,669 19	$12,611 29	$8,096 64	$41,076 74

Of the lands sold, there have been forfeited 720 acres, valued at $5,580, which amounts deducted from the whole amount of sales, as above stated, leaves 14,713.96 acres, sold for $73,246 51, which constituted the real amount and value of sales at the close of the year 1857. From this value of the sales, deduct the $8,096 64 endowment fund expended in buildings, &c., and it leaves $65,149 87—the present amount of the fund. Of this amount, $17,572 55 is in the hands of the State, upon which it pays six per cent. per annum—$47,577 32 remaining in the hands of purchasers, and upon which they pay seven per cent.

This makes the income from the Endowment fund for the present year, $4,384 76. But 1,277½ acres of the land appropriated remains unsold; therefore, the income of the School can be but slightly increased without further aid.

It is an old saying, that "there is no royal road to knowledge." Every child must think for himself. But if knowledge can be attained only in the narrow path of study, it is yet doubtless true, that path is made much easier and more attractive, for the pupils in the Primary School, at the present day, than it was when trod by their fathers. This is owing in part to the improvement in the style and construction of School-houses, by which they are rendered more conducive to health, and more inviting to the taste of the young; but also, in a great measure, to the improved skill of their teachers. In proportion as Teaching becomes a profession, instead of an incidental and temporary occupation, will the teacher's powers of imparting instruction be increased. Men who are not yet very old, can remember when *their* "teacher" appeared to have little more thought of teaching *ideas*, than had the mistress who, with the spelling book reversed upon her knee, repeated to the impatient child, "What's that A, what's that B, what's that C," &c. Who that attended the Common School thirty years ago, cannot remember the many times his "master" worked out his "sum," and never uttered the first word as to *why* it was thus and so? Well was such employment called "*keeping* school." *Words* were taught —*ideas came*, as the pupil could find them! Not that all teachers were thus deficient in the first qualification for their duties; but it was true to a very great extent, thirty years ago.

The great change which has taken place, is attributable in part, perhaps, to the general progress in all the improvements of the age; but more directly, to the association of teachers with each other, the exchange of ideas, and to the professional training which they undergo in various ways. To secure this professional instruction to the teachers in this State, is the design of the Normal School. In the short time since the School was opened, several hundred have already received the benefits of its instruction. These go forth to impart the knowledge they have gained, to others; by their personal intercourse, and by Teachers' Institutes and Associations. The Normal School is believed to be doing all that its early friends promised for it; and the future will doubtless make it still more efficient in securing to professional teachers, the highest attainable qualifications for their important and responsible duties.

That this School will be sustained, the general appreciation of the importance of education for the masses, as manifested by the citizens of this State, is a sure promise. The main expenditure for buildings, &c., has already been made. A very slight amount hereafter, in addition to its annual income, will supply all the necessary material aid for its highest success; and its whole tendency will be, to make teaching a profession, to dignify it, and call into its ranks a higher order of natural talent, and give to that talent its highest efficiency.

THE UNIVERSITY OF MICHIGAN, AND ITS FUNDS.

The men whose history immortalized the names of the Mayflower and Plymouth Rock, were by no means ignorant fanatics, to be led away by the impostures of stronger minds. They were men of strong and cultivated minds, no more to be led astray by sophistry, than were their hearts by the blandishments of a court Religion. Their love for purity of heart was scarcely less than their regard for intellectual excellence ; for they esteemed intelligence the best basis upon which to build a religious character. Consequently we find, that from considerations of religious responsibility, even more than from their love of knowledge in itself, they began at once, upon their advent in the new world, to provide measures for the education of their young. Nor were they satisfied with merely making provision for a common education for the masses; but they felt that, while all could not be, some *must be* scholars of a high order: able to understand the Scriptures in their original language, and to cope with error upon whatever ground it might come, and with whatever weapons it might choose.

The country was a wild, inhabited by wild tribes of men; but those heroes of 1620, as though comprehending their mighty mission to this new world, immediately began to lay the foundations upon which our present institutions are based. But sixteen years elapsed before a College was determined upon, and an appropriation made for its establishment; and two years after, an endowment was made by John Harvard; and thus, two hundred and twenty years ago, was founded Harvard College—the pride of Massachusetts, and of the nation.

From that time to the present, a similar spirit has animated the leading minds which in all our history have given shape to our institutions. The several States have always fostered the highest, no less than the lower institutions of learning.

When those great men—great in the truest sense—the Pilgrims of the Mayflower, emancipated themselves from spiritual dominion, and established "a Church without a Bishop," they probably had some conception of what this land would some day become. But for its present greatness, they would probably have assigned a growth of at least a thousand years; not dreaming then of the wonders of railways, telegraphs or steam. Hardly less did those later heroes who carried the country through the revolution, and established "a State without a King," realize what this magnificent "north west," then the abode of savages, wonld become, even while some of them remained upon life's battle ground. But like the men of Plymouth, they saw something of what it would some day be, and they lost no time in commencing the foundations for temples of knowledge and virtue, upon which their posterity might build.

Appropriations of land for the support of Colleges in Ohio—then a Territory—were made in 1787 and 88. In 1804, by an act for the disposal of public lands in the Indiana Territory, of which this State was a part, three townships were reserved "for the use of seminaries of learning"—one of which was for that section now constituting the State of Michigan.

In 1817, Gen. Cass and Duncan McArthur negociated a treaty with several tribes of Indians at Fort Meigs, by which a grant of three sections was secured from Congress, under pretence of furnishing means for educating Indians, "to the rector of the Catholic church at Detroit," (to the *rector*—not to the church,) and also three sections to the "College of Detroit." It is a singular thing that these six sections were granted in common, to be divided as the parties should agree; but so it was. Part of this grant was located on the river Macon, a branch of the Raisin, and the remainder on the Detroit river and in Livingston county. The three sections for the College of Detroit, nominally became a part of the University lands. The other three accrued to the Catholic Church, and is believed to be the only grant ever made by Congress to any Church in this State.*

The Government lands in the Territory were brought into market in 1818. The University township had not been located, up to 1824, and it was thought that a township of good land of which none had been sold, could not be found; and through the exertions of Governor Woodbridge and others, and Hon. Austin E. Wing, delegate to Congress, an act was passed by which permission was given to select the land in detached sections; and at the same time, another township or its equivalent, was granted.

Thus was constituted the basis of the University Fund, consisting of the seventy-two sections granted for a University, and the three sections to the College of Detroit.

In 1821, a University was organized by the Governor and Judges of the Territory, and the control of the University lands, with all the franchises of the College of Detroit, given to its Trustees.

The ordinance of Congress, admitting the State of Michigan into the Union, declared that "the seventy-two sections of land set apart and reserved for the use and support of a University," by the act of Congress of 1826, "are hereby granted and conveyed to the State, *to be appropriated solely to the use and support of such University.*"

* After the death of the "Rector," the title of this property became a question of doubt, and an act was passed by the Legislature in 1841, incorporating "The Catholic Apostolic and Roman Church of St. Anne of Detroit," to which the lands were by the act confirmed.

The original Constitution, under which Michigan became a State, provided that "all lands that have been or may be granted by the United States to this State, for the support of a University, and the funds accruing from the rents or sales of such lands, or from any other source, for the purpose aforesaid, *shall be and remain a permanent fund*, for the support of said University."

Our present Constitution is similar, and declares that the interest and income of all lands granted for educational purposes, "*shall be inviolably* appropriated, and *annually applied to the specific objects of the original gift, grant, or appropriation.*" The present Constitution did not repeat the blunder of the old one, in adding the receipts for rents, to the main fund, instead of using them as income.

Thus it will be seen that the University Fund, arising from these grants of lands, is inalienable, and cannot be diverted from the University without a gross breach of original faith, and a direct violation of the Constitution. Happily very few have ever entertained a wish for such a result. On the contrary, successive Legislatures have given additional aid by direct appropriations, to the amount of many thousand dollars.

The present University of Michigan was established by an act of the Legislature in 1837, and located in the village (now city) of Ann Arbor. The situation is one of much beauty, comprising forty acres of land, donated by the citizens of that vicinity. The same law provided for the creation of "Branches," as intermediate and preparatory schools, to be located in various sections of the State.

Much ridicule—not to say odium—has been cast upon the early rulers of our State for their schemes—so extravagant for so young a State—of internal improvements. Twenty years only have passed away, and those plans, though from unfortunate circumstances and equally unfortunate management, a signal failure then, are now more than realized. Their legislation was a prophecy, since completely fulfilled.

But if they had commercial and business views twenty years in advance of their circumstances, they had hardly less exalted views of what should be done for intellectual development. Had they commenced one railway, it might have been completed. They undertook three, and built none. So in education—with no capital save the anticipated income from sales of land, they established the University *and* Branches. With borrowed capital, according to the order of that day with all our public works, the University buildings were commenced, and several branches set in motion. After expending thirty-six thousand dollars upon the branches, they were all suspended, or assigned to private hands. Had this money been applied to the University, it would have prevented years of anxiety, embarrassment, and at times great danger of the suspension of the institution itself.

The *need* of the branches was by no means unreal. Their creation was only a question of expediency, in view of the means to sustain them. As soon as an end of borrowing came, it was seen that the means did not exist. Their need was real, and the importance of Schools with a similar design is far greater now than then. But the University has not yet, nor is it probable it ever will have, funds to spare for their restoration. Their re-establishment, therefore, may be considered impossible; and the question is, how shall we otherwise provide in the most feasible mannner, for the intermediate course of study for those who wish to enter the University, or who wish, without entering upon a college course, to give their minds a higher discipline than can be obtained in the Primary School?

The Union School is a Primary School; nothing more, except in its superior arrangements. Yet it is believed that these Schools—or the more prominent of them—may have added to them, with no detriment to their primary design, an intermediate and preparatory feature, answering the main purpose of the Branches, with but a mere fraction of their expense. True, no means from the University Fund can be appropriated in such a direction; and it required a pretty broad construction of the Constitution to do it in the case of the Branches. [For a more extended statement of the Superintendent's views upon this subject, see pages 16 to 18 of his Report for 1856, and pages 45 to 63 of his Report for 1857, recently published, in one volume.]

At the organization of the University, no portion of the seventy-two sections had been sold, except to the amount of $5,000 by the Trustees of the old University, and no means existed with which to put the institution in operation. But everything could be done by borrowing. The State was borrowing on its own account, to build railways, canals, and a State prison, and loaning its credit to private railway companies. It could do no less for Education than it did for locomotion; and in 1838, $100,000 was borrowed, for which the State gave its bonds, payable in twenty years. This was reloaned to the University, with the agreement that the principal and interest was to be paid from the income of the University lands, and that the State, though nominally a principal in reference to the loan, was really only an agent and endorser for the University. With this understanding, the business was for several years conducted, and the interest paid from the funds of the University; when a singular change took place, as will be seen hereafter. About $122,000, in interest and discount, has been paid upon this loan, and the whole original sum—save $1,000—is still (in 1858) a debt against the State. Such is the *economy* of borrowing! But it met the necessities of the case; the buildings were erected, and in 1841 the University was duly inaugurated as an acting institution.

The sales of University lands commenced in 1837; and Nov. 30th, 1841, had reached about two hundred thousand dollars, at an average price of $17 42 per acre. Of this, $37,043 22 had been paid in, and loaned principally to several counties, for ten years. The total receipts for interest to this time, were about fourteen thousand dollars, and the interest on the two hundred thousand dollars was the only available resource of the University, except the hundred thousand dollars loan, which was then about exhausted; while the interest on the loan had already reached the sum of eighteen thousand dollars.

The first year in which the lands were offered for sale, the sales were $149,140 51; but the financial revulsion that followed, not only diminished the sales, but rendered purchasers unable to pay their interest; and the receipts of interest, which in 1838 were $8,920 23, were but $2,203 29 in 1841. The interest due the University Fund, from accumulated arrears, was over thirty-three thousand dollars. Added to these unavailable resources, upon which to rely for the coming year, was $13,550 88 accruing interest, of which, like that already past due, it was expected very little would be paid, and that little mainly in State scrip of depreciated value; also, $11,445 18 of the hundred thousand dollars loan rendered unavailable by the failure of the Bank of Michigan.

The estimated expenses for the coming year, including fifteen hundred dollars for the branches, and six thousand to meet the interest on the hundred thousand dollars loan, were $16,724.

The minimum price of University lands, was twenty dollars per acre. In April, 1841, this was reduced to fifteen dollars; yet but 616 acres were sold during the year; upon which $1,015 28 was paid down; and of over thirty-three thousand dollars interest due, but $2,203 29, as above stated, was paid during the year. Well might the Finance Committee report that they would "venture no estimate of the receipts for the coming year!" Their nominal resources for the coming year, including interest due, and funds in the Bank of Michigan, were reported to be $58,210 63. Of this sum, $10,572 74 was paid during the year.*

The expenses of the University were kept within the receipts only by the closest economy.

In this year, 1842, the minimum price of University lands was still further reduced to $12 per acre. At the close of the year, there were five branches in operation, including one in connection with the University—with 174 students, male and female. The year previous, the number was 210. Those who apprehend so much danger from a co-education of the sexes in the University, seem not to have manifested any apprehension in reference to the branches. But two hundred dollars each, was appropriated for the support of the branches this year. The balance of their expense was met by tuition fees. The Faculty of the University consisted of Rev. JOSEPH WHITING, GEORGE P. WILLIAMS, DOUGLAS HOUGHTON and ABRAM SAGER. (Of these, Messrs. Williams and Sager are still Professors in the institution.)

To the 1st of December, 1842, the sales of University lands amounted to 13,013 acres, for $220,496 05. Of this, 3,422 acres which sold for $77,293 92, had been forfeited for non-payment of interest; of which 969 acres had been re-sold for $13,914 95. The purchasers found themselves in the same dilemma with the purchasers of Primary School lands—perhaps worse, as they had bound themselves not only to pay a higher price, but probably higher in proportion to their real value. And to them the Legislature ex-

* It is proper to say that the reports for several years, in the early history of the University, and even up to within six or eight years past, are often very conflicting. In this instance, the State Treasurer reports "Received for interest on University lands sold, and principal loaned $9,946 45." The Superintendent of Public Instruction reports, page 210, Joint Documents, "Receipts on interest for the year, $10,572 74." On page 292, the Superintendent says, "The amount received by the State Treasurer, on account of interest from the fund, is reported at $10,959 53." The author of this article, therefore, will not vouch, in every case, for the absolute correctness of the figures; but they are at least near enough to answer the general purpose in view, of showing the condition of the University.

tended the same relief.* The law of 1842 provided for the appraisal of University lands that had been sold for $20, or more per acre—none, however, to be valued at less than $12 per acre—and the amount of reduction was to be credited to the principal due. The result was, that in the same year the aggregate of credits to purchasers amounted to $34,651 17. This, with the forfeitures, reduced the fund $111,945 09. The account stood thus:

Sold to Dec. 1st, 1841,		$203,471 76
Sold in 1842, to Dec. 1st,		17,024 29
Total,		$220,496 05
Forfeitures,	$77,293 92	
Reduction by appraisal,	34,651 17	
		111,945 09
Amount remaining,		$108,550 96
Add forfeited lands resold,		13,914 95
" paid previous to forfeiture,		9,425 83
" received from old Trustees,		5,000 00
" " for rents,		276 00
Total University Fund,		$137,167 74

This sum afterward became further reduced, till it amounted to only $131,290 60.

In the Report of the Superintendent of Public Instruction for this year, (1842,) he states the total receipts into the State treasury, for principal and interest, of both the University and Primary School Funds, from the first sales to that time, to be $278,905 97
And the disbursements and cash then in the treasury, ... 256,582 39

What had become of the $22,323 58
the Superintendent could not tell. About one-third of the

*See pages 5-7, on the subject of Primary School lands.

6

deficiency is chargable to the "profit and loss account" of the *University.*

The interest to accrue for the coming year, 1843, with that in arrears, would amount to $62,264 17; yet, with all these nominal resources, the Board of Regents expressed the fear that enough might not be realized to meet the expenses; although they had reduced the estimates to the starvation point of $2,700, exclusive of $6,000 to pay the annual interest on the loan.

In 1843, a settlement was effected with the Bank of Michigan, and the balance due the University, $9,204 70, was liquidated, principally in real estate in the city of Detroit. In the meantime, the Michigan State Bank, with which was deposited $6,000 to meet the accruing annual interest on the hundred thousand dollars loan, had failed, and that sum was rendered unavailable. Of the $62,264 17 due for interest, only $7,526 57 was paid during the year.*

The close of the year found the institution over twelve hundred dollars in debt for current expenses, though they had been kept within the estimate above. Well might the Regents report the prospects even more gloomy than at the time of their last previous report!

In this year the State Land Office was organized, and the direct control of the lands, hitherto in the hands of the Superintendent of Public Instruction, was transferred to that Department. In the first Report of the Commissioner of the Land Office, he says: "Upon an examination of the books transferred to this office, it was soon perceived that their keeping was deficient in system, and incapable of affording exact and perfect information of the business transactions of the Department." This should not necessarily be understood as a reflection upon the former Superintendents of Public Instruction, whose integrity and faithfulness has never been questioned; but it shows with what

* This is as reported by the Commissioner of the Land Office. In the Superintendent's Report for 1851, it is stated to have been $5,427 03. The former is probably the correct amount.

an imperfect system the affairs of those times were conducted. The fault was not so much with the Superintendents, as with the Legislature. If they required one mortal man to superintend the formation and development of our whole Educational System, and at the same time manage and dispose of several millions in value of land, partly on credit, with all the changes and embarrassments of default in interest, forfeitures, and reductions in price by appraisal, &c., &c., what could they expect, but duties unperformed, confusion and errors? The real difficulty was, one man was required to perform the labor of several—an example, however, which has been followed by Legislatures of a still later date.

At the close of 1843, there were five branches in existence, in four of which were 133 students. Three of the branches, only, received $200 each from the University fund. The students in the University numbered fifty-three.

It was now seen that relief, in some form, must be given by special legislation, or the University would soon be compelled to suspend operations. The patriotic and philanthropic hearts, who were directly engaged in the enterprise, again appealed to the Legislature for help. But the State itself, was deeply, not to say disgracefully, in debt, and could give no aid, unless it could be obtained from the lands. These were a rich inheritance, but practically valueless until converted into money.

It will be understood that the one hundred thousand dollars loan was obtained by the State. For this its bonds were given, and it held the University lands as security. So the institution owed the debt, not to the bond-holders, but to the State. If the lands could be sold, the debt might so far be liquidated, and the interest thereon stopped. But in the previous year the sales were but $9,685 70. At this rate, over ten years would be required to remove the incubus, though all the sales should be applied to that end.

A scheme was devised, however, by which it was believed the sales could be greatly augmented, the State enabled to redeem its outstanding obligations, the holders thereof obtaining their pay, and all without any cash or credit in the transaction.

The State, after borrowing money to the extent of its credit, had then issued warrants and scrip, bearing interest, to carry on the government and its public works. These evidences of State indebtedness, it was proposed, should be received for the University lands, and the State receive them to apply upon the loan. They were of greatly depreciated value in the market, which fact it was rightly concluded, would invite the holders to part with them at par for land. Thus the University would sell its land for a debt against the State, which would be an offset to its own. An act legalizing such an arrangement was passed, and approved February 28th, 1844.

There is much confusion in the minds of many in relation to the "trust funds," of which our Educational Funds constitute one class. This arises, doubtless, from the fact that the State has the management of these funds, and is at the same time the borrower of them. It was necessary that the University funds, like the Primary School, Asylum, and other funds, should be invested, so as to make the interest available. It was at first proposed to loan them to the counties, to corporations, or to individuals, as occasion might offer; and that system was commenced. But the State itself was in the market as a borrower, and it was justly deemed safer for these several funds, that they should be loaned to the State, than to A, B, and C, with all sorts of security, or no security at all. Under these circumstances, the State determined itself to borrow all the funds of the University, as they should accrue.

We may consider the State in the character of guardian to a minor; and the guardian himself borrows the money of his ward. The State never really owned the University or Primary School lands. True, they were "granted to the State;" but not in fee. They were *in trust*, for specified objects. Hence the term "Trust Funds," or funds held by the State in trust; which, as the trustee, it has loaned for its own use, instead of loaning them to third parties.

In the present case, it was as though the guardian of a child, whose only property consists of wild land, borrows on his own responsibility, say one thousand dollars, for the expense of the child's education. After awhile the guardian becomes deeply in debt on his own account, and his notes are offered in the market for fifty cents on the dollar. At this crisis, he advertises that he will receive his outstanding notes at par, in payment for the land of his ward; with whom he agrees that he will apply the amount upon his indebtedness of the thousand dollars.

By another act, passed eleven days later than the one authorizing the above arrangement, the Seminary lot (so called) in Detroit, which the University had taken of the Bank of Michigan, was transferred to the State, to be applied upon the loan, at $8,095—the same that it had cost the University.

These measures, it was reasonably supposed, would result in extensive sales, and so far relieve the University of its debt; to pay the interest on which, had been absorbing about two-thirds of its annual income. And the result was: in about eight months—the remainder of the same year—the debt was reduced $39,212 48. The total sales for cash and credit during the entire year, amounted to only $5,709 57. This went into the University Fund—the State taking only what was paid in warrants.

The interest upon the loan was thus in the first year of the experiment, reduced $2,352 74, leaving that amount of additional means for the expenses of the University.

In 1845, the debt was further reduced to $43,258 06.*

* The Board of Regents incorrectly reported this sum $37 20 less than the above.

The total sales of University lands reached $27,381. The interest received was $10,007 22. The first class, numbering eleven, graduated this year.

The crisis of the institution was now passed; and its officers, who had been long trembling for its fate, found a burden which other minds could hardly appreciate, removed from their hearts. The only danger they had now to fear, was that the number of students would increase more rapidly than their means. And some embarrassment was afterward experienced from this cause; but not such as in previous years, to threaten the suspension of the institution.

In 1846, the debt was reduced to $33,850; and the receipts to the interest fund were $10,274. This gave the University the means of paying all its local debts, with a surplus of nearly three thousand dollars. But the number of students had increased to seventy; and the Board of Regents voted to make no further appropriations to the Branches. It had become evident that the original plan of the Branches, to be sustained from the University Fund, could never be accomplished; that whatever might be its future increased resources, they would all be required to meet its increased expenses which the future number of students would involve. From this time, therefore, the Branches were donbtless wisely, however reluctantly, abandoned to their fate, or to such an existence as they could maintain in private hands. The graduating class of this year numbered seventeen.

In 1847, the debt was reduced to $20,628.

The same terms are here used, in speaking of the hunhred thousand dollars loan, that are used in all the reports of the State officers, and by the officers of the University. They invariably speak of it as a loan, upon which the University was paying interest, and which the institution was anxious to liquidate, as it was now fortunately doing, by the process above described. The reader is here reminded of this fact, as in the further history of affairs, he will find the subject presented in a somewhat different aspect.

The debt which had rested so like an incubus upon the institution, and through the interest annually due upon it, had endangered its very continuance, now ceased to be a subject of anxiety, as it was certain in a short time to be entirely cancelled. At the same time, the receipts to the University interest fund were slowly increasing—being this year about a thousand dollars advance upon those of 1846. But the number of students was now eighty-three —a greater number than the capacity of the buildings could well accommodate; and it was deemed indispensable to commence at once the erection of another main building. Accordingly, over sixteen thousand dollars was thus expended in 1847 and '48. The graduates of 1847 numbered twelve.

In 1848 the number of students was eighty eight, and the number of graduates sixteen. There were now seven Professors. The debt was reduced to less than fifteen thousand dollars. The receipts to the interest fund were $10,829 44. The total sales of land amounted to but $8,432 88.

The sales in 1849 amounted to but $6,560. The receipts for interest were $10,907 34. The graduating class numbered twenty-four. The Freshmen numbered but twenty, leaving the total of number students four less than in the previous year. To meet the wants of the Laboratory, the Board of Regents appropriated six thousand dollars for a building for that purpose.

In 1850 the receipts for interest were $10,473 21—the sales of land, $13,621 58. The Medical building was nearly completed, and a Medical Department was organized with eighty students. The number of students in the other departments was reduced to seventy-two.

Under the old Constitution, the Board of Regents had consisted of twelve members, appointed by the Governor.

In them were vested the corporate powers of the University. But by a change in the new Constitution of 1850, the Board consisted of one member from each judicial district in the State, elected by the people for six years. Hitherto the institution had never had a President as a distinctive officer; and the new Board of Regents, under the requirements of the Constitution, elected Rev. HENRY P. TAPPAN, D. D., President. This gentleman soon after entered upon the duties of his office, which he still holds with much credit to himself, and advantage to the institution.

It will be seen that though the available resources of the University had increased from three, four, and five thousand dollars per annum, to about ten thousand, its expenses had also increased, and the demand for additional buildings had at this time involved it in a debt of over twelve thousand dollars. For ten thousand dollars of this, warrants were drawn, payable in three years. Upon these warrants the money was obtained, and temporary relief gained.

We now come to a point where history seems to repudiate itself. For six successive years, after the passage of a law providing a way for the payment of the hundred thousand dollars loan, the various reports agree in speaking of so much being paid in one year, and so much in another, the University ceasing to pay interest on the amount paid from year to year—the whole matter appearing to be as well understood by all, as would be the simplest transaction between man and man. The reader can, therefore, hardly fail to be surprised to find the following singular remarks in the Report of the Superintendent of Public Instruction, for 1850:

"The estimated receipts [of the University] for the coming year, are calculated at $17,088 23. The estimated expenses, $16,263 33. The former exceeds the receipts of last year by $5,088 23, while the expenses are also increased $4,973 92. *The sum of* $6,010 *is set apart*, in this estimate, *to pay interest upon the loan of* $100,000, and the balance for the support of Professors, &c. It would be of no utility at this time, perhaps, to discuss the financial or general policy which has been adopted by successive Boards of Regents. The heavy loan early contracted, and the large amount invested in buildings, has proved a serious detriment to the interests of the institution, and will continue to embarrass its legitimate field of operations until effectual provision is made for sinking the debt. *What provision has been made for this purpose, is unknown to this Department.* Information in this respect, was required from the Board of Regents, but not in season for that body to prepare and submit it at this time. It is believed, however, that the importance of *relieving the University* from this burden, must be apparent to all."

To this time, the public had been informed, and all supposed, that the hundred thousand dollars loan was nearly paid to the State. The same Superintendent of Public Instruction reported, but the last previous year, that "The *weight of a heavy debt,* and improvident expenditures contracted *at an early period,* has been gradually *removed,* by the prudence and discretion of the Board entrusted with its management and supervision."

That this referred to the hundred thousand dollars loan, does not admit of a question; as that was the *only* heavy debt incurred at an early or any other period.

It is deemed fitting to enlarge somewhat upon this subject, by reason of the singular change in its aspect, the large pecuniary considerations involved, and the legislative action that has already resulted from it.

The hundred thousand dollars loan was obtained for *six* per cent. interest, payable in twenty years; that is, in 1858. Had the lands which had now been sold for State warrants, to an amount nearly equal to the loan, been sold for *cash,* and that placed in the University Fund, it would have been drawing *seven* per cent. But they could not have been sold for cash; and were sold for warrants, only because the State was willing to receive that sort of depreciated paper at par. But it had counted dollar for dollar to all parties. The University had stopped six thousand dollars annual interest on the loan, but the means with which it was done, would have been earning seven thousand, had they gone into the University Fund instead of the State treasury. But it was only by assigning those means to the State treasury, they could be brought into existence or made available at all; and though nominally, the University was losing a thousand dollars per annum, by paying its debts, it was really realising five thousand. It had been relieved from great embarrassment, perhaps from suspension, by the arrangement; the State credit was relieved, by redeeming its obligations, and thousands of individuals were benefitted by obtaining the par value for the warrants in their hands.

Before making their Annual Report for 1852, the Finance Committee consulted the Attorney General, who expressed the opinion that the payment which had been made to the State, could not be repudiated. They complained of a hard bargain, and petitioned the Legislature to pay to the University the one per cent. which it was apparently losing upon the hundred thousand dollars in question. This would be one thousand dollars per annum, from the time of sale of the lands which had been purchased with warrants, till 1858, or till the State should pay the original loan.

The Legislature of 1853 more than answered this appeal, by an act directing the Auditor General to credit the University Fund for that and the next year, with the full amount of interest *on all the University lands that had been sold.* This was treating the matter (for two years) as though the debt had not been paid. It showed in a striking light, the readiness of the Legislature to extend aid to the University.

The Auditor General, *Hon. John Sweegles*, in his next report, used the following language:

"The total amount due from the State to the University Fund is $73,504 46. In addition to the interest on this sum, the last Legislature (Act No. 60) required the Auditor General to draw his warrant on the State Treasurer for interest on $100,000 of bonds, heretofore issued by the State for the benefit of the University, and upon which the State pays interest to the holders thereof—thus making the State pay double interest on that amount. This is the plain and simple meaning of the act, although it is so drawn up, as in a measure to disguise the fact. It is true the act is limited to the period of two years; and if it was only intended by those officers of the University who drafted the bill, as a donation to the University of $14,000, to relieve it from present embarrassment, it is well—but if it was intended as a precedent for future legislative action, it is wrong. It would bring the State in debt to the University $100,000 in addition to the $73,504 46 above stated to be due, and the State would also have to pay the $100,000 bonds heretofore assumed."

The next Legislature, in 1855, however, seemed to be neither convinced or alarmed by this report, and passed an act continuing the payment for another *two years*. The phraseology of the bill was similar to the act of 1853; virtually admitting that the State should pay interest on funds which the records showed to be its own.

The Legislature of 1857 again renewed the grant, to continue for *four years* longer.

Thus the State is bound to pay the University seven thousand dollars per annum, for eight years—or sixteen thousand dollars more than has been appropriated from the Treasury to put the Agricultural College in operation. That this money is well expended, it is probable that almost universal enlightened public sentiment will agree. But that it is secured by any *legal claim* of the University upon the State, will not bear investigation, except upon one ground; and one that has never been asserted in any of the reports or memorials. That ground, which may be debatable, is the question of constitutionality.

It may be said, in the exact language of the Constitution, under which the law was enacted, which is similar to the terms of the original grant from Congress, as well as the present Constitution, that "the funds accruing from the sales of such lands shall be and remain a *permanent fund* for the support of said University." If this is to be literally construed, was not the sequestration of one hundred thousand dollars of the University fund for the payment of a loan which had been expended in buildings, apparatus, &c., a violation of the Constitution, and therefore void? If so, then the University still owes the State the hundred thousand dollars; and its only means with which to pay it, are in its yearly interest fund; and a measure so detrimental to the usefulness of the institution as the requiring of payment from this fund, will probably never be entertained by the people or their Legislature. If so, also, the University fund is one hundred thousand dollars greater than appears upon all the State records, and all the reports of the Auditor General; and the sooner the record and the fact are made to agree, the better.

The action of several Legislatures would indicate that they either took the unconstitutional view of the subject, *or* voted under a misapprehension of the facts in the case.

But it may be asked again, on the other hand, was the appropriating of one hundred thousand dollars to necessary buildings and apparatus, any infringement upon the "permanency" of the fund? Suppose, instead of this, they had loaned it to the State, or other parties, and *rented* their buildings, &c. Whatever might be said of the necessity of such a policy, its *impolicy* would be apparent to all. But had not the course been adopted which was adopted, this would have been the only alternative; and what more permanent investment could be made, than to put it into the necessary buildings and conveniences for operating the institution; *saving* thereby in rents, more than the money would *earn* if loaned?

Thus the case now stands before the people, whose institution the University is, and whose money the funds are—whether in the University Fund, or in the State treasury. It is for them to decide in which pocket the money belongs. If they decide that it belongs in the State pocket, there is little danger that they will see the University pocket empty, without replenishing it, with a liberal hand. It is truly to be hoped that the educational spirit of the citizens of Michigan will ever see to it, that the increasing reputation and usefulness of its University, already imparting its blessings to nearly five hundred students, are not blighted for want of all necessary means. But from the importance of this subject, and the circumstance of its having been very little discussed by the people, and consequently not understood by them, the Superintendent of Public Instruction deems it desirable that all the facts in the case should be laid before them, with a view to an early and equitable settlement.

The following table shows the number of acres of land disposed of, and the amount for which it was originally sold, the amount received for principal, and for interest, with the average price per acre for the several years, from the first sales in 1837, to Dec. 1st, 1857—the receipts for interest including the amount granted by the Legislatures of 1853, '55 and '57—to the close of 1857. The table is compiled from the Superintendent's Reports, up to the time the Land Office was established, and the remainder from the Reports of the latter office:

Year.	No. of Acres sold.	Amount of sales.	Principal received.	Interest received.	Av'ge price per acre.
1837	6,492.92	$149,140 51	$14,922 05		$22 97
1838	507.72	10,304 40	14,635 40	$8,920 23	20 29
1839	181.75	3,872 00	1,089 85	2,433 63	21 30
1840	4,786.72	30,457 95	5,380 64	2,142 50	6 36
1841	(*a*)615.92	9,696 90	1,015 28	2,203 29	16 18
1842	1,428.50	17,024 29	3,489 91	10,572 74	11 91
1843	924.59	9,685 70	1,964 08	7,526 57	10 47
1844	4,155.57	44,922 05	21,451 83	8,617 54	11 05
1845	2,259.25	27,381 00	17,561 66	10,007 22	12 12
1846	1,335.21	16,254 52	9,375 86	(*b*)10,274 00	12 17
1847	1,182.59	13,540 10	13,221 99	(*c*)11,177 19	11 45
1848	702.74	8,432 88	11,586 72	(*d*)10,829 44	12 00
1849	382.48	6,560 09	10,233 67	(*e*) 10,928 34	17 20
1850	865.85	13,621 58	9,881 39	10,473 21	15 73
1851	1,257.06	15,501 72	11,674 72	(f)10,414 06	12 33
1852	1,143.05	13,756 60	16,511 48	(*g*)12,755 41	12 03
1853	7,361.49	95,042 20	34,984 44	19,939 76	12 91
1854	6,363.55	76,647 68	31,384 79	26,485 34	12 04
1855	2,288.14	29,013 05	24,199 48	32,871 07	12 68
1856	1,209.41	14,512 92	8,171 13	34,511 29	12 00
1857	679.25	8,151 00	9,032 47	35,201 96	12 00
	46,123.76	$613,519 14	$271,771 84	$278,284 79	

NOTES ON THE FOREGOING TABLE.

(*a*) In another place in the same Report of the Superintendent of Public Instruction, from which this statement is taken, the acres sold are said to be 696, at $10,896 93; the receipts for principal are stated in another place, to be $2,831 69; while the State Treasurer's books give yet a third amount—$1,025 00. The receipts for interest, the Superintendent gives in another place, at $248 50, while the Treasurer's books give here also a third variation, or $2,463 61. These disagreements between the Superintendent and himself, and the Treasurer, will be made more apparent by the following table:

	Acres.	Amount.	Rec'd on principal.	Rec'd on Interest.
Superintendent,	615.92	$9,696 90	$1,015 28	$2,203 29
Superintendent,	696.00	10,896 93	2,831 69	248 50
Treasurer,......			1,025 00	2,463 61

This is but an extreme case of the embarrassment met

with, in attempting to collate *exact* and reliable statements through all the early history of the University funds.

(*b*) The old Constitution made the receipts for rents a part of the principal; but the Reports this year, show that the receipts for rents were added to the interest fund.

(*c*) This year the State Treasurer's books show $221 24 less interest received than is reported by the Commissioner of the Land Office. The rents this year also, went into the interest fund.

(*d*) The receipts are here again placed to the interest fund, and $136 29 received for penalty, appears not to have been received by the Treasurer.

(*e*) The rents again go to the interest fund, and the Treasurer's books show $186 54 less interest paid into the treasury than is reported received by the Commissioner of the Land Office.

(*f*) The Treasurer's books show his receipts $129 50 less for principal, and $689 53 less for interest, than is reported by the Commissioner of the Land Office.

(*g*) For this year the Treasurer reports, as coming into his hands, $602 75 less for principal, and $1,110 72 less for interest, than is given by the Commissioner of the Land Office; and the Finance Committee of the University state the amount different from either.

The aggregate of these discrepancies between the Commissioners of the Land Office and the Treasurer (with whose books the Auditor General's agree) is $3,076 57. All of this, save $732 25 is in the interest account. This may all be mere errors of the Land Office; but it is, to say the least, somewhat singular, that in seven errors, varying from a hundred and twenty-nine, to over eleven hundred dollars, every one is against the University.

The average price of lands sold in 1840 was but $6 36 per acre. This was in consequence of a pre-emption law, allowing "squatters" to take the land by appraisal. The presumption is fair that these were among the most valuable of the University lands.

The foregoing table shows the result according to the original sales, to December 1st, 1857; but a portion of the forty-six thousand one hundred and twenty-three and three-fourths acres is reckoned twice, having been forfeited and resold. The amount actually sold, after deducting forfeitures, is 41,320 acres. To this, add the three sections, which do not appear on the Land Office records—making 43,240 acres.

The grants from Congress were the three sections to the College of Detroit, and seventy-two sections to the University—or 48,000 acres. The University lands yet unsold amount to 2,749 acres; showing the lands selected to be 45,985 acres. This would leave 2,011 acres still due from the General Government. But from this should be deducted 429 acres, less the amount for which the "Toledo lands" and Detroit "Ship-yard" were received.

The true account, then, stands thus:

Original grant—75 sections—acres,.............		48,000
Acres sold,............................	43,240	
" unsold,............................	2,749	
Less on Toledo lots and "Ship-yard,".......	429	
		46,418
Actual deficiency—acres,......................		1,582

This shows 1,582 acres—or about two and a half sections—still really due from the General Government to the University.

It has at all times been known that a small portion of the University lands had not been selected. It has been neglected because it was a fraction of the whole, and not especially needed, while large quantities of selected lands were yet unsold; but the lands selected are now nearly all disposed of, and measures will probably soon be taken, to have the unselected 1,582 acres selected, in accordance with the original design of Congress.

The above table shows the original sales to have amounted to $613,519 14. In this, there is probably no material error. But the sum has been reduced, by forfeitures and appraisal, to $503,121 56.

The table shows the amount *received* upon sales from the beginning, to be $271,771 84. It would be unsafe to vouch for the perfect accuracy of the figures in this column; but they are obtained from what are believed to be the most reliable of the conflicting records of past years, and the aggregate is probably not far from the truth. Only $246,161 33, however, has made its appearance upon the books of the State treasury. What has become of the $25,590 51 deficit? It probably must go to swell the amount reported unaccounted for, by the Superintendent of Public Instruction in 1842.

The amount received to the interest fund from the beginning, appears to be $278,284 79. This includes $7,000 per annum for the last five years, paid in accordance with acts of the Legislatures of 1853, '55 and '57. But from this should be deducted $1,910 63, paid for expenses chargable to the fund, leaving the amount which the University is supposed to have received, at $276,374 16.

The present University Fund, exclusive of the $100,000 paid to the State upon the loan, is $403,121 56. Of this, $146,161 33 is loaned to the State at seven per cent. interest. This has been used toward paying other State indebtedness; so the interest is no additional tax upon the people. A small amount was loaned to various counties at an early day. The remainder of the fund consists of unpaid balances due from about twelve hundred individual purchasers of University lands, and is tantamount to a loan to them. This class of debtors to both the University and Primary School Funds, number between eight and nine thousand. The State assumes all the care and expense connected with these funds, (with a very trifling exception,) selling the lands, keeping the accounts with the purchasers, and collecting the yearly interest, &c., without charge.

The income of the University at the present time, including the $7,000 paid by act of the Legislature, is $35,218 50.

The following table shows the sales of University lands for the several years, after deducting forfeitures:

Year.	Acres.	Amount.
Total sales from July, 1837, to Nov. 30th, 1843,	11,063.90	$131,290 60
1844,	4,155.57	44,154 05
1845,	1,881.53	23,296 19
1846,	1,323.21	16,020 52
1847,	1,017.46	11,839 77
1848,	662.74	8,075 46
1849,	322.48	5,800 09
1850,	781.22	12,896 52
1851,	1,289.59	15,266 29
1852,	1,049.55	12,453 35
1853,	7,361.09	95,042 20
1854,	6,343.55	76,288 03
1855,	2,259.42	28,754 57
1856,	1,129.41	13,792 92
1857,	679.25	8,151 00
Total,	41,319.97	$503,121 56

It will here be seen that the sales in 1853, '54 and '55, reached $200,084 80, or about two-fifths of the whole amount for twenty-one years. The avails gave opportune relief to the University, as well as substantial aid to the State, toward the establishment of her Agricultural College, Asylums, &c.

Below will be found the location of University lands, remaining unsold, Dec. 1st, 1857:

Township.	Acres.	100ths.	On Sec.	Township.	County.
5 s. 7 w.	120		24	Union,	Branch.
4 s. 8 w.	160		26	Athens,	Calhoun.
5 s. 9 w.	80		15	Leonidas,	St. Joseph.
5 s. 9 w.	275	39	30	"	"
6 s. 9 w.	40		5	Colon,	"
1 s. 10 w.	197	36	26	Richmond,	Kalamazoo.
1 s. 10 w.	40		34	"	"
4 s. 10 w.	400		13	Brady,	"
4 s. 10 w.	200		19	"	"
4 s. 10 w.	520		21	"	"
4 s. 10 w.	40		29	"	"
5 s. 10 w.	120		25	Mendon,	St. Joseph.
7 s. 17 w.	31	30	22	Buchanan,	Berrien.
7 n. 10 w.	280		27	Ada,	Kent.
7 n. 14 w.	40		12	Allendale,	Ottawa.

In and adjoining the village of St. Joseph are eighty-five acres, and village lots 1, 2, 5, 6, 7, 8, 9, 10, 13, 14, 15, 16 and 17.

The three sections granted to the College of Detroit appear to have been sold, but nothing has been found in the public records in relation thereto, or of anything paid over on their account, except perhaps $5,000. But the Trustees received also $5,000 for the land sold at Toledo; and nowhere is found any mention of their transferring but once, that sum to the present University.

The University lands at Toledo, from their present value, are perhaps worthy of a special notice. They were selected as a part of the seventy-two sections, in 1827. This was before Toledo had a name in history; but at that time it was perceived by men of sound judgment, that an important commercial town must ere long grow up in that immediate vicinity.

The lands were described as "river lots 1, 2, 7, 8, 9 and 10, in the United States reserve of twelve miles square, lying on the Maumee river," then in the Michigan Territory. These lots comprised nine hundred and sixteen acres, but were accepted by the Trustees of the old University of 1821, as two sections, or twelve hundred and eighty acres. The Wabash and Erie Canal was at the time projected, and Congress had just made grants of land to aid in its construction. It was expected that this canal would cross these lands, and form its junction with the waters of Lake Erie, in very close proximity. From these considerations, the lands were thought to be very desirable, and were therefore accepted for considerably more than the actual amount.

A town had been commenced adjoining lot 1—known afterward, for many years, as "the lower town" of Toledo—and Wm. Oliver and others, of Ohio, wished to obtain lots 1 and 2 on which to commence a rival town, or a rival section of the same town, believing that to be the most natural location for the centre of a great future city. Their negotiations with the Trustees resulted in a trade, in 1830, by permission of Congress, by which the Trustees exchanged lots 1 and 2, containing four hundred and one acres, for lots 3 and 4, (lying west,) and the southwest quarter of section two, and the west half of section three, township number three, of the same reserve, containing in all, seven hundred and seventy-seven acres.

In 1835, the Trustees were authorized by Congress to sell the University lands at auction; but in 1836, the law was repealed, and the Trustees were, by implication, required to sell back to Oliver, and others, the lands they had received from them in 1830, according to a contract *assumed to have been made* nearly two years previous. They were accordingly redeeded to Oliver, (the late Hon. Wm. Oliver, of Cincinnati,) for which the Trustees received $5,000; or six dollars and forty-five cents per acre.

Thus lots 1 and 2 were practically sold for $5,000. Upon this tract, what was long known as the "upper town," is situated. These technical divisions of the city are now mostly obsolete, the whole space between having grown into a compact settlement. The far greater business portion of the city, however, is upon lots 1 and 2. To those familiar with the streets of Toledo, the following description will be sufficient:

Commencing on the bank of the Maumee, near the foot of Cherry street, (about midway between the mouth of Swan creek and the "American Hotel,") thence up the river to the mouth of Swan creek, including some three hundred and fifty or four hundred feet of the point of land between said creek and the Maumee, about five-eights of a mile; thence west, crossing the foot of St. Clair street, about one mile; thence north half a mile; thence east to the place of beginning, crossing Washington street at its junction with 17th street, Monroe street at its junction with 14th street, Jefferson street between 10th and 11th streets, Madison street between Erie street and the canal, Adams street at its junction with Superior street, and Summit street a little west of Oak street, striking the river near the foot of Cherry street. The tract includes the northwest quarter, and fractional northeast quarter of section one, and the northeast quarter of section two, of township three of the twelve mile square reservation, containing four hundred and one and a half acres.

It will thus be seen that this now constitutes the most important part of the city, including over half a mile of the upper part of Water and Summit streets. The whole includes nearly a thousand lots, according to the city map. And all this, but twenty-eight years ago, was purchased of the University in exchange for another tract, which six years after was bought back for $5,000. By that time, it is probable that lots 1 and 2 could not have been bought, exclusive of improvements, for half a million! At the present time, its value cannot be estimated lower than from two to three millions!

Lots 3 and 4 lay directly west of 1 and 2, with the quarter of section 2 on their rear, making a tract of 457 acres, fronting over half a mile on the river upward from near the mouth of Swan Creek, and extending back on both sides of said Creek about one and one-fourth miles. It includes all the high land (except a few rods at the point,) between Swan Creek and the Maumee, directly against the "middle ground" where the railway improvements are located. Upon it also, is situated the magnificent hotel recently erected.

The half of section three, which accompanied the above, was farther back, but within two miles of the river, and is now crossed by the railroads to Chicago, Detroit, and Jackson.

The remainder of the University lands at Toledo, were situated still farther west, and adjoining the above mentioned tracts. The whole, comprising lots 7, 8, 9 and 10, is now within the city limits. These lots, when accepted, were supposed to contain 515 acres; but a survey made in 1848, showed them to contain 621. The first sales were made in 1849; and in that and the following year, all were sold except one lot of 44½ acres, which was a marsh or wet meadow, extending into the river, and at that time considered of no especial value. At the time of these sales, Toledo containined a population of seven to nine thousand souls, and was rapidly growing in importance. Its commerce at that time exceeded that of any other port save one, upon Lake Erie. The lands were sold for twelve to twenty-five dollars per acre—but one lot of twenty-seven acres going above the last named sum. That sold for $30 per acre. The average price was $19 62 per acre. These lots are now valued at $300 to $1,000 per acre.

The 44½ acres above mentioned, was claimed by an individual on a pre-emption right. A suit had been instituted in the Courts of Ohio, and a judgment was rendered in his favor. An appeal was taken, which was pending in 1855;

when a citizen of Toledo proposed to give $1,000 for the tract, and himself assume all risk as to the title. It was accordingly sold for that sum—closing up the ownership of the University in the Toledo lands.

When these lands were selected, they were not in Ohio, but in the Territory of Michigan, as bounded by more than one Congressional enactment. But the State of Ohio wished to possess the outlet of the Maumee, as well as to have within her borders the important commercial city which it was seen must grow up upon its banks. The old boundary, of a line drawn due east from the south end of Lake Michigan, ran some three miles south of Toledo; and when the people of Michigan Territory began to talk of organizing a State government, the citizens of Ohio claimed that their State extended five or six miles north of Toledo, and attempted to exercise jurisdiction over the Territory in dispute. The history of that contest is familiar to all. The people of Michigan raised an army, and prevented the holding of a Court in the disputed Territory.

When the Territory was admitted into the Union of States, Ohio influence was sufficient in Congress, to obtain her demands, and the line, as claimed by her, was declared to be the Southern boundary of the State of Michigan. As a virtual confession however, that Michigan was robbed of the Territory in question, the whole "Upper Peninsula," was thrown in as an offset, to appease the outraged feelings of the Wolverines.

The University lands were then *de facto*, if not *de jure* in the State of Ohio, and subject to her taxation. Our State officers, whose duty it was to attend to the business, neglected to pay the taxes, and they were sold, and bid in by the State of Ohio. This was in 1839. Thus the matter stood till 1842, when the authorities of Ohio, having doubts as to the legality of the forms under which they were sold, determined to sell them again. The taxes, interest, &c., then claimed, amounted to $550 79. When it was found that the lands (comprising all the original tract save lots 1 and 2) were in danger of being lost, an appeal was made to the Legislature of Ohio, which remitted the amount. From that time, the lands were looked after, and the Commissioners of the Land Office reported upon them from year to year—advising that they should not be sold—till 1849; when they were required by the Legislature to be appraised and offered at public sale. They were appraised at the average price of $19 66 per acre. One hundred and ten acres sold at auction, at an average price of $24 19 per acre. The Commissioner of the Land Office reported that the time was "not far distant when the lands would be worth three times their present value," and approved of their sale at the time, only because they were situated in another State. Nine years have passed, and they are worth fifteen or twenty times the sum for which they were sold.

Such is the history of the University lands at Toledo. All the Fund has realised therefrom, is $17,311 37; or about $17 00 per acre, for what is now worth on an average, more than THREE THOUSAND DOLLARS per acre! Thus narrowly did the University of Michigan escape from becoming rich!

THE OBSERVATORY.

The Observatory, in connection with the University, but recently added to its other attractions and means of influence, by the liberality of the citizens of Detroit, may appropriately be noticed in this place. Such is the magnitude of this Department, and such the interest that can but be felt by the public in its explorations among the heavenly bodies, that it seems befitting to give its history, and to place on record the munificence of the generous donors who have borne the expense of the enterprise. At the request, therefore, of the Superintendent of Public

Instruction, the following statement has been prepared by Mr. James C. Watson, the Assistant Observer:

The project of erecting an Astronomical Observatory originated with Dr. Tappan, of the University. In his inaugural address delivered on the 21st of December, 1852, he showed how advantageously private munificence might be admitted into a State Institution. The same day, after his inauguration, he recieved a visit from Hon. Henry N. Walker, of Detroit, who expressed his deep interest in the University, and his wish to do something for its advancement, in accordance with the suggestion of the inaugural address. Whereupon Dr. Tappan inquired whether the citizens of Detroit would subscribe money for establishing an Observatory, to which Mr. Walker promptly answered in the affirmative. An appointment was then made to meet friends of the enterprise at the Michigan Exchange, in Detroit, a few days afterward. At this meeting Dr. Tappan unfolded the project, addresses were made by several gentlemen, and much enthusiasm was manifested.

The result of the meeting was the following subscription:

"DETROIT, December 29, 1852.

The undersigned, being desirous of obtaining the erection of an Observatory on the University grounds, at Ann Arbor, to be connected with the University of Michigan, do hereby agree to pay to the President of the University the sums set opposite our respective names, to be paid one half on or before the first day of July next, and one half on or before the first day of October next, to be expended under the direction of the President of the University, in the erection and furnishing of an Observatory to be called the DETROIT OBSERVATORY, to be forever connected with the University of Michigan; such payments to be made only in case at least ten thousand dollars is subscribed for that purpose. [Signed.]

Henry N. Walker,........................$500 00

H. P. Baldwin,	500 00
Z. Chandler,	500 00
Elisha C. Litchfield;	500 00
F. & C. H. Buhl,	500 00
Catharine H. Jones,	500 00
B. Wight,	500 00
Smith, Dwight & Co.,	500 00
J. W. Brooks,	500 00
E. A. Bush,	500 00
Franklin Moore,	250 00
J. A. Van Dyke,	200 00
Shubael Conant,	100 00
C. C. Trowbridge,	100 00
J. W. Tillman,	100 00
B. Hubbard,	100 00
S. Barstow,	100 00
Samuel T. Douglass,	100 00
C. A. Trowbridge,	100 00
Henry Ledyard,	100 00
S. N. Kendrick,	100 00
Lothrop & Duffield,	100 00
Duncan Stewart,	100 00
Wm. M. Whitcomb,	100 00
Henry D. A. Ward,	100 00
C. Howard,	100 00
John Owen,	100 00
E. N. Wilcox,	50 00
Total,	$7,000 00

The plan originally proposed, as may be readily inferred from the amount of money contemplated to be raised by subscription, was to purchase only a large telescope and erect a building sufficient for its accommodation. The unexpected liberality, however, with which the project was received by those who were both willing and able to carry it into effect, soon induced President Tappan to enlarge the plan so as to embrace nothing less than the erection and equipment of a first class Astronomical Observatory.

On mentioning his views to Mr. Walker and several other friends of the enterprise, they encouraged him to proceed. In the month of February following, Dr. Tappan, then on his way to Europe, was accompanied to New York, by Mr. Walker, and at a meeting which took place at the residence of Col. Livingston, in that city, where several scientific gentlemen were present, a contract was made with Mr. Henry Fitz, 237 Fifth Street, New York, to furnish an Achromatic refracting telescope, equatorially mounted, of at least twelve inches clear aperture, to be delivered in that city, ready for transportation, on or before the first day of June, 1854. The amount which Mr. Fitz was to receive for this instrument, when completed, was six thousand one hundred and fifty dollars.

In view, therefore, of the superior dimensions of the Equatorial contracted for, which was to be second only to the great Refractors at Cambridge, Massachusetts, and at Pulkowa, in Russia, it seemed extremely desirable that the other equipments of the Observatory should be correspondingly extensive. The amount already subscribed, would not allow of the perfection of such a liberal and extended plan. Mr. Walker, however, immediately furnished Dr. Tappan with funds to purchase, while in Europe, a Meridian Circle of the largest and most expensive kind.

Having thus already contracted for a great Refracting Telescope to be made by an American artist, Dr. Tappan sailed with his family for Europe, where they duly and safely arrived. After having visited the principal observatories in England, France, and Italy, leaving his family at Geneva, in Switzerland, he repaired to northern Germany, and upon arriving at Berlin, visited the Royal Observatory in that city, where he became acquainted with Professor Encke, the celebrated Astronomer, and his assistant, Dr. Brunnow. He had no sooner made known his plans to these gentlemen than they at once recommended him to employ Messrs. Pistor and Martins, of Berlin, to construct the Meridian Circle, and, at his request, they very kindly consented to supervise its construction in every particular. The result of this recommendation was the following contract with the above named artists:

"We do hereby engage to make for the University of Michigan, in the United States of America, a Transit instrument [Meridian Circle] with a telescope of eight feet focal length, English measure, with an object-glass of seventy-two French lines, in diameter, with two divided circles of three feet diameter each, with eight microscopes and complete furniture, throughout as described under number one of our *Preis Verzeichniss.* We engage to furnish and deliver the same by May 1st, 1854, and to pack and forward the same to New York to the care of Messrs. Sturges, Bennett & Co., unless in the mean time otherwise directed. We accept Professor Encke and Dr. Brunnow, of Berlin, as the judges of the instrument, and engage to furnish one with which they shall be satisfied. The above instrument we engage to make for the sum of four thousand Prussian Thalers, to be paid us upon delivery of the instrument. Dated Berlin, July 15th. 1853.

In witness whereof, we have set the hand and seal of our firm.

[Signed.] PISTOR & MARTINS, [Seal.]"

Witness—[Signed,] Dr. Brunnow.

By the terms of this contract, it will be perceived that the instrument was not to be paid for until approved and delivered. Dr. Tappan, therefore, brought back and returned to Mr. Walker the Bill of Exchange with which he had furnished him. After the instrument was received at Ann Arbor, Mr. Walker paid for it, and donated it to the Observatory.

At the recommendation, also, of Professor Encke, Dr. Tappan purchased of Mr. Tiede, of Berlin, an Astronomical Clock, which was thoroughly tested at the Royal Observatory, before its acceptance and shipment to this country. After his return, he also engaged Messrs. Pistor & Martins to furnish two collimators, at a cost of $375 00.

Having thus accomplished the object of his visit, so far as it related to the Observatory, he spent the remaining portion of his stay in Europe in visiting the schools and in examining into the system of public instruction. He returned to Ann Arbor in the month of September, 1853, after an absence of only seven months.

While the instruments were in process of construction, the Regents of the University purchased about five acres of ground, situated a little more than a quarter of a mile northeast from the University grounds, including an eminence high above the surrounding country, and commanding, in every direction, a clear and unobstructed view of the horizon. The plans and drawings for the building having been completed by Professor Bull, of New York, whom Dr. Tappan had employed to superintend its construction, before leaving for Europe, ground was broken for laying the foundation of the great central pier, which was to support the great equatorial telescope, early in May, 1853. From this time onward the work of constructing the building progressed favorably and rapidly until its completion, which was in due time for the reception of the instruments.

The amount of money, however, as we have previously remarked, which had, up to this time, been subscribed, was not sufficient to defray the additional expense arising from the extended plan which was being carried out, and it became necessary, under these circumstances, to appeal to those who were liberal and wealthy, that the deficiency should no longer exist. The result of this appeal was the following:

"DETROIT, May, 1854.

"The undersigned, being desirous of finishing and furnishing the Observatory now constructing at Ann Arbor, called the Detroit Observatory, upon the improved and extended plan now in course of being carried out, agree to pay the sums set opposite to our names, on or before the first day of September next, to the President of the University of Michigan, to be expended by him in the completion and furnishing of the Observatory aforesaid:

M. Weston Field,	$100 00
J. M. Harmon,	100 00
W. S. Driggs,	100 00
J. W. Brooks,	100 00
Theodore H. Eaton,	100 00
E. W. Hudson,	50 00
T. H. Hinchman,	50 00
John Winder,	50 00
Eliza E. Stuart,	50 00
Pittman, Trowbridge & Jones,	50 00
C. A. Trowbridge,	50 00
Henry Doty,	50 00
James H. Hicks,	50 00
James H. Armstrong,	25 00
George Doty,	25 00
B. C. Whittemore,	25 00
Sylvester Larned,	25 00
E. A. Lansing,	25 00
B. B. &. W. R. Noyes,	25 00
J. C. Holmes,	25 00
Edwin Noyes,	25 00
James V. Campbell,	25 00
Bridge & Lewis,	25 00
Total,	$1,150 00"

To this must be added Mr. Walker's draft for the amount which was to be paid for the Meridian Circle, making the total amount of his subscription *three thousand seven hundred dollars.*

The building and instruments were now rapidly arriving toward completion, and it remained, therefore, before the latter could be mounted and prepared for use, to procure the services of an Astronomer competent to undertake the future scientific direction of the Observatory. The great neglect which had been shown to astronomical science in our country, rendered it necessary to look abroad for some one qualified to undertake this duty; and very naturally, of course, the name of Dr. Brunnow, who, from the very beginning, had so disinterestedly exerted himself, as far as it lay in his power, to perfect the plans of the liberal and enlightened donors, appeared most conspicuous among the brilliant array of European astronomers. The fitness of such a selection received the cordial and unanimous approval of the friends of the enterprise, and at a meeting of the Board of Regents, held in March, 1854, he was unanimously elected Director of the Observatory and Professor of Astronomy in the University of Michigan. The official announcement of his appointment, was communicated to him by President Tappan, and received his acceptance. He arrived at Ann Arbor in July, 1854, and immediately assumed the duties pertaining to his office.

The Meridian Circle was received in September following, and was mounted as soon as the stone piers, upon which it rests, were prepared for its reception. The great refracting telescope being yet unfinished, a temporary one was loaned to the Observatory by Mr. Fitz, and was received in April, 1855. This instrument was superseded in December following by the one which had been contracted for. The mounting of the latter, with the exception of the position circles and the appendages belonging to the tube, was of cast iron, and the experience of a few months having clearly demonstrated its inferiority, rendering the instrument nearly, if not entirely useless, for making very accurate astronomical observations, a new contract was made with Mr. Fitz, by which he agreed to make a new instrument, to be mounted wholly in brass and bell-metal. For this, when completed, he was to receive the one already in use and the additional amount of six hundred dollars, making the total cost of the new instrument six thousand seven hundred and fifty dollars. The new contract was successfully complied with by Mr. Fitz, and the equatorial instrument, which was finally accepted, arrived at Ann Arbor and was mounted in November, 1857.

In the meantime, a meeting of the subscribers to the Observatory was held at the National Hotel, in the city of Detroit, on the evening of the 13th of March, 1856, and the following resolution was unanimously adopted:

"*Resolved*, That the subscribers to the 'Detroit Observatory' hereby express their entire satisfaction with the manner in which President Tappan has executed the trust reposed in him, in relation thereto, and cordially congratulate the friends of the University, and the citizens of the State, on the successful completion of an Observatory in which we all may take great pleasure."

A committee was then appointed to solicit subscriptions to liquidate a balance still due on the Observatory, which amounted to about eight thousand dollars. This committee consisted of President Tappan, and Messrs. F. Buhl, Theodore H. Eaton, C. I. Walker and C. A. Trowbridge. The subscriptions obtained were the following:

A. Sheley,...............................	$500 00
I. F. Joy,...............................	500 00
Gen. Cass,...............................	500 00
I. W. Waterman,..........................	500 00
S. M. Holmes,............................	200 00
Elon Farnsworth,.........................	200 00
D. Cooper,...............................	200 00
F. Buhl,.................................	125 00
Theodore H. Eaton,.......................	100 00

A. C. McGraw,	$100 00
Wm. A, Butler,	100 00
Philo Parsons,	100 00
Walker & Russell,	100 00
George E. Hand,	100 00
George B. Russell,	100 00
Campbell & Linn,	50 00
W. N. Campbell,	25 00
Total,	$3,500 00

To complete the outline of the history of the establishment of the Observatory, it remains only to add that, at the meeting of the Board of Regents held on March 26, 1858, Mr. James C. Watson, a graduate of the University, in the class of 1857, who had been carefully trained by Dr. Brunnow, and had become familiar with the use of the instruments, was appointed, on his recommendation, Assistant Observer. We shall now proceed to describe, as briefly as possible, the instruments belonging to the Observatory, and, also, to give a summary of the principal contributions to astronomical science, which have emanated from it.

The building is of brick, stuccoed, and consists of a main part 32 feet square and 23 feet high, and two wings, one on the east and one on the west side, each 20 feet wide, 18 feet long, and 15 feet high. The east wing contains the Meridian Circle Collimators, Astronomical Clock, a standard Barometer, and an external and internal Thermometer. The meridian opening extends entirely across the roof and down each side to a point below the plane of the horizon. It is thirty inches wide, the portions in the sides of the building being closed by shutters sliding in grooves in the casings, and the portion which extends across the roof being closed by two shutters hung on hinges, so that each may be raised or lowered by means of a crank and a rope, which, passing through a hole in the roof and over a pulley, is attached to the upper side. The west wing was fitted

10

up into apartments for the observer, to contain the books and charts belonging to the Observatory.

The main part of the building is surmounted by a hemisperical revolving dome, 23 feet in diameter, in which there is an opening 18 inches wide, extending from the horizon to the zenith, closed by a single curved shutter, which, by means of rack-work, may be made to travel to the opposite side of the dome. Through the centre of the main building, rises the great central pier which supports the Equatorial Telescope. This pier is built of brick, and has its foundation fifteen feet below the surface. It rises completely detached from the building to the height of nearly forty feet, and is constructed in the form of a frustum of a cone, twenty feet in diameter at the base, and ten feet in diameter at the top. It is surmounted by a circular cap of limestone, quarried at Sandusky, Ohio. Upon this capstone stands a pier of limestone nine feet in height, weighing over four tons, to the top of which the base-plate of the equatorial mounting of the great Refracting Telescope is secured.

There are also in the east wing five piers of the same stone, and of similar dimensions, two for the Meridian Circle, one for each Collimator, and one for the Astronomical Clock.

The large Equatorial, which was constructed by Mr. Fitz, has an Achromatic Refracting Telescope of 12⅝ inches clear aperture, and 17 feet 8 inches focal length. It has seven negative and six positive eye-pieces, the highest magnifying power being 1200 times, and the lowest 50 times. There is also a ring-micrometer, sun-shades, and a filar-micrometer of the German construction, which has one vertical wire, one movable and three fixed horizontal wires, and also a position circle reading by two verniers to single minutes. The Telescope has an achromatic finder 2½ inches in clear aperture, and 36 inches in focal length.

The equatorial mounting is after the plan originally prepared by the celebrated Fraunhofer, of Munich. The polar axis is five inches in diameter at the larger bearing, two and a half inches in diameter at the smaller end, and thirty-five inches long. The declination axis is four and a half inches in diameter at the larger bearing, and two and a half inches at the smaller end. Both axes are made of bell metal. The hour circle is made of brass, 18 inches in diameter, graduated on an inlaid band of silver, to single minutes, and reads by means of two verniers to single seconds of time. The declination circle is also of brass, 20 inches in diameter, graduated on a band of silver to 10 minutes of arc from 0 to 360 degrees and reads by means of two verniers to 10 seconds of arc. To the hour circle is attached a tangent screw for slow motion in a direction parallel to the equator, and to the declination circle a tangent screw for slow motion in declination. There is also clock-work connected with the hour circle, which gives to the telescope a slow motion, corresponding exactly to the diurnal motion of the heavenly bodies arising from the rotation of the earth about its axis.

The Meridian Circle constructed by Messrs. Pistor and Martins, of Berlin, is mounted in the east wing. It has an Achromatic Telescope eight feet in focal length, and $6\frac{3}{8}$ inches in clear aperture, situated at the middle of the horizontal axis, with four positive eye-pieces, magnifying from 85 to 288 times. The horizontal axis is perforated so that the light emanating from a lamp, placed at either extremity, and passing to the centre of the tube, is reflected to the eye-piece, by a mirror inclined to the axis at an angle of 45 deg., and thus illuminating the field of view of the Telescope. The mirror is also perforated at its centre so as not to interfere with the rays of light coming from the object-glass. There is also a contrivance for illuminating the wires and leaving a dark field, which is employed in observing very faint objects. The circles are firmly attached by screws to each end of the horizontal axis. They are three feet two inches in diameter, divided on an inlaid band of silver to two minutes, and reading by means of four microscopes to the nearest tenth of a second. The entire mounting of the instrument is of brass, with the exception of the axis, which is of bell metal.

Directly opposite to the Meridian Circle, and in the plane of the meridian, are mounted two collimators, one on the north side and one on the south side, which are employed for determining the error of collimation of the telescope, and the amount of flexure in the tube. Besides the collimators, there is an apparatus for observing stars, and for finding the nadir point, by reflection from a basin of mercury. The east wing contains also the siderial clock, made by Tiede, in Berlin, and the standard barometer and thermometers.

In addition to the instruments already enumerated, the Observatory possesses a siderial chronometer, made by Messrs. Negus, of New York, and a comet-seeker of four inches clear aperture and forty-four inches focal length, made by Mr. Fitz, of New York.

This Observatory has undertaken to observe all the double stars south of the equator which are visible in this latitude—the only observations of these which have hitherto been made, being those taken by Sir John Herschel, at the Cape of Good Hope. In addition to this, the Director has engaged that the Observatory shall furnish regular observations of the following planets: *Astrœa, Flora, Hebe, Metis, Clio, Calliope, Proserpina, Euphrosyne;* besides observations of all newly-discovered asteroids and of comets.

The principal contributions to Astronomical Science, which have emanated from the Observatory, up to the present time, (September, 1858,) are the following:

(1.) Tables of Flora, with reference to the perturbations by Jupiter and Saturn, by Professor F. Brunnow. Published by the Royal Academy of Berlin; quarto, 1855.

(2.) Tables of Victoria, with the pertubations by Jupiter and Saturn, by Professor F. Brunnow. Published by authority of the Board of Regents of the University of Michigan; quarto, 1858.

(3.) In the *Astronomische Nachrichten*, published at Altona, in Denmark:

General perturbations of Victoria by Jupiter and Saturn, and Ephemeris for the opposition in 1857, by Professor Brunnow.

Ephemeris of Victoria for the opposition in 1858–9, by Professor Brunnow.

Observations of the Fourth Comet of 1857, by James C. Watson.

Elements and Ephemeris of the Fifth Comet of 1858, by James C. Watson.

(4.) In the *Astronomical Journal*, published at Albany, N. Y., the following:

Observations of Flora, by Professor Brunnow.

Elements of the First Comet of 1857, by James C. Watson.

Elements of Ariadne, by James C. Watson.

Elements and Ephemeris of the Fourth Comet of 1857, by James C. Watson.

Elliptic elements of the Fourth Comet of 1857, by James C. Watson.

Elements of Victoria, by Professor Brunnow.

Observations of Victoria, by James C. Watson.

Elements and Ephemeris of the Sixth Comet of 1857, by James C. Watson.

Observations of Metis and Flora, by Professor Brunnow.

Elements of the First Comet of 1858, by James C. Watson.

Elliptic elements of the First Comet of 1858, by James C. Watson.

Observations of the Comets 1857 IV and 1857 V, Letitia, Virginia, Hestia, Aglaia, and Calliope, by James C. Watson.

Elements and Ephemeris of Nemausa, by James C. Watson.

Elements and Ephemeris of Calypso, by James C. Watson.

Elements and Ephemeris of the Third Comet of 1858, by James C. Watson.

Observations of Calliope, Thalia, Massalia, Hebe, and the Comets 1858 I, 1858 II, and 1858 III, by Prof. Brunnow.

Observations of the Comets 1858 I, 1858 II, and 1858 III, and the Asteroids Europa, Nemausa, and Atalanta, by Jas. C. Watson.

On the orbit of Hestia, by James C. Watson.

Elements and Ephemeris of the Fifth Comet of 1858, by James C. Watson.

Such is the Detroit Observatory of the University of Michigan; an institution of which the State may well be proud, since, although it is less than two years since it commenced active operations, it has already taken a position which ranks among the first in the world.

THE STATE AGRICULTURAL COLLEGE.

The State of Michigan has a greater extent of coast upon navigable waters, and more harbors, than any other State in the Union. But that very fact prevents her from engaging extensively in commerce, except so far as it is created and sustained by her own enterprise. Being almost surrounded by water, the commerce of the lakes created by other States, has little occasion to pass through her ports.

But what is thus lost is more than gained, in point of State wealth, by the facilities afforded for her domestic trade, and the aid thus given in the development of her internal resources, naturally great, and already sufficiently improved to give an extensive trade upon her railroads, and a very large domestic commerce to her port towns—numbering ten or twelve places of considerable importance, and as many more whose business is increasing, as the country tributary to them becomes improved. Her vast quantities of lumber, and minerals, and her agricultural products, form an important item in the commerce of other States. Yet Michigan cannot be called a commercial State.

The growing importance of her mines—her iron ore, equal in excellence to any in the world—is destined yet to make her mineral resources as world-wide as they are inexhaustible. Yet, her mines, with all their anticipated importance and unlimited wealth, are mainly in one locality, and can never be the most important feature of State prosperity. She can never be known distinctively as a mining State.

It can hardly be foretold what Michigan will yet become in her manufactures. Her vast mineral resources—her water-power, which is considerable—her vast forests for wood, and her extensive beds of coal, which wait only the demand, to supply whatever amount is required—her economical production of most of the wants of life, and her easy communication with other States in every direction, would seem to point her out as destined at some day to become engaged in manufactures to a very great amount. But as yet, with the exception of lumber, she manufactures but little except for her own consumption. She is, therefore, not yet at least, a manufacturing State.

Her access from every part to navigable waters, the variety and richness of her soil, her railroads, which have been and are building, to a great extent, in advance of settlement, unitedly invite the Agriculturist to make Michigan his home. For the cereal grains, and all the coarser productions of the soil, the State is doubtless equal to any other ; while for fruit, from the peach to the most hardy fruit of the northern climes, it is in some respects superior to all. While in northern Michigan the excellence of the common potatoe is unrivalled, in southern Michigan the sweet potatoe can be raised with ample success. Extending from a latitude of 41 degrees and 43 minutes northward about six and a half degrees, it gives a variety of climate from that in which the grape is successfully cultivated, with an average season of sleighing not exceeding four weeks per annum, to the invigorating atmosphere of Lake Superior.

Therefore, notwithstanding her unlimited mineral resources, her vast lumber interests, her important fisheries, her inducements to manufactures, and her unparalleled commercial facilities, Michigan is, and probably will be for years to come, an *Agricultural State.*

Nor is she so, because men are driven from other occupations, and compelled reluctantly to apply to an equally reluctant soil for subsistence. It might almost be said of many, that they make Agriculture a passion! Consequently we see in nearly every organized county an Agricultural Society—and in some counties two—where the farmers exhibit and compare their productions, enlighten and stimulate each other, creating a public sentiment which makes labor honorable, and diffusing knowledge which makes it more profitable. The State Agricultural Society, also, which receives from the State two thousand dollars per annum toward its support, continues its operations from year to year, with unabated interest, and publishes annually, a large volume of its proceedings, for public benefit.

There are classes of men of certain occupations, who delight to exhibit their ability and skill, but show no disposition to aid others in arriving at a like standard of excellence. It is a selfish spirit of competition, that desires a monopoly of whatever advantage may be gained, regardless of the welfare of others, or of the general good. There are large classes of men who should be natural allies, who treat each other like natural enemies. Thrown together by an affinity of pursuits, and really benefitting by each others' prosperity, if careful in any respect, it is *not* to "play into each others' hands;" and they rather prefer to see men of other professions prosper and receive promotion to office and influence. There are large numbers in our land, who as a class (of course, with many individual exceptions,) are pursuing this suicidal policy and destroying their own success and influence among men—living as though they suppose they will rise, just in proportion as they can pull their fellows down.

Whether men have noticed it or not, such is a sad fact in the social world. Men are often willing to ignore their own good, if they can prevent others from obtaining an equal degree of prosperity with themselves; and it is here alluded to, not to preach them a lecture upon their folly, or their wrong, but as showing the contrast between them and the agricultural class. They, as a class, are actuated by no such short-sighted evil policy. With them, what one knows, all may know. They rally without jealousy, to each others' aid, socially and politically. Legislative bodies invariably show from five to ten times as many members from among the farmers, in proportion to numbers, as from another class which might be named, who have equal, yes, superior advantages for qualifying themselves for stations of honor and influence.

The only enemies of this class are themselves; but the farmer has no enemies, and no rivals, in the obnoxious sense of the term. All men, of all classes, wish him success; and all are benefitted in his prosperity.

Commerce *produces* no wealth to the country; it only *exhibits* the prosperity created by the artisan and farmer. Like the piles of gold in the banker's window, it *shows* the riches, and aids in exchanging the products of labor; but it does not produce them. Commerce is like the farmer's wagon, upon which he carries his productions to market. So far from its creating the products, the expense of its own dead weight must be subtracted from their avails. It is a convenience, a necessity; and the means of making wealth more available; but it never doubles a grain of wheat. On the other hand, its use is attended with a constant waste. True, it may make a bushel of wheat, worth but one dollar in Michigan, worth two dollars in a distant market; but it has *created* no gains; the apparent gain is a loss to somebody else.

The real source of wealth is in a power which creates, or produces—which fills the pocket of one man without emptying that of another. Such production is real gain to the world, while the wealth acquired by Commerce is, to a great extent, at the expense of some other interest. The man who raises a bushel of wheat, creates it, under Providence, out of the earth ; but the man who transports it to market, adds nothing to its intrinsic value ; it will feed no greater number of persons in New England than in Michigan ; and what he indvidually gains in the transaction, comes out of the pocket of the consumer or producer, or is shared between them.

Such being the case, it has ever been considered that the agriculturist is more emphatically a *producer* of wealth than any other class. But while the importance of his class, both from this fact and from its numbers, has always been admitted, it is surprising how slow is the progress that has been made. Not that the progress in agriculture has not in some respects been great. As far as improvement in the implements of his labor is concerned, the change since the remembrance of some who still "hold the plow," is astonishing. From the old sickle, with which he cut his fingers when a boy, he has seen the change to the giant reaper, that can do a giant's work. He has seen the water-pail, from which handful by handful he spread his seed broadcast upon the ground, exchanged for the seed-drill, which, by horse power, leaves every seed in its proper place. So with the plow, and other implements. But it cannot fail to be observed that all these improvements are mainly physical, or mechanical. The great study of cause and effect, with reference to vegetable growth, as well as the acquisition of general knowledge, has been strangely disregarded.

A man may learn from their effects alone, that certain medicines are good for certain diseases ; and he may thus apply remedies, often with benefit and success ; yet knowing nothing of the human system, the nature of disease, or the nature of the remedy. Too much in this manner has the agricultural world, in all the past, pursued its way.

But it has occurred to some minds that the farmer-whose sphere is in Nature's laboratory, should know some, thing of Nature ; in the constitution of the soil she gives him ; something of the nature of the remedies he applies for its renovation, and from a knowledge of both, be able to decide without the slow, expensive, uncertain process of repeated experiments alone, to what productions his soil is, or may be made adapted, how most certainly to apply the remedy, and how to secure the greatest result with the least labor.

The quack may give his patient (and patient must he be who suffers it) twenty "remedies" by way of experiment. It is the best he can do ; he may succeed, or he may "kill on the first fire ;" when the scientific practitioner might perceive the true nature of the disease, and from his knowledge of the nature of medicine, be able to give that which will on the first trial effect a cure. The same principles will apply to the agriculturist, with a similar difference in his success.

To acquire this knowledge, schools are as necessary for the farmer as for the physician. And it is indeed a wonder in our land, that schools for systematic instruction of the Agricultural Class were not instituted generations since! In organizing new States, liberal grants of land have been made for a great variety of purposes ; for schools of Latin and Greek, and Law, and Medicine, as well as the Primary School for all ; but knowledge for the farmer, as such, has been ignored, and the wants of the most numerous class in society forgotten. By a strange infatuation, the world has seemed to think that "any fool could be a farmer," and therefore, it was no matter if all the farmers, as such, were fools!

But yet the world moves! Men are beginning to grasp a new idea, in the appreciation of which, the citizens of Michigan stand foremost. Late as we have been, in the movement, we may well be proud of the fact, that first in the Union has been the inauguration of the MICHIGAN AGRICULTURAL COLLEGE!

The incipient steps for the establishment of an Agricultural School in Michigan, were taken over eight years since, by a provision of our present State Constitution, which required the Legislature, as soon as practicable, to establish such an institution. The question of practicability was one upon which opinions probably differed; but nothing was done till 1855,* when the Legislature decided to establish the School; the same to be located within ten miles of the State Capital. Twenty-two sections of Salt Spring lands were appropriated, to meet the expense of putting the School in operation.

The law was approved February 12th, by GOVERNOR BINGHAM—who from the first has been a warm and efficient friend of the enterprise—and in June, the Executive Committee of the State Agricultural Society—the agents designated by the law for that purpose—selected and recommended the purchase of a farm of six hundred and twenty-three and fifty-six one-hundredths acres, situated upon each side of Cedar river, three and one-half miles due east from the capital; and in pursuance of the law, the State Board of Education approved of the selection, and concluded the purchase of the same, for $9,353 55—or fifteen dollars per acre. This was considered by all acquainted with the circumstances, to be a reasonable price. It was thought very desirable to procure, in addition to the above, an adjoining tract of fifty-three and one one-hundredth acres, upon which some improvements had been made; but which the Board could not buy—fifteen dollars per acre being as high as they were allowed to pay, by the act authorizing the purchase. This was, however, procured, and $1,059 92 paid therefor, agreeable to a Joint Resolution of the Legislature; making the whole amount six hundred and seventy-six and fifty-seven one-hundredths acres, and a total expense of $10,413 47.

* A bill establishing an Agricultural College in 1853, passed the Senate by a vote of 17 to 14, and was lost in the House by a vote of 36 to 24.

In 1856, a large boarding-house, and the west wing of the College buildings, one hundred by fifty feet, and four stories high, including a high basement, were erected, and nearly ready for use when the Legislature convened in January, 1857. The sum of $34,181 50 was expended in 1856.

The aggregate minimum price of the twenty-two sections of Salt Spring lands was $56,320; and the Legislature of 1857 further appropriated $40,000 from the treasury, to meet the wants of the institution, in completing the necessary improvements, furnishing apparatus, &c., and sustaining the current expenses of the School in operation for the years 1857 and 1858.

The farm was new, and a heavy expense was required to bring a portion of it under immediate cultivation. Barns, &c., were to be built, with dwellings for the officers; (for until this was done, they must reside at Lansing,) and about the time the School was to be opened, provisions, and almost everything required in commencing farm operations, rose to unprecedented high prices. The contractors who erected the College buildings had performed some of their work insufficiently, and $1,546 13 had been deducted from their pay, in a settlement with the Board of Education; but the cost of repairing their deficiences was found to be much more than was anticipated, involving additional expense.

The Board of Education elected Hon. JOSEPH R. WILLIAMS, President, and *J. C. Holmes, Esq.*, *Calvin Tracy, Esq.*, *Robert D. Weeks, Esq.*, and *Rev. L. R. Fisk*, Professors of the Institution: which was opened by appropriate exercises, with sixty-one students, on the 13th of May, 1857.

The second term commenced in December of the same year, with one hundred students.

The third term commenced in April, 1858, with no increase of numbers, for the reason that the buildings were already crowded to their utmost capacity. Had the accommodations been sufficient for all who made application for admission, the number of students at the third term would have been not less than two hundred.

The amount paid upon previous contracts, expended in improvements, and for the support of the school, in 1857, and till April, 1858, was $52,931 66.

Thus the institution was put in operation, a large College building, four Professors' houses, a boarding house, a brick barn and out-houses, were erected; one of the best laboratories in the country purchased; nearly 200 acres of land cleared and brought under cultivation; an orchard planted, and the farm stocked with horses and cattle; and the school conducted one year, at an expense, including the cost of the magnificent farm, of $97,526 63. This is less, exclusive of the farm, than was the expense of putting the State University in operation, and sustaining it one year, with ten students. The University now boasts of its four hundred and fifty students, and holds an enviable rank among the highest Schools in the land. Yet its commencement was far more unpromising, and its pecuniary embarrassments were vastly greater, than have been those of the Agricultural College.

The actual wants of the Agricultural College required at least ten thousand dollars more than has been provided, to carry it to the spring of 1859 without embarrassment, and anxiety on the part of its officers. But in this, it has only encountered the same misfortune that has attended the early days of every State institution.

Sunlight and rain are the free gifts of God. Money cannot buy them, nor the want of it deprive us of their blessings. But Providence does not furnish the farmer with his plow growing by his gateway, or the blacksmith with his forge ready built. Neither does Providence build us Churches, Asylums, or School houses. But a munificent Creator has given us the means by which with our own hands to procure these and other social blessings, and left us to a great extent, to have them or not, according to our appreciation of their benefits. The rich fruits are placed within our power to obtain, and we may reach forth our hand and feast upon their luxuriance, or we may starve on in moral and intellectual poverty as whole ages and races have done before us.

The liberal hand with which the citizens of Michigan have dispensed the means for public improvements, public charities and Schools, is proof beyond dispute that in these things the question with them is not, "will they cost money?" but only this: "will they be worth the money expended?" This is a legitimate caution, which they will consider as well in reference to the Agricultural College as any other enterprise.

That the establishment of this institution was called for by public sentiment, as it was imperatively demanded by the Constitution, there can be no doubt. The year 1855 found the State Treasury in an apparently well replenished condition. True, a large portion of the funds were borrowed money, upon which the State was paying six and seven per cent., while they were earning the State but one per cent. per annum. But it was not optional with the State to borrow the money or not; it had long before agreed to loan all the trust funds as they accumulated; and for some years previous to 1855, they had increased rapidly, from the general prosperity of the country and consequent extensive sales of land. These funds were still flowing into the treasury, and but comparatively a small portion would be soon required to meet the State indebtedness, most of which was not for several years due.

The question then very naturally arose with the Legislature of 1855—shall these hundreds of thousands still remain in the treasury, earning but *one per cent.*, while the State is paying six and seven per cent. for them—or shall a liberal portion be used in building up those important State institutions demanded by our Christianity, by philanthropy, by public sentiment, and by the Constitution? It was decided with great unanimity that a portion should be thus used; and that what remained in the treasury should be made to earn *five per cent.* per annum. The bill passed the Senate by a vote of *twenty-four* to *five*, and the House by a vote of *forty-four* to *fourteen*. The amount of the five per cent. earned by the money in the treasury, after the withdrawal of all that was used in carrying on the public institutions, and for the expenses of the government, in 1855, '56 and '57, was $61,484 98—or $51,237 49 more than the same amount would have earned at one per cent., as by the previous law. The *difference, alone*, is more than will have been drawn from the treasury (exclusive of the avails of salt spring lands) to place the Agricultural College free from all debts at the commencement of its third school year in 1859. This may be considered a sufficient comment upon the financial policy of the Legislature which inaugurated the institution. As to the economy that has been practiced in putting the School in operation, it is believed that, considering the difficulties to be overcome, the Board of Education have acquitted themselves well, and to the satisfaction of a candid public.

All was new—the character of the School itself, not less so, than the lands upon which it was to be located. It *was*, in 1855, in most of its features, an experiment. It *is*, in 1858, no longer so. It had then no precedents upon which to rely. It has now furnished successful precedents which several other States are already taking measures to follow. Experiment has changed to demonstration. Never was the figure of the wilderness blossoming like the rose, more literally manifested. Where in 1855, was the wild forest farm, are now the smiling fields, elegant College buildings, and one hundred students, who, as a body, are proud of the institution, and indignant at any attempts to decry its benefits, or injure its reputation. With three hours per day of field labor, it is the testimony of the officers, who have had experience in other institutions, that the students come to their recitations with clearer minds, and as great advancement as in other Schools.

Discipline is said also to be easier than in Colleges generally. The relaxation from study, which so often leads to irregularity and mischief, here takes another direction, and the physical demands for action, like the steam in the boiler, which must be discharged to prevent danger, is here expended in useful labor. But there are other causes also, which contribute to the good deportment of the students. Colleges are usually in cities or large towns, where every temptation is at hand, soliciting the student to sensual indulgence and mischief. The Agricultural College is in the country, three and a half miles from any settlement, except here and there the farm house of a respectable citizen, entirely away from town temptations, and where the practice of many of the vices of youth in towns is next to impossible.

There is also a difference in the character of the students themselves. The largest portion are from the country—from the seclusion of the farmer's home—and have not so much acquired town habits, or been so much subject to town temptations, and consequently are less inclined to town vices.

The Agricultural College, like the State University, is under the control of no religious denomination or sectarian influence. Yet like that, it is designed to be in the hands of men who recognize the claims of a common Christianity, and will recommend its principles with true catholicity, by precept and by example. No College, therefore, is a safer place for a parent to send his son, with reference to moral influence upon his character.

The Agricultural College of Michigan is now in successful operation. The only questions are; Shall it be sustained? and how?

To the question—shall it be sustained?—it is believed that the people of Michigan will give but one answer. When a State suffers its Schools to expire, (unless superceded by others,) it gives fearful tokens of decay, and a relapse toward, if not actually to, public ignorance and barbarism. Blot out the State University, the Normal School, and the Agricultural College, and the same public sentiment that will *thus* assassinate the GENIUS OF MIND, will lift no hand to save local Seminaries and Primary Schools from a similar fate. Well may we look with honest pride at the State University, and rejoice in the great work it is doing; but the genius of its system is not specially adapted to the wants of the farmer. Its main design is in other directions. The Agricultural College, while it designs to discipline the mind of the student, and impart generally, the most useful practical knowledge of men and things, makes his instruction in those branches of science most useful to him *as a Tiller of the Soil*, a primary object. That the College shall be sustained, therefore, is believed to be a proposition that requires little argumentation with an intelligent people.

This question, however, in view of the other, may admit of a division, which is debatable. Shall the College be sustained only with its present capacity—or shall it be made commensurate with the wants and wishes of the class for whom it is instituted?

It has now one hundred students; and this is the utmost limit of its capacity. At the commencement of the last term, about one hundred and fifty applicants were rejected or discouraged from appearing at examination, for no other reason than because there was no room to receive them. As many will probably be refused admittance in April next, unless the applications shall be withheld, from a knowledge that the institution is full. To meet the full demand, requires that further additions to the College buildings should be immediately erected, and the boarding accommodations increased three-fold, with additional barns, and other incidental expenses. Fifty thousand dollars would probably no more than make such additional improvements as might be fully occupied as soon as completed. (Such increased accommodations as would admit of two hundred students, might probably be secured for twelve to fifteen thousand dollars.) Thus this question involves the other: How shall the College be sustained?

The Agricultural College has no endowment. Until it has, its current expenses must be a charge upon the treasury, if tuition is to remain free. The State has no more unappropriated lands from which to create an endowment fund, as has been done for the University and Normal School; and their funds, even, are not sufficient for their wants. The Educational funds from Congressional grants are all pledged to their appropriate ends. The seventy-two sections of Salt Spring lands have been appropriated—twenty-two sections to the Agricultural College, twenty-five to the Normal School, and twenty-five to the Asylums for the Deaf and Blind, and the Insane. The avails of the Internal Improvement lands have been expended in various ways, and are a matter of history. The will of the people appears decisive that such portion of the avails of the Swamp Lands as are not required for reclaiming the lands, shall be added to the Primary School Fund; as thus imparting the greatest good to the greatest number. The State has no more lands from which to create an endowment for this, or any other institution.

As members of a great confederacy we have an interest in many hundred millions of acres of land, several millions of which lie within our own borders, but of which the State has no exclusive ownership, or power even of taxation. In all these untold millions we have only an equal ownership, according to population, with Vermont or Georgia. Congress has for years been well granting an immense amount of these lands to aid in internal improvements. But this has not been done exactly as a gift, or as distributing to "the people" that which is their own; but rather with the expectation that the remaining lands would be thereby increased in value equal to, or exceeding the whole.

But what real difference would it make, whether the grant of land to build a railway increases the value of the remaining lands, or adds an equal amount to the wealth of the country in some other way? And may we not justly claim that the wealth of the country is increased by the education of the people? Especially will this be true in reference to Agricultural Schools. As is Michigan, so is our nation essentially an Agricultural Nation. As a Nation, we buy more manufactured productions than we sell, and sell more of the earth's productions than we buy. The farmers cannot be educated—and especially if educated in reference to their profession—without adding materially to national wealth and power. Therefore, if the public lands are to be regarded only in the sordid view of dollars and cents, a portion can be appropriated in no wiser direction than for the education of that class whose numbers, physical strength and general political integrity, have given them the cognomen of "the bone and sinew of the land."

But a grant of lands for Agricultural Schools may be claimed upon still other and higher grounds. In addition to the proposition that it will add directly to the national wealth and power, we may urge the value of Education itself; in the comfort and happiness it brings to individuals; in making them better citizens; and the new guaranties it creates of the perpetuity as well as the prosperity of our boasted institutions. Like the former proposition, this would seem to need no argument. It is not proposed to argue either of them here. These remarks are designed rather as suggestions of facts, the truth of which must be apparent to every intelligent mind. The man who would require argument to convince him of their truth, must be one who has never heard the maxim, "Knowledge is power!"

But we have yet another claim to urge for a grant of land to Agricultural Colleges. The benefits derived from grants of lands to railways are to a great extent local—being made only for sections where the lands are situated—while a grant for the education of the farmers in all parts of the country, will be general and equal. As has been said, these lands belong not to the States or Territories in which they lie, nor do they belong to Congress. They are the property of the people—as much of the people of Massachusetts and Georgia as of Michigan or Kansas. A great portion of the people are agriculturists; and those who are not, are equally benefited by their prosperity, and equally ready to see Schools endowed for their education. None would rejoice more sincerely in their prosperity than the manufacturers of New England, the miners of Pennsylvania, or professional men everywhere. In establishing the Agricultural College of Michigan—as was well shown in an article from the pen of a member of the present Legislature from Ionia county, published some months since—all other classes were even more interested than the farmers themselves. This proves what has been before stated, that the farmer has no enemies.

The public lands, then, belong entirely to the farmers and their friends. And shall not Congress, which is only their agent, or trustee, give to the people a portion of that which is their own—which will make them wiser and happier—which will teach them how to lighten the fatigue of labor, while it makes them more valuable citizens, increases the aggregate wealth of the nation, and forms new guaranties of its perpetuity and future greatness? If refused, it will be in defiance of public sentiment, and a great want of the age; and give evidence that the rulers we have placed in power have a higher appreciation of internal improvements than they have of the intelligence and prosperity of the people. In other words, that they think more of the value of railways than of *men!*

We ask it not for Michigan alone; though were there to be an exclusive privilege, we might cite the fact, that she has been the pioneer in the inauguration of an Agricultural College, and risked the liabilities incident to every new enterprise; but we ask it upon the above considerations, *for* every State in the Union. We ask it as their right, as States and as individuals, as a means of social happiness and general improvement; and as the highest benefit that can be derived from a portion of the public lands, in securing the greatest good of the greatest number, and the wisest means of making our great community of States a rich, happy, intelligent, and powerful people among the nations of the earth.

HOUSE OF CORRECTION FOR JUVENILE OFFENDERS.

Had this institution been denominated, by the Act establishing it, the *State Reform School*, it would have been a more appropriate name, and more expressive of its true design. That design, with reference to those under its influence, is scarcely different, in its moral and intellectual character, from what the Primary School should be, in relation to its pupils. The aim of each should be to educate both the intellect and the heart. Moral discipline ought everywhere to be united with intellectual culture. While the latter, in the Primary School, is more apparent in the machinery, so to speak, by which it is effected, it will still fail of its highest end, unless moral instruction is constantly blended with it. The moral influences may not come with as much observation, but they are no less important. Improve the intellect of a morally bad person, without any cultivation of the moral qualities, and while he may be able more successfully to evade the penalties of law, he is, in some respects, only a more dangerous man in society than before.

Hence, we see what a Primary School should be; and this it is designed the House of Correction *shall be*. In one respect, however, it goes further than is to be expected of the Primary School. The latter makes intellectual culture its more apparent object; but should consider the training of the moral nature equally important. The former places the two considerations on a more equal basis than is done in Primary Schools, as a matter of fact, both in real importance, and in prominence. But to these features is added another. It is also an Industrial School. Morality, Intelligence, and Industry. Truly, this is a worthy trinity of considerations to impress upon the youthful mind anywhere! If the boy who has fallen into crime needs these teachings, to reform him, the child in the Primary School, who has not yet fallen, needs the same to fortify him against temptation, and insure his safety.

If any one supposes that the House of Correction is some modern Bastile, where unfortunate or guilty boys are immured behind bolts and bars, like a criminal in his dungeon, with nothing to do but to mourn over his loss of liberty, and his far greater loss of the sympathies of his race, and to plot revenge upon society when he shall escape—a more hardened and desperate character than before—he has something to unlearn before he can understand what the institution is; what its aims, or its operations. It is probable that many persons form their opinion of a State Penitentiary, not a little from their ideas of some unfortunate captive, entombed alive by a cruel tyrant; and then imagine that a House of Correction for juvenile offenders must be similar to their imaginary penitentiary. It will be the design of these remarks to correct such impressions, by a brief review of the establishment of the Michigan House of Correction, and its practical workings in the education and reclaiming of those who come under its influence.

The main object which is, or should be designed, in the punishment of adult violators of law, is a question upon which men differ. Some hold that the great object of punishment is the reformation of the offender; that a State Prison is scarce else than a moral Asylum, where the morally insane may be taken to be treated for the obliquities of their hearts, as the intellectually insane are sent to their appropriate Asylum. Others contend that, while everything should be done that can be, to reclaim the heart, as well as to reform the manners and conduct of the culprit, the greatest design of punishment is the protection of society; not only by restraining, and if possible, reforming the man, but by making him an example of terror to evil doers, with whom moral considerations are not sufficient to restrain from crime.

Whether the world will ever agree upon this subject, is perhaps doubtful—unless they meet upon the more rational intermediate ground, that both objects are of equal importance. But in reference to those who, from their youth, are sent to the House of Correction, all will probably agree that their reformation should be the great object. Hence, the necessity of the institution; for all agree that, to send them to the penitentiary, is but to hasten and perfect their ruin.

As a School, the House of Correction is designed to do all that the Primary School can do, and more. As a Prison, it is divested, to a very great extent, of those obnoxious features, and degrading associations and influences that attach to the penitentiary, and seeks hopefully to accomplish results, which the penitentiary either regards as of secondary importance, or in which it most signally fails of its end. As to the bare fact of personal restraint, the House of Correction has the character of a prison; and in this it is only like the Asylum for the Insane. But farther than this, it more resembles an industrial school for boys. The appearances of restraint are, as far as possible, avoided. They wear no stripes, or other sign of disgrace, to remind them of their fall, and make them despise themselves; their honor, and their better, higher nature—not rendered obtuse, like the matured man of crime—are happily appealed to, and all their associations and surroundings are designed as much as possible, to cultivate their self-respect, and stimulate them to high and noble thoughts and aspirations.

The law of hereditary descent is no less certain in its effects upon the moral than upon the physical nature. Diseased parents semetimes give birth to comparatively healthy offspring, but such cases are regarded as exceptions to the general rule; and it is more than probable that if we fully understood the subject, we should find no exceptions. All our race is to a greater or less degree morally diseased. This disease is comprehended in the simple term *self;* and it descends from father to child. So well aware is the world of this, that every prudent, thoughtful parent begins in the earliest years of his child to apply the remedies for counteracting the natural evil tendencies of his nature, and *educate* him into the love and practice of virtue, and the avoidance of vice. His first object is to invest his exposed moral nature with armor, both defensive and offensive; so that he may be able to stand unharmed and uncorrupted in the battle of life. Unfortunately, many fail in their design; some from undervaluing its importance, and others from a mistake in the means which they employ; and others, perhaps, from unfortunate counteracting influences, which they cannot control. And not a few parents are themselves so far lost to any just appreciation of the superiority of right over wrong, that the teachings of their own lives are continual practical lessons of vice to their children; and they are daily offering them a living sacrifice upon the altar of self-indulgence and vice.

But there are thousands of the young, whose parents are removed by death before they have formed a self-reliant character, and learned to resist the enticements of others, or of their own wayward nature. Some of these find protectors who supply their loss, and train them to respectability and usefulness. But many others wander forth, as it were, from the very graves of their parents, one or both, unprotected, to become an easy prey to bad examples, and every temptation.

Under all these circumstances, is it strange that so many fall victims to evil passions, and become involved in crime? Who has ever carefully and kindly taught them fully to comprehend the enormity of vice, and the moral beauty of purity of heart and life? If they were ever told that the wages of vice is disgrace and woe, the serpent of temptation whispered, "it is not so; *gratification* is happiness!" and as do many who claim to have come to years of discretion, they believed the declaration most in accordance with their inclinations, and were lost.

In contemplating the situation and future prospect of this large class of the young, the humane and Christian heart regards their depredations upon society of trifling importance compared with the moral, and often physical ruin, they are developing for themselves and their associates. They differ from the adult criminal, both in the fact that their moral responsibility is less, and there is a hundred fold more hope, with proper means, of reforming and restoring them to virtue and a useful life. If they have fallen into serious crime, doubtless they should be restrained; but to *punish* them as we do the adult offender, and imprison them together, has been found the most certain method of making their absolute ruin more certain, and fitting them for a life continuance in the school of vice to which we send them.

With the light which the world now has upon this subject, these simple facts need only to be suggested to obtain the assent of every candid mind. And the State which now fails to provide the best means yet discovered for the protection and reclamation of its youth, is as false to itself, and its aims, as a social compact, as it is to the claims of humanity in its most tender aspects, or to the Christianity which as a people we profess.

Probably the same minds which first conceived the idea of Asylums for the Insane, and other unfortunates, comprehended the thought of the practicability of saving this equally unfortunate class, by some similar institution. It now seems strange that in this State a Reform School for juvenile offenders was not established at as early a day, or at least nearly so, as was the State Prison; and the neglect can only be accounted for in the supposition that our early rulers in the State thought more of punishing crime than of preventing it, and more of preventing it by the terrors of the law than by educating its young to virtue; that they regarded the reformation of any class hopeless; or if they deemed reform possible, they designed for the first fifteen years to try the experiment upon the most hopeless subjects.

For fifteen years after the organization of the State government of Michigan, the State Prison was considered the proper place for all offenders against the law, of all ages, from the stripling of eleven years, to the man of gray hairs. For fifteen years, the attention of the public or the Legislature was never called to the subject by any report from the officers of the State Prison, or any Governor's message.

The State Prison Inspectors in their report for 1851, speak as follows:

"There are among the convicts five or six boys, one of whom is only *eleven* years of age; and the records of the institution show that others have been brought into it at that tender age. The propriety of this is indeed questionable. What can be expected of a child whose nursery has been the State Prison? If he be naturally wayward, the contamination with the hardened villains with whom he is associated is fatal. He is sent out of Prison with the brand of disgrace upon him, and suspicion lurking continually at his heels. The probability is, that he has no friends, and being shunned by all good influences, he necessarily leads a life of crime. For such youthful offenders there should certainly be some milder, or at least less disgraceful and withering punishment provided. The subject is commended to the consideration of the Legislature."

This is believed to be the first official notice taken of the subject in this State. By sad observation, the Inspectors of the State Prison were made sensible of the importance of the subject, as above expressed; and in their next report, the same language is repeated to the Legislature of 1853. Governor McClelland, in his message to the same body, says:

"Many boys of a tender age have been sent to Prison. It is no fit place for them. A milder and less infamous punishment should be provided. A House of Correction, conducted as some of them are in older States, would be more suitable, and its moral influences more salutary."

The attention of the Legislature of 1853 being thus officially called to the subject, it came before that body, and somewhat singular action was taken upon it. Probably few persons are aware that in the Session Laws of 1853, is an act with the following title:

"*An Act to provide for the erection of a Prison for the purpose of solitary confinement,* AND A HOUSE OF CORRECTION FOR JUVENILE OFFENDERS, *and making an appropriation therefor.*"

An act with this title passed both Houses, and was signed by the Governor. It appropriated $5,000 for a Prison for solitary confinement of murderers, but contained not the most remote allusion to a House of Correction, except in the title, and of course, made no provision for it. Had it made such provision, the entire act would have been void, as the Constitution declares that "*No law shall embrace more than one object,* which shall be embraced in its title." The "title" is thus left free to embrace any number of objects that may be desired.

By reference to the journals of the Legislature, the history of this bill appears to be as follows: A bill was before the Senate, entitled "*A bill to provide for the erec-*

tion of a Prison for the purposes of solitary confinement." In the course of its passage, it was amended so as to embrace the other object, and thus passed the Senate, by a vote of nineteen to twelve. In the House, the provision for the House of Correction was stricken out, but without altering the title; and on the return of the bill to the Senate, that body unanimously concurred in the amendment, and thus the one body with two heads found its place among the laws.

In 1854, the Chaplain of the State Prison recommended to the Inspectors, that there being no proper House of Correction for the boys, they should spend one hour in each day in study.

Governor Parsons, in his retiring message to the Legislature, in 1855, said:

"I believe it to be the duty of the Legislature to establish a House of Correction for Juvenile Offenders."

In this opinion Governor Bingham fully concurred, as will be seen by the following extract from his message to the same body:

"The presence of several boys and youth among the more hardened criminals in the State Prison, induces me to urge upon your attention the propriety of establishing a House of Correction, where a milder course of treatment, more especially adapted to their reformation, can be employed. The State has not performed its duty to these unfortunate victims of ignorance and temptation, until it has made provision by a proper system of discipline, for their instruction, in useful knowledge, morals and piety—taught them some mechanical trade, or other proper employment, and prepared them upon their release from confinement, to become good citizens and useful members of society, as they return to its duties and privileges."

To these humane sentiments, the Legislature cordially responded, and appropriated twenty-five thousand dollars to establish a "*House of Correction for Juvenile Offenders,*" to which all persons under fifteen years of age committing a Prison offence should be sent, together with such of those as were from fifteen to twenty years of age, as the Court before which they were tried should think fit. The bill passed the Senate by a vote of *twenty-six* to *two;* and the House, by a vote of *fifty-eight* to *five.* Such unanimity is rare in the appropriation of large sums for a new enterprise.

The site selected consists of thirty acres of high land on the eastern border of the village of Lansing, which it overlooks for a distance of about two miles along the Grand River. The main building and north wing were at once commenced, and the institution was ready for the reception of *scholars* on the second of September, 1856. The main building is 48 by 55 feet, and the wing 94 by 35 feet, the whole four stories high, and covering 5,930 square feet of ground. The plan is in good style, but comparatively plain, with no extravagant expense incurred for show. When the corresponding south wing shall be erected, as it ought soon to be, it will be quite an imposing edifice, beautifully situated, showing a front of 236 feet. The present edifice contains a chapel, with seats for 400 persons; rooms for the accommodation of two familes; office, kitchen, dining-room, bathing-room, sitting-room, hospital, tailor's shop, a school room, with seats for 80 scholars, and other necessary rooms, together with dormitories for 76 boys, each boy occupying a room. The "yard" is inclosed by a high board fence, and comprises nearly two acres of land. In this yard is a brick shop, 25 by 60 feet, one story high, and another, also of brick, 25 by 50 feet, and two stories high, with an engine room attached.

The entire expense to the State up to Dec. 1st, 1857, (the date of the latest reports,) was $46,701 45. This includes all the cost of grounds, (a large portion of which was donated by the citizens of Lansing,) buildings, superintendence, salaries of officers, and everything to put the institution in operation, and pay the current expenses for fifteen months after being opened. It is estimated from the expenditures of the past year, that the annual current expense with the present number, 53, will be about $6,000. The boys will earn from $500 to $1,000.

In 1857 the law was so amended that all delinquents not over sixteen years of age shall be sent to the House of Correction—nominally till they are twenty-one, but the Board of Control have power to dismiss them whenever in their discretion their reformation will warrant them in so doing, and such action promises their highest good. The happy influence which this must have upon the boys, in stimulating them to establish a good character, is apparent. If they are without friends, to throw around them their aid and protection, or for other reasons, the Board of Control may apprentice them to some trade or occupation, as they think best.

The number now in the institution (October, 1858) is fifty-four. The whole number admitted since it was opened, two years ago, is seventy-three. Of this entire number, *nine only* had never been in jail for previous offences. Thirty-three had been in jail once; thirteen, twice; seven, thrice; seven, five times; one, six times; one, nine times; and one, *ten times!* Nearly all were sent for larceny. But fourteen were over fifteen years of age, and but one under ten years. The age of one was nine years. Such is the *material* which this institution designs to reform, and send forth into the world to become good citizens. That in some cases it will fail, is to be expected; but that in many others it will meet with the happiest success, reason, no less than the history of older Reform Schools, gives a sure promise.

The history of these seventy-three youth—but three of whom were girls—leads us to regard their misfortunes in quite as striking a light as we do their crimes. Less than half of the number have both parents living; and of those whose parents are living, those of four had separated. Less than half are of American birth. The fact that all, save four or five, were sent for larceny, indicates that they were led into crime, to a very great extent, through poverty. Most of the number were convicted of crimes which would have consigned an adult to the State Prison. Yet it is probable that not one-eighth of these delinquents would have been thus sentenced had there been no House of Correction to receive them. They would still have been sent to jail, from time to time, till increased depravity and greater age fitted them for that College of crime where they would ultimately have graduated with sad honor, unless as they grew wicked, they should become crafty enough to escape the grasp of the law.

But look at their prospect now. They have a home, away from the evil examples and influences that, like an armed host, have invested them hitherto. In the place of idleness, they find industry; in the place of want, plenty. Indeed, a greater contrast than really exists between their former woes and their present comforts, cannot well be imagined. On entering the institution, their daguerreotypes are taken, their history ascertained, and briefly recorded. The fact is explained to them that they are not sentenced from a vindictive spirit of vengeance, that would torment them for their past crimes, but mainly for their highest good—to save them from ruin, and enable them to become respectable men; and that they will be dismissed as soon as, from their improvement, their truest friends deem compatible with their highest welfare. Every inducement that can be devised is set before them, to stimulate to virtuous thought and action. It is the design not to treat them in a mass, but each individual is made a special object of solicitude—his disposition studied, and in view of his particular case, such remedial influences applied as give the highest promise of success. To do otherwise, the institution would greatly fail in its aim of restoring its patients. The physician might almost as well go through the wards of a hospital and give the same medicine to its sufferers, as to expect to accomplish the highest good with fifty wayward boys by dealing with them all alike, and in the mass. In many respects, their treatment must of course be uniform; but it may not be forgotten, they are to be reformed as individuals. It is believed that the officers in charge realize the importance of this consideration.

On entering the institution, each boy commences in class "6," which figure, in German silver, is worn on the breast upon the Sabbath and holidays. At the end of a month, if his conduct justifies it, he is promoted to class "5," and the figure changed. At the close of another month, he is promoted to "4," or remains stationary, or is set back, according to his conduct. Thus he goes on from month to month, till he reaches number "1." Next comes the star, (*) the degree of honor; and high are the aspirations of many of the number to gain this token of their character, and the confidence of their teachers. Some of the boys are often sent into the village upon errands, or otherwise trusted, and never yet has the Superintendent found his confidence betrayed.

They are not locked into "cells" to sleep. Their dormitories are single, and large enough for comfort, with a window, and open into a spacious hall, two, and part of the way, three stories high, with tastefully constructed galleries. They have a better bedstead and bed than are the lot of half the boys in our land. The doors, it is true, are locked at night, but they appear like light lattice work, and are painted green. They are allowed to adorn their rooms according to their taste, and not a few are ornamented with pictures.

They rise at 5 to 6½ o'clock, according to the season, and breakfast at 6½ to 7 o'clock. From 7 till nine they are in school, where they are taught the branches usually pursued in the Primary School. In their education, the development of their moral faculties, and an inculcation of their responsibilities as beings destined to an endless existence, are kept constantly in view. From 9 till 12, the time is devoted to labor. Then comes dinner.

And here is a scene well worth a journey from any part of the State to behold. Cold indeed, must be the heart which can witness it without emotion! One forgets to mourn over their "imprisonment," and rather finds the eye moistening at the thought of their future hopes, in contrast with the inevitable ruin from which they have been rescued. They march around the long table, and take their places in perfect order, and most of them with cheerful countenances. At a signal they are seated; another, and fifty heads are bowed, and fifty voices rise in unison to their Creator in a short, appropriate prayer. The meal is eaten in silence, and with a decorum that would put many a fashionable hotel dinner party to the blush. All their meals are taken in the same manner. From one o'clock to four, the time is again devoted to labor. From four to five o'clock, the hour is for recreation and supper, when they return to the school-room, where they study till eight, and retire for the night, after a short recess. This system gives them *six* hours per day for labor, *five* in school, and two and a half to *four* for recreation.

The institution has a library of about 175 volumes, from which the boys draw books every Saturday. They have also a common room where they can go when not otherwise engaged, to sit, or read the papers of the day, and learn what is going on in the world. In the State Prison, it is deemed the best policy, as far as possible, to exclude from the prisoners, all knowledge of what is passing outside of their walls. But here it is evidently wise to keep the boys informed of what is passing in the busy world upon which it is hoped they will ere long enter, to be good citizens and virtuous men. To keep them ignorant of the world, would be a poor method of fitting them for its duties and trials. They are encouraged to keep up a correspondence with their friends; and can write monthly without expense to themselves or friends, and oftener if they wish, by providing for their own postage.

On the Sabbath morning, they thoroughly wash themselves in a large bathing tank, and the day is spent in reading, religious instruction, Sabbath-School teaching, singing, &c., under the direction of the Chaplain, Teacher, and others. They *appear* to be under no more *restraint* than are the pupils of a well conducted boarding-school.

Much has been said and written upon the reformation of criminals. But whatever may be thought of the possibility of reforming adults, it is a sad fact, that for every one who is reformed, either in heart, or only in his conduct, many are made more desperate in wickedness, by imprisonment. And in those cases where the reform is genuine, what infinite loss has the man still sustained? Like him who recovers from the small-pox, to go through life with the scars upon his face, so he is saved, but with those fearful scars upon his character, which time can never efface. But with the young delinquent, there is hope. The disease with him, is not yet as deap seated; his recuperative powers are greater; and his past moral injuries, if not entirely obliterated, may be measurably so.

The design of the House of Correction is the salvation of the young from ruin. It is not to create a revenue to the State Treasury. No school was ever organized for that purpose, though the wealth, as well as the happiness of the State is vastly augmented by the knowledge and virtue of its citizens. Yet it is designed to train these boys to habits of industry, and teach them the practice of useful labor. In 1857 a portion of them were contracted at twelve and a half cents per day of seven hours, for making boots and shoes; in which business however, the contractors did not succeed. A contract has been recently entered into, with Messrs. Woodhouse, Butler & Co., for twenty to forty boys, for five years, at eight cents per day of six hours, in manufacturing chairs; to be instructed, so that they may be able to obtain a livelihood at the business, when they go out into the world, dependent upon themselves. This looks like a small price, but considering their age and inexperience, and the fact, that six hours constitutes a day, that the more competent and faithful they are, the sooner the contractors will lose their services by their dismissal—their places to be continually supplied by inexperienced hands—it is believed to be as high a price comparatively, as is paid by contractors in the State Prison.

Few of the blessings of life, either moral or physical, are obtained without labor and expense. The poor we have always with us; and one of the highest duties of a State, is to protect its poor and unfortunate, and to educate its youth. But Schools and Asylums are not expected to be sources of revenue. The House of Correction is both a School and an Asylum. A School, in which these boys,—equal in native intellect, to boys in general,—are given a good Common School education, and taught some useful occupation; an Asylum, where the unprotected orphan, and the boy doubly orphaned in a besotted or depraved parent, may find a refuge from the ten thousand lures set by his poverty or by bad men, to entrap his unwary feet. Perhaps there are men who cannot appreciate this; but there are *boys* who can. During the brief period since the institution was opened, several homeless lads have presented themselves at its door, begging admission to its protection. Unfortunately they could not be received, under the law as it now stands. All the worthy Superintendent could do, was to interest himself unofficially, to obtain them a home. It is to be hoped that the next Legislature will make provision for this class of orphans, who wish even at the cost of personal freedom, to escape the ruin that overtakes so many of their class. A few months since, an orphan boy stole a horse from the most public street in Lansing, in broad day, on purpose, as he stated, to be arrested and sent to the protection of the House of Correction!

Shall such an institution be decried because it is attended with expense? Then abandon, for the same reason, our other Asylums. Nay, let us pay out money for nothing that does not bring a money return, with interest! Abolish all our Schools and Churches; let all our public and private charities cease; let us pay no more taxes for the support of the Government, or for building Court Houses, Jails, or other local public buildings, or for roads and bridges; let us invest all our money where it will promise us a direct money profit in return! Who is so poor a philosopher as not to see that such economy would most signally defeat its own end, and that we should speedily sink to a nation of barbarians, where there would be no security for property, and every man's hand would be against his neighbor, and his neighbor's against him? Who doubts that such a withholding would tend to poverty?

But what is the burden of expense which we must bear to support this institution. To complete the south wing of the building, and fit the whole for the accommodation of one hundred and fifty inmates, with shops and all necessary appurtenances, will require, from the commencement of the enterprise, not more than $65,000. This is a permanent investment, and will amount to not over ONE-THIRD OF A MILL *upon the dollar* of the property in the State! The current annual expenses, with 175 inmates, which it ought to provide for, will not exceed $10,000; and this amounts to not over *one mill* on every *eighteen dollars* of property in the State!

Some of these very boys may yet be in positions to to render our children the same protection we now extend to them. The wheel of life in society revolves; let us see to it now, that the wretched appeal to us not in vain, as we may hope for succor for our ourselves, or our posterity, when the wave of misfortune rolls over us or them.

ASYLUM FOR THE DEAF AND DUMB, AND THE BLIND.

Article *Thirteen* of the Constitution of the State of Michigan is entitled "EDUCATION." Section *ten* of this Article, reads as follows:

"Institutions for the benefit of those persons who are Deaf, Dumb, Blind or Insane, shall always be fostered and supported."

The Asylum for the Insane perhaps cannot strictly be called an educational institution; yet it is so in this important sense: Its design is to restore wandering Reason to its dominion in the Mind. As a hospital, it deals with physical disease, which is the cause of the loss of reason; but that very disease is often the result solely of the mind's action upon the brain, and probably in all cases aggravated by it; and the restorative means are quite as much of an intellectual, as of a physical character. There is therefore, evidently no impropriety in classing the Asylum for the Insane, as is done by the Constitution, among the educational institutions of the State.

But the institution for the Deaf and Dumb, and the Blind, though popularly styled an Asylum—"a place of retreat, or security"—is strictly a School, according to the popular usage of that term. It is a School for the intellectual development of a class physically unable to receive the benefits of the Primary School. It is the boast of our institutions, that all classes shall have the means of education. Here are large numbers who, of all classes, need an education the most. They are to a great extent, deprived of the ordinary means of improvement from observation and daily intercourse with the world, and are thus robbed, not only of their mental, but likewise of their physical resources. In this sad state, unable by their peculiar misfortune, to avail themselves of the ordinary means of an education, they may justly claim that the obligations of the Social Compact impose upon the State increased responsibilities to provide such other means as are within its power, for the improvement of those powers of mind that lie undeveloped in the midnight of blindness, or in the living death of perpetual silence.

The State Census of 1854 gives us the information that there were at that time one hundred and seventy-six blind, and two hundred and six deaf and dumb persons in Michigan—in all, three hundred and eighty-two. Since that time, the population of the State has increased nearly fifty per cent.* Allowing a proportional increase to these classes, we have at the present time, nearly *six hundred* who must have aid from the State, or go down to the dark grave, scarcely darker than the mental and moral entombment in which they live and die!

It were a great thing for a State to speak into being six hundred souls, and clothe them with knowledge and joy! It were a more glorious deed could it raise that number from the dead, and give them back, with renewed life and youth, to their rejoicing friends! It can do neither literally; but figuratively, it can accomplish both. It can restore those who exist, but can hardly be said to live; it can perform the miracle of making the sense of feeling see, and the sense of sight hear! It can call to the soul, imprisoned in its temple of darkness, chained like a body of death to the charity of friends, and bid it to go forth disenthralled, to be a joy to itself and its kindred. By giving

* The actual increase is probably not so great as this; but the increase upon the number reported by the census of 1854 doubtless is. That census was notoriously defective. Yet it gave a population of 509,374 To this, add fifty per cent, and it gives 764,061—which cannot much exceed the present population of the State.

to the Deaf and Blind a substitute for their absent senses, we create them anew to the world and its enjoyments, and develope a new world to them. We open the darkened chambers of the soul to the light of moral and spiritual truth, and furnish appropriate aliment for the soul's immortal yearnings.

To be born deaf a hundred years ago, was to come into the world apparently more like an unfortunate animal than like an offspring of humanity, and with hardly an animal's prospect for enjoyment in life. To be born blind was to open the eyes upon rayless darkness—only conscious, like Tantalus, that just beyond the reach, were innumerable fruits never to be obtained.

But the Genius of Invention in these last days, has not expended all its power upon dead matter, though it has well nigh imbued that with life and thought. Its most glorious experiments have been successfully made with Humanity. It has sought out the insulated soul, and lighted up the deep dungeon of the mind with the electricity of Thought. It is not only spanning seas with messages of fire, but it is bridging that deeper, broader ocean, whose turbid waters roll between the soul of the Deaf and Blind, and the shores of Science and Revelation! It not only makes dead matter supply the place of lost members of the body, but it furnishes a substitute for those almost spiritual mechanisms, the eye and ear!

Men are still living who can remember when the Abbe De L'Epee, of France, first conceived the idea of a system for educating the Deaf and Dumb. It is little more than forty years since the noble Gallaudet, of Hartford, Conn., established the first School in America for their benefit. The invention of a system for instructing the Blind originated also in France. Not far from the same time that the good Abbe De L'Epee was perfecting his scheme for educating the Deaf and Dumb, the Abbe Hauy was inventing the plan of embossed printing for the Blind. But fifteen years later, Dr. Howe established a School for the Blind, in Boston, Mass. We can well afford to forgive "fickle France" for the folly of the fashions which she gives us, for these glorious inventions, which our country has copied as readily as we do her fashions.

The State of Michigan has perhaps little to boast of, in the fact that about twenty years elapsed after the State organization before she had any School for the Deaf and Dumb, and the Blind; certainly not, that eight years passed between the making of the first appropriation, and the completion of one wing of a building for their accommodation. The first movement was in 1848, when the Legislature adopted a Resolution, asking a grant of land from the General Government in aid of the enterprise, together with that of an Asylum for the Insane. At the same time, an appropriation of eight sections of Salt Spring lands was made toward the same objects. Nothing was done however, during the year, to carry the law into effect; and Governor Ransom in his message to the Legislature in 1849, recommended that nothing should be done until the lands could be sold, or other means provided.

The Legislature nevertheless increased the appropriation of Salt Spring lands from eight sections to fifteen, and directed the Trustees to commence the erection of an Asylum for the Insane as soon as the receipts from sales of the land would warrant—virtually abandoning the Asylum for the Deaf and Dumb, and the Blind, for the time. During the year, however, the citizens of the village of Flint and vicinity made an offer of ten acres of land, and three thousand dollars in money, to secure the location of the last named Asylum at that place; and the Trustees went so far as to decide upon that location. In 1850, they urged upon the Legislature the importance of providing the means for putting the School in operation without delay. The Legislature further increased the appropriation of Salt Spring lands for the Asylums, to twenty-five sections, and enacted to advance five thousand dollars from the State treasury—the same to be refunded from the first receipts upon sales of the lands. At the same time it was provided that not more than one thousand dollars of the amount should be used in the first year, and not more than three thousand in any one year thereafter. This was not a very large beginning for institutions which could hardly be made available for limited use, for less than a hundred thousand dollars, and to complete which, would require from three to four hundred thousand. But it may be said that the finances of the State were in a deranged condition, and the increase of its debt more than the available resources during the previous year, was $109,718 58, while the State direct tax was over one hundred thousand dollars.

Up to 1851, nothing had been done toward the Asylum for the Deaf and Dumb, and the Blind, except to obtain the subscriptions above named, from the citizens of Flint, and to decide upon its location at that place; and in 1851, the Trustees reported to the Legislature, that the Asylum for the Insane was of the most pressing importance, and they had given their first attention to that object. That is the last that was heard officially, of the subject, till 1853, when the Trustees reported that two hundred dollars of the donation from the citizens of Flint had been expended in improving the grounds. This was a discouraging prospect for the five or six hundred unfortunates who for five years, had been promised a School adapted to their wants.

The commencement of 1853 found $116,555 21 in the State Treasury; and during the year, this was increased to $375,773 07. This increase was owing to the sales of the public lands. Of the State indebtedness, with the exception of $100,000 due in 1856, there would be nothing due until 1858; and it would seem that something practical and positive might have been done for the enterprise, in 1853. But Governor McClelland made no allusion to the Asylums in his Message of that year, to the Legislature. That body however voted to levy a direct tax as follows:

For the Asylum for the Deaf and Dumb, and the Blind,..	$3,000
For the Asylum for the Insane, in 1853,.........	10,000
" " " " 1854,..........	10,000

But this was not to be an appropriation from the Treasury; but a tax to go ultimately into the Treasury; for it was only to be *loaned* to the Asylums, to be refunded out of the first avails of the Salt Spring lands which had been appropriated. It seemed still to be the policy of the State, that the cost of these noble and humane institutions should never exceed the avails of twenty-five sections of land. But even the three thousand dollars thus voted as a loan, was useless until it should be collected—which would require almost a year. So nothing was done during the year 1853; and by the time the State had collected the three thousand dollars, so generously to loan to the institution, about four hundred thousand dollars was lying idle in the Treasury, or earning but one per cent. to the State.

But in 1854, the work was really commenced. Six years had passed away since the first appropriation of land, and now the Trustees found themselves in command of means sufficient to make a beginning—though that was about all. Without waiting longer, however, they rented a building, and Feb. 1st, 1854, a School was opened, with eleven deaf mutes and one blind person for pupils. Slow as the progress was, that of the Asylum for the Insane had hardly been greater.

In 1855, Governor Parsons, the retiring, and Governor Bingham, the incoming Executive, both recommended to the Legislature to give the Asylums the necessary aid to make them competent for their high design. These two gentlemen were supposed to represent the views of all the voters in the State. It was evident to all, that the finances of the State, so abundantly replenished by the sale of the School, and other lands, were now in a condition to warrant substantial aid, and that the progress of the age imperatively demanded it. Accordingly, thirty-three thousand dollars was appropriated from the treasury to complete the School wing, which had been commenced, for the Deaf and Dumb, and the Blind, and to sustain the institution in 1855 and '56. The bill passed the Senate by a vote of 25 to 2, and the House by a vote of 52 to 14. It was in no respect a party measure—the majority of both parties in both Houses voting for the bill.

In one year the wing was completed, and occupied by forty-seven pupils, and four teachers. By Autumn, the number was increased to seventy-seven pupils, and six teachers. These, with the Principal and his family, and help, numbered ninety persons; which were more than could be comfortably situated, but the importunities for admission were so numerous and urgent, that the chapel was converted into a sleeping-room, and on the 1st of January, 1858, there were sixty-two Deaf, and twenty-eight Blind, in the institution.

The Legislature in 1855 appropriated in all, one hundred and twenty-five thousand dollars for the Asylums and the House of Correction. None of these appropriations were made a party measure, and a majority of both the political parties voted for them. It is to be recorded to the honor and humanity of all, that these institutions, promising so much for the relief of human woe, were placed above all party considerations, and the appropriations were made simply upon the merits of each several case. All the circumstances indicated it as the settled policy of the State to press forward these institutions to completion, as rapidly as prudence would warrant. During the exciting political contest of 1856, no one complained of the heavy appropriations of the previous year—still fresh in the public memory—no one considered the expenditure an extravagance, or a waste.

With such a public sentiment, and so well understood by the members of the Legislature in 1857, that body, with remarkable unanimity, with the same union as in 1855, made large appropriations for the Asylums, of which seventy-five thousand dollars was for the Asylum for the Deaf and Dumb, and the Blind—to erect the main building, and sustain the School in 1857 and '58. The bill making this appropriation passed the House by a vote of fifty-nine to eleven; and the Senate, by the unanimous vote of all the members present.* Until 1857, both of the Asylums had been under the control of one Board of Trustees. The bad policy of this—one institution being located at Flint, and the other at Kalamazoo—had become apparent, and the two were placed under the care of separate Boards.

On the 15th of July, 1857, the corner-stone of the main buildings for the Asylum for the Deaf and Dumb, and the Blind, was laid, with appropriate ceremonies, in the presence of the Governor and other distinguished gentlemen. Letters of congratulation upon the progress of the enterprise, from distinguished citizens of our own and other States, were read upon the occasion.

The buildings thus commenced, are the main front and wings. One of these wings is now (November, 1858,) roofed, and the other almost ready for covering in; the main building is so far advanced that it also, will be roofed this fall.

The main building, which covers an area of 50 by 100 feet, independent of its projections, will consist of four stories above the basement—the whole surmounted by a dome 120 feet high from the ground. The basement is designed

*The bill appropriating $50,000 for the Asylum for the Insane, passed the House by a vote of 45 to 6; and the Senate by a vote of 21 to 7. The appropriation for the House of Correction was with similar unanimity.

for shops for the instruction of pupils in mechanical trades, store rooms, hot air chambers for regulating the temperature of the rooms, &c. The first floor consists of reception rooms and music rooms for the use and recreation of pupils; the second floor is appropriated to the family purposes of the Principal and Assistants, and the third to the use of the Teachers.

One of the side wings is designed for male, the other for female pupils; they will accommodate from 350 to 400 persons. Each wing covers an area of 50 by 80 feet, and consists of three stories above the basement. The basement story is designed for bathing, washing and ironing rooms; the first story for exercise and study; the second for hospital and dormitories; the third for dormitories.

The central building, which is not yet commenced, will communicate by covered corridors, in front with the main building, or in rear with the side and school wings. The basement is designed for the kitchen, the first story for the dining hall, and the second for the chapel—covering an area of 40 by 70 feet.

The school wing, completed in 1856, is in the rear. The whole will show a front of two hundred feet. The style is good, but comparatively plain, with no wasteful extravagance for mere ornament. The original estimate of the cost of the buildings and appurtenances was $120,000 00; but thus far, the expenses have been kept considerably within the estimates, (a very rare thing in public works,) and it is believed that not more than $110,000 will be required in all. This speaks well for the economy and faithfulness of the Board, and especially of the acting Commissioner, Hon. J. B. Walker.

The design of this institution is not merely to impart intellectual light to the darkened minds of its unfortunate pupils; but likewise, as soon as suitable conveniences can be prepared, to teach them such occupations as will best enable them to earn their own support in after life. Even the Blind will be taught simple trades, such as making baskets, brooms, and brushes, which will make them, thereafter, less dependent upon others. In this, it is like the House of Correction, an *Industrial* School. The man who gives his son no occupation, whereby he may honestly provide for his own wants, is justly regarded as recreant to his high responsibility as the natural protector of his offspring. He places himself below the parental instincts of some of the brute creation. And he who denies his son the time and means to cultivate properly his intellectual powers, is regarded as a sordid wretch, almost deserving of a place in the pillory. But it is the duty of the State to do in the general, what the parent is expected to do in particular. All should be educated, but all cannot be educated to professional life. Especially is this true of the Deaf and the Blind. Hence, as a majority of fathers should educate their sons to *labor*, so should the State thus educate these classes, who are peculiarly its children. We talk of intellect as resident in the brain; but who does not know that the *hand* can be educated till it almost shows signs of intelligence in itself? A wonderful thing, indeed, is the human hand! What is there grand in architecture, or beautiful in artistic display, not wrought by the hand? From the boy's shingle, with its paper sail, to the leviathan steamer—from the infant's block house to the proudest palace—from the most insignificant to the most stupendous material works of man—all is due to the skill of the human hand. Sad, indeed, would be the condition of our race, were the hand to "forget its cunning!" It is true that the hand is dependent upon the intellect for its power; (though the most skillful hand and the weakest intellect are often found united;) but, though the intellect may be equal to an angel's, the hand itself must be educated, ere it can accomplish its wonderful works. It is, therefore, evidently due to the Deaf and Blind that they shall receive such a labor education as may be best adapted to their condition and wants.

All acknowledge the obligation of the State to provide for the physical necessities of those who, from any misfortune, are unable to provide for themselves. Hence our County poor-houses; and officers in every township to become the protectors of the poor and helpless. Probably not a man could be found in the State who will object to all the expense thus incurred for the unfortunate. And shall we place the physical wants of our humanity above its moral and intellectual hungerings? Shall we show such solicitude for this animal frame, which, at the best, soon lies down to mix again with its kindred dust, and ignore all the demands of that higher nature, upon which is stamped the seal of immortal being? We make no "appropriations" for the support of the poor—saying they shall be provided for so far, but no farther; but we agree to support them, and pay the bills as properly presented, be they less or more. And can we do less for those, many of whom are equally helpless, and all of whose higher natures are starving, and when nothing short of the power of the State can give them relief? Each man cannot provide teachers for his deaf or blind child; nor is it often that a town or county can do it. The State only—except in rare instances—can build and support Asylums.

The Deaf, Blind and Insane, are fully equal in numbers to those who receive aid from the county funds. The three classes in this State, at the present time, number probably not less than one thousand. The number of the Insane is about equal to that of the Deaf and Blind united. It cannot be assumed that these classes are any better qualified for their own support than are the county poor. Will it be said that the Deaf should be excepted in this comparison? Then it may be replied with confidence, that an equal number of the least helpless of the county poor should be excepted; for doubtless there are many of that number who could "get along in some way," by their own exertions.

The fable represents a traveler wandering into distant climes till he became lost in the world's wide desert. After hair-breadth escapes from barbarian tribes, he came suddenly upon a populous city. Uncertain of the character of its inhabitants, he approached fearfully, until his eye caught the sight of a Church and a Prison. Then he rejoiced; for he knew he had found a Christian people.

Back of the irony here intended, lies a truth, perhaps not discovered by the author, which does honor to the Christianity of the age. Prisons and chains have not been wanting in all ages, almost from the time when the first distinguished fratricide went forth from the presence of his Maker, a vagabond upon the earth; and probably they will be required until the promised millenium shall obviate their necessity, by the abolition of crime. But until the advent of the Man of Nazareth—and even now, where his Religion is unknown or unappreciated—they were as likely to be employed for the persecution of good men, as for the restraint or punishment of the bad. Churches, therefore, are a sign that there are those who are striving to promulgate and practice the principles of a higher law than that of *self*, regardless of the rights of others, or the claims of God; and Prisons show that these principles are not universal--that there still exist bad men to be punished and restrained. Our traveler—or his historian—must have lived long ago, or he would have seen by the side of the Church, indicating love to God, the Asylum, speaking of good will to man.

Hospitals and Asylums are not the offspring of Heathenism. There have been tribes of men, where the infirm and helpless were put to death, with the sanction of law—if law it could be called, where justice and humanity were thus set at naught. And from that state of diabolism, as our race has progressed in intelligence and virtue, we find first the rights, and then the wants, of the weak, regarded; and Prisons are put more exclusively to their appropriate use. Hospitals, for the sick and disabled, were of an early date. It needed but a heart of humanity to conceive of *their* benefits. Asylums for the Deaf, Blind and Insane, are of modern origin; not because the warm heart of Christianity did not feel for the woes of these classes, but because no inventive mind had been Heaven inspired to conceive the means of their relief. To conceive the *plan*, was to secure its execution. And if the names of Faust, and Fulton, and Morse, descend to remote posterity, as benefactors of their race, in their inventions, shall they who have invented Asylums, and successful treatment for the Deaf, the Blind, and the Insane—and even for Idiots—ever be forgotten? What say the grateful hearts of those who have had a new existence opened up to their consciousness by their philanthropy?

To the memory of the devoted Gallaudet, the founder of the first Asylum for the Deaf and Dumb in America, at Hartford, Conn., a monument has been erected at an expense of two thousand and five hundred dollars, by the money and labor of Deaf Mutes alone! And how many thousands are there in all enlightened lands, who bless the memory of the Abbe De L'Epee, the inventor of the "deaf and dumb alphabet;" and of his compeer, the Abbe Hauy, who like another Faust, conceived of printing books to be read by the Blind! And is it not safe to predict, that another generation in this State—and especially the thousands who will hereafter find relief from mental bondage, and darkness inconceivable—will send back aspirations of gratitude to the men of those Legislatures who founded and sustained our Asylums, and to their constituents who so cheerfully contributed the means.

The means! Ah, that is the bugbear which stands ever like a devouring lion, before some men's eyes! If they would not themselves live forever in midnight darkness, with worse than iron chains upon their soul, they would let others do so, rather than incur the "expense" necessary for their relief. While such narrow selfishness exists in the world, Prisons must doubtless be built by the side of Churches; for when a man denounces such monuments of enlarged and enlightened Christianized humanity as are our Asylums, and seeks to enlist a popular or party prejudice against them because of their trifling expense, he demonstrates in no small degree, the necessity of Prisons for bad men, or the erection of another Asylum for another class, who were, until a recent date, considered the most hopeless cases of an almost obliterated humanity.

"The *trifling* Expense?"

Yes, the term is used advisedly. A slight consideration of the subject shows that all the expense of our Asylums *is* trifling, compared to our means, and unworthy of a second thought, in view of the blessings these institutions are able to impart.

To complete the Asylums for the Deaf and Blind, and for the Insane, and the House of Correction, and fully furnish them, according to their several plans, competent to meet the wants of the State for a generation to come, cannot, at the highest estimate, cost over six hundred thousand dollars. And what is that upon two hundred millions? Divide it between six years, which is as fast as the means have been and will be required, and five cents upon every hundred dollars of our property, or half of one mill upon every dollar, is all. And will any one who claims affinity to "Godlike humanity," object to a tax so trifling in amount, when productive of so noble results? Taxation is usually most severely felt by men of moderate means; but where is the man worth five hundred dollars, who would object to paying twenty-five cents per annum for six years, to perfect these humane institutions? When they are completed, the current expenses of their maintenance and support for the next twenty years, may average forty thousand dollars per annum. This will amount to less than *two hundredths of one per cent.* upon the value of the property in the State! Nearly half of the above estimated six hundred thousand dollars has already been expended. Not half of the amount hitherto used, has been raised by a direct tax; but as every man is a co-partner, and owner of the public funds, in proportion to the amount of his property, it is essentially the same thing. And who will object to the appropriation annually of an amount equal to *two cents* upon every hundred dollars of his property, to sustain these three noble institutions, and to reveal a new life to the six or seven hundred of our unfortunate fellow beings who will ere long be found within their walls?

Men seem to have an instinctive dread of taxation; and there was, perhaps, never a community where the complaint of "high taxes" was not heard. The money thus paid *appears* to bring no return. Yet our taxes do secure a valuable consideration, as truly as does the money with which we buy our daily food. We do not see it as much in the detail, but in the aggregate result it is no less certain. And our taxes for the support of the government and its works are very insignificant, compared with those we pay on our own direct account. We pay from half a cent to four cents upon the dollar for insurance on our buildings; yet the public taxes of every description, which we pay, averaging perhaps half of one cent upon the dollar in the country, and one cent in the cities annually, constitute really a far better insurance upon the general safety and productiveness of our property, than does any insurance against fire upon our buildings. What would our property be worth without schools, courts, and highways? Yet these are maintained only by taxation. Our taxes keep in motion all the machinery of society, necessary to protect and give value to our possessions. Let a now prosperous community reduce its contributions for churches, schools, courts, roads, and for all county and town purposes, and let every individual reduce his private charities, to one-fourth the amount heretofore paid, and in a very brief space of time, we should see property of all kinds depreciate in value, business would decline, crime would increase, and "for sale or to let" might soon be stereotyped upon a great portion of its dwellings.

All the blessings of life which we enjoy superior to uncivilized tribes of men, come to us through the agency of taxation in its various forms. As an individual, the farmer pays a tax in the purchase of his land; and the seed which he deposits in the soil, is but one of the taxes he must pay to secure a harvest. As a member of society, he must pay a further tax for building roads and bridges, or the harvest, when obtained, will lose a great part of its value. Without taxation of any kind, we should stand upon the earth—if, indeed, we could live under such circumstances—physically inferior to the animal tribes; and less competent than they to enjoy even our animal existence. The wild Indian pays no public taxes, and few upon his own account. And few and small are the blessings he obtains, either for his physical, intellectual, or moral nature! But to make available the blessings which we procure by direct purchase—which may be denominated private taxation—we must consent to pay common or public taxes. What would the surplus crop of the farmer be worth, were there no roads? But free roads can be built only by public taxation. And when the roads are constructed, there is involved the necessity of another private tax for his wagon, or the system is still imperfect, and the other taxes fail in their highest results. Thus are all our expenditures, private and public, intimately related to, and dependent upon each other, in securing the greatest amount of good to ourselves and the community.

As a question of expediency, it is not so much what amount of taxes we pay, as for what objects we pay them. Some young men expend more for cigars than all the public taxes they would pay, if worth twenty thousand dollars! There is little danger of such a tax bringing any better return than a debased taste, a beclouded intellect, a diseased body and poverty. In those nations where the taxes are wrung from the reluctant masses, to aggrandize the few, the people are necessarily impoverished thereby. But in this free land, so called, we the people, *tax ourselves* for our own benefit; and we are our own judges how our revenues can be best applied. When the tax gatherer makes his appearance, he is not always a welcome visitor; but he comes only for that which we have probably voted to pay, and it is seldom that any one would have a single object for which the money is to be raised, abandoned. Who would have a dollar less expended for the support of Schools? Doubly benighted must the man be, who would lessen one cent, the means for educating his children! Who would have a dollar less appropriated for the enforcement of the laws of the land? Surely, our persons and property are even now, none too safe from the assassin and thief! Thus we might go through the long list of objects for which we tax ourselves; and though the aggregate may appear large, and at times onerous, there is seldom a single object we would be willing to see relinquished, merely on the ground of an enlightened economy.

We owe the security of all our rights, and the protection to our persons and property which we enjoy more than that possessed by barbarous nations, entirely to our social compact, sustained in its influences by the virtue and intelligence of the people. To carry out the designs of this compact, while there is so much evil and selfishness in the world, requires all the machinery of government; and the more perfect it is in its operations and results—as a general rule, and perhaps always, if in the hands of honest agents—the more expensive it is. We might elect one or two men to make our laws, at one-fiftieth of the expense incurred by a Legislature. As far as any necessity in the case is involved, this would be the best economy; yet all are aware that the history of the world shows, that as a matter of fact, the "one man power" is the most expensive that can be devised; and that not only financially, but as regards justice and equal rights. Few men can resist the temptation of power, to use it for their own aggrandizement; and the most perfect wisdom and virtue that ever united in mere mortal man, cannot be safely trusted with supreme power. Our fathers who followed their God-like commander through the Revolution, might have trusted Washington, but Washington would not have trusted himself. The possession of power is perhaps the severest trial to which a man's integrity is ever subjected. We often see this illustrated in those who, in obtaining power, or even in the hope of obtaining it, forfeit a character which they have labored many years to acquire.

Hence we perceive the true policy in free institutions, in retaining the power as directly as practicable, in the hands of the people. And as the people must necessarily employ agents to transact their public business, they are elected for short terms; so that, if they fail to reflect the will of the people, they can be displaced before they have time to do extensive injury. Thus the men—the leaders of a party—who fail for any length of time to execute the will of the masses, will be hurled from power, and their places bestowed upon new parties and new men. Even judicial tribunals—the strongest holds of civil power—will be overthrown if they continue to outrage united public sentiment. If one Legislature makes laws in opposition to the will of the people, men will be elected to the next, to repeal them. It is therefore impossible for a body of legislators long to misrepresent the will of their constituents, by taxation or otherwise.

When we see successive Legislatures making the establishment of our humane institutions a marked feature of their policy, with no remonstrance, it is fairly to be inferred

—were other proof wanting—that they are executing the public will. Even the strife of political partizanship has not reached the ground of our Asylums and Schools. So well are politicians aware that they are founded in reason, justice, humanity, and the hearts of the people, that they dare not avow opposition to them. The most they dare do, is to appeal to men's passions in reference to some of the details of their management. Such appeals go for about what they are worth, with an intelligent people. The unearthly wail of the Maniac, the sightless look of the Blind, and the mute speech of the Dumb, utter a more impressive voice than ever went up from the hosts of a political battle field. The man who would sacrifice the claims of suffering humanity for party or political considerations, would be likely to commit any crime that seemed to promise him benefit, if he could do it with impunity.

The enlightened and benevolent hearts of the citizens of Michigan who have thus far cordially sustained their public servants in establishing their Asylums, will hardly take a step backward in the noble works now half completed, and thus incur the stigma of going downward in the scale of civilization and humanity. Michigan has no cause to be ashamed of her institutions. She has set an example for her sister States in her Agricultural College—her University ranks among the first in the land—her Normal School is raising still higher the standard of education in the Primary Schools, which, with her local Colleges and Seminaries, will compare favorably with those of older States. Her public debt is insignificant, compared with that of several other States, and her resources are abundant to meet all the demands of an enlightened State policy. Her general tax is but about half a mill upon the dollar of her property, as assessed at less than two-thirds its value, and the heavier taxes for local objects, are only such as her citizens voluntarily impose upon themselves, as they deem best for their highest prosperity. With all her past acts of enterprise, intelligence and benevolence, it can hardly be ever said that her reformatory and humane institutions are not sustained with all the promptitude and liberality that is warranted by her ability, demanded by her Christianity, and by the obligations of the social compact, whose Constitution—which demands their support—is but the written recognition of the mutual obligations of dependent humanity.

ASYLUM FOR THE INSANE.

The Asylum for the Insane being classed among the educational institutions of the State, by the Constitution, the Superintendent of Public Instruction has deemed it fit and desirable that some notice of it should be given in connection with other kindred institutions, in this work. Having consulted with the officers of the Asylum, who entertain like views, the following article prepared by the Medical Superintendent, is here submitted.

The discovery and settlement of Michigan date far back in our national history, and yet only half a century has passed since its constiution as a territory, and but twenty-two years since its admission into the Union as a separate and independent State. Though Detroit was founded as early as 1670, in 1810, one hundred and forty years afterward, the population of the entire State was only four thousand seven hundred and sixty-two. The occurrence of the last war with Great Britain, and the unsettled state of the country consequent thereon, so far interrupted immigration, that in ten succeeding years the population was scarcely doubled. The growth of the State was thenceforward more rapid; the census returns showing a population in 1830 of 31,639, and in 1840 of 212,267.

The statistics of nativity, occupation, education, and other points more or less directly connected, etiologically or otherwise, with the subject of insanity, are presented as follows, in the United States Census of 1850. In an entire population of 397,654, 341,596 were born in the

United States, 54,703 were of foreign birth, and 1295 unknown. About one-half of those of foreign birth were originally from Great Britain. The male adult population of the State was 108,978, of whom 65,709 were farmers, about two thousand professional men, nearly four thousand were engaged in the different branches of mercantile pursuit, and about the same number are classed as laborers. Of the male adult population, 8,000, about three-eighths of whom were of foreign birth, were found entirely destitute of education, and unable to read or write. At the date of the Census Report, June 1st, 1850, the whole number of paupers receiving support was four hundred and twenty-nine—two hundred and forty-eight of whom are of native and one hundred and eighty-one of foreign birth.

No special attempt seems to have been made to procure a full and reliable enumeration of the Insane in the State of Michigan. The statistics presented, however, it is presumed, are as correct as those usually compiled under similar circumstances, and for purposes of comparison fully as reliable. In 1840 the number of Insane and Idiots, as presented in the United States Census, was but sixty-five, only seven of whom were supported at public charge. In the next decennial census and statistical returns made to the Department of State, in pursuance of an act of the Legislature, the whole number of Insane and Idiots, in May, 1854, was found to be four hundred and twenty-eight. The annexed table is a compilation of the foregoing data, and shows the ratio of Insane and Idiotic to the existing population:

Year.	Number of Insane.	Total Population.	Proportion of Insane and Idiots to the entire Population.
1840	65	212,267	1 to 3265
1850	326	397,654	1 to 1190
1854	428	509,374	1 to 1119

In 1850 the ratio of Insanity in the United States was 1 in 1,280. Assuming the population of Michigan to be at the present time 725,000, and taking the same ratio, the number of Insane in our State is more than 550. In the most recently settled of the western States, statistics have shown the rates of insanity to be 1 in 1,400. Taking a more favorable ratio even than this, 1 in 1,500, we have the Insane population in Michigan numbering 480. The question presents itself, what is the State doing for this most unfortunate and helpless class of her citizens? Where are these 480 lunatics? What is their condition?

On account of the almost universally received idea that the term *idiocy* is applicable to all forms of mental imbecility, and the great difficulty usually experienced in instructing census marshals to make a proper distinction between idiots and the demented, no attempt was made, in compiling the statistical tables from the returns of the State census, to separate the one class from the other. With a view of presenting the matter more fully to the Legislature, and to arrive at the facts with greater minuteness than was exhibited in the returns of the census, the Board of Trustees of the Michigan Asylum for the Insane, during the summer of 1856, instituted inquiries, by means of circulars, in every township of the State. Returns were received from only about one-third of the organized townships.

Comparing previous results with those deducible from the statistics thus obtained, the Board came to the conclusion that the number of insane in the State was not less than four hundred, three hundred and fifty of whom they consider proper subjects for immediate medical treatment. It was further ascertained that about one-half of this number were maintained by their friends at home, the remainder being county and town paupers. Of those supported in the poor houses and other similar receptacles, the Board remark, "very few receive any medical treatment whatever, and are subject to influences which tend rather to confirm than to remove their disease, while the worst possible moral effect is produced upon all who are thus associated."

The subject of public provision for the Insane of the State of Michigan was first introduced for legislative action in 1848. A joint resolution of the Senate and House of Representatives made it the duty of the assessors, in their annual assessment rolls, to report the number of the Insane, Deaf and Dumb, and Blind, in their respective townships. The laws of that session also established the Asylums, and appropriated eight sections of "Salt Spring lands" (5120 acres) for the erection of buildings. The government of the institution was vested in a Board of Trustees, empowered to establish rules and regulations, appoint officers, and to report to the Legislature annually.

In 1849 the amount of lands appropriated was increased to fifteen sections, (9600 acres,) and the immediate selection of the land required. The proceeds of sale were to be passed to the credit of the "Asylum Fund;" and at this session it was also made the duty of the Board of Trustees to select suitable locations. At the next session of the Legislature ten additional sections of land were appropriated, making a total of sixteen thousand acres, also $5,000 as a loan, from the general fund, to be used by the Trustees in the construction of the Asylums, and in defraying other expenses.

In 1851, the Board reported to the Legislature that they had ascertained the number and wants, as far as possible, of the Insane, Deaf and Dumb, and the Blind, and recommended the immediate erection of institutions for their care and treatment. They found in the State between three and four hundred Insane persons, some of whom were with their friends and relatives, but the greater number confined in county houses and jails. "The wants of this class being of pressing necessity, particular attention was directed to the obtaining of information on the organization and construction of institutions for the Insane, and communication had with several medical superintendents. As the result of their labors, they recommend the immediate erection of an institution capable of accommodating two hundred patients; to have attached not less than one hundred and sixty acres of land, located near some town or village; built substantially, and upon the general plan of the most perfect building in the country; to be warmed by steam or hot water apparatus, and ventilated upon the most improved modern plan."

The citizens of Kalamazoo, in addition to the sum of $1,380, had donated for the site of the Asylum for the Insane, ten acres of land in the central portion of the village. This, being unsuitable for the location of an institution, was disposed of, and one hundred and sixty acres purchased about one mile from the village.

The Legislature of 1853 made another appropriation from the General Fund of twenty thousand dollars, as a loan, and appointed a second Board of Trustees, and made it their duty to adopt plans for the buildings, and advertise for proposals.

The first Board of Trustees had presented to the Legislature the plans of two of the most approved institutions for the Insane in the United States, but without making any specific recommendation. With a view of obtaining the best information, and collecting data which should govern their action, the second Board deemed it necessary that one or more of their number should visit some of the eastern Asylums. Accordingly, the Board deputed one of its members to visit some of the best eastern institutions. In referring to this subject in their report to the Legislature of 1855, the Board remark: "Of existing institutions for the Insane in the United States, that established at Trenton, New Jersey, a plan of which was submitted to the late Board, is probably best adapted, in its general features, to the wants of this State; but the present Board came to the conclusion that none of the existing institutions combine all the improvements which are important to be adopted. It further seemed to them advisable to secure the early appointment of the Medical Superintendent, in order that the building might be erected so far under his supervision as to secure his approbation when completed. The frequent and expensive repairs of institutions erected without such supervision led them to look upon this as a matter of the greatest economy. Many of the Asylums of the United States were erected according to plans furnished by architects only, or by trustees without practical medical experience, and when supposed to by finished, have been found so ill-arranged and defective as to call for very large additional expenditures before the building could be used."

Acting upon these suggestions, the Board of Trustees, in January, 1854, appointed Dr. John P. Gray, then Acting Superintendent of the New York State Lunatic Asylum, to the post of Superintendent. Dr. Gray agreed to devote as much of his time and attention to the buildings and fixtures as should be necessary. As early as practicable in the following spring, the erection of the centre building was commenced, and proceeded with, as energetically as possible, until September, when the work was discontinued.

The Legislature of 1855 made an appropriation of sixty-seven thousand dollars to continue the construction of the institution, and as soon after as the weather would permit, the extreme transverse portion of the south wing was built and roofed, with a view of finishing it, together with the centre building, for immediate occupation. This course seemed very desirable, in order to meet the pressing demands of the Insane in the State even then awaiting admission, but upon consultation with several medical Superintendents of Asylums, it was found to be impracticable. A proper classification of patients is the first requisite in the care of the Insane, and a curative treatment is in a measure based thereon. To have finished the limited portion designated, and opened it for the reception of patients as intended, would have been entirely subversive of the purposes of the institution. To have assembled patients together without the facilities requisite to a proper degree of classification; to have associated the quiet and orderly, the melancholy and sensitive, with the raving and boisterous, the filthy and profane, would have made all more wretched, and in many confirmed the disease, which without such harmful association might have proved but temporary. A proper regard, therefore, for the greatest good both of the patients and the institution, induced the Trustees to abandon the design, and apply the balance of the appropriation to the completion of the remainder of the institution.

In the following year, Dr. Gray was elected to the Superintendency of the New York State Lunatic Asylum, and Dr. E. H. Van Deusen, first Assistant Physician at the same institution, was appointed to succeed him in the Michigan Asylum. The appointment of Dr. Van Deusen is considered a very judicious one. He brings to the service of the institution a long and tried experience, acquired during an official connection of five years with the New York State Asylum, at Utica.

The institutions for the Deaf and Dumb, and the Blind, at Flint, and for the Insane, at Kalamazoo, were commenced under one Board of Trustees, and continued under a joint control until the winter of 1855, when the Legislature judiciously severed this unnatural connection. The wants of the two classes are entirely dissimilar, and there is nothing in common between them, except that both are under the fostering care, and receive their inmates from among the citizens of the same State. In order to save the institutions from the loss and embarrassment inseparable from frequent and entire changes in their management, the same Legislature very wisely varied the manner of appointing Trustees, and so arranged it that whenever a member of the Board assigned either Asylum should go out of office, two would still remain with some experience in their official duties.

The appropriation of 1857 was only $50,000; a sum in marked contrast with the wants of the institution. Nevertheless, the Trustees at once set themselves energetically to work, and the portions of the building commenced were pressed on to completion as rapidly as the limited means at their command would permit.

During the year, the applications for the admission of patients were numerous, and many were made under the most afflicting circumstances. "The necessity which first demanded the erection of an Asylum in the State, had yearly become more and more urgent. The causes producing this most afflicting of all diseases had been in constant and uniform operation, and the number of the insane, as shown by statistics, had already more than doubled." The Trustees considered it their duty to make almost any sacrifice that might be required to meet the pressing want. They were aware of all the inconveniences and dangers which would attend the operation of a partially finished institution, but felt that some relief *must speedily* be afforded the many who were absolutely suffering in various parts of the State.

In February, 1858, the institution sustained a severe loss in the destruction of the centre building by fire, whereby nearly one-fifth of the portion erected was laid in ruins. Every precaution had been used to guard against such an accident, and a subsequent investigation showed conclusively that the fire originated above the second story, and was the work of an incendiary. The building is very nearly fire-proof—indeed, more nearly so than any other Asylum in the world—and it is doubtful whether it could have been successfully fired in any other portion. The pecuniary loss was estimated at $22,000. The part destroyed, though small as compared with the remainder of the structure, serves the most important purposes in the economy of the institution. It is the residence and head-quarters of the officers; all accidents and wants are reported there, and thence must issue the orders necessary for the direction and control of the entire household.

In this connection, and as thwarting their cherished desire of receiving patients at an early day, its loss was most deeply felt by the officers. Nevertheless, after careful and mature deliberation, the Trustees still determined to carry their original purpose into execution, and have prepared apartments for the reception of eighty-eight patients, and their necessary attendants, and this number will be received as soon as an appropriation can be secured for the purchase of furniture.

The statistics of insanity in Michigan, and the origin and history of the Asylum as presented in the successive reports of the Trustees, have been given in the preceding pages. Before proceeding to a description of the building, it may be remarked, that none but those who have had an opportunity of acquainting themselves practically with the subject, can form any idea of the close study in detail, which every part of an institution for the care of the Insane requires, and without which, it must necessarily be deficient in some important particular. Take for illustration an Asylum window. The health and comfort of the patient require that it be large, at the same time no subdivision must be small enough to allow one's head to pass. It must be strong and well guarded, and yet all appearance of restraint must be avoided. The sash must be movable, and readily opened, and at the same time must be guarded against injury by being heavily dropped upon the sill. To this end, it must be balanced by a weight, which requires, as a matter of course, a cord; but the cord must be concealed, and beyond the reach of the patient, or it may be removed and used for purposes of suicide. Thus in every part and appointment of the institution, the peculiar character of the inmate must be studied; and while striving to meet each requirement with constant attention to strength and durability, everything forbidding or unpleasant must be carefully avoided.

DESCRIPTION OF THE ASYLUM.

SITUATION.—The Michigan Asylum for the Insane is situated at Kalamazoo, upon the Michigan Central Railroad, one hundred and forty-three miles west of Detroit, and fifty-one miles southwest of the Capitol at Lansing. The location is probably as central and convenient as any that could have been chosen, having reference both to the present means of communication with the various parts of the State, and to any other routes of travel likely to be projected hereafter. The site selected for the building is upon an irregular eminence, about one mile from the village, and sufficiently elevated above the valley of the Kalamazoo river to secure an extended prospect, and yet well sheltered, and easy of access from the plain below. The location is in every respect healthful and desirable, and well adapted to the purposes and objects of an institution for the treatment of mental disease.

FARM.—The amount of land originally purchased for the use of the Asylum was one hundred and sixty acres; but to secure a more desirable site for the buildings, an adjacent tract was subsequently added, making the whole amount of land in the possession of the institution one hundred and sixty-eight acres (167 76-100ths.) Most of this land is finely timbered with the original growth of oak, hickory, and other trees, affording every facility which could be desired for beautifying the grounds. That in the rear of the building is broken, and falls, by a series of ravines covered with trees, about eighty feet to the valley below, through which flows a small but rapid stream of pure warer. The buildings themselves will cover an area of one and one-third acres. It is designed to preserve about fifty acres in groves and woodland, with walks and drives, and the remainder will be devoted to ordinary agricultural purposes.

GENERAL PLAN.—The ground plans were furnished by Dr. John P. Gray. It might here be remarked, that the principles laid down in a series of propositions relative to the construction and arrangement of Hospitals for the Insane, unanimously adopted by the "Association of Medical Superintendents of American Institutions for the Insane," have been fully carried out in the plans adopted by the Board. The form and internal arrangement of the Institution will be readily understood by reference to the accompanying ground-plan. The Asylum building proper, the main front of which has an easterly aspect, consists of a center and six wings. The center portion of the main building is divided by the entrance hall into two nearly equal parts. That to the right contains, in front, the principal office of the Institution, the apothecary shop, and an ante-room communicating by a private stairway with the Superintendent's apartments above; and in the rear. the matron's room and ladies' reception room; while that to the left contains in front the public parlor and officers' dining-room, and immediately behind these, the business office and men's reception room. The second floor is appropriated exclusively to the use of the Medical Superintendent. Upon the third floor are the apartments of the assistant physicians, steward and matron. The basement contains the laboratory connected with the apothecary shop, and the officers' kitchen and store-rooms. Immediately behind the center building is the chapel, and still further in the rear the engine and boiler-house. Extending from the center building, towards the south for males and towards the north for females, are the several wards of the Institution, nine on each side, including the infirmaries.

Architecture.—The plans selected by the Board of Trustees were placed in the hands of A. H. Jordan, Architect, of Detroit, for the necessary elevations, details, &c. The style adopted is the Italian, it being the lightest, most cheerful, and least expensive for the effect required in such an extensive range of building.

Materials.—The material used in construction has been brick, covered with Roman cement and sand, and finished to represent freestone. The window-caps, sills and brackets, belt-courses and capitals in front, are of white limestone, from the Athens quarries, near Chicago. The division walls throughout are of brick. The Asylum is built upon a system of fire-proof construction, nearly all the floors being laid upon brick arches sprung from iron girders, which besides providing against fire, give additional security to the building, and ensure its durability.

Appropriation of Wards.—The various wards in the institution are appropriated as follows:

Nos.	Classification.	No. of Wards.	Number of Beds.		Total of each sex and Class.
			Single Rooms.	Associated Dorm.	
1 and 2	Convalescent and quiet,	4	80	16	96
3 and 4	Less disturbed,.......	4	56	32	88
5 and 6	More disturbed,.......	4	60	......	60
7	Demented,............	2	20	......	20
8	" and infirm,...	2	12	......	12
9	Acute cases, &c., (Infir.)	2	12	......	12
	Total,.............	18	240	48	288

The divisions for the sexes are equal. Eight of these wards, inclusive of the infirmaries, are upon the first floor, six upon the second, and four upon the third floor of the transverse wings. It is considered that by means of these, any desirable classification of patients may be readily carried out.

Arrangement of Wards.—Each ward has the usual

arrangement of corridor, sleeping-rooms, day-rooms, and dining-room; with two stair-ways, clothes-room, lavatory, bath-room, water-closet, soiled clothes-shaft, drying-shaft and dust-flue to each. The corridors in the first, second, and third wings are respectively one hundred and fifty-five, one hundred and sixty, and seventy feet long; and in the third stories of the first and second transverse wings, one hundred and nineteen, and thirty-four feet long. They are uniformly twelve feet wide, and, in common with all other rooms, sixteen feet in hight upon the first and third floors, and fifteen upon the second. The dimensions of the single sleeping-rooms are eight and ten by eleven feet, with an average cubic capacity of fourteen hundred feet. The associate dormitories are fourteen by twenty-one feet, and the parlors, or recreation-rooms, eighteen by twenty. Lateral recesses, extending into the projecting towers in front, form additional day-rooms in the first and second wings, on either side. The dining-rooms are sufficiently capacious to accommodate the number for which they are intended, and are supplied with detached sinks, cupboards, and dumb waiters. The closets, bath-rooms, lavatories, and clothes-rooms open upon an adjacent, and not upon the main hall, giving a very desirable privacy. The bath and closet fixtures are of approved construction, and, to prevent all possible danger from leakage, the service-pipes are conveyed in a separate pipe-shaft—an arrangement which also facilitates and cheapens any repairs that may become necessary. Drying-shafts, having lattice-work floors, and communicating directly with the ventilating cupolas, furnish a ready means of drying mops, wet cloths, damp brooms, &c., and thus materially assist in promoting the cleanliness and healthfulness of the corridors. To prevent exposure, the bath-rooms and lavatories have communicating doors, in order that the latter may serve, on "bathing-days," as dressing-rooms to the former.

References to the Plate.—A, public parlor; B, Superintendent's office; C, Matron's room; D, business office; EE, reception rooms; F, officers' dining room; G, apothecary shop; H, ante-room, communicating by a private stiarway, with the Superintendent's apartments above; I, and II, store-rooms; K, associated dormitories; L, attendants' rooms; M, day and recitation-rooms; N, patients' sitting-rooms; O, dining-rooms; U, Chapel, having beneath it the kitchen, bakery and store-rooms; 1, boiler-room; 2, engine and fire-rooms; 3, laundry; 4, drying-room; 5, ironing-room; 6, workshop; 7, covered corridors.

NOTE.

The preceding "*References to the Plate,*" contemplate the insertion of a ground plan of the Asylum, not in hand at the time this form goes to press, but promised by the Officers of the Asylum on a separate sheet, in season to be bound up with this volume, and facing this page.

INFIRMARY FOR MALES

INFIRMARY FOR FEMALES.

HALL Nº 5.

HALL Nº 3.

HALL Nº 1.

HALL Nº 1

HALL Nº 3

HALL Nº 5

WARDS FOR MALE PATIENTS.

WARDS FOR FEMALE PATIENTS

MICHIGAN ASYLUM FOR THE INSANE, KALAMAZOO.

Scale 100 feet to an inch

A. H. Jordan, Arch^t. Detroit.

LITH OF ENDICOTT & CO N.Y.

INFIRMARIES.—In a detached building, in the rear of the first transverse wings, but connected with the wards by means of a covered corridor, an infirmary is provided for each sex. Fitted up with every convenience, they provide a very desirable place for the treatment of acute cases, of those who are seriously ill, or of any requiring special care and frequent medical attention. They can be reached at all hours of the night without disturbing any other portion of the house; they provide the means of isolation in case of the occurrence of any infectious or contagious diseases in the institution, and give to the friends of dying patients an opportunity of administering to them in their last moments.

WINDOWS.—The windows are fitted throughout with a cast-iron sash, the upper half of which alone is glazed. Posterior to the lower half, and immediately against it, is a wooden sash of corresponding size and shape, moving free, and suspended by a cord and weight; the former being attached to the bottom of the sash, and passing over a pulley near its top, is always entirely concealed. The panes of glass are six by nine inches in size. The windows, where deemed desirable, are protected by a shutter of framed wicker-work, sliding into the wall, and retained there, as also in its position, by one and the same lock.

FLOORING.—The floors in all uncarpeted rooms are formed of one and one-half inch oak plank, grooved and tongued, and none of them being more than three and one-half inches in width. The sleepers and the iron girders supporting the arches rest upon an offset in the wall, which, when finished, also forms the cornice in the room below.

PROVISION AGAINST FIRE.—The horrible sacrifice of human life on the occasion of the burning of an institution for the insane in one of the Eastern States, and the peculiar liability of these buildings to take fire, as shown by the frequent occurrence of such accidents, determined the Board of Trustees, although it would somewhat increase the price of construction, to make the Asylum fire-proof. The more recent partial destruction by fire of another institution has confirmed the wisdom of this decision. The use of iron girders and brick arches as support for the floors, was consequently determined upon, and to secure additional safety, all connection between the wing and the centre building is entirely cut off by the interposition of a verandah of iron and glass, with communication from one to the other only through iron doors. The location of the heating apparatus and the kitchen in detached buildings under the institution, quite exempt them from danger of destruction by fire.

CHAPEL.—A separate building immediately in the rear of the centre building, seventy by forty feet in size, contains upon its first floor a room for Chapel purposes, capable of seating three hundred and eighty persons. It communicates with the different wards by means of covered corridors, is appropriately fitted up, properly warmed, and lighted with gas.

KITCHEN.—One central kitchen is intended to supply the whole institution. It is placed immediately beneath the Chapel room, with store-rooms near at hand, and communicates with the dumb-waiters of the different dining-rooms, by means of a small car moving upon a covered railway. The building containing the Chapel room and kitchen is surmounted by a bell and clock tower.

WARMING AND VENTILATION.—It is now admitted as a principle that the warming and ventilation of buildings corresponding in size and purpose with institutions for the insane, should be effected by one and the same process; and also, that means should be adopted for expelling the foul air to the same extent and simultaneously with the admission of fresh. The fact is also established, and in many Asylums has been confirmed by a costly experience, that the ordinary system of making the ventilation depend upon the spontaneous action of warm air currents, has failed to give satisfactory results. A perfect and equable distribution of fresh air, either warm or cold, or the necessary rapidity in the discharge of foul air, under all circumstances and in all seasons, can be secured only by a system of *forced* ventilation. This is found to be most efficiently and economically effected by means of a fan driven by a steam engine; effectual, because at all times under perfect control, and economical, because the warm air is more thoroughly and rapidly distributed. The primary cost is not great; it is not liable to get out of order, and the motive power is that required for other purposes.

The system decided upon is a modification of that in use at the New York State Lunatic Asylum, the efficiency of which is shown by the fact that in ten similar institutions in other States it has since been adopted, in place of furnaces and other means of heating and ventilation already in operation. It consists of boilers, an engine, a fan, heating surface, and distributing-ducts and inlet-flues, with exit-flues, foul-air ducts, and ventilating cupolas. The boilers are four in number; these, with the engine and fan, (the latter peculiar, from the circumstance of its delivering the air in the direction of its axis,) are all in a separate and detached building. The air, after its delivery from the fan, passes directly forward beneath the chapel. The main duct conveying it gives off a small branch to the chapel, and another to the centre building. It then branches toward either wing, and another sub-division is made, one portion passing beneath the first longitudinal wing, and the other, entering the proximal end of the second wing, passes on to the end of the extreme wing. The air-passage beneath the building occupies the centre of the middle portion of the basement, or rather, the space immediately beneath the floors of the corridors, and the distributing flues pass up in the walls upon either side of them. The heating surface consisting of a series of wrought iron pipe, one inch in diameter, is placed in narrow chambers on either side of the air-chamber. Exit-flues are carried up in the same walls, taking their departure from two points, one near the ceiling, and the other near the floor of the rooms on either side. These again conjoin in the attics to form the foul-air ducts, and empty out into the open air through the ventilating cupolas. Downward currents of air, for the ventilation of the water-closets, will be secured in the usual manner. This very important department has been intrusted to Joseph Nason, Esq., of New York City.

WATER.—Water is forced up to the institution through a cast-iron pipe three inches in diamater, from a stream flowing in the valley immediately in the rear of the building.

COST.—It is estimated, and the experience thus far acquired in the progress of construction has shown the estimate to be a liberal one, that the entire cost of the institution, with all necessary out-buildings, farm implements, farm stock, fences, gas-fixtures and pipes, a complete system of drainage and sewerage, warming and ventilating, and furnished throughout, ready for the occupation of two hundred and eighty-eight patients, will be about three hundred and thirty thousand dollars.

Of the sum thus stated as the entire cost of the establishment, the amount properly belonging to the *cost of erection* would be $270,000.

For the purpose of comparing this with the cost of simlar institutions in other States, the following table is subjoined:

Name of Asylum.	Land.	Capacity.	Cost.
State Lunatic Asylum, Utica, New York,............	130 acres.	440 patients.	$517,400 00
Maryland Hospital, Baltimore,.....................	12 "	130 "	213,600 00
McLean Asylum ,Somerville, Massachusetts,.........	32 "	200 "	321,000 00
Pennsylvania Hospital, Philadelphia,..............	113 "	230 "	330,000 00
Friends' Asylum, Frankfort, Pa.,..................	62 "	60 "	85,593 00
State Lunatic Asylum, Trenton, New Jersey,........	100 "	250 "	250,000 00
Maine Hospital for the Insane,....................	115 "	17[illegible] "	150,712 00
Mt. Hope Institution, Baltimore, Maryland,........	18 "	120 "	100,000 00
Butler Hospital, Providence, R. I.,...............	115 "	140 "	116,000 00
State Lunatic Asylum, Taunton, Mass.,.............	120 "	250 "	250,000 00

Experience in the erection of Asylums for the Insane,

both in this country and elsewhere, has shown that the average cost of such institutions is about one thousand dollars for each patient accommodated; though in several of the larger Asylums in the United States, it has been much greater. In the Michigan Asylum, it will be observed that the cost has not exceeded this average.

Reviewing the architectural details of the building, and its general arrangement, and recollecting that the amount of cubic space allotted to each patient, is about one-third more than usual; that the number accommodated in single, instead of associated dormitories, is proportionably greater, (being 214 of the whole number;) also, that the estimate includes the erection of a well arranged infirmary for each sex, external to the walls, (a very important feature, peculiar to this institution, though common to all recently erected Asylums in England,) it will be observed that the plan is most complete, and embraces all the modern improvements.

The following is an extract from a recent article in the editorial department of the "PENINSULAR AND INDEPENDENT MEDICAL JOURNAL," published at Detroit.

"That our readers may know how our State Asylum is regarded by those who have studied its construction, on the other side of the Atlantic, we subjoin the following extract from the *Dublin Medical Quarterly:*

"'Great good sense was shown respecting the Michigan Asylum, at the commencement, by the appointment of an experienced Medical Superintendent. This was done with the view of the building being erected so far under his supervision as to secure his approbation when finished, than which nothing could have been more judicious. And another and equally wise course was carried out, that of taking as a basis of action the principles embodied in the series of propositions adopted by the Assoc. of Med. Superintendents of American Institutions for the Insane; which we considered sufficiently important and practical at the time of their publication, to transcribe *in extenso* into our Annual Review on Insanity in 1851. We wish our authorities at home would take a lesson from our far-seeing trans-Atlantic brethren, in such matters.

"'In the appropriation of the wards, we find that the greater portion of accommodation consists in single rooms, there being as many as two hundred and forty, leaving but forty-eight to be located in dormitories. This is in the opposite degree to what prevails in these countries, the Asylums in which, we consider, are entirely too much limited in single rooms, and too abundant in dormitories. But this is done for economy, which is an injurious and mistaken one of its kind, and but ill calculated to promote either the recovery or comfort of the patients.

"'Altogether, this Asylum will be, from all appearances, most complete in its several arrangements—in fact, will be a model one for the New as well as the Old World!'

"It will be seen by this extract that Michigan not only excels in her educational institutions, but that her Insane Asylum is an acknowledged model, not only for the New but the Old World."

OFFICERS.

Charles T. Gorham, Esq., President of Board of Trustees.
I. P. Woodbury, Esq., Secretary of Board of Trustees.
Henry Montague, Esq., Acting Commissioner.
E. H. Van Deusen, M. D., Medical Superintendent.

PART II.

CONSTITUTIONAL PROVISIONS RELATING TO EDUCATION;

DUTIES OF SUPERINTENDENT OF PUBLIC INSTRUCTION;

LAWS RELATING TO PRIMARY SCHOOLS;

PROVISIONS FOR LIBRARIES AND LYCEUMS;

TEACHERS' ASSOCIATIONS AND TEACHERS' INSTITUTES;

THE STATE NORMAL SCHOOL;

THE UNIVERSITY OF MICHIGAN;

AGRICULTURAL COLLEGE OF MICHIGAN;

INCORPORATED INSTITUTIONS OF LEARNING;

INSTRUCTIONS FOR CONDUCTING PROCEEDINGS UNDER THE PRIMARY SCHOOL LAWS.

PROVISIONS OF THE CONSTITUTION RELATIVE TO EDUCATION.

Article Thirteen of the Constitution of Michigan, under the head "Education," makes the following provisions:

Section 1. The Superintendent of Public Instruction shall have the general supervision of public instruction, and his duties shall be prescribed by law. Superintendent.

Sec. 2. The proceeds from the sales of all lands that have been or hereafter may be granted by the United States to the State, for educational purposes, and the proceeds of all lands or other property given by individuals, or appropriated by the State for like purposes, shall be and remain a perpetual fund, the interest and income of which, together with the rents of all such lands as may remain unsold, shall be inviolably appropriated and annually applied to the specific objects of the original gift, grant or appropriation. School Fund Perpetual.

Sec. 3. All lands, the titles to which shall fail from a defect of heirs, shall escheat to the State; and the interest on the clear proceeds from the sales thereof, shall be appropriated exclusively to the support of Primary Schools. Escheats.

Sec. 4. The Legislature shall, within five years from the adoption of this Constitution, provide for and establish a system of Primary Schools, whereby a School shall be kept without charge for tuition, at least three months in each year, in every School District in the State; and all instruction in said Schools shall be conducted in the English language.(1) Free schools

(1) The Legislature has not, as yet, fully complied with the requirements of this Section.

Dist. schools

Sec. 5. A School shall be maintained in each School District at least three months in each year. Any School District neglecting to maintain such School, shall be deprived for the ensuing year of its proportion of the income of the Primary School Fund, and of all funds arising from taxes for the support of Schools.

Penalty.

Election of Regents of University.

Sec. 6. There shall be elected in each judicial circuit, at the time of the election of the Judge of such circuit, a Regent of the University, whose term of office shall be the same as that of such Judge. The Regents thus elected shall constitute the Board of Regents of the University of Michigan.

Regents a body corporate.

Sec. 7. The Regents of the University, and their successors in office, shall continue to constitute the body corporate, known by the name and title of "The Regents of the University of Michigan."

Reg'ts elect President of University.

Sec. 8. The Regents of the University shall, at their first annual meeting, or as soon thereafter as may be, elect a President of the University, who shall be *ex-officio* a member of their board, with the privilege of speaking, but not of voting. He shall preside at the meetings of the Regents, and be the principal executive officer of the University. The Board of Regents shall have the general supervision of the University, and the direction and control of all expenditures from the University Interest Fund.

Supervison.

State Board of Education

Sec. 9. There shall be elected at the general election in the year one thousand eight hundred and fifty-two, three members of a State Board of Education—one for two years, one for four years, and one for six years; and at each succeeding biennial election there shall be elected one member of such Board, who shall hold his office for six years. The Superintendent of Public Instruction shall be *ex-officio* a member and Secretary of such Board. The Board shall have the general supervision of the State Normal School, and their duties shall be prescribed by law.

Sec. 10. Institutions for the benefit of those inhabitants who are deaf, dumb, blind or insane, shall always be fostered and supported. Asylums.

Sec. 11. The Legislature shall encourage the promotion of intellectual, scientific and agricultural improvement; and shall, as soon as practicable, provide for the establishment of an Agricultural School. The Legislature may appropriate the twenty-two sections of salt spring lands now unappropriated, or the money arising from the sale of the same, where such lands have been already sold, and any land which may hereafter be granted or appropriated for such purpose, for the support and maintenance of such School, and may make the same a branch of the University, for instruction in agriculture and the natural sciences connected therewith, and place the same under the supervision of the Regents of the University.(1) Agricultural School.

Sec. 12. The Legislature shall also provide for the establishment of at least one library in each township; and all fines assessed and collected in the several counties and townships for any breach of the penal laws, shall be exclusively applied to the support of such libraries. Township Libraries.

(1) The Agricultural College, as organized, is entirely distinct from the State University.

SUPERINTENDENT OF PUBLIC INSTRUCTION.

By an Act approved April 4th, 1851, (page 708 Compiled Laws,) the duties of the Superintendent of Public Instruction are thus defined:

Superintendent to have general supervision of Public Instruction. Annual Report.

Section 1. The Superintendent of Public Instruction shall have general supervision of Public Instruction, and it shall be his duty, among other things, to prepare annually and transmit a report to the Governor, to be transmitted by him to the Legislature at each biennial session thereof, containing:

1. A statement of the condition of the University, and its branches, of all incorporate Literary Institutions, and of the Primary Schools;

2. Estimates and amounts of expenditures of the School money;

3. Plans for the improvement and management of all educational funds, and for the better organization of the educational system, if in his opinion the same be required;

4. The condition of the Normal School;

5. All such other matters relating to his office, and the subject of Education generally, as he shall deem expedient to communicate.

Report to embody abstracts of reports of Inspectors.

Sec. 2. He shall make all necessary abstracts of the reports of School Inspectors, transmitted to him by the clerks, and embody so much of the same in his report as may be necessary.

Sec. 3. He shall prepare and cause to be printed, with

the laws relating to Primary Schools, all neccessary forms, regulations and instruments for conducting all proceedings under said laws, and transmit the same with such instructions relative to the organization and government of such Schools, and the course of studies to be pursued therein, as he may deem advisable, to the several officers entrusted with their care and management.

To prepare forms, regulations, etc., for School Officers.

Sec. 4. School laws, forms, regulations and instructions shall be printed in pamphlet form, with a proper index, and shall have also annexed thereto a list of such books as the Superintendent shall think best adapted to the use of the Primary Schools, and a list of books suitable for township libraries, with such rules as he may think proper for the government of such libraries.

School laws, forms, etc., to be printed.

Sec. 5. He shall annually, on receiving notice from the Auditor General of the amounts thereof, apportion the income of the Primary School fund among the several townships and cities of the State, in proportion to the number of scholars in each between the age of four and eighteen years, as the same shall appear by the reports of the several Township Inspectors of Primary Schools, made to him for the year last closed.

Apportionment of Primary School Fund.

Sec. 6. He shall prepare annually a statement of the amount in the aggregate, payable to each county in the State from the income of the Primary School fund, and shall deliver the same to the Auditor General, who shall thereupon draw his warrant upon the State Treasurer in favor of each county for the amount payable to such county.

To furnish Aud. General with annual statement of the amou't payable to each county.

Sec. 7. He shall also send written notices to the clerks of the several counties, of the amount in the aggregate, to be disbursed in their respective counties, and the amount payable to the townships therein respectively; which notice shall be disposed of as directed by an act entitled, "An Act to amend Chapter fifty-eight of the Revised

Notices to Co. Clerk of amount to be disbursed in each county.

Statutes of one thousand eight hundred and forty-six," approved March twenty-eight, one thousand eight hundred and fifty.(1)

Rates of apportionment, how ascertained when Reports defective.

Sec. 8. Whenever the returns from any county, township or city, upon which a statement of the amount to be disbursed or paid to any such county, township or city, shall be so far defective as to render it impracticable to ascertain the share of public moneys which ought to be disbursed or paid to such county, township or city, he shall ascertain, by the best evidence in his power, the facts upon which the ratio of such apportionment shall depend, and shall make the apportionment accordingly.

In what cases deficiency may be apportioned the next year.

Sec. 9. Whenever, by accident, mistake, or any other cause, the returns from any county, township or city, upon which a statement of the amount to be disbursed to any such county, township or city, shall not contain the whole number of scholars in such county, township or city, between the age of four and eighteen years, and entitled to draw money from said fund, by which any such county, township or city, shall fail to have apportioned to it the amount to which it shall justly be entitled, the Superintendent, on receiving satisfactory proof thereof, shall apportion such deficiency to such county, township or city, in his next annual apportionment; and the conditions of this section shall extend to all cases which accrue in the year one thousand eight hundred and fifty.

Interest on Educational Fund; how computed and how paid.

Sec. 10. Upon all sums paid into the State Treasury upon account of the principal of any of the educational funds, except where the provision is or shall be made by law, the Treasurer shall compute interest from the time of such payment, or from the time of the last computation of interest thereon, to the first Monday of April in each and every year, and shall give credit therefor to each and every School fund, as the case may be; and such interest shall be paid out of the general fund.

(1) Section 112, Primary Schools.

Sec. 11. The Superintendent shall, at the expiration of his term of office, deliver over, on demand, to his successor, all property, books, documents, maps, records, reports, and all other papers belonging to his office, or which may have been received by him for the use of his office.

Superintendent at the expiration of his term to deliver to successor books, papers, etc.

Sec. 12. Chapter fifty-six of the Revised Statutes of one thousand eight hundred and forty-six, and an Act to amend said chapter fifty-six, approved March twenty-ninth, one thousand eight hundred and fifty, are hereby repealed.

Certain enactments repealed. R. S. of 1846, Chap. 56. 1850, p. 181.

PRIMARY SCHOOL LAW.

The following Laws relating to Primary Schools, are copied from the Revised Statutes of 1846, as since amended, from time to time.(1)

DISTRICTS.

When new district is formed Township Clerk to deliver notice to taxable inhabitant.

Section 1. Whenever the Board of School Inspectors of any township shall form a School District therein, it shall be the duty of the Clerk of such Board to deliver to a taxable inhabitant of such District a notice in writing of the formation of such District, describing its boundaries, and specifying the time and place of the first meeting, which notice, with the fact of such delivery, shall be entered upon record by the Clerk.(2)

Inhabitant to serve notice.

Sec. 2. The said notice shall also direct such inhabitant to notify every qualified voter of such district, either personally or by leaving a written notice at his place of residence, of the time and place of said meeting, at least five days before the time appointed therefor; and it shall be the duty of such inhabitant to notify the qualified voters of said district accordingly.(3)

Duty to serve; see section 129.

Return of notice.

Sec. 3. The said inhabitant, when he shall have notified the qualified voters as required in such notice, shall endorse thereon a return, showing such notification, with the date or dates thereof, and deliver such notice and return to the Chairman of the meeting.(4)

Notice and return to be recorded.

Sec. 4. The said Chairman shall deliver such notice and return to the Director chosen at such meeting, who shall

(1) Compiled Laws, Chapter 78.

(2) See Forms Nos. 1 and 2.

(3) See Forms Nos. 1 and 2.

(4) See Forms Nos. 1 and 3.

record the same at length in a book to be provided by him, at the expense of the District, as a part of the records of such District.[1]

Sec. 5. The qualified voters of such District, when assembled pursuant to such previous notice, and also at each annual meeting, shall choose a Moderator, Director, and Assessor, who shall be residents of said District, and who shall, within ten days after such meeting, severally file with the Director a written acceptance of the offices to which they shall have been respectively elected, which shall be recorded by said Director.[2] **Election of officers.**

Sec. 6. Every such School District shall be deemed duly organized, when any two of the officers elected at the first meeting shall have filed their acceptance as aforesaid.[3] **When district deem'd organized.**

Sec. 7. In case the inhabitants of any District shall fail to organize the same in pursuance of such notice as aforesaid, the said Clerk shall give a new notice in the manner hereinbefore provided, and the same proceedings shall be had thereon as if no previous notice had been delivered.[4] **New notice in case of failure to organize.**

Sec. 8. Every School District organized in pursuance of this chapter, or which has been organized and continued under any previous law of the State or Territory of Michigan, shall be a body corporate, and shall possess the usual powers of a corporation for public purposes, by the name and style of "School District Number (such number as shall be designated in the formation thereof by the Inspectors), of ," (the name of the township or townships in which the district is situated), and in that name shall be capable of suing and being sued, and of holding such real and personal estate as is authorized to be purchased by the provisions of this chapter, and of selling the same. **Corporate powers of districts.**

Sec. 9. The record made by the Director, as required in the fourth section of this chapter, shall be *prima facie* evi- **Director's record evidence.**

(1) See Form No. 1.
(2) See Form No. 4, Note A, and Sec. 130
(3) See Note A, and Sec. 149.
(4) See Form No. 1, Sec. 149 and Note A.

dence of the facts therein set forth, and of the legality of all proceedings in the organization of the District prior to the first District meeting; but nothing in this section contained shall be so construed as to impair the effect of the record kept by the School Inspectors, as evidence.

Rresumpti'n of legal organiaztion. Sec. 10. Every School District shall, in all cases, be presumed to have been legally organized, when it shall have exercised the franchises and privileges of a District for the term of two years.

DISTRICT MEETINGS.

Annual meeting. Sec. 11. The annual meeting of each School District shall be held on the last(1) Monday of September in each year, and the School year shall commence on that day.(2)

Special meeting. Sec. 12. Special meetings may be called by the District Board, or by any one of them, on the written request of any five legal voters of the District, by giving the notice required in the next succeeding section, and in all notices of special meetings the object of the meeting shall be stated.(3)

Notice of meetings. Sec. 13. All notices of annual or special District meetings, after the first meeting has been held as aforesaid, shall specify the day and hour, and place of meeting, and shall be given at least six days previous to such meeting, by posting up copies thereof in three of the most public places in the District; and in case of any special meeting called for the purpose of establishing or changing the site of a School-house, such notice shall be given at least ten days previous thereto.(4)

When meeting not illegal for want of notice. Sec. 14. No district meeting shall be deemed illegal for want of due notice, unless it shall appear that the omission to give such notice was willful and fraudulent.

Who entitled to vote. Sec. 15. Every white male inhabitant of the age of twenty-one years, residing in the District, and liable to pay a

---

(1) This word was erroneously printed "first," in the Compiled Laws.

(2) See Form No. 5 and Note A. (3) See Form No. 6 and Note A.

(4) See Note A, and Forms Nos. 5 and 6.

School District tax therein, shall be entitled to vote at any district meeting.[1]

Challenges to persons offering to vote.

Sec. 16. If any person offering to vote at a School District meeting shall be challenged as unqualified, by any legal voter in such district, the chairman presiding at such meeting shall declare to the person challenged the qualifications of a voter, and if such person shall state that he is qualified, and the challenge shall not be withdrawn, the said chairman shall tender to him an oath in substance as follows: "You do swear (or affirm) that you are twenty-one years of age, that you are an actual resident of this School District, and liable to pay a School District tax therein;" and every person taking such oath, shall be permitted to vote on all questions proposed at such meeting.

Oath.

False oath to be deemed perjury.

Sec. 17. If any person so challenged shall refuse to take such oath, his vote shall be rejected, and any person who shall willfully take a false oath, or make a false affirmation under the provisions of the preceding section, shall be deemed guilty of perjury.

When challenge may be made in certain cases.

Sec. 18. When any question is taken in any other manner than by ballot, a challenge immediately after the vote has been taken, shall be deemed to be made when offering to vote, and treated in the seme manner.

Powers of voters at meetings.

Sec. 19. The qualified voters in such School District, when lawfully assembled, shall have power to adjourn from time to time, as may be necessary; to designate a site for a School-house, by a vote of two-thirds of those present, and to change the same by a similar vote at any regular meeting.[2]

When Inspectors to determine site of School House.

Sec. 20. When no site can be established by such inhabitants as aforesaid, the School Inspectors of the township or townships in which the district is situated shall determine where such site shall be, and their determination shall be certified to the Director of the District, and shall

(1) See Forms Nos 1, 2 and 3.

(2) See Form No. 19 and Note B.

be final, subject to alteration afterwards by the Inspectors only, if necessary.(1)

Qualified voters may direct purchasing of site, etc., and prescribe the amonnt of fuel, and how furnished.

Sec. 21. The said qualified voters shall also have power at any such meeting to direct the purchasing or leasing of an appropriate site, and the building, hiring, or purchasing of a School-house, and the amount of fuel to be furnished, and the time and mode of furnishing it for the succeeding year; whether by apportionment to persons having scholars to send to such School, in wood, to be delivered at the School-house, or in money, to be assessed on a rate bill, or by a tax on the property of the District, and to impose such tax as may be sufficient for the payment thereof, subject to the limitation contained in the succeeding section.

Limitation of tax for School House, etc.

Sec. 22. The amount of taxes to be raised in any District for the purpose of purchasing or building a School-house, shall not exceed the sum of two hundred dollars in any one year, unless there shall be more than thirty scholars residing therein, between the ages of four and eighteen years; and the amount thereof shall not exceed three hundred dollars in any one year, unless there shall be more than fifty scholars residing in the District between the ages last aforesaid; and no sum shall be raised exceeding one hundred and eighty dollars, for the purpose of building or purchasing a School-house of less dimensions than twenty-four feet by thirty feet, and ten feet between floors; nor exceeding seventy-five dollars for the purpose of building or purchasing a School-house, constructed of round or hewn logs.(2)

Tax for repairs, and or apparatus, etc., for use of school.

Sec. 23. Such qualified voters, when assembled as aforesaid, may from time to time impose such tax as shall be necessary to keep their School-house in repair, and to provide the necessary appendages, and to pay and discharge any debts or liabilities of the District lawfully incurred; and in Districts containing more than fifty scholars between

(1) See Form No. 19 and Note B. (2) See Note B.

the ages of four and eighteen years, may raise a sum not exceeding twenty dollars in any one year for the purchase of globes, maps, or any apparatus for the purpose of illustrating the principles of astronomy, natural philosophy, and agricultural chemistry or the mechanic arts.

Voters may determine the length of time a School shall be taught, etc.

Sec. 24. They may also determine, at each annual meeting, the length of time a School shall be taught in their District during the ensuing year, which shall not be less than three months; and whether by male or female teachers, or both; and whether the moneys apportioned for the support of the School therein shall be applied to the winter or summer term, or a certain portion of each.(1)

When district board may determine.

Sec. 25. In case any of the matters in the preceding section mentioned are not determined at the annual meeting, the District Board shall have power, and it shall be their duty, to determine the same.(2)

When voters may direct sale of property.

Sec. 26. Said qualified voters may also, at any regular meeting, authorize and direct the sale of any School-house, site, building or other property belonging to the District, when the same shall no longer be needed for the use of the District.(3)

Directions in regard to suits.

Sec. 27. They may also give such directions, and make such provision as they shall deem necessary, in relation to the prosecution or defense of any suit or proceeding in which the District may be a party, or interested.

DISTRICT OFFICERS, THEIR POWERS AND DUTIES.

District officers.

Sec. 28. The officers of each School District shall be a Moderator, Director and Assessor, who shall hold their respective offices until the annual meeting next following their election or appointment, and until their successors shall have been chosen, and filed their acceptance, but not beyond ten days after the time of a second annual meeting

(1) See Note C. (2) See Note C. (3) See Note C.

after their election or appointment, without being again elected or appointed.(1)

MODERATOR.

Moderator's powers and duties.

Sec. 29. The Moderator shall have power, and it shall be his duty, to preside at all meetings of the District, to sign all warrants for the collection of rate bills after they shall have been prepared and signed by the Director, and to countersign all orders upon the Assessor for moneys to be disbursed by the District, and all warrants of the Director upon the Township Treasurer for moneys raised for District purposes, or apportioned to the District by the Township Clerk; but if the Moderator shall be absent from any District meeting, the qualified voters present may elect a suitable person to preside at the meeting.(2)

Moderator to keep order, etc.

Sec. 30. If at any District meeting any person shall conduct himself in a disorderly manner, and after notice from the Moderator or person presiding, shall persist therein, the Moderator or person presiding may order him to withdraw from the meeting, and on his refusal, may order any constable or other person or persons to take him into custody until the meeting shall be adjourned.

Penalty for disturbing meeting.

Sec. 31. Any person who shall refuse to withdraw from such meeting on being so ordered, as provided in the preceding section, or who shall willfully disturb such meeting, shall, for every such offence, forfeit a sum not exceeding twenty dollars.

ASSESSOR.

Assessor to collect and pay over moneys.

Sec. 32. The Assessor shall pay over all moneys in his hands belonging to the District, on the warrant of the Director, countersigned by the Moderator; and shall collect all rate bills for tuition and fuel, in obedience to the command contained in the warrant annexed thereto.(3)

Sec. 33. In case any person shall neglect or refuse to pay

(1) See Notes A. and D.

(2) See Note P. and Forms Nos. 7, 10 and 11.

(3) See Form No. 7.

the amount on such rate bill for which he is liable, on demand, the Assessor shall collect the same by distress and sale of any goods or chattels of such person, wherever found, within any county in which the District, or any part of it, is situated.(1)

On refusal to pay, Assessor to collect by distress.

Sec. 34. The Assessor shall give at least ten days' notice of such sale, by posting up written notices thereof in three public places in the township where such property shall be sold.(2)

Notice of sale.

Sec. 35. At the expiration of his warrant, the Assessor shall make a return thereof, in writing, with the rate bill attached, to the Director; stating the amount on said rate bill collected, the amount uncollected, and the names of the persons from whom collections have not been made.(3)

Assessor to make r'turn to Director.

Sec. 36. The Assessor shall appear for and on behalf of the District in all suits brought by or against the same, when no other directions shall be given by the qualified voters in District meeting, except in suits in which he is interested adversely to the District, and in all such cases the Director shall appear for such District, if no other direction be given as aforesaid.

When Assessor to appear for Director.

DIRECTOR.

Sec. 37. The Director shall be the clerk of the District Board, and of all District meetings when present, but if he shall not be present at any District meeting, the qualified voters present may appoint a clerk of such meeting, who shall certify the proceedings thereof to the Director, to be recorded by him.

Director to be Clerk.

Sec. 38. The Director shall record all the proceedings of the District, in a book to be kept for that purpose, and preserve copies of all reports made to the School Inspectors, and safely preserve and keep all books and papers belonging to his office.

To record proceedings, etc.

Sec. 39. By and with the advice and consent of the Mod-

(1) See Form No. 7. (2) See Form No. 7. (3) See Form No. 7.

To contract with Teachers. erator and Assessor, or one of them, the Director shall contract with, and hire qualified teachers for, and in the name of the district, which contract shall be in writing, and shall have the consent of the Moderator and Assessor, or one of them endorsed thereon, and shall specify the wages per week or month as agreed by the parties, and a duplicate thereof shall be filed in his office.(1)

To ascertain requisite quantity of fuel for each person, and give notice to furnish, etc. Sec. 40. He shall ascertain, as near as practicable, before the commencement of each School Term, if the District at any regular meeting so direct, the just proportion which each person having scholars to send to the School ought to furnish, of the fuel for such term, and give each such person at least five days' notice of the time within which he is required to deliver the same at the School-house; and if any person shall not deliver his proportion as required, the same shall be furnished by the Director, and the amount thereof shall be assessed on the rate bill to the person neglecting to deliver his proportion as aforesaid.

To take census of district, and make list. Sec. 41. Within ten days next previous to the annual District meeting, the Director shall take the census of his District, and make a list in writing of the names of all the children belonging thereto between the ages of four and eighteen years.(2)

To furnish copy of list to Teacher, and require Teacher to note attendance and make return. Sec. 42. He shall furnish a copy of such list to each Teacher employed in the District, and require such Teacher carefully to note the daily attendance of each scholar, and to make return thereof to him, including the ages of all scholars whose names are not on such list; and such Teacher shall also certify and return, according to his best information and belief, the name of the person liable for the tuition of each scholar.

When Teacher to keep list, etc. Sec. 43. In case the Director shall not have furnished such list as aforesaid, the Teacher shall keep a list of all the scholars attending School, and the number of days each

(1) See Note O, and Forms Nos. 8 and 17. (2) See Form No. 22 and Note M.

scholar shall attend the same, with the age of each, and the name of the person liable for the tuition of each, according to his best information and belief, which list he shall return to the Director as aforesaid.

Sec. 44. The Director shall ascertain from the return of such Teacher, the number of days for which each person not exempted shall be liable to pay for tuition, and the amount payable by each. Director to ascertain amount due for tuition.

Sec. 45. Within twenty days after receiving such list and certificate from the Teacher, the Director shall make out a rate bill, containing the name of each person so liable, and the amount due from him for tuition and fuel, or either, adding thereto five cents on each dollar of the sum due, for Assessor's fees, and shall annex thereto a warrant for the collection thereof, to be signed by him and the Moderator.(1) Rate bill for tuition and fuel, and warrant for collection.

Sec. 46. Such warrant shall command the Assessor that within sixty days he collect of the persons named in said rate bill the amount set opposite their respective names, and that if any person shall neglect or refuse, on demand, to pay the amount on said rate bill for which he is liable, he collect the same by distress and sale of the goods and chattels of such person wherever found within the county or counties in which the District is situated, first publishing such sale at least ten days, by posting up notices thereof in three public places in the township where such property shall besold.(2) Contents of warrant.

Sec. 47. In case the Moderator and Director shall deem it necessary, they may, by an endorsement on such warrant signed by them, extend the time therein specified for the collection of such rate bill, not exceeding thirty days.(3) Renewal of warrant.

Sec. 48. The Director shall provide the necessary appendages for the School-house, and keep the same in good condition and repair during the time a School shall be Director to provide appendages, etc., and keep account.

(1) See Form No. 7. (2) See Form No. 7. (3) See Form No. 9.

taught therein, and shall keep an accurate account of all expenses incurred by him as Director.(1)

Allowance of Director's account.

Sec. 49. He shall present said account for allowance to the qualified voters of the District, at a regular meeting, and the amount of such account, as allowed by such meeting, shall be assessed and collected in the same manner as other District taxes; but no such account shall be allowed at a special meeting, unless the intention to present the same shall be expressed in the notice of such meeting.(2)

Director to give notice of meetings.

Sec. 50. He shall give the prescribed notice of the annual District meeting, and of all such special meetings as he shall be required to give notice of in accordance with the provisions of this chapter, one copy of which for each meeting shall be posted on the outer door of the District School-house, if there be one.(3)

To draw books from Township Library, and return the same.

Sec. 51. The Director shall draw from the Township Library the proportion of books to which his District may be entitled, and return the same to the Township Library at the expiration of three months, and shall continue to draw books in like manner, at the expiration of every three months, and to return the same as aforesaid.(4)

Distribution of books.

Sec. 52. He shall distribute the books drawn out by him to the parents or guardians of the children of the District of the proper age, for the time and under the restrictions contained in the rules prescribed by the Board of School Inspectors.(5)

Director to draw and sign warrants on Treasurer.

Sec. 53. He shall draw and sign all orders upon the Assessor for all moneys to be disbursed by the District, and all warrants upon the Township Treasurer for moneys raised for District purposes, or apportioned to the District by the Township Clerk, and present the same to the Moderator, to be countersigned by him.(6)

Sec. 54. The Director shall also, at the end of each

(1) See Note E.

(2) See Note E.

(3) See Forms Nos. 5 and 6.

(4) See Note K.

(5) See Note K.

(6) See Note P. and Forms Nos. 10 and 11.

School year, deliver to the Township Clerk, to be filed in his office, a report to the Board of School Inspectors of the township, showing: (1) Director to report to Township Clerk.

1. The whole number of children belonging to the District, between the ages of four and eighteen years, according to the census taken as aforesaid; Contents of report.

2. The number attending School during the year, under four, and also the number over eighteen years of age;

3. The whole number that have attended School during the year;

4. The length of time the School has been taught during the year by a qualified Teacher, the name of each Teacher, the length of time kept by each, and the wages paid to each;

5. The average length of time scholars between four and eighteen years of age have attended School during the year;

6. The amount of money received from the Township Treasurer, apportioned to the District by the Township Clerk;

7. The amount of money raised by the District, and the purposes for which it was raised;

8. The kinds of books used in the School;

9. Such other facts and statistics in regard to Schools, and the subject of education, as the Superintendent of Public Instruction shall direct.

DISTRICT BOARD.

Sec. 55. The Moderator, Director and Assessor shall constitute the District Board. District board.

Sec. 56. Said Board shall, between the last Monday of September and the second Monday of October, in each year, make out and deliver to the Supervisor of each township in which any part of the District is situated, a report in writing under their hands, of all taxes voted by the Board to report amount voted by district, etc.

(1) See Form No. 22, and Note M.

District during the preceding year, and of all taxes which said Board is authorized to impose, to be levied on the taxable property within the District.(1)

Purchase of books for poor children.

Sec. 57. The District Board may purchase, at the expense of the District, such School books as may be necessary for the use of children admitted by them to the District School free of charge, and they shall include the amount of such purchases, and the amount which would have been payable for fuel and Teachers' wages, by persons exempted from the payment thereof, together with any sums on the district rate bills, which could not be collected, in their report to the Supervisor or Supervisors, to be assessed as aforesaid.(2)

Exemption of Poor Persons from payment of Tuition, etc.

Sec. 58. Said Board shall exempt from the payment of Teachers' wages, and from providing fuel for the use of the District, all such persons residing therein as in their opinion ought to be exempted, and shall certify such exemptions to the Director; and the children of such persons shall be admitted to the District School free of charge during the time of such exemption.(3)

Board shall purchase or hire site for School House, etc.

Sec. 59. They shall purchase or lease a site for a School-house, as shall have been designated by the District, in the corporate name thereof, and shall build, hire or purchase such School-house out of the fund provided for that purpose, and make sale of any site or other property of the District, when lawfully directed by the qualified voters at an annual or special meeting: *Provided*, That the District Board shall not in any case build a stone or brick School-house upon any site, without having first obtained a title in fee to the same, or a lease for ninety-nine years; and also that they shall not in any case build a frame School-house upon any site for which they have not a title in fee, or a lease for fifty years, without securing the privilege of removing the said School-house when lawfully

(1) See Form No. 12.
(2) See Form No. 12.
(3) See Forms Nos. 7 and 12.

directed so to do by the qualified voters of the District, at any annual or special meeting.(1)

Sec. 60. The District Board shall apply and pay over all School moneys belonging to the District, in accordance with the provisions of law regulating the same, as may be directed by the District; but no School moneys apportioned to any District shall be appropriated to any other use than the payment of Teachers' wages, and no part thereof shall be paid to any Teacher who shall not have received a certificate as required in this chapter, before the commencement of his School.(2) Board to apply School Moneys.

Sec. 61. The Moderator and Director shall require of the Assessor, and the Assessor shall execute to the District, a bond in double the amount of money to come into his hands as such Assessor during the year, as near as the same can be ascertained, with two sufficient sureties, to be approved by the Moderator and Director, conditioned for the faithful application of all moneys that shall come into his hands by virtue of his office.(3) Bond to be required of Assessor.

Sec. 62. Such bond shall be lodged with the Moderator, and in case of any breach of the condition thereof, the Director shall cause a suit to be commenced thereon in the name of the District, and the money, when collected, shall be paid into the Township Treasury, for the use of the District, subject to the order of the proper District officers.(4) Where Bond to be lodged, and when sued, etc.

Sec. 63. Said Board shall present to the District, at each annual meeting, a report in writing, containing an accurate statement of all moneys of the District received by them, or any of them, during the preceding year, and of the disbursement made by them, with the items of such receipts and disbursements. Report of Receipts and Disbursements.

Sec. 64. Such report shall also contain a statement of all taxes assessed upon the taxable property of the District Statement of Taxes, etc.

(1) See Forms No. 20 and 21.
(2) See Note O. and Form No. 8.
(3) See Form No. 13.
(4) See Form No. 13.

during the preceding year, the purposes for which such taxes were assessed, and the amount assessed for each particular purpose, and said reports shall be recorded by the Director in a book to be provided and kept for that purpose.

Board to have custody of District Property.

Sec. 65. The said District Board shall have the care and custody of the School-house and other property of the District, except so far as the same shall be specially confided to the custody of the Director, including all books purchased for the use of pupils admitted to the School free of charge.[1]

To fill Vacancies.

Sec. 66. The Board shall have power to fill by appointment, any vacancy that shall occur in their own number, and it shall be their duty to fill such vacancy within ten days after its occurrence.[2]

Board may appoint Assessor in certain cases.

Sec. 67. If the Assessor shall fail to give bond as is required in this chapter, or from sickness or any other cause shall be unable to attend to the duty of collecting any District rate bill, the said Board shall appoint an Acting Assessor to collect the same, who shall possess all the powers of the District Assessor for that purpose, and shall, before proceeding to the collection thereof, give bond to the District in double the amount of money to be collected, in the same manner, and with the same effect as the District Assessor is required to give such bond. Every School District office shall become vacant upon the incumbent ceasing to be a resident of the District for which he shall have been elected, or upon the happening of either of the events specified in section three of chapter fifteen of the Revised Statutes of 1846.[3]

When District Offices to become vacant.

TOWNSHIP BOARD OF SCHOOL INSPECTORS.

Board of School Inspectors.

Sec. 68. The Inspectors elected at the annual township meetings, together with the Township Clerk, shall constitute the Township Board of School Inspectors; and the

(1) See Note E. (2) See Form No. 15, and Note D.
(3) See Note D.

Inspector elected at the annual township meeting, having the shortest time to serve, shall be Chairman of said Board, and the said Township Clerk shall be the Clerk thereof.(1)

Chairman of Board to be Treasurer and give bond.

Sec 69. The Chairman of said Board shall be the Treasurer thereof, and shall give bond to the township in double the amount of library moneys to come into his hands during his term of office, as near as the same can be ascertained, with two sufficient sureties, to be approved by the Township Clerk, conditioned for the faithful appropriation of all moneys that may come into his hands by virtue of his office.(2)

In case of breach, Bond to be sued.

Sec. 70. Said bond shall be filed with the Township Clerk, and in case of the non-fulfillment thereof, said Clerk shall cause a suit to be commenced thereon, and the moneys collected in such suit shall be paid into the Township Treasury for the benefit of the Township Library.(3)

Formation of Districts.

Sec. 71. The Inspectors shall divide the township into such number of School Districts as may from time to time be necessary, which Districts they shall number, and they may regulate and alter the boundaries of the same as circumstances shall render proper; but no District shall contain more than nine sections of land, and each District shall be composed of contiguous territory, and be in as compact a form as may be; but no land shall be taxed for building a School-house, unless some portion of every legal subdivision of said land shall be within two and one-half miles of said School-house site.(4)

2 Douglass, Mich. 121.

Persons residing out of District, may be attached to District in certain cases.

Sec. 72. They may attach to a School District any person residing in the township, and not in any organized District, at his request; and for all district purposes, except raising a tax for building a School-house, such person shall be considered as residing in such District; but when set off to a new District, no sum shall be raised for such person as his proportion to the District property.(5)

---

(1) See Form No. 14. (2) See Form No. 14. (3) See Form No. 14.
(4) See Note F. (5) See Note M.

Inspectors to receive and appropriate Library Money.

Sec. 73. The Inspectors shall apply for and receive from the Township Treasurer all moneys appropriated for the Township Library of their township, and shall purchase the books, and procure the necessary appendages for the Township Library, and make such rules for the regulation thereof, and the preservation of the books contained in it, as they may deem proper.(1)

To appoint one of their number to visit Schools.

Sec. 74. They shall appoint one of their number to visit each School in the township having a qualified Teacher, at least once in each School term in which a School is taught, who shall inquire into the condition of such Schools, examine the scholars, and give such advice to both Teachers and pupils as he may think beneficial.(2)

When part of District set off, value of Property to be apportioned.

Sec. 75. When a new District is formed, in whole or in part, from one or more Districts possessed of a School-house, or entitled to other property, the Inspectors, at the time of forming such new District, shall ascertain and determine the amount justly due to such new District from any District out of which it may have been, in whole or in part formed, as the proportion of such new District, of the value of the School-house and other property belonging to the former District at the time of such division.(3)

How proportion to be ascertained.

Sec. 76. Such proportion shall be ascertained and determined according to the value of the taxable property of the respective parts of such former District at the time of the division, by the best evidence in the power of the Inspectors; and such amount of any debt due from the former District, which would have been a charge upon the new, had it remained in the former District, shall be deducted from such proportion: *Provided*, That no real estate thus set off, and which shall not have been taxed for the purchase or building of such School-house, shall be entitled to any portion thereof, nor be taken into account in such division of District property.

Sec. 77. The amount of such proportion, when so ascer-

(1) See Note K. (2) See Note G. (3) See Note F.

tained and determined, shall be certified by the Township Clerk to the Supervisor of the Township, whose duty it shall be to assess the same upon the taxable property of the District retaining the School-house or other property of the former District, in the same manner as if the same had been authorized by a vote of such District, and the money so assessed shall be placed to the credit of the taxable property taken from the former District, and shall be in reduction of any tax imposed in the new District on said taxable property for School District purposes. Proportion to be certified to Supervisor; How disposed of.

Sec. 78. When collected, such amount shall be paid over to the Assessor of the new District, to be applied to the use therefore, in the same manner, under the direction of its proper officers, as if such sum had been voted and raised by said District for building a School-house, or other District purposes. When apportionment collected to be paid over.

Sec. 79. Between the first and fifteenth days of October in each year, the Inspectors shall make out and deliver to the Township Clerk duplicate reports to the County Clerk, setting forth the whole number of Districts in their townships, the amount of money raised and received for the Township Library, together with the several particulars set forth in the reports of the School Directors for the preceding year.(1) Report from Inspectors to Township Clerk.

Sec. 80. The Board of Inspectors, before making their annual report to the County Clerk, shall examine the record of Teachers to whom certificates have been given by them, and if in any School District a School shall not have been taught for three months during the preceding school year by a qualified Teacher, no part of the public money shall be distributed to such District, although the report from such District shall set forth that a School has been so taught; and it shall be the duty of the Board to certify the facts in relation to any such District in their reports to the County Clerk.(2) Record of Teacher to be examined before Report made, etc.

(1) See Form No. 23. (2) See Notes C. and M.

Formation of Districts in two or more Townships.

Sec. 81. Whenever it shall be necessary or convenient to form a District from two or more adjoining townships, the Inspectors, or a majority of them, of each of such adjoining townships, may form such District, and direct which Township Clerk shall make and deliver the notice of the formation of the same to a taxable inhabitant thereof, and may regulate and alter such District as circumstances may render necessary. The Director of such District shall make his annual report to the Clerk of the Township in which the School-house is situated.(1)

To whom Report to be made.

Director to Report to each Township.

Sec. 82. The Director of every District formed as provided in the preceding section, shall also report to the clerk of each township in which the District is in part situated, the number of children between the ages of four and eighteen years in that part of the District lying in such township, and books shall be drawn from the Library of each township for the use of such District; but the District shall have access to but one such library at the same time, and the said Inspectors shall establish the order in which books shall be drawn from each Township Library.(2)

Districts, formed from two or more Townships; How regulated.

Sec. 83. Such School Districts already formed from two or more townships, shall continue to be governed by the regulations already established according to law, in relation to the annual reports, and the drawing of books from the Township Libraries, subject to such changes as may be made in respect thereto by the said Inspectors, in conformity with the preceding provisions.(3)

Amount of Taxes; How certified and apportioned.

Sec. 84. The full amount of all taxes to be levied upon the taxable property in such District, shall be certified by the District Board to the Supervisor of each of such townships, and each of said Supervisors shall certify to each other Supervisor within whose township such District is in part situated, the amount of taxable property in that part of the District lying in his township; and such Su-

(1) See Notes H., M. and O. (2) See Note H. (3) See Note H.

pervisors shall respectively ascertain the proportion of such taxes, to be placed on their respective assessment rolls, according to the amount of taxable property in each part of such District.(1)

Sec. 85. It shall be the duty of the Inspectors to examine annually all persons offering themselves as candidates for Teachers of Primary Schools in their township, in regard to moral character, learning and ability to teach a School; and they shall deliver to each person so examined and found qualified, a certificate signed by them, in such form as shall be prescribed by the Superintendent of Public Instruction; which certificate shall be in force for two years from the date thereof, unless annulled within that time, and no person shall be deemed a qualified Teacher within the meaning of this chapter, who has not such a certificate in force.(2) Examination of Teachers.

Sec. 86. For the purpose of making such examination, the Board of School Inspectors shall meet on the second Saturday of April and first Saturday of November in each year, at the office of the Township Clerk, or at such other place as they shall designate, of which meetings the Township Clerk shall give at least ten days' notice in writing, by posting up the same in three public places in the township.(3) Meetings for examining Teachers, and Notice thereof.

Sec. 87. The Inspectors may make such examination at such other times as they may designate for that purpose, but shall make no charge against the township for examining Teachers at any other times than those specified in the preceding section.(4) Examination at other times.

Sec. 88. The examination of Teachers shall be public, and no certificate shall be given by the Inspectors, unless they are satisfied that the applicant possesses a good moral character, and a thorough and accurate knowledge of the several branches of study usually taught in Primary Examination to be Public; Qualifications of Teachers.

(1) See Note H.

(2) See Note O. and Forms Nos. 8 and 17.

(3) See Notes F. and O. and Forms Nos. 17, 18.

(4) See Note O., and Form No. 17.

Schools, and is competent in other respects to teach and govern a School.[1]

Where Teacher to be examined for District situated in two or more Townships.

Sec. 89. When a District is situated in two or more townships, the Teacher for such District shall be examined by the Inspectors of the township to which the Director is required to make his annual report.[2]

Inspectors may re-examine Teacher, and annul certificate.

Sec. 90. Whenever the Inspectors shall deem it necessary to re-examine any Teacher of a Primary School in their township, they shall give five days' notice to such Teacher of the time and place of such re-examination, and of their intention to annul his certficate if they find him deficient in the requisite qualifications; and at the time and place specified in the notice, if such Teacher shall not appear and submit to such re-examination, or if he shall be found deficient as aforesaid, the Inspectors shall annul the said certificate.[3]

Number of Meetings of Board.

Sec. 91. The whole number of meetings of said Board of Inspectors during any one year, at the expense of the township, shall not exceed six; and whenever said Board shall meet for the purpose of forming or altering School Districts, they shall cause the like notice to be given as is required for meetings to examine Teachers.[4]

Notice in certain cases.

Districts may be formed from two or more Districts, and pupils classified.

Sec. 92. Whenever the Board of Inspectors of any township shall deem that the interests of any of the Schools will be best promoted by so doing, they may form a single District out of any two or more Districts therein, and classify the pupils in such District into two or more classes, according to their proficiency and advancement in learning, and require that such pupils be taught in distinct[5] Schools or departments as classified by them, and such District may have the same number of School-houses, if necessary, and raise the same amount of taxes, which the original Districts forming the same could raise if not united.[6]

---

(1) See Note O., and Form No. 17.

(2) See Note O., and Form No. 17.

(3) See Note O., and Form No. 17.

(4) See Note F

(5) The word "distinct" was incorrectly printed "district" in the Compiled Laws.

(6) See Note I.

1. In Districts containing more than one hundred scholars between the ages of four and eighteen years, the District Board may be enlarged by adding thereto four Trustees: *Provided*, The District determine to do so, by a two-third vote, at any annual meeting; When additional Trustees may be appointed.

2. The additional Trustees first elected shall serve severally, one, two, three and four years, to be determined by lot, immediately on filing their certificate of acceptance with the Director. After the first election, each Trustee elected shall serve four years; Term of service.

3. All vacancies that may occur in the office of Trustee shall be filled according to existing provisions for filling vacancies in the District Board; How vacancies filled.

4. Rate bills shall be collected, and all moneys shall be drawn and applied according to existing provisions of law, but in the employment of Teachers the Director shall have the approval of the Moderator or Assessor, according to provisions of law heretofore existing, and of at least two of the Trustees; and the authority to classify pupils in such cases shall be transferred from the School Inspectors to the enlarged District Board; Employment of Teachers, etc.

5. The boundaries of Districts that may avail themselves of this Act, shall not be enlarged nor diminished without the written approval of a majority of the enlarged District Board.(1) Boundaries; How changed.

Sec. 93. The said Inspectors may also, on the application of the District Board of any District, classify the pupils therein in the manner prescribed in the preceding section, and require that such pupils be taught in distinct departments, whenever they shall judge that the interests of the School will be best promoted thereby; and in case of any such classification as is provided for in this or the preceding section, as many teachers may be employed for each District as there are departments in which Teachers are required.(2) On application of District Board, Inspectors may classify Pupils in any District, etc.

---

(1) See Sec. 141, and Note O. (2) See Sec. 141.

Inspectors to account to Township Board.

Sec. 94. It shall be the duty of the Board of Inspectors to render to the Township Board, on the Tuesday next preceding the annual township meeting, a full and true account of all moneys received and disbursed by them as such Inspectors during the year, which account shall be settled by said Township Board, and such disbursements allowed, if the proper vouchers are presented.

When Inspectors to supply vacancy in District Board; Power to appoint Librarian.

Sec. 95. Whenever any District Board shall fail to supply any vacancy that shall occur in their own number, within ten days after the time of its occurrence, the Board of Inspectors shall fill the same by appointment.(1)

CERTAIN DUTIES OF TOWNSHIP CLERK.

Clerk of Board of Inspectors.

Sec. 96. The Township Clerk shall be the Clerk of the Board of School Inspectors by virtue of his office, and shall attend all meetings of said Board, and under their direction prepare all their reports and record the same, and shall record all their proceedings, including the names of Teachers to whom certificates shall have been given, with the date of each certificate, and the name of each Teacher whose certificate shall have been annulled, with the date of such annulment.

Clerk to apportion School Moneys.

Sec. 97. On receiving notice from the County Treasurer of the amount of School moneys apportioned to his township, he shall apportion the same amongst the several Districts therein entitled to the same, in proportion to the number of children in each between the ages of four and eighteen years, as the same shall be shown by the annual report of the Director of each District for the School year last closed.

To apportion School Moneys raised by Township, and Record apportionment.

Sec. 98. Said Clerk shall also apportion, in like manner, on receiving notice of the amount from the Township Treasurer, all moneys raised by township tax, or received from other sources for the support of Schools, and in all cases make out and deliver to the Township Treasurer a

(1) See Note D, and Form No. 16.

written statement of the number of children in each District drawing money, and the amount apportioned to each District, and record the apportionment in his office.

Sec. 99. He shall receive and keep all reports to the Inspectors from the Directors of the several School Districts in his township, and all the books and papers belonging to the Inspectors, and file such papers in his office. To keep books and papers.

Sec. 100. He shall receive all such communications as may be transmitted to him by the Superintendent of Public Instruction, and dispose of the same in the manner directed therein. To receive and dispose of communications from Superintendent.

Sec. 101. He shall transmit to the County Clerk all such reports as may be delivered to him for that purpose by the Inspectors, within the time limited in this chapter. To transmit Inspectors' Report.

Sec. 102. Each Township Clerk shall cause a map to be made of his township, showing by distinct lines thereon the boundaries of each School District, and parts of School Districts therein, and shall regularly number the same thereon as established by the Inspectors. To make Map of Districts.

Sec. 103. One copy of such map shall be filed by the said Clerk in his office, and one other copy he shall file with the Supervisor of the township; and within one month after any division or alteration of a District, or the organization of a new one in his township, the said Clerk shall file a new map and copy thereof as aforesaid, showing the same. To file copy of Map, and deliver copy to Supervisor.

Sec. 104. The Clerk shall also certify to the Supervisor the amount to be assessed upon the taxable property of any School District retaining the District School-house or other property, on the division of the District, as the same shall have been determined by the Inspectors, and he shall also certify the same to the Director of such District, and to the Director of the District entitled thereto. To certify amount to be collected on division of a District.

Sec. 105. Said Clerk shall also be the Township Librarian, and as such, shall have the custody of the Township Library; and he shall do and execute all such other acts Clerk to be Librarian.

and things pertaining to his office, as may be required of him by the Inspectors.

OF TAXES FOR SCHOOL PURPOSES.

Assessment and collection of Taxes for School purposes.

Sec. 106. It shall be the duty of the Supervisor of the township to assess the taxes voted by every School District in his township, and also all other taxes provided for in this chapter, chargeable against such District or township, upon the taxable property of the District or township respectively, and to place the same on the township assessment roll in the column for School taxes, and the same shall be collected and returned by the Township Treasurer, in the same manner and for the same compensation as township taxes.(1)

Assessment of Mill Tax: how applied.

Sec. 107. The Supervisor shall also assess upon the taxable property of his township one mill upon each dollar of the valuation thereof, in each year; and twenty-five dollars of the same shall be applied for the purchase of the books for the Township Library, and the remainder thereof shall be apportioned to the several Districts in the township, for the support of Schools therein; and the same shall be collected and returned in the same manner as provided in section one hundred and six of chapter fifty-eight of the Revised Statutes of eighteen hundred and forty-six; and all School taxes returned for non-payment shall be collected in the same manner as State and county taxes.(2)

Statement to be delivered to Treasurer with Warrant, etc.

See Sec. 144.

Sec. 108. The Supervisor, on delivery of the warrant for the collection of taxes to the Township Treasurer, shall also deliver to said Treasurer a written statement of the amount of School and Library taxes, the amount raised for District purposes on the taxable property of each District in the township, the amount belonging to any new District on the division of the former District, and the names of all persons having judgments assessed under the provisions of this chapter upon the taxable property of any District,

(1) See Note J, and Form No. 12.

(2) See Notes J. and K.

with the amount payable to [each] such person on account thereof.(1)

Sec. 109. The Township Treasurer shall retain in his hands, out of the moneys collected by him, after deducting the amount of the tax for township expenses, the full amount of the School tax on the assessment roll, and hold the same subject to the warrant of the proper District officers, to the order of the School Inspectors, or of the persons entitled thereto.(2) School Tax to be retained by Treasurer, subject to Warrant, etc.

Sec. 110. Said Treasurer shall, from time to time, apply to the County Treasurer for all School and Library moneys belonging to his township, or the Districts thereof; and on receipt of the moneys to be apportioned to the Districts, he shall notify the Township Clerk of the amount to be apportioned. Township Treasurer to apply to County Treasurer for Moneys, etc.

CERTAIN DUTIES OF THE COUNTY CLERK.

Sec. 111. It shall be the duty of each County Clerk to receive all such communications as may be directed to him by the Superintendent of Public Instruction, and dispose of the same in the manner directed by said Superintendent. County Clerk to receive and dispose of communications from Superintendent.

Sec. 112. The Clerk of each county shall, immediately after receiving the annual reports of the several Boards of School Inspectors, transmit to the Superintendent of Public Instruction one of the duplicate reports of each of the said several Boards, and the other he shall file in his office; and on receiving notice from the Superintendent of the amount of moneys apportioned to the several townships in his county, he shall file the same in his office, and forthwith deliver a copy thereof to the County Treasurer. County Clerk to Report to Superintendent. Notice of School Moneys apportioned.

Sec. 113. [This section has been repealed.]

LIBRARIES.

Sec. 114. A Township Library shall be maintained in each organized township in this State, which shall be the property of the township, and the parents and guardians Library to be maintained in each Township.

(1) See Form No. 12.

(2) See Form No. 11.

of all children therein, between the ages of four and eighteen years, shall be permitted to use books from such Library without charge, being responsible to the township for the safe return thereof, and for any injury done thereto, according to such rules and regulations as are or may be established by the Board of School Inspectors of the township.(1)

Books to be drawn once in three months, and returned by Directors.

Sec. 115. The books in such Library shall, once in three months, be distributed by the Township Librarian among the several School Districts of the township, in proportion to the number of children in each between the ages aforesaid, as the same shall appear by the last report of the Director thereof, and said books shall be drawn and returned by the several Directors for their respective Districts.(2)

Proceeds of fines, etc., to be apportioned by County Treasurer among Townships for purchase of books.

Sec. 116. The clear proceeds of all fines for any breach of the penal laws of this State, and for penalties, or upon any recognizances in criminal proceedings, and all equivalents for exemption from military duty, when collected in any county, and paid into the County Treasury, together with all moneys heretofore collected and paid into said Treasury, on account of such fines or equivalents, and not already apportioned, shall be apportioned by the County Treasurer, between the first and tenth days of April in each year, among the several townships in the county, according to the number of children therein, between the ages of four and eighteen years, as shown by the last annual statement of the County Clerk on file in his office; which money shall be applied to the purchase of books for the Township Library, and for no other purpose.(3)

Director to distribute books of District Library, and collect damages for injury done to any books belonging to Township Library.

Sec. 117. In each District in which a District Library has been established, the Director shall, as the Librarian of the District, distribute the books therein to the children of his District of proper age, and shall collect from the parents or guardians of such children, all such damages as they may respectively become liable to pay on account of

(1) See Note K. (2) See Section 146. (3) See Note K.

any injury done to, or loss of, or neglect to return any of such books, or any books belonging to the Township Library, pursuant to such rules and regulations as shall be prescribed by the Board of School Inspectors.([1])

Sec. 118. If such damages shall have occurred by reason of any injury to, or loss of, or neglect to return any books belonging to the Township Library, they shall be collected in the name of the township, and paid into the Township Treasury for the benefit of such Township Library, and if the same shall have accrued by reason of any injury to, or loss of, or neglect to return any books belonging to the District Library, the same shall be collected in the name of the District, for the benefit of the District Library.([2]) Damages to books; how collected and applied.

DISTRIBUTION OF THE INCOME OF THE SCHOOL FUND.

Sec. 119. The interest of the Primary School Fund shall be distributed on the first Monday of May, or as soon thereafter as is practicable, in each year, for the support of Primary Schools in the several townships in this State, from which reports have been received by the Superintendent of Public Instruction, in accordance with the provisions of this chapter, for the School year last closed, in proportion to the number of children in such townships, between the ages of four and eighteen years; and the same shall be payable on the warrant of the Auditor General to the Treasurers of the several counties.([3]) Interest of School Fund to be distributed. Payable to County Treasurers on Warrant of Auditor General.

Sec. 120. The several County Treasurers shall apply for and receive such moneys as shall have been apportioned to their respective counties, when the same shall become due; and each of said Treasurers shall immediately give notice to the Treasurer and Clerk of each township in his county, of the amount of School moneys apportioned to his township, and shall hold the same subject to the order of the Township Treasurer. County Treasurer to receive Moneys and notify Clerk of each Township.

Sec. 121. [This section has been repealed.]

(1) See Note L. (2) See Note K and L. (3) See Note M.

OF SUITS AND JUDGMENTS AGAINST SCHOOL DISTRICTS.

Justices to have jurisdiction in certain cases.

Sec. 122. Justices of the Peace shall have jurisdiction in all cases of assumpsit, debt, covenant, and trespass on the case against School Districts, when the amount claimed, or matter in controversy shall not exceed one hundred dollars, and the parties shall have the same right of appeal as in other cases.

Suit against District; how commenced.

Sec. 123. When any suit shall be brought against a School District, it shall be commenced by summons, a copy of which shall be left with the Assessor of the District, at least eight days before the return day thereof.

No execution to issue against District.

Sec. 124. No execution shall issue on any judgment against a School District, nor shall any suit be brought thereon, but the same shall be collected in the manner prescribed in this chapter.

Judgments against District to be certified to Supervisor by Assessor

Sec. 125. Whenever any final judgment shall be obtained against a School District, if the same shall not be removed to any other Court, the Assessor of the District shall certify to the Supervisor of the Township, and to the Director of the District, the date and amount of such judgment, with the name of the person in whose favor the same was rendered, and if the judgment shall be removed to another Court, the Assessor shall certify the same as aforesaid, immediately after the final determination thereof against the District.

If Assessor fails to certify, party may get certificate from Justice or Clerk.

Sec. 126. If the Assessor shall fail to certify the judgment as required in the preceding section, it shall be lawful for the party obtaining the same, his executors, administrators or assigns, to file with the Supervisor the certificate of the Justice or Clerk of the Court rendering the judgment, showing the facts which should have been certified by the Assessor.

If District in two or more Townships, Certificate to be made to Supervisor of each.

Sec. 127. If the District against whom any such judgment shall be rendered, is situated in part in two or more townships, a certificate thereof shall be delivered as aforesaid to the Supervisor of each township in which such District is in part situated.

Sec. 128. The Supervisor or Supervisors receiving either of the certificates of a judgment as aforesaid, shall proceed to assess the amount thereof, with interest from the date of the judgment to the time when the warrant for the collection thereof will expire, upon the taxable property of the District, placing the same on the next township assessment roll, in the column for School taxes, and the same proceedings shall be had, and the same shall be collected and returned in the same manner as other District taxes. Supervisors to assess amount of judgment and interest; How collected and returned.

PENALTIES AND LIABILITIES.

Sec. 129. Every taxable inhabitant receiving the notice mentioned in the first and second sections of this chapter, who shall neglect or refuse duly to serve and return such notice, and every Chairman of the first District meeting in any District, who shall willfully neglect or refuse to perform the duties enjoined on him in this chapter, shall respectively forfeit the sum of five dollars.(1) Penalty for neglecting to serve Notice of First Meeting, etc.

Sec. 130. Every person duly elected to the office of Moderator, Director or Assessor of a School District, who shall neglect or refuse, without sufficient cause, to accept such office and serve therein, or who, having entered upon the duties of his office, shall neglect or refuse to perform any duty required of him by virtue of his office, shall forfeit the sum of ten dollars.(2) Penalty on District Officers for neglect, etc.

Sec. 131. Every person duly elected or appointed a School Inspector, who shall neglect or refuse, without sufficient cause, to qualify and serve as such, or who, having entered upon the duties of his office, shall neglect or refuse to perform any duty required of him by virtue of his office, shall forfeit the sum of ten dollars.(3) Penalty on Inspectors for not qualifying, or neglecting duty.

Sec. 132. If any Board of School Inspectors shall neg-

(1) See Forms No. 1 and 2. (2) See Forms Nos. 4, 5 and 23, and Note A. (3) See Form No. 23, and Notes K. and O.

25

Board of School Inspectors liable for neglect. lect or refuse to make and deliver to the Township Clerk their annual report to the County Clerk, as required in this chapter, within the time limited therefor, they shall be liable to pay the full amount of money lost by their failure, with interest thereon, to be rcovered by the Township Treasurer in the name of the township, in an action of debt, or on the case.(1) [See section 79.]

Township Clerk neglecting to transmit Reports liable for amount lost. Sec. 133. If any Township Clerk shall neglect or refuse to transmit the report mentioned in the preceding section to the County Clerk, as required in this chapter, he shall be liable to pay the full amount lost by such neglect or refusal, with interest thereon, to be recovered in the manner specified in the preceding section.(2)

County Clerk neglecting to make Annual Report liable for amount lost. Sec. 134. Every County Clerk who shall neglect or refuse to transmit the report required in this chapter, to be made by him to the Superintendent of Public Instruction, within the time therefor limited, shall be liable to pay to each township the full amount which such township, or any School District therein, shall lose by such neglect or refusal, with interest thereon, to be recovered in the manner specified in the last two preceding sections.

Money collected on account of neglect, how disposed of. Sec. 135. All the moneys collected or received by any Township Treasurer under the provisions of either of the three last preceding sections, shall be apportioned and distributed to the School Districts entitled thereto, in the same manner, and in the same proportion, that the moneys lost by any neglect or refusal therein mentioned would, according to the provisions of this chapter, have been apportioned and distributed.

Removal of Officers for illegal use of Money. Sec. 136. The Township Board of each township shall have power, and is hereby required, to remove from office, upon satisfactory proof, after at least five days' notice to the party implicated, any District officer or School Inspector who shall have illegally used or disposed of any of the public moneys entrusted to his charge.

(1) See Form No. 23.

(2) See Form No. 23.

MISCELLANEOUS PROVISIONS RELATING TO PRIMARY SCHOOLS.

Persons paying Taxes in District may send to School, and be rated therein.

Sec. 137. Any person paying taxes in a School District in which he does not reside, may send scholars to any District School therein, and such person shall, for that purpose, have and enjoy all the rights and privileges of a resident of such District, except the right of voting therein, and shall be rated therein for Teachers' wages and fuel, and in the census of such District, and the apportionment of moneys from the School fund, scholars so sent, and generally attending such School, shall be considered as belonging to such District: *Provided*, That a majority of the qualified voters attending at any regular meeting in the District in which such person resides, shall have determined that no School shall be taught in said District for the year: *Or provided, further*, That such persons shall not reside in any organized School District.(1)

Proviso.

When District shall be divided, after Tax assessed and not collected; how Tax collected and apportioned.

Sec. 138. Whenever any portion of a School District shall be set off and annexed to any other District, or organized into a new one, after a tax for District purposes other than the payment of any debts of the District shall have been levied upon the taxable próperty thereof, but not collected, such tax shall be collected in the same manner as if no part of such District had been set off, and the said former District, and the District to which the portion so set off may be annexed, or the new District organized from such portion, shall each be entitled to such proportion of said tax as the amount of taxable property in each part thereof bears to the whole amount of taxable property on which such tax is levied.(2)

District in two or more Townships, Income of School Fund; how apportioned, etc

Sec. 139. For the purpose of apportioning the income of the Primary School Fund among the several townships, a District situated in part in two or more townships shall be considered as belonging to the township to which the annual report of the Director is required to be made; [but

(1) See Note N.

(2) See Note F.

money raised in any one of such townships for the support of Schools therein, shall be apportioned to the Districts and parts of Districts therein, according to the number of children of the proper age in each.](1)

What Tax voters may raise for support of Schools.

Sec. 140. The qualified voters of any School District may, by vote at their Annual District Meeting, raise by tax upon the taxable property of the District a sum not exceeding one dollar for every scholar in the District between the ages of four and eighteen years, for the support of Common Schools in the District, and such tax shall be reported to the Supervisor of the proper township, and shall be levied, collected and returned in the same manner as township taxes are levied, collected and returned.(2)

Price of Tuition in School Districts may be graduated by Board.

Sec. 141. The District Board in any School District in which the scholars have been or may be classified as provided in section number ninety-two or ninety-three of chapter number fifty-eight of the Revised Statutes, and the act or acts amendatory thereto, shall have power to graduate the price of tuition according to the studies pursued by the scholars respectively, in such manner as the said Board shall deem just.(3)

Secs. 92 and 93 above.

Rate bills; how collected in such case.

Sec. 142. The rate bills made out in accordance with the graduation provided for in the preceding section, shall have the same force, and be collected in the same manner, as the rate bills in other cases.

Supervisor liable for neglect to assess certain Taxes.

Sec. 143. If any Supervisor shall neglect or refuse to assess the taxes provided for in section one hundred and seven of chapter fifty-eight of the Revised Statutes, he shall be liable to pay to any School District the full amount lost to such District by such neglect or refusal, with the interest thereon, to be recovered by the Assessor in the name of the School District, in an action of debt, or on the case.(4)

Sec. 107 above.

(1) See Notes H., M. and O. The latter clause of section 139, embraced in brackets, is practically repealed, for reasons stated in Note O, which see.

(2) See Note J.

(3) Sections 141 and 142 were passed Feb. 18, 1850. [Compiled Laws, p. 758.] These sections were not embraced in the School Law as published in 1852.

(4) Sections 143 to 146, inclusive, were passed April 2, 1850. [Compiled Laws, p. 758.]

Sec. 144. The Supervisor of each township, on the delivery of the warrant for the collection of taxes to the township Treasurer, shall also deliver to said Treasurer, a written statement, certified by him, of the amount of the taxes levied under section one hundred and seven of said chapter, upon any property lying within the bounds of a fractional School District, a part of which is situate within his township, and the returns of which are made to the clerk of some other township; and the said Township Treasurer shall pay to the Township Treasurer of such other township the amount of the taxes so levied and certified to him for the use of such fractional School District.

Supervisor to give statement to Township Treasurer of certain Taxes.

Sec. 108 above.

Sec. 145. Each Treasurer of a township, to the clerk of which the returns of any fractional School District shall be made, shall apply to the Treasurer of any other township in which any part of such fractional School District may be situate, for any money to which such District may be entitled; and when so received it shall be certified to the Township Clerk, and apportioned in the same manner as other taxes for School purposes.

Town Treasurer's duties.

Taxes in fractional Districts.

Sec. 146. The Board of School Inspectors shall have power to suspend the operation of section one hundred and fifteen of said chapter, whenever they shall be of opinion that the convenience or the interests of the people of their township will be promoted thereby, and to restore the same, as in their judgment they shall think best.

School Inspectors may suspend the operation of Section 115.

Sec. 147. The words "qualified voters," as used in chapter fifty-eight of the Revised Statutes of eighteen hundred forty-six, entitled, "Of Primary Schools," except in the fifth section thereof, shall be taken and construed to mean and include all taxable persons residing in the District of the age of twenty-one years, and who have resided therein for the period of three months next preceding the time of voting.(1)

Who are qualified voters in School Districts.

Sec. 148. In all cases where the Board of School Inspec-

(1) Sections 147, 148 and 149, were passed Feb. 8, 1855. [Compiled Laws, p. 759.]

When School Inspectors shall appoint District Officers.

tors of any township shall form a School District therein, and where no election for School District officers shall be held, and where any School District shall neglect or refuse to elect, at the proper time, the necessary School District officers, it shall be the duty of the Township Board of School Inspectors of the township in which such District is situated to appoint the officers of such District from among the male persons residing in such District, of the age of twenty-one years, who are tax payers therein; which officers thus appointed shall severally file with the Director a written acceptance of the offices to which they shall have been appointed, which shall be recorded by the Director.(1)

Acceptance; where filed.

When District deemed to be organized.

Sec. 149. Every such School District shall be deemed duly organized, when any two of the officers thus appointed shall have filed their acceptance as aforesaid; and such School District and its officers shall be entitled to all the rights, privileges and immunities, and be subject to all the duties and liabilities conferred upon School Districts by law.(2)

Voters may designate site for School-house by two-thirds vote.

Sec. 150. The qualified voters in any School District, having more than three hundred children between the ages of four and eighteen years residing in such District, shall have power, when lawfully assembled, to designate by a vote of two-thirds of those present, any number of sites for School-houses, including a site for a Union School-house, and to change the same by a similar vote, at any regular meeting: *Provided*, That the whole number of sites or School-houses in any one District shall not exceed five: *Provided, further*, That in case two-thirds cannot agree upon a site for said School-house, that a majority of the voters of said District shall have power to instruct the District Board to locate said site.(3)

When District Board may designate site.

---

(1) See Form No. 4. (2) See Note A.

(3) Sections 150 to 168, inclusive, were passed Feb. 7, 1855. [Compiled Laws, p. 762.] See Note B.

Sec. 151. Whenever a site for a School-house shall be designated, determined or established, in any manner provided by law, in any School District, and such District shall be unable to agree with the owner of such site upon the compensation to be paid therefor, or in case such District shall, for any cause, be unable to purchase or procure a title to such site, the District Board of such District may authorize any one or more of its members to apply to the Circuit Judge, if there be one in the county, or to a Circuit Court Commissioner of the county, or to any Justice of the Peace of the city or township in which such School District shall be situated, for a jury to ascertain and determine the just compensation to be made for the real estate required by such School District for such site, and the necessity for using the same, which application shall be in writing, and shall describe the real estate required by such District as accurately as is required in a conveyance of real estate.[1]

Compensation for site; how ascertained.

Application for Jury.

Sec. 152. It shall be the duty of such Circuit Judge, Circuit Court Commissioner, or Justice of the Peace, upon such application being made to him, to issue a summons or venire, directed to the Sheriff or any constable of the county, commanding him to summon eighteen freeholders residing in the vicinity of such site, who are in nowise of kin to the owner of such real estate, and not interested therein, to appear before such Judge, Commissioner or Justice, at the time and place therein named, not less than twenty, nor more than thirty days from the time of issuing such summons or venire, as a jury to ascertain and determine the just compensation to be made for the real estate required by such School District for such site, and the necessity for using the same, and to notify the owner or occupant of such real estate, if he can be found in the county, of the time when, and the place where such jury is sum-

Jury to be summoned.

Owner to be notified.

(1) See Note B.

moned to appear, and the object for which said jury is summoned; which notice shall be served at least ten days before the time specified in such summons or venire for the jury to appear, as hereinbefore mentioned.

Notice in cases where owner is unknown.

Sec. 153. Thirty days' previous notice of the time when, and the place where such jury will assemble, shall be given by the District Board of such District, where the owner or owners of such real estate shall be unknown, non-residents of the county, minors, insane, *non compos mentis*, or inmates of any prison, by publishing the same in a newspaper published in the county where such real estate is situated; or if there be no newspaper published in such county, then in some newspaper published in the nearest county where a newspaper is published, once in each week for four successive weeks, which notice shall be signed by the District Board, or by the Director or Assessor of such District, and shall describe the real estate required for such site, and state the time when, and place where such jury will assemble, and the object for which they will assemble, or such notice may be served on such owner personally, or by leaving a copy thereof at his last place of residence.

Return of venire, and the proceedings thereon.

Sec. 154. It shall be the duty of such Judge, Commissioner or Justice, and of the persons summoned as jurors, as hereinbefore provided, and of the Sheriff or Constable summoning them, to attend at the time and place specified in such summons or venire; and the officer who summoned the jury shall return such summons or venire to the officer who issued the same, with the names of the persons summoned by him as jurors, and shall certify the manner of notifying the owner (or owners) of such real estate, if he was found, and if he could not be found in said county, he shall certify that fact; either party may challenge any of the said jurors for the same causes as in civil actions. If more than twelve of said jurors in attendance shall be found qualified to serve as jurors, the officer in attendance, and who issued the summons or venire for such jury, shall strike from the list of jurors a number sufficient to reduce the number of jurors in attendance to twelve; and in case less than twelve of the number so summoned as jurors shall attend, the Sheriff or Constable shall summon a sufficient number of freeholders to make up the number of twelve; and the officer issuing the summons or venire for such jury, may issue an attachment for any person summoned as a juror who shall fail to attend, and may enforce obedience to such summons, venire or attachment, as Courts of Record or Justice's Courts are authorized to do in civil cases.

Attachment may issue to enforce obedience to process.

Sec. 155. The twelve persons selected as the jury shall be duly sworn by the Judge, Commissioner or Justice in attendance, faithfully and impartially to inquire, ascertain and determine, the just compensation to be made for the real estate required by such School District for such site, and the necessity for using the same in the manner proposed by such School District, and the persons thus sworn shall constitute the jury in such case. Subpœnas for witnesses may be issued, and their attendance compelled by such Circuit Judge, Commissioner or Justice, in the same manner as may be done by the Circuit Court or by a Justice's Court in civil cases. The jury may visit and examine the premises, and from such examination and such other evidence as may be presented before them, shall ascertain and determine the necessity for using such real estate in the manner and for the purpose proposed by such School District, and the just compensation to be made therefor; and if such jury shall find that it is necessary that such real estate shall be used in the manner or for the purpose proposed by such School District, they shall sign a certificate in writing, stating that it is necessary that said real estate (describing it) should be used as a site for a School-house for such District, also stating the sum to be paid by

Jury to be sworn.

Subpœna for witnesses.

Jury to determine necessity for taking Land and compensation therefor.

such School District as the just compensation for the same.

Court to make Certificate.

The said Circuit Judge, Circuit Court Commissioner, or Justice of the Peace, shall sign and attach to, and endorse upon the certificate thus subscribed by the said jurors, a certificate stating the time when, and the place where the said jury assembled, that they were by him duly sworn as herein required, and that they subscribed the said certificate; he shall also state in such certificate who appeared for the respective parties on such hearing and inquiry, and shall deliver such certificate to the Director, or to any member of the District Board of such School District.

Judgment; collection thereof.

Sec. 156. Upon filing such certificates in the Circuit Court of the county where such real estate is situated, such Court shall, if it finds all the proceedings regular, render judgment for the sum specified in the certificate signed by such jury, against such School District, which judgment shall be collected and paid in the manner as other judgments against School Districts are collected and paid.

When owner is unknown, etc., Money to be deposited with County Treasurer.

Sec. 157. In case the owner of such real estate shall be unknown, insane, *non compos mentis*, or an infant, or cannot be found within such county, it shall be lawful for the said School District to deposit the amount of such judgment with the County Treasurer of such county, for the use of the person or persons entitled thereto; and it shall be the duty of such County Treasurer to receive such money, and at the time of receiving it to give a receipt or certificate to the person depositing the same with him, stating the time when such deposit was made, and for what purpose; and such County Treasurer and his sureties shall be liable on his bond, for any money which shall come into his hands under the provisions of this act, in case he shall refuse to pay or account for the same as herein required: *Provided*,

How to be drawn from County Treasurer.

That no such money shall be drawn from such County Treasurer, except upon an order of the Circuit Court,

Circuit Court Commissioner, or Judge of Probate, as hereinafter provided.

Sec. 158. Upon satisfactory evidence being presented to the Circuit Court of the county where such real estate lies, that such judgment, or the sum ascertained and determined by the jury as the just compensation to be paid by such District for such site, has been paid, or that the amount thereof has been deposited according to the provisions of the preceding section, such Court shall, by an order or decree, adjudge and determine, that the title in fee of such real estate shall, from the time of making such payment or deposit, forever thereafter be vested in such School District and its assigns; a copy of which decree, certified by the clerk of said county, shall be recorded in the office of the Register of Deeds of such county, and the title of such real estate shall thenceforth, from the time of making such payment or deposit, be vested forever thereafter in such School District and its assigns in fee.

On payment Court may decree that Title be vested in School District.

Sec. 159. Such School District may, at any time after making the payment or deposit hereinbefore required, enter upon, and take possession of such real estate, for the use of said District.

When District to take possession.

Sec. 160. In case the jury hereinbefore provided for shall not agree, another jury may be summoned in the same manner, and the same proceedings may be had, except that no further notice of the proceedings shall be necessary; but instead of such notice, the Judge, Commissioner, or Justice, may adjourn the proceedings to such time as he shall think reasonable, not exceeding thirty days, and shall make the process to summon a jury returnable at such time and place as the said proceedings shall be adjourned to; such proceedings may be adjourned from time to time by the said Judge, or Commissioner, or Justice, on the application of either party, and for good cause, to be shown by the party applying for such adjournment,

When Jury cannot agree, proceedings may be adjourned, and new Jury summoned.

Adjournments not to exceed three months.

unless the other party shall consent to such adjournment; but such adjournments shall not in all exceed three months.

District Board may fix amount of Tuition to be paid by Scholars in certain cases.

Sec. 161. The District Board of any School District shall have power to fix the amount of tuition to be paid by non-resident scholars attending any of the Schools in said District; and in cases where there shall be a Union School in any such District, to be paid by scholars attending such Union School, and to make and enforce suitable by-laws and regulations for the government and management of such Union School, and for the preservation of the property of such District. Such District Board shall also have power to regulate and classify the studies, and prescribe the books to be used in such School.

Make laws for School.

How boundaries of District altered.

Sec. 162. No alteration shall be made in the boundaries of any School District having a Union School, without the written consent of a majority of the District Board of such District.

Districts having three hundred children between four and eighteen years, may borrow Money.

Sec. 163. Any School District having more than three hundred children, between the ages of four and eighteen years, residing in such District, shall have power and authority to borrow money to pay for a site for a Union School-house, to erect buildings thereon, and to furnish the same, by a vote of two-thirds of the qualified voters of said District present at any annual meeting, and by a like vote at any other regular meeting: *Provided*, That the times of holding such meetings shall not be less than five days, nor more than six months apart, and that the whole debt of any such District, at any one time, for money thus borrowed, shall not exceed fifteen thousand dollars.

Limitation of amount.

How Money deposited with County Treasurer may be drawn from him.

Sec. 164. The Circuit Judge, Judge of Probate, or Circuit Court Commissioner of any county where any money has been deposited with the County Treasurer of such county, as hereinbefore provided, shall, upon the written application of any person or persons entitled to such money, and upon receiving satisfactory evidence of the right of such applicant to the money thus deposited, make an order, directing the County Treasurer to pay the money thus deposited with him to said applicant; and it shall be the duty of such County Treasurer, on the presentation of such order, with the receipt of the person named therein endorsed on said order, and duly acknowledged, in the same manner as conveyances of real estate are required to be acknowledge, to pay the same; and such order, with the receipt of the applicant or person in whose favor the same shall be drawn, shall, in all Courts and places, be presumptive evidence in favor of such County Treasurer, to exonerate him from all liability to any person or persons for said money thus paid him.

Sec. 165. Circuit Judges, Circuit Court Commissioners, and Justices of the Peace, for any services rendered under the provisions of this Act, shall be entitled to the same fees and compensation as for similar services in other special proceedings; Jurors, Constables and Sheriffs, shall be entitled to the same fees as for like services in civil cases in the Circuit Court.

Compensation of Officers and Jurors on proceedings to obtain site for School-house.

Sec. 166. In case any Circuit Judge, Circuit Court Commissioner, or Justice of the Peace, who shall issue a summons or venire for a jury, shall be unable to attend to any of the subsequent proceedings, in such case, any other Circuit Court Commissioner or Justice of the Peace may attend and finish such proceedings.

When Judge or Justice unable to attend, another may finish proceedings.

Sec. 167. Whenever any School District shall have voted to borrow any sum of money, the District Board of such District is hereby authorized to issue the bonds of such District in such form, and executed in such manner by the Moderator and Director of such District, and in such sums, not less than fifty dollars, as such District Board shall direct, and with such rate of interest, not exceeding ten per centum per annum, and payable at such time or times as the said District shall have directed.

Bonds may be issued for Money Loaned.

Interest thereon.

Sec. 168. Whenever any money shall have been borrowed by any School District, the taxable inhabitants of

District may raise Tax to pay Loan.

such District are hereby authorized, at any regular meeting of such District, to impose a tax on the taxable property in such District for the purpose of paying the principal thus borrowed, or any part thereof, and the interest thereon, to be levied and collected as other School District taxes are collected.

Superintendent authorized to subscribe for Journal of Education for Districts.

Sec. 169. The Superintendent of Public Instruction is authorized to subscribe for one copy of the Michigan Journal of Education, a periodical published under the direction of the Michigan State Teachers' Association, for each School District in this State, to be sent by mail, the postage being prepaid by the publisher, to the Directors of the said Districts, the price of such subscription to be sixty cents a year for each copy, and such subscription to begin with the January number of the present year.(1)

Laws relating to Public Instruction to be published in Journal.

Sec. 170. All general laws relating to public instruction which shall hereafter be passed in this State, and all general notifications or instructions issuing from the Department of Public Instruction, shall, when directed by the Superintendent of Public Instruction, be published in said Journal of Education, free of charge to the State.

Certificate of Superintendent to be delivered to publisher.

Sec. 171. Upon making such subscription, the Superintendent of Public Instruction shall make and deliver to the publisher of said Journal of Education, quarterly, his certificate in writing, stating the number of copies so subscribed for and sent as aforesaid, and the amount due therefor at the time of making such certificate; and the Auditor General, on presentation to him of such certificate, shall draw his warrant upon the State Treasurer for the amount named in said certificate, and said Treasurer is directed to pay the amount of the said warrant to the holder thereof, out of any moneys in the Treasury not otherwise appropriated.

---

(1) Sections 169, 170 and 171 were passed Feb. 14, 1857. [Compiled Laws, p. 760.]

LIBRARIES AND LYCEUMS.

Sec. 172. Any seven or more proprietors of a Library may form themselves into a Corporation, under such corporate name as they may adopt, for the purpose of enlarging, regulating and using such Library; and for that purpose any Justice of the Peace may, on the application of five or more of the proprietors, issue his warrant to one of them, directing him to call a meeting of the proprietors at the time and place expressed in the warrant, for the purpose of forming such Corporation; and such meeting shall be called by posting up a notice containing the substance of such warrant, in at least two public places in the township where such Library is kept, at least seven days before the time of meeting.(1) Meeting of proprietors to form Corporations; how called.

Sec. 173. Any seven or more of the proprietors of such Library, met in pursuance of such notice, may choose a President, a Clerk, a Librarian, Collector, Treasurer, and such other officers as they may deem necessary; and they may also determine upon the mode of calling future meetings of the proprietors; and the proceedings of such first meeting, containing a specification of the corporate name adopted by such proprietors, shall be certified by the Clerk of such Corporation, and recorded by the County Clerk of the county within which the same is formed, who shall be entitled to receive seventy-five cents for recording the same. Proprietors may choose officers.

Sec. 174. When such proprietors shall be organized as a Corporation in the manner hereinbefore provided, they Powers and privileges of corporation.

---

(1) Sections 172 to 177, inclusive, from Compiled Laws, pp. 568 to 570

shall have all the powers and privileges, and be subject to all the duties of a Corporation, according to the provisions of chapter fifty-five,(1) so far as such provisions shall be applicable in such case, and not inconsistent with the provisions of this chapter.

Bond of Collector and Treasurer.

Sec. 175. The Treasurer and Collector shall give bond to such Corporation, with sufficient sureties, to the satisfaction of the President, for the faithful discharge of their duties.

Certain powers of corporation.

Sec. 176. The said proprietors may raise such sums of money, by assessment on the shares, as they shall judge necessary for the purpose of preserving, enlarging and using the Library; and the shares may be transferred according to such regulations as they may prescribe, and such Corporation may hold real and personal estate to any amount not exceeding five thousand dollars, in addition to the value of their books.

Lyceums; how organized.

Sec. 177. Any fifteen or more persons, in any township or county within this State, who shall, by writing, associate for the purpose of mental improvement, and the promotion of Education, may form themselves into a Corporation by the name of "The Lyceum of ," (the name of the place where the meetings of the Corporation are to be holden,) by calling their first meeting and being organized in like manner as is provided in this chapter, in the case of Library Corporations; and every Lyceum, upon becoming a Corporation as aforesaid, shall have, during the pleasure of the Legislature, all the like rights, powers and privileges, as the proprietors of such Libraries, and may hold real and personal estate, not exceeding six thousand dollars.

---

(1) Chapter 72, Compiled Laws.

TEACHERS' ASSOCIATIONS.

Sec. 178. Any fifteen or more Teachers, or other persons residing in this State, who shall associate for the purpose of promoting Education and Science, and improvements in the theory and practice of Teaching, may form themselves into a Corporation, under such name as they may choose, providing they shall have published, in some newspaper printed at Lansing, or in the county in which such Association is to be located, for at least one month previous, a notice of the time, place and purpose of the meeting for such Association, and shall file in the office of the Secretary of State a copy of the Constitution and By-Laws of said Association.(1) **Fifteen or more Teachers may form Corporation.** **Notice to be published.**

Sec. 179. Such Association may hold and possess real and personal property to the amount of five thousand dollars; but the funds or property thereof shall not be used for any other purpose than the legitimate business of the Association in securing the objects of its Corporation. **May hold Real and Personal Property.** **Restrictions upon its use.**

Sec. 180. Upon becoming a Corporation, as hereinbefore provided, they shall have all the powers and privileges, and be subject to all the duties of a Corporation, according to the provisions of chapter fifty-five of the Revised Statutes(2) of this State, so far as such provisions shall be applicable in such case, and not inconsistent with the provisions of this act. **Privileges and liabilities of Corporation.**

---

(1) Sections 178, 179 and 180, passed Feb. 12, 1855. [Compiled Laws, p. 671.]

(2) Chapter 73, Compiled Laws.

TEACHERS' INSTITUTES.

When Superintendent to appoint and make arrangements for Institute.

Sec. 181. Whenever reasonable assurance shall be given to the Superintendent of Public Instruction that a number not less than fifty, or in counties containing a population of less than twelve thousand inhabitants, whenever twenty-five Teachers of Common Schools shall desire to assemble for the purpose of forming a Teachers' Institute, and to remain in session for a period of not less than ten working days, said Superintendent is authorized to appoint a time and place for holding such Institute, to make suitable arrangements therefor, and to give due notice thereof.(1)

Money for expenses, etc.; how to be drawn, and to what amount.

Sec. 182. For the purpose of defraying the expenses of rooms, fires, lights, attendance, or other necessary charges, and for procuring Teachers and Lecturers for said Institute, the Auditor General shall, upon the certificate of the Superintendent of Public Instruction, that he has made arrangements for holding such Institute, draw his warrant upon the State Treasurer for such sum as said Superintendent shall deem necessary for conducting such Institute, which sum shall not exceed two hundred dollars for any one Institute, and shall be paid out of the general fund.

Superintendent may appoint suitable persons to make arrangements for the same.

Limitation as to Moneys that may be drawn.

Sec. 183. Said Superintendent, in case of inability personally to conduct any Institute, or to make the necessary arrangements for holding the same, is authorized to appoint some suitable person or persons for that purpose: *Provided*, That not more than eighteen hundred dollars shall be drawn from the Treasury in any one year, to meet the provisions of this act.

---

(1) Sections 181. 182 and 183, passed Feb. 10, 1855. [Compiled Laws, p. 769.]

STATE NORMAL SCHOOL.

An Act to Consolidate and Amend the Laws Relative to the Establishment of a State Normal School.

[Compiled Laws, p. 715.]

Scetion 1. *Be it enacted by the Senate and House of Representatives of the State of Michigan,* That all acts done and contracts made by and with the Board of Education under and by virtue of "An Act to establish a State Normal School," approved March twenty-eighth, eighteen hundred and forty-nine, and the Act supplementary thereto, approved March thirty-first, eighteen hundred and forty-nine, be and they are hereby ratified and confirmed.

Acts and contracts of Board of Education confirmed.

1849, p. 157.
1849, p. 221.

Sec. 2. That a State Normal School be established and continued at Ypsilanti, in the county of Washtenaw, upon the site selected by said Board of Education, the exclusive purposes of which shall be the instruction of persons, both male and female, in the art of teaching, and in all the various branches that pertain to a good common school education. Also to give instruction in the mechanic arts, and in the arts of husbandry and agricultural chemistry; in the fundamental laws of the United States, and in what regards the rights and duties of citizens.

State Normal School, where established.

Its design.

Sec. 3. The said Normal School shall be under the direction of a Board of Education, and shall be governed and supported as herein provided. Said Board shall provide for the erection of suitable buildings on the site selected as soon as the title thereto is vested in them in fee, and the means in their hands for that purpose are sufficient; and they may appoint a suitable person to superintend the erection of said buildings.

To be under direction of Board of Education.

Board to provide for erection of buildings.

State Board of Education

Sec. 4. There shall be elected at the general election in the year one thousand eight hundred and fifty-two, three members of a State Board of Education. one for two years, one for four years, and one for six years; and at each succeeding biennial election there shall be elected one member of such Board, who shall hold his office for six years. The Superintendent of Public Instruction shall be *ex-officio* a member and Secretary of such Board. The Board shall have the general supervision of the State Normal School, and their duties shall be prescribed by law.[1]

Powers of Board of Education.

Sec. 5. Said Board of Education shall have power to appoint a Principal and assistant to take charge of said School, and such other Teachers and officers as may be required in said School, and fix the salary of each, and prescribe their several duties. They shall also have power to remove either the Principal, assistant, or Teachers, and to appoint others in their stead. They shall prescribe the various books to be used in said School, and shall make all the regulations and by-laws necessary for the good government and management of the same.

Experimental School to be established.

Sec. 6. Said Board shall also establish an experimental School in connection with the Normal School, and shall make all the regulations necessary to govern and support the same, and may, in their discretion, admit pupils free of charge for tuition.

Powers and duties of Board to provide grounds, buildings, etc., for instruction in Agriculture and Mechanic Arts.

Sec. 7. Said Board shall have power, and it shall be their duty, from time to time, as the means at their disposal may warrant, to provide suitable grounds and buildings, implements of husbandry and mechanical tools, either by purchase or lease, for the purpose of more effectually and experimentally carrying out the provisions of the second section of this act, "To Give Instruction in the Mechanic Arts, and in the Arts of Husbandry and Agricultural Chemistry."

---

(1) The original Section 4 of this Act has been superceded by Section 9, Article *thirteen*, of the Constitution—which is here given in its stead. The Constitution also somewhat contravenes some of the details of other Sections of the Act.

Sec. 8. As soon as said Normal School is prepared to receive pupils, the Superintendent of Public Instruction shall give notice of the fact to each County Clerk in the State, and shall publish said notice in a newspaper published in each Senatorial district. Notice to be given when School ready for Pupils.

Sec. 9. The Board of Education shall ordain such rules and regulations for the admission of pupils to said School as they shall deem necessary and proper. Every applicant for admission shall undergo an examination in such manner as may be prescribed by the Board; and if it shall appear that the applicant is not a person of good moral character. or will not make an apt and good Teacher, such applicant shall be rejected. The Board of Education may, in their discretion, require any applicant for admission to said School—other than such as shall, prior to such admission, sign and file with said Board a declaration of intention to follow the business of teaching Primary Schools in this State—to pay, or secure to be paid, such fees for tuition as to said Board shall seem reasonable. Rules and Regulations for admis- of Pupils. Certain Pupils to pay or secure Tuition fees.

Sec. 10. Any person may be admitted a pupil of said School who shall pass a satisfactory examination: *Provided*, That the applicant shall, before admission, sign a declaration of intention to follow the business of teaching Primary Schools in this State: *And provided, further*, That pupils may be admitted without signing such declaration of intention, on such terms as the Normal School Board may prescribe; and that each county shall be entitled to send pupils in the ratio of the Representatives in the State Legislature to which it may be entitled, not to exceed such number as the Board may prescribe. Pupils to sign declaration of intention to become Teachers. But may be admitted without. Ratio of Pupils from each County.

Sec. 11. After said School shall have commenced its first term, and at least once in each year thereafter, it shall be visited by three suitable persons, not members, to be appointed by the Board of Education, who shall examine thoroughly into the affairs of the School, and report to the Superintendent of Public Instruction their views with re- Board of Visitors; how appointed.

gard to its condition, success and usefulness, and any other matters they may judge expedient. Such Visitors shall be appointed annually.

Superintendent of Public Instruction to visit School, and make Report.

Sec. 12. It shall be the duty of the Superintendent of Public Instruction, once at least in each term, to visit said School; and he shall annually make to the Legislature a full and detailed report of the doings of the Board of Education, and of all their expenditures, and the moneys received for tuition, and the prospects, progress and usefulness of said School, including so much of the reports of said Visitors as he may deem advisable.

Lectures.

Sec. 13. Lectures on chemistry, comparative anatomy, astronomy, the mechanic arts, agricultural chemistry, and on any other science, or any branch of literature that the Board of Education may direct, may be delivered to those attending said School, in such manner, and on such terms and conditions as the Board of Education may prescribe.

Examination of Pupils.

Sec. 14. As soon as any person has attended said institution twenty-two weeks, said person may be examined in the studies required by the Board, in such manner as may be prescribed; and if it shall appear that said person possesses the learning and other qualifications necessary to teach a good Common School, said person shall receive a certificate to that effect from the Principal, to be approved by the Superintendent of Public Instruction.

Certificate of qualifications.

Board may receive Donations and Subscriptions.

Sec. 15. The Board of Education shall have the power and authority to demand and receive the sum or sums donated and subscribed by the citizens of Ypsilanti and its vicinity, in such manner as said Board may prescribe, and apply the same to the erection and completion of the necessary buildings, the purchase of the necessary books, apparatus, furniture and fixtures, and for various other incidental expenses to be incurred by said Board in pursuance of the provisions of this act; and if any surplus shall remain, to apply the same in defraying the expenses of conducting said School. And any deficit which may arise

How to apply them.

in the erection and completion of said buildings and purchases aforesaid, shall be paid out of the principal to be received on the sale of lands hereinafter mentioned, not to exceed the sum of ten thousand dollars. Such sum shall be paid from time to time on the warrant of the Auditor General, to be drawn in pursuance of the certificate of the Superintendent of Building, or Secretary of the Board, and countersigned by the President of the Board of Education; and no such certificate shall be issued until work shall be done, or services rendered, or buildings erected, or books, apparatus, fixtures, or furniture purchased for the Normal School, under the direction of the Board of Education, entitling the applicant to such certificate, according to a contract or agreement with said Board for that purpose, or for services and expenses of the Board or some member thereof, in connection with the selection of the site, or the erection of the Normal School buildings, or the improvement of the grounds.

Deficit in erection of buildings, etc; how paid.

Sec. 16. The ten sections of Salt Spring lands, located by the Board of Education under the provisions of sections fifteen and sixteen of "An Act to establish a State Normal School," approved March twenty-eight, eighteen hundred and forty-nine, together with the fifteen sections of Salt Spring lands located under the provisions of section sixteen of said Act, and all such lands as may be granted by Congress, or received or set apart (in any manner,) in lieu of any portion of said land to which the title may prove insufficient, and all donations, in land or otherwise, to the State in trust, or to the Board of Education for the support of a Normal School, shall constitute a fund, to be called the Normal School Endowment Fund, and shall be reserved from sale until the same shall be appraised. The minimum price of said lands shall be four dollars per acre; and it shall be the duty of the officer authorized to sell said lands, to cause the same to be appraised as soon as practicable, in the manner provided for the appraisal of other lands.

1849, p. 157.

What Lands to constitute Endowment Fund.

Minimum price of Lands, and how sold.

None of said lands shall be sold for less than the minimum price fixed by law. It shall not be necessary to appraise any of said lands which have heretofore been appraised under existing provisions of law; and the proceeds of sales of any of said lands heretofore appraised and sold, shall constitute a part of the fund herein provided. After such appraisal, such land shall be and remain subject to sale at the State Land Office, as is now, or shall be hereafter provided by law; and the principal shall be and remain a perpetual fund for the use of said institution (except as herein provided.) The instalments of principal paid by the purchasers, shall be paid into the State Treasury; and the interest thereon from the time of its receipt, or from the time of the preceding computation of interest, as the same [case] may be, shall be computed by the Auditor General and State Treasurer, at the close of each fiscal year, at the rate of six per cent. per annum, and together with all interest paid by purchasers of any portion of said lands, shall be passed to the credit of the Normal School interest fund, to be drawn therefrom upon the warrant of the Auditor General, issued in pursuance of a certificate of the Board of Education, signed by their Secretary and countersigned by their President, that the money is due and payable to the Principal of the Normal School, or his assistants, or the Teachers or officers employed, or to the members of the Board, or the Board of Visitors, as herein authorized, or for necessary incidental expenses in the support or maintenance of said School, or some of its departments.

Funds under control of Board of Education.

Sec. 17. Said funds shall be under the direction and control of the Board of Education, subject to the provisions herein contained. The Treasurer of said Board shall pay out of the proper fund all orders or drafts for moneys to be expended under the provisions of this act. Such orders or drafts to be drawn by the Auditor General, on the certificate of the Secretary, countersigned by the President of the Board. No such certificates shall be given, except upon accounts audited and allowed by the Board at a regular meeting.

Expenses of Board of Education and Visitors; how paid.

Sec. 18. The services, and all necessary traveling and other expenses, already or hereafter to be incurred by any member of the Board of Education, or the Board of Visitors, shall be paid on the proper certificate out of any funds belonging to said Institution in the hands of the Treasurer, until the erection and completion of the necessary buildings. The Principal, Assistants, Teachers and other officers employed in said School, shall be paid out of the Normal School Interest Fund, and from receipts for tuition; and the services and expenses of the Board of Education, after the erection of the necessary buildings, and other expenses incident to said Institution, shall be paid for out of the Normal School Interest Fund, in the same manner, as near as may be, as is required in regard to moneys drawn for the payment of the Principal or other Teachers. The members of the Board of Education and the Visitors, shall be entitled to two dollars per day for their actual services, and to their necessary traveling and other expenses.

Instructors and Officers; how paid.

Pay of Members and Visitors.

"The Board of Education" to be body Corporate; their powers, etc.

Sec. 19. For the purpose of rendering more efficient their organization, and to enable them the more fully to carry into effect the provisions herein contained, the members of the Board of Education, now holding their offices under the provisions of "An Act to establish a State Normal School," approved March 28th, 1849, and their successors in office, are hereby constituted a body politic and corporate, by the name of "The Board of Education," for the purposes herein contemplated, and subject to such modifications as may be made thereto, and in that name shall have perpetual succession, and shall be, and they are hereby empowered to purchase, have, hold, possess and enjoy to themselves and their successors, lands, tenements, hereditaments, goods, chattels and effects of every kind, and the same to grant, alien, sell, invest and dispose of, to sue and be sued, plead and be impleaded in all Courts in this State, to have and to use a common seal, and the same to change, alter and renew at pleasure, and to make such by-laws and regulations as they may deem proper for the well ordering and government of said Corporation and the transaction of its business: *Provided*, The same be not repugnant to the Constitution or laws of this State or of the United States.

To be subject to provisions of Chap. 55 of Revised Statutes of 1846. Chapter 73, Compiled Laws.

Sec. 20. Said Corporation shall be subject to the provisions of chapter fifty-five of the Revised Statutes of 1846, so far as the same can apply, and are not inconsistent with the provisions of this act. They shall have power to transact all necessary business at any meeting, a quorum being present; and meetings may be called in such manner as their by-laws may provide, and a quorum shall consist of a majority of the members.

First Meeting; when held.

The first meeting under this act may be held at such time and place as may be directed by the Secretary, and no publication of notice thereof shall be necessary; and the attendance of a quorum shall render valid the proceedings of such meeting.

Process against Board; how served.

All process against said Corporation shall be served on the President or Secretary thereof.

Certain enactments repealed. 1849, p. 157. 1849, p. 221.

Sec. 21. Sections four, fifteen and sixteen of "An Act to establish a State Normal School," approved March 28th, 1849, and all of the provisions of said act, and the act supplementary thereto, which are inconsistent with the provisions of this act, are hereby repealed.

Legislature may alter, etc., this Act.

Sec. 22. This act shall take effect and be in force from and after its passage, and the Legislature may at any time alter, amend or repeal the same by a vote of two-thirds of the members present in each House.

Diplomas may be granted to graduates from Normal School.

Sec. 23. The Board of Instruction of the State Normal School are authorized to grant to graduates of said Institution Diplomas, which, when signed by the members of the State Board of Education, shall be regarded as evidence that such graduates have completed the prescribed course of study in said Institution.[1]

Sec. 24. Each Diploma so conferred shall be accompanied by a certificate, signed by the Board of Instruction, which, when recorded in the office of the Clerk of any township in this State, shall serve the holder as a certificate of qualification to teach in any Primary School of said township, until the same shall be amended [annulled] by the School Inspectors of such township under the provisions of law for annulling certificates.

Diplomas to be accompanied by Certificate, which shall serve as Certificate of qualification to Teach.

---

(1) Sections 23 and 24 passed Feb. 13, 1857. [Compiled Laws, p. 722.]

THE UNIVERSITY OF MICHIGAN.

An Act to Provide for the Government of the State University.

[Compiled Laws, p. 711.]

University continued.

SECTION 1. *The People of the State of Michigan* **enact**, That the institution established in this State, and known as the University of Michigan, is continued under the name and style heretofore used.

Its objects.

Sec. 2. The University shall provide the inhabitants of this State with the means of acquiring a thorough knowledge of the various branches of Literature, Science and Arts.(1)

Government vested in Board of Regents.

Sec. 3. The government of the University is vested in the Board of Regents.

Regents to be a body Corporate.

Sec. 4. The Board of Regents shall constitute the body corporate, with the right as such of suing and being sued, of making and using a common seal, and altering the same.

Regents to make By-Laws, etc., elect President, Professors, etc., and fix salaries.

Sec. 5. The Regents shall have power to enact ordinances, by-laws and regulations for the government of the University; to elect a President, to fix, increase and reduce the regular number of Professors and Tutors, and to appoint the same, and to determine the amount of their salaries: *Provided,* That there shall always be at least one Professor of Homœopathy in the department of Medicine.

May remove President, Professors, etc.

Sec. 6. They shall have power to remove the President, and any Professor or Tutor, when the interest of the University shall require it.

---

(1) See note to Section 13.

Sec. 7. They shall have power to appoint a Secretary, Librarian, Treasurer, Steward, and such other officers as the interests of the institution may require, who shall hold their offices at the pleasure of the board, and receive such compensation as the board may prescribe.

May appoint other Officers, and prescribe their compensation.

Sec. 8. The University shall consist of at least three departments:

Of what departments University to consist

1. A department of Literature, Science and the Arts;
2. A department of Law;
3. A department of Medicine;
4. Such other departments may be added as the Regents shall deem necessary, and the state of the University fund shall allow.

Sec. 9. The Regents shall provide for the arrangement and selection of a course or courses of study in the University, for such students as may not desire to pursue the usual collegiate course, in the department of literature, science and the arts, embracing the ancient languages, and to provide for the admission of such students without previous examination as to their attainments in said languages, and for granting such certificates at the expiration of such course or term of such students, as may be appropriate to their respcctive attainments.

Regents to prescribe Course of Study for Students who do not desire to pursue Collegiate Course.

Sec. 10. The Regents shall make provision for keeping a set of meteorological tables at the University, after the forms adopted and furnished by the Smithsonian Institution, the record of which shall be transmitted with their report to the Superintendent of Public Instruction, who shall embody the same into his report.

To make provision for Meteorological Tables.

Sec. 11. The immediate government of the several departments shall be entrusted to the President and the respective faculties; but the Regents shall have power to regulate the course of instruction, and prescribe, under the advice of the Professorship, the books and authorities to be used in the several departments; and also to confer such

General direction of Institution.

degrees and grant such diplomas as are usually conferred and granted by other similar institutions.

Admission Fees.

Sec. 12. The fee of admission to the regular University course in the department of literature, science and the arts, shall not exceed ten dollars, but such course or courses of instruction as may be arranged under the provisions of section nine of this act, shall be open without fee to the citizens of this State.

What Students admitted without Fee.

University to be open to Citizens of the State without charge.

Sec. 13. The University shall be open to all persons resident of this State, without charge of tuition, under the regulations prescribed by the Regents; and to all other persons under such regulations and restrictions as the Board may prescribe.(1)

Moneys to whom paid, and how applied.

Sec. 14. The moneys received from such source shall be paid to the Treasurer, and so much thereof as shall be necessary for the purpose, shall be expended by the Regents in keeping the University buildings in good condition and repair, and the balance shall be appropriated for the increase of the library.

Annual Report of Regents.

Sec. 15. The Board of Regents shall make an exhibit of the affairs of the University, in each year, to the Superintendent of Public Instruction, setting forth the condition of the University and its branches; the amount of receipts and expenditures; the number of Professors, Tutors and other officers, and the compensation of each; the number of students in the several departments, and in the different classes; the books of instruction used; an estimate of the expenses for the ensuing year; a full transcript of the journal of their proceedings for the year; together with such other information and suggestions as they may deem important, or the Superintendent of Public Instruction may require to embody in his report.

Buildings may be erected from increase of University Fund.

Sec. 16. From the increase arising from the interest of the University fund, the Board of Regents may erect, from

(1) For the views of the Superintendent of Public Instruction as to the rights of "persons" to admission to the University, see his Report for 1857, pp. 27 to 34.

time to time, such buildings as are necessary for the uses of the University, on the grounds set apart for the same; but no such buildings shall be erected until provision shall be made for the payment of the existing indebtedness of the University, nor until one branch of the University shall be established in each judicial circuit of the State.

Sec. 17. The Board of Regents shall have power to expend so much of the interest arising from the University fund, as may be necessary for the improving and ornamenting of the University grounds, for the purchase of philosophical, chemical, meteorological, and other apparatus, and to keep the same in good condition. Interest of Fund; how expended.

Sec. 18. As soon as the income of the University interest fund will admit, it shall be the duty of the Board of Regents to organize and establish branches of the University, one at least in each judicial circuit or district of the State, and to establish all needful rules and regulations for the government of the same. They shall not give to any such branch the right of conferring degrees, nor appropriate a sum exceeding fifteen hundred dollars, in any one year, for the support of any such branch. Board of Regents may establish Branches.

Sec. 19. The Regents may establish and organize a branch or branches, by the creation of a Trusteeship for the local management of the same, or they may in their discretion select for a branch, under the restrictions aforesaid, any chartered literary institution in the State. Ibid.

Sec. 20. The meetings of the Board may be called in such manner as the Regents shall prescribe; five of them shall constitute a quorum for the transaction of business, and a less number may adjourn from time to time. Meetings of Board.

Sec. 21. A Board of Visitors, to consist of three persons, shall be appointed biennially at the commencement of the collegiate year, by the Superintendent of Public Instruction. It shall be their duty to make a personal examination into the state and condition of the University in all its departments and branches, once at least in each year, Board of Visitors appointed.

THE AGRICULTURAL COLLEGE.

An Act for the Establishment of a State Agricultural School.

[Compiled Laws, p. 723.]

Section 1. *The People of the State of Michigan enact,* That the President and Executive Committee of the Michigan State Agricultural Society be, and are hereby authorized to select, subject to the approval of the State Board of Education, a location and site for a State Agricultural School, within ten miles of Lansing; and subject to such approval, contract for and purchase for the State of Michigan such lands, not less than five hundred acres, nor more than one thousand acres, in one body, for the purpose of an experimental farm and site for such Agricultural School: *Provided,* That the amount to be paid for such farm and site shall not exceed fifteen dollars per acre, and that the conveyance or conveyances be made to the State of Michigan. **Selection of location for School.** **Farm to be purchased.**

Sec. 2. That there is hereby appropriated twenty-two sections of salt spring lands, or the money arising from the sale thereof, referred to in article thirteen, section eleven, of the Constitution of the State of Michigan, for the purchase of land for such site and location, and the preparation thereof, the erection of buildings, the purchase of furniture, apparatus, library and implements, payment of Professors and Teachers, and other necessary expenses, to be incurred in the establishment and successful operation of said School; which sum shall be drawn from the State Treasury on the presentation of the proper certificates of **Salt Spring Lands appropriated for purchase of Land, erection of Buildings, etc.**

the Board of Education to the Auditor General, and on his warrant to the State Treasurer; but not to exceed in the whole amount the sum of fifty-six thousand, three hundred and twenty dollars, the minimum price of said twenty-two sections, unless the whole proceeds of the sales of said sections shall exceed that sum, and then not to exceed the amount of such proceeds.(1)

On execution and approval of conveyance, Auditor General to draw Warrant to pay for same.

Sec. 3. Upon the execution and delivery to the Secretary of State of the proper conveyance or conveyances of the land, the purchase of which is provided for in the first section of this act, and the certificate of the Attorney General that he has examined the title to the same, and finds it unencumbered, and that the conveyance or conveyances are executed in due form, and a certificate from the President and Secretary of the Board of Education, that the same is in accordance with the contract or contracts for the purchase of the same, and that the location has been approved by them, the Auditor General shall draw his warrant or warrants on the State Treasurer for the amount of such purchase, in favor of the party or parties to whom such sum or sums shall be due, payable out of said salt spring lands, or money accruing from the sale of the same; and the said certificates in this section mentioned, shall be filed and preserved in the office of the Secretary of State.

Agricultural College to be established, its purpose and design.

Sec. 4. Upon the purchase of such location and site, there shall be established on such site, under the direction and supervision of the State Board of Education, an Agricultural School, by the name and style of the Agricultural College of the State of Michigan, and the chief purpose and design of which shall be, to improve and teach the science and practice of Agriculture.

Sec. 5. The course of instruction in said College shall

(1) As amended by "An Act making an Appropriation for the State Agricultural School, and to amend the Act entitled, 'An Act for the Establishment of a State Agricultural School, Approved February twelfth, eighteen hundred and fifty-five,'" approved February 16, 1857, Laws of 1857, p. 385.

the Board of Education to the Auditor General, and on his warrant to the State Treasurer; but not to exceed in the whole amount the sum of fifty-six thousand, three hundred and twenty dollars, the minimum price of said twenty-two sections, unless the whole proceeds of the sales of said sections shall exceed that sum, and then not to exceed the amount of such proceeds.(1)

On execution and approval of conveyance, Auditor General to draw Warrant to pay for same.

Sec. 3. Upon the execution and delivery to the Secretary of State of the proper conveyance or conveyances of the land, the purchase of which is provided for in the first section of this act, and the certificate of the Attorney General that he has examined the title to the same, and finds it unencumbered, and that the conveyance or conveyances are executed in due form, and a certificate from the President and Secretary of the Board of Education, that the same is in accordance with the contract or contracts for the purchase of the same, and that the location has been approved by them, the Auditor General shall draw his warrant or warrants on the State Treasurer for the amount of such purchase, in favor of the party or parties to whom such sum or sums shall be due, payable out of said salt spring lands, or money accruing from the sale of the same; and the said certificates in this section mentioned, shall be filed and preserved in the office of the Secretary of State.

Agricultural College to be established, its purpose and design.

Sec. 4. Upon the purchase of such location and site, there shall be established on such site, under the direction and supervision of the State Board of Education, an Agricultural School, by the name and style of the Agricultural College of the State of Michigan, and the chief purpose and design of which shall be, to improve and teach the science and practice of Agriculture.

Sec. 5. The course of instruction in said College shall

(1) As amended by "An Act making an Appropriation for the State Agricultural School, and to amend the Act entitled, 'An Act for the Establishment of a State Agricultural School, Approved February twelfth, eighteen hundred and fifty-five,'" approved February 16, 1857, Laws of 1857, p. 385.

include the following branches of education, viz: An English and scientific course, natural philosophy, chemistry, botany, animal and vegetable anatomy and physiology, geology, mineralogy, meteorology, entomology, veterinary art, mensuration, leveling and political economy, with book-keeping and the mechanic arts, which are directly connected with Agriculture, and such others as the Board of Education may from time to time see fit to prescribe, having reference to the objects specified in the previous section; and the said Board may establish such professorships, and employ such Professors and Teachers, to be called the Board of Instruction of said College, for the instruction aforesaid, as they may judge best for such object: *Provided,* The sum paid such Professors and Teachers, for the first year after said College shall go into operation, shall not exceed the sum of five thousand dollars, and for the next year, not exceeding the sum of six thousand dollars, and for any years thereafter, such a sum as the State Board of Education may deem necessary, for the successful operation of the Institution. Tuition in said Institution shall be forever free to pupils from this State, and any number of pupils may be admitted who shall apply from any part of this State: *Provided,* That in case more pupils apply than can be accommodated or taught, then said Board shall adopt some equitable plan, giving to each county a number according to the ratio of population, as it shall appear from the census last taken; and in that case, those from each county shall be admitted in the order in which they shall apply, until the quota of such county be full.

Course of Instruction. Professorships. Compensation of Professors. Pupils and Tuition.

Sec. 6. There shall be two scholastic terms in each year, the first term commencing on the first Wednesday in April, and ending on the last Wednesday in October; the second term commencing the first Wednesday in December, and ending on the last Wednesday in February; and no pupil shall be received for less than one term, unless by special permission from the Board of Instruction.

Terms of School. Pupils not to be received for less than term, except by special permission.

Hours for labor, study, etc.

Sec. 7. The Board of Education, upon consultation with the Board of Instruction, shall, from time to time, fix and establish rules as to the number of hours which shall be devoted to manual labor and to study, which may be different in different terms or seasons; but during the first term in such year, the time devoted to labor shall not be less than three, nor more than four hours each day; and no student or pupil of said College shall be exempt from such labor, except in case of sickness or other infirmity.

Board of Education to appoint Officers of College.

Establish Rules and Regulations, etc.

Sec. 8. The Board of Education shall appoint one of the Professors in said College to be the President thereof, and one to be its Secretary, and one to be its Treasurer; and the Board of Instruction may establish such rules and regulations from time to time, for the government of said College and instruction therein, as they may deem proper in any matter not regulated by the Board of Education; and the rules and regulations adopted by such Board of Instruction, shall remain in full force until altered by said Board of Education. And said Board of Instruction shall have power, subject to the approval of the Board of Education, to establish by-laws for the government and discipline of the pupils of said College, in regard to conduct and behavior, and to affix such pecuniary penalties as they may deem proper, and to prescribe the causes for expulsion or dismissal of any such pupil, which by-laws shall have the force of law, unless altered, modified or repealed by the Board of Education or the Legislature; and the Board of Education shall fix the compensation to be credited or paid for the labor performed by pupils, under the provisions of section seven of this act.

To fix compensation for labor of Pupils.

Duties of President.

Sec. 9. The President of said Board of Instruction shall preside at all meetings of said Board, except in case of sickness or absence; in which case the Board may elect one of their number President *pro tempore;* and it shall be the duty of the President to see that all the regulations established by this act, by the Board of Education, and by the Board of Instruction, in regard to the government and instruction in said College, be enforced.

Duties of Secretary.

Sec. 10. The Secretary of said Board of Instruction shall record all the proceedings of said Board, and all regulations and by-laws for the government of said College, and shall publish the same, and furnish a copy thereof to the Governor of this State, to each member of the Board of Education, to the County Clerk of each county, and to the Clerk of each organized township in this State. He shall also keep a full record of all improvements and experiments made on said lands, their cost and results. He shall also keep a careful account with each field, in connection with a plan of the farming lands or farm, exhibiting the position of each, in which shall be shown the manner and cost of preparing the ground, the kind of crop, time of planting or sowing, the after condition, the time and manner of harvesting, the labor devoted to each process, and its cost price, with the cost of preparing the matured crop for market, and the price for which it was sold, and of such other matters as the Board of Education and of Instruction, or either of them, may require of him; and he shall furnish a copy thereof at the end of each term to the President of the Board of Education; and the said record shall, at all reasonable hours, be open to the inspection of any citizen of this State.

Duties of Treasurer.

Sec. 11. The Treasurer shall receive and keep all moneys arising from the sale of products of the farm, and from fines and penalties that may be imposed; and shall give bonds in such sum as the Board of Education may require. He shall pay over all moneys upon the warrant of the President, countersigned by the Secretary, on account of such contingent expenses of the institution as may arise. He shall render annually, in the month of December, to the Board of Education, and as often as required by said Board, a full and true account of all moneys received and disbursed by him; stating for what received and paid, and shall produce vouchers for such payments. The surplus money, if any remain in his hands at the time of rendering such account, shall, if required by said Board, be paid over to the State Treasurer, to be placed to the credit of said institution.

Visitors to be appointed.

Sec. 12. After said College shall have commenced its first term, the Superintendent of Public Instruction shall appoint Visitors for the same, who shall perform the like duties required of such Visitors by law, in reference to the State Normal School.(1)

Their duties

(1) For An Act making appropriations for the School for 1857 and 1858, see Laws of 1857, p 385.

"INSTITUTIONS OF LEARNING."

An Act to Provide for the Incorporation of Institutions of Learning.

[Compiled Laws, p. 564.]

Section 1. *The People of the State of Michigan enact*, That any number of persons not less than five, may become a Corporation for the purpose of founding and establishing a College, Seminary, Academy, or other Institution of Learning, by complying with the provisions of this Act. When stock, legacies, bequests or donations, to the amount of thirty thousand dollars for any such College, or five thousand dollars for any such Seminary, Academy, or other Institution of Learning, so intended to be founded and established, shall be in good faith subscribed or given, and twenty per cent. thereon actually paid in, as herein required, such persons may elect Trustees for such College, Seminary, Academy, or other Institution of Learning; and thereupon said Trustees shall severally, subscribe articles of association, in which shall be set forth the name, character, and object of the Corporation, the amount of capital stock so subscribed, bequeathed, donated or given, and the amount paid in; the names and place of residence of the Trustees; the length of time they shall continue in office, not to exceed thirty years; the manner in which their successors shall be elected, who shall not be less than five, nor more than thirty-five, and the place where such College or other Institution is to be located. Said articles of association, when subscribed as aforesaid, may be filed in the office of the Secretary of State; but such articles

How may be incorporated.

Articles of association, what to set forth and where to be filed.

shall not be so filed until there is annexed thereto an affidavit, made by at least three of such Trustees, that the amount of stock required by this section has been in good faith subscribed, and that twenty per cent. thereon has been paid in; and thereupon the persons who have subscribed said articles, with such other persons as may from time to time become donors to such Institution, or if said articles of association so declare, the Trustees elected as herein provided, shall be a body corporate and politic, capable of suing and being sued, and may have a common seal, which they may make and alter at pleasure, and be capable in law of receiving by gift, subscription, bequest, will, donation or devise, and of purchasing, holding and conveying any real estate or personal property whatever, for the purpose of founding, establishing and conducting any such College, Seminary, Academy, or other Institution of Learning.

Powers of corporation.

Certified copy of Articles and affidavit made evidence.

Sec. 2. A copy of any such articles of association filed in pursuance of this Act, with a copy of the affidavit annexed thereto, and certified by the Secretary of State to be a copy, shall, in all Courts and places, be presumptive evidence of the incorporation of such Institution, and of all the facts therein stated.

Additional powers of College or Seminary incorporated under this act.

Sec. 3. The Trustees of any College or Seminary incorporated under the provisions of this Act, besides the general powers and privileges of a Corporation, shall have power:

1. To elect their own chairman or clerk;

2. Upon the death, resignation, or other vacancy in the office of any Trustee, to elect another in his place;

3. To declare vacant the seat of any Trustee who shall absent himself from five successive meetings of the Board;

4. To take and hold, by gift, grant, or devise, any real or personal property, the annual income or revenue of which shall not exceed twenty-five thousand dollars;

5. To sell, mortgage, let, or otherwise use such property,

in such manner as they shall deem most conducive to the educational interests of such Corporation;

6. To direct and prescribe the course of study and discipline to be observed in the College, Seminary or Academy: *Provided*, That no religious test whatever shall be required of any pupil in such Institution;

7. To appoint a President, Professors, Tutors, and such other officers and agents as they may deem necessary, who shall hold their offices during the pleasure of the Trustees;

8. To grant such literary honors as are usually granted by any such College, or similar Institutions in the United States, and in testimony thereof to give suitable Diplomas, under their seal, and the signatures of such officers of the Institution as they may deem expedient: *Provided*, That the course of study pursued in such College be, in all respects, as thorough and comprehensive as is usually pursued in similar Institutions in the United States;

9. To ascertain and fix the salaries of the President, Professors, and other officers and agents;

10. And to make all ordinances and by-laws necessary and proper to carry into effect the foregoing powers.

Effect of Diploma.

Sec. 4. Every Diploma granted by such Trustees, shall entitle the possessor to all the immunities which, by usage or statute, are allowed to possessors of similar Diplomas granted by any similar Institution in the United States.

Additional powers of Trustees of Academy incorporated under this act.

Sec. 5. The Trustees of any Academy incorporated under the provisions of this Act, besides the general powers and privileges of a Corporation, shall have power:

1. To take and hold, by gift, grant, subscription, bequest, or devise, any property, personal or real, the annual income or revenue of which shall not exceed four thousand dollars;

2. To sell, mortgage, let, or otherwise use and dispose of such property for the benefit of such Academy;

3. To direct and prescribe the course of study and discipline in such Academy;

4. To appoint a Treasurer, Clerk, Principal, and such other officers and agents as they shall deem necessary, who shall hold their offices during the pleasure of the Trustees;

5. To ascertain and fix the salaries of all the officers of the Academy;

6. To make all ordinances and by-laws necessary to carry into effect the foregoing powers.

Corporation subject to Visitation and Examination.

Sec. 6. Any institution incorporated under the provisions of this Act, shall be always subject to the visitation and examination of the Superintendent of Public Instruction, and also to a Board of Visitors (three in number,) to be annually appointed by said Superintendent; and said Visitors shall report to said Superintendent as soon after an examination as practicable.

Funds, how to be applied.

Sec. 7. The Trustees of any institution incorporated under the provisions of this act, shall apply all funds and property belonging thereto, according to their best judgment, to the promotion of its objects and interests: *Provided*, That any gift, bequest or donation to such institution for any specific object, shall be faithfully applied to the object specified by such donor.

Officers may be required to give bond, etc.

Sec. 8. The Trustees of any institution incorporated under the provisions of this act, may require the Treasurer, and all other officers and agents, before entering upon the duties ot their respective offices, to give bonds and securities in such sums as they may deem proper and sufficient.

Trustees to report to Superintendent of Public Instruction.

Sec. 9. Such Trustees shall be required, on or before the first day of December, annually, to report to the Superintendent of Public Instruction, a statement of the name of each Trustee, Officer, Teacher and student of such Institution, with a statement of its property, the amount of stock subscribed, donated and bequeathed, and the amount actually paid in, and such other information as will tend to exhibit its condition and operations. And said Trustees shall be severally and jointly liable for all the labor performed for the Corporation; but no execution shall issue against any Trustee, till an execution against the Corporation shall have been returned unsatisfied, in whole or in part; and no such Trustee shall be thus liable, unless suit for the collection of such debt shall have been brought against said Corporation within one year after such debt shall have become due.

Liability of Trustees for labor performed. Const. Art. 15, Sec. 7.

Sec. 10. Service of legal process on any such Corporation, may be made on any one of the Trustees thereof, if such Trustee be in the county in which the Institution is located; but if not, then by leaving a copy of such process with any officer in the employ thereof, at its principal place of business.

How service of process to be made on corporation.

Sec. 11. Any Institution of Learning now in existence in this State, whether incorporated or not, shall be entitled to all the benefits of this act, by complying with the provisions of this act; and may, by a vote of the majority of such Corporation or unincorporated Company or Association, to be taken according to the act of incorporation, by-laws, or other legal regulations thereof, determine to avail itself of the provisions of this act, and to take and assume corporate name and powers thereunder, and may, by a like vote, transfer to such Corporation, formed under this act, all its property, both real, personal and mixed; and thereupon said Corporation, to which such property is so transferred, shall take the same in the same manner, to the same extent, and with the like effect as the same was previously owned and held by the Corporation, Company or Association so transferring the same, and may, in its own corporate name, sue for and collect all debts, dues, demands, subscriptions, devises and bequests thereof. The said Corporation so taking such property as aforesaid, shall take the same subject to all liens, trusts, and limitations, both legal and equitable, to which the same was subject before such transfer, and shall also be liable for all the debts and obliga-

Existing institutions may become incorporated under this act.

Rights, powers and liabilities of such new corporation.

tions of such previous Corporation, Company or Association, and shall pay the same to the full extent of the value of such property at the time of so taking the same.

Restriction upon powers of corporation.

Sec. 12. Nothing in this act shall be construed as granting banking powers, or as allowing the business of brokerage, or any other powers not usually granted to, or exercised by institutions for educational purposes.

Report to be made to Superintendent of Public Instruction.

Sec. 13. It shall be the duty of the President of the Board of Trustees of every organized Academy, or Literary or Collegiate Institution, heretofore incorporated or hereafter to be incorporated, to cause to be made out by the principal Instructor, or other proper officer, and forwarded, by mail or otherwise, to the office of the Superintendent of Public Instruction, between the first and fifteenth days of December, in each year, a report, setting forth the amount and estimated value of real estate owned by the Corporation, the amount of other funds and endowments, and the yearly income from all sources, the number of Instructors, the number of students in the different classes, the studies pursued, and the books used, the course of instruction, the terms of tuition, and such other matters as may be specially requested by said Superintendent, or as may be deemed proper by the President or Principal of such Academies or Institutes, to enable the Superintendent of Public Instruction to lay before the Legislature a fair and full exhibit of the affairs and condition of said Institutions.(1)

Contents of Report.

(1) Section 13, passed March 4, 1859. [Compiled Laws, p. 768.]

NOTES ON THE SCHOOL LAW.

OFFICE OF PUBLIC INSTRUCTION,
Lansing, Mich., Nov. 6th, 1858.

The Superintendent of Public Instruction, in obedience to Chapter 56, Section 2, of the Revised Statutes, [Compiled Laws, Chapter 74, Section 3,] has prepared Notes on the foregoing Laws, with Forms and instructions for conducting proceedings under them, and has caused the same to be printed, together with other laws now in force relating to Education. These laws, as here printed, will be found to differ in several Sections from the Revised Statutes, and in a few instances from the Compiled Laws, being here printed as amended from time to time. These amendments have become so numerous, that the Revised Statutes of 1846 are no longer a safe guide for School Officers.

The words "the purchase of," which were omitted in the eighth line of Section 23, Chapter 78, of the Compiled Laws, are here inserted, between the words "for" and "globes;" and the words "the purpose of" have been omitted in the next line, to correspond with the enrolled copy of the Revised Statutes, in the office of the Secretary of State, passed and approved May 18th, 1846. For a like reason, the word "reserving" has been stricken out of Section 59, and "securing" has been inserted in its stead. The word "five" has likewise been stricken out of Section 22, and "four" has been inserted in its place. The last correction specified is made in the Compiled Laws. But by mistake, the word which is printed "first," in Section

11 of the same Chapter of the Compiled Laws, should have been "last." This correction is here made. A few other typographical errors have also been corrected. But these corrections have generally been stated in notes appended to the sections where they occur.

In printing this edition of the Primary School Laws, the sections of the recent enactments have been consecutively numbered, and appended to those of Chapter seventy eight of the Compiled Laws. But a foot note in each instance shows when the sections inserted were enacted, and where they may be found.

Questions frequently arise in the administration of the School Law which cannot be satisfactorily settled in the districts and townships in which they originate. The Superintendent is, hence, frequently called upon to give his opinion in relation to the true meaning and proper construction of the School Law. This has given rise to a very extensive and laborious correspondence. And yet, hundreds of letters of inquiry, have often too long remained unanswered, for the want of clerical assistance to perform the necessary business of this office. In the publication of this edition of the School Law, the Superintendent has endeavored to anticipate and answer such questions as most commonly arise, and he hopes the following NOTES will not only save the trouble and expense of a correspondence hitherto deemed necessary, but, what is frequently an object of greater importance and solicitude, obviate a tedious delay, and facilitate the dispatch of business. It is thought they may also be instrumental in inducing greater uniformity in the administration of the School Law, and save many a School District from dissentions which frequently terminate in their disorganization.

IRA MAYHEW,
Superintendent of Public Instruction.

NOTE A.

[See Sections 5, 6, 7, 11, 12, 13, 28, 130 and 149]

WHEN A DISTRICT IS ORGANIZED—WHAT BUSINESS MAY BE TRANSACTED AT THE FIRST MEETING OF A DISTRICT.

The following questions are frequently asked at this office:

1st. Can a District at its first meeting for organization, having elected its officers, proceed to the transaction of other business as at annual or special meetings?

It cannot.

In case the officers elected at the first meeting of a School District after its formation, are present, and certify their acceptance of the offices to which they have been respectively chosen, the District may be considered duly organized. If, however, the officers chosen are not present, or being present, do not file with the Director certificates of acceptance, the District is not organized. In neither case does the law contemplate the transaction of other business at the first meeting. Officers may be elected at the first meeting of a District, and at annual meetings, but not at special meetings. Any lawful business may be transacted at an annual meeting. But all business to be done at special meetings must be set forth in the notices calling the same. In case two, at least, of the officers elected at the first meeting of a School District, file their certificate of acceptance with the Director, within ten days from the time of their election, the District is duly organized. A special meeting may then be called, as in other cases, for the transaction of any lawful business. Otherwise it will be necessary to commence proceedings anew, according to the provisions of section 7.

2d. May District officers be elected by a plurality vote?

They may be so elected.

As far as the Constitution or Laws of our State make specific provision in relation to the election of State, county, or town officers, it is by a plurality of votes.

Section 3, of Article 5, of the Constitution, in providing for the election of Governor and Lieut. Governor, says, "The person having the highest number of votes shall be elected."

Sections 7 and 52, of Chapter 6, and section 45, of Chapter 12, of the Compiled Laws, provide that all officers elected at general and township elections, shall be chosen by a plurality vote, the person having the greatest number of votes being elected. As this is the only manner of electing officers known to our laws, it may be inferred that all officers shall be elected in like manner.

3d. Who are eligible to hold office in a School District?

All qualified voters. No other conclusion can be drawn from sections two, five and fifteen.

4th. Who are qualified voters?

Section 15 provides that "every white male inhabitant of the age of twenty-one years, residing in the District, and liable to pay a School District tax[1] therein, shall be entitled to vote at any District meeting." Section 147 further provides that the words "qualified voters," as here used, "shall be taken and construed to mean and include all taxable persons residing in the District, of the age of twenty-one years, and who have resided therein for the period of three months next preceding the time of voting," without any restriction on account of nationality or sex.

5th. May a Director file his acceptance of office with himself? He may.

Sections 5 and 28 seem to contemplate that the incoming officers shall file their acceptance with the outgoing Director. But if, from the absence of the old Director, or from other cause, the books and papers of the office come into the hands of the Director elect within ten days, on filing his acceptance within that time, the design of the law will be fully met, and he may properly be regarded as a qualified officer.

(1) For liability to taxation, see Compiled Laws, pp. 287 to 291.

6th. Can an annual District meeting be legally held in case the Director omits to give the notice required by sections 13 and 50?

It can be legally held.

The time of holding the annual meeting is fixed by law. The neglect of the Director to give notice may subject him to a fine, but it cannot deprive the inhabitants of the District of the exercise of a legal right. They may lawfully meet at the usual time and place of holding meetings, and transact all necessary business. See sections 11, 13, 14 and 50.

NOTE B.

[See Sections 19, 20, 22, 150 and 151.]

SITE FOR SCHOOL-HOUSE—WHAT AMOUNT MAY BE RAISED FOR BUILDING A SCHOOL-HOUSE.

Section 19 provides that a site for a School-house may be established, or changed, by a vote of two-thirds of the voters present at any regular meeting. In case no site can be thus established, Section 20 authorizes the School Inspectors to locate a site, which shall be subject to alteration only by the Inspectors.

Section 150 provides that Districts containing more than three hundred children within the legal ages, may establish any number of sites they may deem necessary, not exceeding five; and that in case *two-thirds* of the voters cannot agree upon a site, a *majority* shall have power to instruct the District Board to locate a site.

Section 151, and Sections following, provide for determining the price of a site in case of a disagreement between the owner thereof and the District.

Although but $200 can be raised in any one year in a District where there are not more than thirty scholars between the ages of four and eighteen years, and but $300 where there are but fifty scholars between those ages, yet a more valuable house may be built, provided the District desire it, by raising these sums annually, until a sufficient amount is collected.

In case the number of scholars in the District between the ages of four and eighteen years, exceeds fifty, there is no limitation to the tax for purchasing or building a School-house. The qualified voters of a School District may, in such cases, raise for that purpose any sum which, in their judgment, may be necessary. Section 163 empowers Districts having more than three hundred children within the legal ages, to loan money for the purpose of purchasing sites and building School-houses, in certain cases.

NOTE C.

[See Sections 24, 25, 26 and 80]

A SCHOOL MONTH—A SCHOOL DAY—POWER OF SPECIAL MEETINGS.

There is a great diversity of opinion and practice in relation to the word "month," when applied to Schools. In some cases a School is taught five days in a week for four weeks, making twenty days for a month. More commonly, however, the School is taught four weeks for a month, allowing the Teacher to dismiss the School Saturday afternoon, or all day every other Saturday, without losing time, which gives twenty-two working days to a month. In other instances, the School is taught twenty-six working days for a month.

The following is the law on this subject, with the construction of this Department: [See Compiled Laws, Chapter 1, Section 3, Subdivision 10 :] "In the construction of the statutes of this State, the following rules shall be observed, unless such construction shall be inconsistent with the manifest intent of the Legislature, that is to say: * * * * 10. The word 'month' shall be construed to mean a calendar month," &c. This gives, on an average, four and one-third weeks, or twenty-six days, for a month, exclusive of Sundays.

From a long established and time-honored usage, however, School may be dismissed every Saturday afternoon, or all day every other Saturday, where the latter custom prevails, without the Teacher's losing time. A School may also be omitted, without loss of time, on days ordinarily observed as holidays, embracing the 4th of July, New Year's, Christmas, and days appointed by the Chief Magistrate for public thanksgiving.

According to Section 80, no District is entitled to draw public money unless a School has been taught therein three months by a qualified Teacher, during the School year last closed, at the time of each annual distribution of School moneys.

In the absence of specific legislation, common usage has established the custom of teaching School six hours a day, commencing at nine o'clock in the morning, and at or about one o'clock in the afternoon. This, then, may be considered as constituting a school-day, in the absence of a specific agreement between the Teacher and the School District. It is competent, however, for School Districts to vary these hours, and to contract with their Teachers, accordingly.

The opinion of this Department has been repeatedly solicited concerning the validity of instructions given by a special meeting in relation to the length of time a School shall be taught, the employment of a male or female Teacher, or both, and the application of the public money to the winter or summer School, or to both, when no instructions had been given at the annual meeting.

From the specific language of section 25, the Superintendent entertains the opinion that whenever these matters are not determined at the annual meeting, the District Board has sole power, and that it is their duty to determine them. A special meeting may advise or recommend, but not direct. The Superintendent will add: If the winter and summer Schools are taught about the same length of time—say four or five months each—and a Teacher is employed in the winter for $17 a month, and in the summer for $2 a week, (which is $8 67 per month,) an equitable division would, in ordinary cases, give two-thirds of the public money to the winter School, and one-third to the summer School.

Any and all business that may lawfully come before an annual meeting, may be transacted at special meetings, provided proper notice has been given, except such as is specifically restricted by law to annual meetings. (See Sections 5, 24 and 25.)

NOTE D.

[See Sections 28, 66, 67 and 95.]

WHEN A DISTRICT LOSES ITS ORGANIZATION—WHEN VACANCIES OCCUR—HOW SUPPLIED.

The opinion of this Department is frequently solicited in relation to the proper construction of section 28. The Superintendent entertains the opinion that if a District is properly organized, it does not lose its organization by neglecting to hold *one* annual meeting. In such cases, the District Officers hold over a second term, and are the legal officers of the District for two years from the time of their election, but not to exceed ten days thereafter, without being again elected or appointed.

In case ten days elapse after the time for holding the *second* annual meeting of a School District, without an election of officers, the District loses its organization. A new organization can then be had, only in accordance with the provisions of the first five sections of the Primary School Law.

The occurrence of any of the following events will create a vacancy in a School District office:

1. The death of the incumbent;
2. His resignation;
3. His removal from office;
4. His removal from the District;
5. His conviction of any infamous crime;
6. His election or appointment being declared void by a competent tribunal;
7. His neglect to file his acceptance of office, or to give or renew any official bond, according to law. (Compiled Laws, Chap. 11, Sec. 3, p. 219.)

Section 66 authorizes the District Board to fill, by appointment, any vacancy that shall occur in their number, and makes it their duty to do so within ten days after its occurrence. Either two members of the Board may fill any vacancy that shall occur by the legal inability of the third to discharge the duties of his office.

In case the District Board do not supply any vacancy within ten days after its occurrence, Section 95 further provides that the School Inspectors shall fill the same by appointment. (See Forms Nos. 15 and 16.)

IRREGULARITIES.

An irregularity in the manner of electing District Officers does not render their official acts void; and where a District Officer fails to file his acceptance of office, or where an Assessor fails to give bonds, his acts are not hence illegal.

A person who has been elected at a District meeting to any office, and who has the general reputation of being such officer, is an officer *in fact*, although he may not be an officer by right; and all his acts, so far as the District and third persons are concerned in them, are legal and binding.

If the meeting at which a person was elected was not

strictly legal; or if an officer fails to file his acceptance of office according to law; or if an Assessor fails to give bonds; or, if such persons are elected as are incapable of holding such office, as minors, non-residents, &c., such want of compliance with law, or irregularity, does not render their official acts illegal, although it be established that the *holding* of such office *is* illegal. If an officer fails to comply with the requirements of law, he is liable to its penalties; and if an acting officer holds an office by an illegal tenure, his right to hold said office may be determined by an appeal to the proper tribunal; but no person would be justified in withholding a District tax, because of some irregularity in the election of officers who levied it, or of the Assessor who is collecting it.

In a decision of the Supreme Court of New York, (5 *Wendell*, p. 234,) after citing many cases involving the above principle, the Court said:

"It will be observed that these cases do not go upon the ground that the claim by an individual to be a public officer, and by acting as such, is merely *prima facia* evidence that he is an officer *de jure*, (of right,) but the principle they establish is this: that an individual coming into office by color of an election or appointment, is an officer *de facto*, (in fact,) and his acts in relation to the public, or third persons, are valid, until he is removed, although it be conceded that his election or appointment was illegal."

Another case was decided as follows:

"In the case of *Trustees* and *Collectors* of *School Districts*, general reputation of their being such officers, and proof of their acting as such, is *prima facia* sufficient, without producing evidence of their election, especially where there is evidence of their acting under color of an election." (7 Wendell Rep., p. 341.)

NOTE E.

[See Sections 48, 49 and 65.]

SCHOOL-HOUSES, RELIGIOUS MEETINGS, REPAIRS, ETC.

Questions like the following are often asked:

1st. May School-houses be used for religious worship, Sunday schools, temperance meetings, etc., when there is a respectable minority of the District opposed?

2d. Have a portion of the inhabitants of a District the right to use a false key, or break a lock to obtain possession of a School-house?

The reply has been substantially as follows:

1st. The Director of a School District and the District Board have the care and custody of the School-house, according to Sections 48 and 65. But they have the custody of it only for the purposes specified in the act from which they derive their authority, viz: for Common School purposes. They have strictly no more right to allow it to be used for religious meetings, than the Trustees of a religious society have to allow the church or meeting-house to be used for School purposes. There would be no impropriety in allowing each to be used for both purposes, if there were no objection on the part of the District or members of the society.

In country neighborhoods and small villages, where there are no meeting-houses, and the citizens of a District consent to the occupancy of the School-house for the purposes named in the first question above, I can see no impropriety in its being thus used. The object of Sunday schools is so nearly identical with that of Common Schools, that it would seem hardly proper to close the School-house against them. But when controversies grow out of the occupancy of a School-house for other purposes than those contemplated by law, it is the duty of the District Board to confine its use strictly to legitimate objects. The law has determined the purposes for which a School-house may be used. It may be otherwise used only by general consent. It should not be opened on a majority vote, or even on a two-thirds vote, for any purpose that is likely to distract the District or breed dissensions.

2d. Every School-house should be furnished with a lock and key, and be kept locked whenever it is not occupied. No person is justifiable in breaking a lock, or otherwise forcibly obtaining possession of a School-house.

These views are in unison with the decisions of the School Department in New York and other States, and if properly heeded, will, doubtless, in many cases obviate serious difficulties.

Sections 48 and 49 make it the duty of the Director to provide the necessary appendages for the School-house, and keep the same in good repair during the time a School shall be taught therein. They also make it his duty to keep an accurate account of all expenses incurred by him as Director, and present the same for allowance to the qualified voters of the District, at a regular meeting. They further provide that the amount of such account, as allowed by the meeting, shall be assessed and collected in the same manner as other District taxes. These provisions, however good, are nevertheless defective, unless supplemental action is taken on the part of the District. There may arise cases, and do not unfrequently, in which it becomes necessary for the Director to advance money, and lay out of the use of the same more than a year. The duties of the Director are onerous, and it is unjust to require him to advance money. Many Districts have hence very appropriately anticipated the probable expense it would be necessary to incur for repairs, and have voted a tax to cover the same, at the annual meeting. This tax is collected early in the winter, and placed at the disposal of the Director, who, at the end of the year, is required to account therefor. The propriety of the general adoption of this course is commended to whom it may concern.

NOTE F.

[See Sections 71, 75, 86, 91 and 138]

ALTERATION OF SCHOOL DISTRICTS — DIVISION OF DISTRICT PROPERTY — APPORTIONMENT OF SCHOOL MONEYS — DRAWING BOOKS.

School Inspectors, by examining Section 71 alone, sometimes proceed to district a township, and to alter the boundaries of Districts already established, without giving any notice thereof. Great dissatisfaction is frequently and justly the result of such a course. The School Inspectors may not be able to please every person residing in Districts they are required to establish. This, indeed, might often be incompatible with the conscientious discharge of their official duty. They should, nevertheless, do what they reasonably can to harmonize conflicting interests; and in order to do this, they must give aggrieved individuals, and all others interested, a reasonable opportunity for a hearing. This they may do by giving the notice required by Sections 86 and 91, which should invariably be done.

The Superintendent would caution Inspectors against subdividing Districts any farther than becomes actually necessary to accommodate the citizens of a township. Large and populous Districts are able to build good School-houses, and employ well qualified Teachers; while small and feeble Districts sometimes feel compelled to occupy unsuitable houses, and to depend upon the services of incompetent Teachers. It is better to go a mile and a half, or even two miles, if need be, to reach a good School, than to reside within half a mile of an indifferent one. But where the citizens of a neighborhood are so situated as to be practically unable to avail themselves of the advantages of any existing School District, and wish to be set off, and can be without detriment to the rights of others, the Inspectors should pay a due regard to their wishes.

Section 71 provides that no land shall be taxed for building a School-house, unless some portion of every legal subdivision of said land shall be within two and a half miles of said School-house site.

The smallest "legal subdivision" of land is one-fourth of a quarter section, or forty acres.

Section 75 provides that when a new District is formed, wholly or in part, from one or more Districts possessed of a School-house, or entitled to other property, it shall be the duty of the Inspectors, at the time of forming such new District, to ascertain and determine the amount justly due to it from any District out of which it may have been wholly or in part formed, as the proportion to which such new District is entitled of the value of the School-house and other property belonging to the former District at the time of such division.

The mode of ascertaining the amount due to said new District, and of collecting and paying over the same, is pointed out in the three following sections, to wit: 76, 77 and 78. But as the frequent inquiries made of this Department indicate an imperfect understanding of the subject, an effort is here made to elucidate it.

Absolute justice cannot always be done in case of the division of Districts. The law seems to contemplate that when a part of a District, possessed of a School-house, or owning other property, is set off and attached to another District owning a School-house, or other property, the interest received is an equivalent for the interest left, although one house may be more valuable than the other. But in case the old District has a School-house, or other property, which it retains, and the part set off goes to a new District which has no such property, it is the intention of the law to remunerate that part of the old District thus set off, for the interest it had in a School-house it leaves, to associate itself with a new District possessing no such property. This remuneration is reached on this wise: Let A. B. represent the District possessed of a School-house, and let C. represent an adjacent unorganized territory owning no School-house. The Inspectors set off that portion of the former District represented by B., and unite it with the previously unorganized territory C., and form a new District, represented by B. C., possessing no School-house, or other property. The sections referred to make it the duty of the Inspectors to decide what the School-house owned by the original District A. B., is worth, and the value of the interest B. had in the same, after the payment of any debts the original District A. B. may have owed. The District A., which retains the School-house, owes the new District B. C. for interest left by B. This amount is assessed by the Supervisor on the District A., and when collected it is paid to the Assessor of the new District B. C. This amount the new District B. C. receives as an equivalent for what B. relinquishes in the old District A. B. This amount is retained by the new District B. C., until they require more money for building a School-house, or for other District purposes. The amount, then, which the new District B. C. received from A., is to be placed to the credit of the property represented by B., in reduction of what would otherwise have been a tax thereon. Thus, District A. pays the new District B. C. for the interest B. had in their School-house, and when B. C. raises a District tax, C. remunerates B. for the money received of A. in reduction of the amount that would otherwise have been a tax upon B.

A neglect on the part of the Board of School Inspectors to determine the amount due to a new District at the time of making the division, does not invalidate the proceedings, nor render void the claim of the new District upon the old. The claim of the new District upon the old should be provided for at the time of making the division. But if neglected then, it should be estimated and determined by the Inspectors making the division, at the earliest practicable period thereafter.

The principle here illustrated applies in the division of taxes under the provisions of Section 138.

The following embrace the substance of a large number of questions that have been forwarded to this office from time to time:

1st. When a regularly organized School District, in which a School has been taught the time required by law, is divided so late in the school year, as not to allow time for a School to be taught three months before the expiration of the year, does the part set off lose its School money for the ensuing year?

2d. If the division takes place after the annual report is made, and before the School money is received, does the original District receive all the public money, or is the part set off entitled to a portion of it?

3d. Is the part set off entitled to draw books from the Township Library, before the beginning of a new School year; or, in other words, until after the Director makes his annual report to the School Inspectors? or can the original District claim and receive, to the end of the year, all the books it would have been entitled to, had there been no division?

The opinion of the Superintendent, in relation to these several questions, is as follows:

1st. Whenever a School District is divided, each of the Districts formed from it has a right, in making its annual report, to embrace the time a School was taught between the commencement of the School year, and the time the division was made, and to add thereto the time a School has been taught in said District subsequently to the division. If each District, reckoning time thus, is enabled to report a School taught three months or more, by qualified Teachers, each is entitled to draw public money. But if either District, reckoning time thus, is unable to report a School taught three months by qualified Teachers, said District is not entitled to draw public money.

2d. In the distribution of School moneys to said Districts, the same sum should be apportioned to the two, that the original District would have been entitled to receive had there been no division. This sum should be divided between them according to the rules of justice and equity. If the division of a District takes place immediately after the commencement of a School year, and before a School has been opened, the public money should be apportioned to the new Districts in proportion to the number of scholars within the legal ages residing in each of them at the time of the division. But if the division is made at the close of the winter School, and two thirds (more or less) of the public money has been apportioned to said School, in which both of the Districts were entitled to share equitably, the remaining one-third should be apportioned in proportion to the number of children within the legal ages, in the Districts at the time the division is made.

3d. Whenever a District is divided, the part set off, when duly organized, is entitled to draw books from the Township Library at the time for quarterly distribution among the Districts of the township, provided the Director files with the Township Librarian a statement of the number of scholars within his District at the time the division was made. The Director of the other District should do the same. The original District has no advantage over the one set off in relation to the use of the Library, nor in any other respect.

NOTE G.

[See Section 74.]

VISITING SCHOOLS.

Section 74 makes it the imperative duty of the Board of School Inspectors to "appoint one of their number to *visit each School in the township* having a qualified Teacher, *at least* ONCE *in each School term* in which a School is taught, who shall inquire into the condition of such Schools, examine the scholars, and give such advice to both Teachers and pupils as he may think beneficial."

Hitherto, in the majority of cases, so far as this Department has the means of knowing, no visitor has been appointed. Moreover, the majority of the Schools in the State have not been visited officially by the School Inspectors, once a year, according to the reports received at this office.

If the citizens of townships throughout the State would, at their annual township meeting, select good practical men for School Inspectors—the men best qualified to discharge the duties of the office, without any regard to personal or political considerations—and if the Inspectors would be faithful in the discharge of this duty, there can be but little reason to doubt that the Schools of the State would advance *twenty per cent.* in excellence, each of the next three years.

The Inspectors should, at their first meeting every year, appoint the best and most practical and efficient member of the Board, a VISITOR; and he should visit *every School* ONCE at least, as the law directs. It would be well for Inspectors to invite the citizens of Districts, so far as practicable, and especially District Boards, to accompany them in their visits.

The visiting of Schools is very commonly neglected from the mistaken impression that Inspectors are not entitled to pay while engaged in the discharge of this duty. But section 91, limiting the meetings of the Board of Inspectors at the expense of the township to six, has exclusive reference to *meetings of the Board.* This is a service not contemplated in that limitation. School Inspectors engaged in visiting Schools are entitled to pay for their services as when engaged in the discharge of other official duties. [See Compiled Laws, Title 5, Chapter 12, Sections 95 and 96.]

NOTE H.

(See Sections 81, 82, 83, 84, 139 and 146.)

FRACTIONAL SCHOOL DISTRICTS.

Section 81 has, in very many cases, been disregarded, and much perplexity and not a little inaccuracy has resulted from the organization of *Fractional Districts.* These difficulties might be almost entirely obviated by complying with the requisition of the law relating to them. If a township can be conveniently districted without, fractional Districts should not be formed. But, according to section 81, "whenever it shall become necessary to form a District from two or more adjoining townships, the Inspectors, or a majority of them, of each of such adjoining townships, may form such District, and direct which township Clerk shall make and deliver the notice of the formation of the same to a taxable inhabitant thereof, and may regulate and alter such District as circumstances shall render necessary. The Director of such District shall make an annual report to the Clerk of the towship in which the School-house is situated." In this report he should embrace all the children within the legal ages residing in the District, without regard to the township in which they live ; and none of them should be embraced in a regular report to any township in which the School-house is *not* situated.

Mark the following particulars:

1. In the formation of a fractional School District, the

concurrence of a *majority* of the Inspectors from *each* of *all* the townships from which it is formed, is necessary. Suppose it is contemplated to form a fractional District embracing a portion of the territory of three townships, and suppose *all* of the Inspectors from two of the townships, and *one* from the third, were in favor of its formation, (making 7-9ths of all the Inspectors from the three towns,) said District could not be formed. A District might be established from the two towns whose Inspectors approve of it. But if a majority of the Inspectors of any township, a portion of whose territory it is desirable should be embraced in a fractional District, are opposed to it, said territory must be omitted, unless the consent of said majority can be obtained.

2. Whenever and wherever a fractional District exists, said District cannot be dissolved, nor its boundaries be in any way modified, without the consent of a majority of the School Inspectors of *each township* from which the District is in part formed. The propriety of avoiding their organization, when it can be done without special inconvenience, is hence manifest.

3. Section 81 makes it the duty of the Director of a fractional District, to make his annual report "to the Clerk of the township in which the School-house is situated." No full report should be made by the Director to the Clerk of any other township than the one in which *the School-house is situated*, and if such report be made, it should be rejected by the Township Clerk. The report of the number of children within the legal ages, provided for by section 82, is of no use when the operation of section 115 is suspended by the Inspectors as provided for in section 146. But (see Sec. 82,) in addition thereto—

4. It is the duty of the Director to "report to the Clerk of each township in which the District is in part situated, the number of children between the ages of four and eighteen years in that part of the District lying in such town-

ship, and books shall be drawn from the library of each township for the use of such District; but the District shall have access to but one such library at the same time, and the said Inspectors shall establish the order in which books shall be drawn from each township library." Hence arises another inconvenience connected with Fractional Districts. They are entitled to draw books from the libraries of both or all of the townships in which they are in part situated, and hence have access to a greater number of books, it is true; but still, they are not, according to the provisions of the section under consideration, (82,) entitled to draw so many books at a time as single Districts of the same size. Suppose a District is situated in part, in each of three townships, having in the township A. 40 scholars between the ages of four and eighteen years, and in the townships B. and C. each 20, making 80 in all. The year the District draws books from township A., they are entitled to receive but *one-half* (40 is ½ of 80) of their equitable quota of books; and the years they draw from townships B. and C. but *one-fourth* (20 is ¼ of 80) their equitable proportion. Whatever might have been the *intention* of the Legislature, this is the only construction the language of the section will warrant.

Some School Inspectors will not allow books drawn from their Township Library to circulate in those parts of Fractional Districts situated in other townships. The statutes of the State provide that the Libraries of each of the several townships in which a Fractional District is in part situated, may circulate *throughout* said District; and this provision Inspectors consent to whenever they form a Fractional District. The only way of restricting the circulation of Township Libraries to the townships to which they belong, (in harmony with existing provisions of law,) is, to dispense with Fractional Districts.

5. For the manner of raising taxes for building School-houses and other purposes, see section 84.

6. In the formation of a new township from one or more towns, if the boundary line passes through an organized School District, said District is not hence dissolved, but it becomes a Fractional District, subject to the joint action of the Inspectors of both townships, as other Fractional Districts.

7. Joint Boards of Inspectors may attach to a Fractional District any person who may wish to be attached. They may also fill vacancies in such Fractional Districts.

8. The law does not provide specially for notices of meetings of joint Boards; but it would seem to be wise to pursue the same course the law requires of whole Districts, as far as it can be done, where the law has made no provisions.

9. Fractional Districts have the same powers as whole Districts, and their proceedings are the same in all cases, where the law does not direct otherwise.

10. A Fractional District may be formed out of two adjoining townships, in two adjoining counties.

11. For the manner of apportioning the income of the Primary School Fund, and moneys raised in the township, see section 139. The public money is distributed to the townships to which the annual report is made.

NOTE I.

[See Section 92.]

UNION SCHOOLS.

Section 92 contemplates the establishment of what are commonly known as "Union Schools," and which may be made to combine all the advantages of the ordinary Primary or Common School, the Acadamy for young gentlemen, and the Seminary for young ladies.

When two or more Districts are united in a Union District, all the property and liabilities of each are assumed by the new District thus formed.

For the Superintendent's views in relation to the utility of these Schools, course of study, and plans for School-houses, warming, ventilation, &c., see his Report, recently published, page 47 to 69, inclusive, and Part III, of this volume.

—

NOTE J.

[See Sections 97, 98, 106, 107, 140, 143, 144 and 145.]

MILL TAX—TAX OF ONE DOLLAR A SCHOLAR—OTHER TAXES—DUTIES OF THE SUPERVISOR, TREASURER AND CLERK.

The mill tax specified in section 107, has hitherto been unassessed, in many instances. Supervisors have sometimes excused themselves by saying it was not the wish of the citizens of their township that the tax should be assessed. It is made the imperative duty of the Supervisor to assess this tax, and a neglect or refusal to do so, renders him liable, as in other cases, for neglect of official duty.

By an amendment to section 140, in 1848, "the qualified voters of any School District may, by vote at their annual District meeting," raise a tax, on the taxable property in the District, as high as one dollar per scholar in the District. Under the previous law, but fifty cents per scholar could be raised, and that only at a township meeting, and to apply to every District in the township. Now, each District acts for itself, and may raise the means for educating its youth without asking the concurrence of other, and perhaps less enterprising Districts.

It is earnestly recommended to all the Districts of the State to avail themselves of this provision of law, and to do what they can toward rendering the instruction afforded in our Common Schools as *free* to all classes of children *as the air we breathe.*

In case the taxes required to be assessed by Section 106, are not reported to the Supervisor within the time specified in Section 56, it will be lawful and proper for him to make the assessment, if the amount is reported to him by the District Board at any time before he makes out his assessment roll.

And when the mill tax has been assessed and collected, it has often been erroneously applied, and especially in the case of fractional Districts. These Districts have sometimes drawn their *full proportion* of the mill tax from one township, and then drawn an additional sum from other townships in which they have been in part situated; and in other cases they have been deprived of their just dues. No uniform usage seems to have prevailed in its apportionment. The following exposition is therefore given, which it is hoped will lead to a uniform, equitable, and legal mode of apportioning the mill tax, which already amounts to considerably more than $100,000 a year.

1. Section 106 makes it the duty of the Supervisor to assess certain taxes that have been *voted by School Districts.* But Section 107 makes it his duty to assess upon the taxable property of his township, one mill on each dollar of the valuation thereof, *without any vote.* Twenty-five dollars of the mill tax is to be applied to the purchase of books for the Township Library, and the remainder thereof is to be apportioned to the several School Districts of the township for the support of Schools therein, as explained below.

Section 144 makes it the duty of the Supervisor, on the delivery of the warrant for the collection of taxes to the Township Treasurer, to deliver to said Treasurer a written statement, certified by him, of the amount of the mill tax levied upon any property lying within the boundaries of a fractional School District, a part of which is situated within his township, and the returns of which are made to the Clerk of another township *in which the School-house is situated;* and the said Township Treasurer is required to pay to the Treasurer of the township in which the School-house is situated, the amount of the taxes so levied, and certified to him by the Supervisor, for the use of such fractional School District.

2. Section 145 makes it the duty of each Treasurer of a township, to the Clerk of which the returns of any fractional School District shall be made, to apply to the Treasurer of any other township in which any part of such fractional District shall be situated, for any money raised thereon; and all moneys so received, said Treasurer must certify to the Township Clerk. There is thus brought into the treasury of each and every township, all the mill tax raised upon the property of all the whole Districts of each township, and upon all the property of all fractional Districts *whose School-houses are in the township;* and no Treasurer holds any money raised from a fraction of a District whose School-house is in *another* township. Sections 98 and 110 contemplate that the Treasurer shall notify the Township Clerk of the amount to be thus apportioned.

3. Section 98 then makes it the duty of the Township Clerk to apportion all such moneys among the several Districts in his township entitled to the same, in proportion to the number of children residing in the several Districts between the ages of four and eighteen years, as shall appear from the annual reports of Directors of School Districts, and in the same manner that Primary School Interest moneys are apportioned. It is apparent, hence, that *fractional* Districts are to be considered in every respect the same as *whole* Districts. And, *practically*, for School purposes, each township is treated as though it embraced all the territory of all fractional Districts *whose School-houses are in the township*, and none of the territory of any District whose School-house is in *another* township.

It is proper here to remark that the statutes relating to fractional School Districts are somewhat confused, and perhaps contradictory. It is evident that the *idea* of the law has somewhat changed in relation to them, since the publication of the Revised Statutes of 1846. Several sections have since that time been modified. Some have been repealed. Two were added in February, 1850, and four were added in June of the same year. These six added sections have been numbered 141, 142, 143, 144, 145 and 146, in the order of their enactment; and other sections have since been added.

It is a principle of law that whenever later enactments seem to conflict with the provisions of previous statutes, said statutes must be so interpreted as to harmonize with the later enactments. Thus, the latter clause of Section 139, enacted in 1846, must be so interpreted as to harmonize with the evident idea of Sections 144 and 145, these having been enacted in 1850. And especially will this be apparent, when we bear in mind that Section 140, as originally passed, provided for a *township tax* to be apportioned among the Districts of the township, whole and fractional, which tax might be voted in some townships and not in others; and that this Section has since been repealed, and with it, essentially, the latter clause of Section 189, (embraced in brackets,) upon which it depended. When Section 140 stood, as originally enacted, *the ends of justice* required the application of the preceding clause in its apportionment. But Section 140, as it now stands, provides that *each District*, whether whole or fractional, may vote a *District tax* for the support of Schools in the District. Said clause is now not only unnecessary, but it is incompatible with the manifest intent of Sections since enacted. It is hence to be regarded as *void*.

NOTE K.

[See Sections 51, 52, 73, 107, 114, 116, 118 and 131.]

TOWNSHIP LIBRARIES.

Section 114 provides that "a Township Library shall be established in each organized township in this State."

Township officers, charged with the assessment of taxes for Township Libraries, and with the application of the same and other moneys required by law to be appropriated to the purchase of said Libraries, and not otherwise, have sometimes taken the responsibility, contrary to the express provisions of the Constitution and statutes of the State, to apply those moneys to meet current county and township expenses. This, I am informed, has been done for the purpose of establishing the reputation of conducting an economical administration, and of thereby securing the continuance of their places!!

It is not the prerogative of any man or set of men to say whether they will have a Library established in their township or not. The Section referred to requires their establishment; and Sections 107 and 116 provide that certain moneys "shall be applied to the purchase of books for the Township Library, and for no other purpose."

Article 13, Section 12 of the Constitution of the State also expressly provides that "all fines assessed and collected in the several counties and townships for any breach of the penal laws, shall be exclusively applied to the support of such Libraries."

Boards of Supervisors have, in several instances that have come to my knowledge, applied these moneys to other purposes. They are individually liable to forfeit one hundred dollars for each such offence. [See Compiled Laws, p. 197, Sec. 31.]

The reports of the Superintendent for past years clearly show that wherever Township Libraries have been established and properly maintained, they have been productive of incalculable good.

A misapprehension seems to have arisen in the minds of many persons, (and some School officers charged with the purchase and care of Township Libraries,) in relation to the design of their establishment. The phraseology of Sections 52, 114 and 117, has evidently a tendency to mislead. It was never the design of the Legislature to have the Township Libraries distributed, indiscriminately, among the children of the townships between the ages of four and eighteen years, and to no others, as has been, in some instances, practiced.

It is the design of our Township Libraries to furnish profitable and instructive reading to all persons who have access to them.

The great majority of the children of the State between the ages of four and ten years, cannot, perhaps, read ordinary Library books with either interest or profit. For such these Libraries were never designed. But young persons *over eighteen years of age*—members of families that are entitled to draw books belonging to Township Libraries—(as well as younger ones who are able to read understandingly,) should be encouraged to avail themselves of the privilege of these Libraries, until they contract the *habit* of reading; and the character of our Libraries should be such as to afford readers generally, entertaining, instructive, and profitable employment. Then, and not till then, will the design of their establishment be fully met.

INCREASE OF TOWNSHIP LIBRARIES.

Section 107 of the Primary School Law provides that $25 of the mill tax, which is raised every year, shall be applied to the purchase of books for the Township Library. Section 116 provides that the clear proceeds of fines, penalties, etc., be also applied to the purchase of books for the Township Library, and for no other purpose. The amount of Library money arising from these two sources often exceeds $50 a year.

The School Inspectors are charged with the application of these moneys in the purchase of books for the Library, which imposes upon them a difficult and important duty. They may consult the lists recommended pursuant to provisions of law by this Department, and other lists. But they must decide for themselves what they will have, and make the purchase.

The Superintendent would counsel the Inspectors to purchase chiefly standard works; and when they have an opportunity of doing so advantageously, they may anticipate moneys to come into their hands, and give their warrant on the Township Treasurer therefor, in payment of books so purchased.

The following, and other similar questions, have been repeatedly proposed to the Superintendent:

1st. "Are the School Inspectors liable for dividing the Library money among the Districts, to be used for School purposes, after the township has voted it to be done?"

2d. "When the town has voted to have the Township Library divided among the School Districts, what is the duty of the School Inspectors?"

My reply has uniformly been substantially as follows:

1st. The School Inspectors are liable to any aggrieved party for appropriating the Library money to any other purpose than the purchase of a Township Library. A vote of the annual township meeting to have the Inspectors disregard the Constitution and Statutes of the State affords no sufficient reason for their doing so. They should obey the law of the State while it remains law, and keep inviolate their official oaths.

2d. In case the citizens of a town vote to have their Township Library divided among the School Districts of the township, it is the duty of the School Inspectors to do just as though no such vote had been taken,—viz: to discharge their duty according to law,—and they are amenable to any aggrieved person or persons if they neglect or refuse to do so.

But old and damaged books, and books that are deemed unsuitable for the Township Library, in case such have at any time been purchased, may be disposed of in the discretion of the Inspectors, and the proceeds thereof be applied to the purchase of new books.

The Superintendent, in pursuance of the requirements of chapter 74, section 3, of the Compiled Laws, recommends the following

RULES FOR THE GOVERNMENT OF TOWNSHIP LIBRARIES.

1. *Duties of Librarian.*

1. The Township Librarian shall keep a catalogue of all the books belonging to the Township Library, in a blank book to be provided for that purpose, and he shall be accountable to the township for their safe keeping. In said book he shall enter in a legible hand, the *title* and *number* of each book belonging to the Library, with such additions as may from time to time be made thereto.

2. He shall label each book belonging to the Township Library, before it is drawn therefrom, thus :

"*Lansing Township Library.* *No.*——

"This book is returnable to the Director the last Saturday of every month. The drawer is responsible for all damages done to it while in his possession."

The preceding label should, if practicable, be *neatly printed*, and snugly pasted on the inner side of the cover. Where "Lansing" is used, the name of the township to which the Library belongs should be inserted. The number of the several volumes should be filled with a pen, commencing with No. 1.

3. Section 51 provides that "the Director shall draw from the Township Library, the proportion of books to which the District may be entitled, and return the same to the Township Library at the expiration of every three months." The times for drawing books from the Township Library, and returning the same, shall be the first Saturday of January, April, July and October, between the hours of 12 M. and 3 o'clock P. M.

According to section 115, the books of the Township

Library are to be distributed by the Township Librarian among the several Districts of the township, in proportion to the number of children in each, between the ages of four and eighteen years, as the same shall appear by the last report of the Director thereof. [See Note H., 4th particular.] But all maps, charts, engravings and lexicons, belonging to the Library shall remain therein, and at all proper times be open to inspection by the citizens of the township.

4. The Librarian shall, in a book to be provided for that purpose, charge every Director with the books he may draw from the Township Library, by their *numbers;* and in like manner credit the same when they shall be returned.

5. He shall make a written report to the School Inspectors, between the 25th and 31st days of March in each year, setting forth the number of books in the Library, and their condition. The report shall also state what books have been added to the Library during the year; what books have been lost, if any; what injured; and what amount of fines have been imposed and collected; together with such other particulars as the Inspectors shall direct; which report shall be placed on file with the papers of their office.

2. *Directors to Draw Books.*

1. No person, except Directors of School Districts, shall be permitted to draw books from the Township Library; nor shall *they* be entitled to draw at any other times than specified above. Nevertheless the Librarian may allow Directors who have not drawn books for any quarter, to receive them at other times.

2. None but inhabitants of School Districts shall be entitled to draw books from the Directors; and no Director shall loan a book to any person who is not a resident of his District.

3. No person shall be permitted to draw more than one

book at a time, unless there are books enough in the library to accommodate all persons that are entitled to draw therefrom. And in no case shall any person be permitted to draw, at one time, more than one book for himself, and one for each member of his family that is able to read.

4. The library shall be open for drawing and returning books, every Saturday, (except those days when the Director returns books to the township library, and draws anew,) from 12 o'clock, M., until 2 o'clock, P. M., unless the Director, with the consent of the District Board, shall change the time, in which case he shall give due notice thereof. The Director may, at his discretion, allow persons entitled to receive books, to draw them at other times as may suit the convenience of the parties. But all books, whenever drawn, shall be returned to the Director the last Saturday of every month.

5. Different persons wishing any book or books shall be entitled to draw the same according to the priority of their application.

3. *Fines and Damages.*

1. For every volume retained beyond the time established by these rules, a fine of five cents shall be imposed for the first day, and a fine of ten cents per week thereafter until the book shall be returned.

2. For turning down leaves, tearing, greasing, or in any way mutilating or injuring books beyond their natural wear, the Director is authorized to impose a fine of not less than five cents, nor more than twenty, for each and every offence. No person, against whom fines stand unpaid, shall be entitled to draw books. But any person dissatisfied with fines imposed by a Director, shall be entitled to appeal to the Township Librarian, whose decision shall be final.

3. Any person losing a book belonging to the Township Library, shall pay therefor not less than the first cost of the

same, and not more than twice that amount, to be determined by the Director; or, if lost by a Director, to be determined by the Librarian; and if lost by a Librarian, to be determined by the Board of School Inspectors.

4. All fines received by Directors shall be paid to the Township Librarian, who shall pay the same into the township treasury for the benefit of the township library.

SUSPENSION OF SECTION 115.

Whenever the School Inspectors suspend the operation of Section 115, [and 51,] as provided for in Section 146, the citizens of the township draw books directly from the Township Library, under such rules as shall be established by the Board of School Inspectors.

In case the Inspectors of one of the townships in which a fractional District is situated, suspend the operation of Section 115, all the citizens of said township draw books directly from the Township Library, under rules established by the School Inspectors; and the fraction of any District situated in the township in which the Section is not suspended, draw books from the Library of their own township, and not from the township in which the operation of Section 115 is suspended.

NOTE L.

(See Sections 117 and 118.)

DISTRICT LIBRARIES.

For the Superintendent's views in relation to District libraries, and rules for their government, the reader will please see that portion of the rules recommended for the government of township libraries, [Note K.] that relates to the duty of Directors.

The law originally contemplated District Libraries; but at the present time there are no legal provisions for their increase. The Superintendent is of the opinion that District Libraries would be more acceptable and useful than Township Libraries now are, and especially in the older and more densely settled portions of the State.

NOTE M.

(See Sections 41, 54, 72, 80, 81, 97, 98, 119 and 139.)

INCOME OF THE SCHOOL FUND—ITS DISTRIBUTION—WHO MAY PARTICIPATE IN IT—WHEN TO BE APPLIED.

Section 119 makes the interest of the Primary School Fund distributable on the first Monday of May, or as soon thereafter as is practicable, in each year. It has not usually been "practicable" to do this till some weeks later than the first Monday of May, in consequence of the interest from purchasers of Primary School lands not being received at that time.

The question, "Are children under four and over eighteen years of age, entitled to attend Primary Schools and participate in the avails of the School Fund?" has been frequently proposed to the Superintendent, from various parts of the State.

In the opinion of this Department, all children and persons residing in School Districts, having a desire and capacity to receive instruction, are entitled to enjoy the same and equal privileges. These ages are not fixed upon for the purpose of determining who may attend school, and who may not; but for the purpose of establishing an equitable data for the distribution of the income of the School Fund.

It is the evident design of our SCHOOL SYSTEM, the foundation of which is laid in the thirteenth Article of the Constitution, to furnish the means of obtaining a good English Education, not only to all children between the ages of four and eighteen years, but to all persons residing within the State, who are desirous of receiving instruction —married and single, old and young. And I may here add—one of the most gratifying scenes I have ever witnessed, was a *grandmother* attending a Primary School in this State, and receiving instruction from an assistant pupil in learning to read the English language.

The majority of children under four years of age are doubtless better off at home than in School. Still, there may be cases where it is proper to send them. There are also many young men over eighteen, and, in some cases, married persons of both sexes, who desire to attend School for the purpose of receiving instruction in branches ordinarily taught in our Primary Schools. In such cases it is the opinion of this Department that they should be allowed to attend School on the same terms as children between the ages of four and eighteen. But should idiots or insane persons between those ages—or any other individuals incapable of learning, and especially disorderly persons who will not comply with good and wholesome rules—disturb any School, it would be right to exclude them; and it is proper for the District officers, in all such cases, to render the Teacher any assistance he may need.

There must needs be some equitable basis for the apportionment of the School fund. The object of Section 119 is to fix this basis, and not to determine who may participate in the avails of said fund.

The School money received into Districts from year to year, should be applied for the support of Schools taught by qualified Teachers, and no others, during the year next ensuing the date of the report upon which the money is drawn.

The following, and similar questions, have frequently been proposed to the Superintendent:

1st. "Have the taxable inhabitants of a School District a legal right to receive children from without the District into their families to board and attend School?"

2d. "Have Districts a legal right, at an annual or special meeting, to pass a resolution and enforce the same, to exclude scholars from without the district, from School?"

3d. "Have the District Board authority to expel such scholars from School, provided they are in all respects obedient to the rules thereof?"

The following is the substance of replies to such interrogatories:

1st. Taxable inhabitants of such Districts have not the right to take children from without their Districts, into their families to board and send to School.

2d. Any District has the right, at an annual or special meeting, to pass a resolution excluding from their School all children that do not reside within the District. Children should never be sent from one District into another, to attend School, without the consent of the District Board where they thus attend. Moreover, the District Board should not allow such children to attend School, without the consent of the District, in case the question has ever come up for consideration at an annual or special meeting, and action has been taken thereon.

A District may admit children from other Districts to the privileges of its School on such conditions as it may prescribe. But should it permit such children to attend its School, without imposing any conditions upon them, they would stand on the same footing in relation to the rate bill, and the public moneys, as resident children.

The children of one organized District, by going into another District to board and attend School therein, do not by this means become residents of said District. [See Constitution of Mich., Art. 7, Sec. 5.]

In apportioning the Primary School interest money by the Superintendent of Public Instruction to the townships, and in apportioning the same, and also the moneys raised by the mill tax, by the Township Clerk to the Districts, those Districts only are to be embraced that have maintained a School taught by a qualified Teacher, at least three months during the preceding year, as shall appear from their report.

The same rule is to be observed in the apportionment of all moneys accruing from fines, etc., under the provisions of Section 116.

Section 72 provides that persons residing in a township, and not in any organized District, may, at their request, be attached to an organized District. In such cases, their children have a right to attend any Primary School that may be taught therein. They cannot, however, in any case, claim the privilege of sending from one *organized* District into another. Nor can they claim the privilege specified in Section 72, without the official sanction of the School Inspectors.

3d. In case children who are not residents of the District where they attend School, are sent without the consent of the District, as above, the District Board may direct them to leave, and they have no right to remain.

The following question has often been asked:

"Is it the duty of the Director to report the colored children of his District between the ages of four and eighteen years, and are such children entitled to the privileges of the School?"

Section 41 makes it the duty of the Director to take the census of his District, and section 54 makes it his duty to make a report, at the end of the School year, setting forth, among other particulars, "The whole number of children belonging to the District, between the ages of four and eighteen years, according to the census taken as aforesaid." This census should embrace all the resident children of the District, including the children of Americans and Foreigners, of Colored persons and Indians, (if such reside within the boundaries of the District,) all of whom have, under the general provisions of the Statutes of this State, a right to attend the Primary or Common Schools of the

State, and to participate equally in the avails of the School fund. The only exception to this rule is when a special act of the Legislature has been passed, for a city or village, as in case of colored persons in the city of Detroit.

To the question, whether persons having children between the ages of four and eighteen years, and sending them to school, are individually entitled to the money their children draw, and can have the same apply on their tuition, or whether public money is to be applied equally in paying the tuition of all children attending School, who are residents of the District, the reply has been: The public money drawn into a District, is to be applied equally, in reduction of the tuition of all residents of the District attending School, without regard to their ages.

In taking the census the Directors of School Districts have sometimes embraced children under sentence of law in the House of Correction for juvenile offenders, and in county jails. This usage is unjust, and in clear violation of the Constitution and laws of the State.

NOTE N.

[See Section 137.]

RIGHTS OF PERSONS PAYING TAXES IN A DISTRICT WHERE THEY DO NOT RESIDE.

Persons paying taxes in a District in which they do not reside, are entitled to send their children to School in said District, if their residence is in no organized District, or if the qualified voters of the District in which they reside have voted at a regular meeting to have no School for the year; and they will thus be entitled to all the privileges of residents of the District to whose School they send, except the right of voting.

NOTE O.

(See Sections 39, 60, 81, 85, 86, 87, 88, 89, 90, 92, 131 and 139.)

EMPLOYMENT AND EXAMINATION OF TEACHERS—STUDIES.

The following question has, in some instances, arisen:

In case neither the Moderator nor the Assessor can unite with the Director in the employment of a teacher, can the former two employ a teacher without the consent of the Director?

The statutes of this State very appropriately assign to each member of the District Board specific duties; and neither can lawfully discharge the duties of another. Section 39 makes it the duty of the Director, "by and with the advice and consent of the Moderator and Assessor, or one of them, to contract with and hire qualified teachers, for and in the name of the District." Teachers may be employed in this manner, and in no other. The Moderator and Assessor are not authorized by law to employ a teacher. In case the Director cannot act in concert with one, at least, of the other officers of the District, in the employment of a teacher, the Superintendent has, in a few instances, suggested the propriety of his resignation. This will give the District Board an opportunity of appointing a Director in accordance with the provisions of section 66, with whom they may be able to harmonize their views.

But the contract between the teacher and the Director, who acts as an agent of the District Board, and of the District, does not necessarily imply that the teacher employed is the choice of the Director. If the Director and *either* of the other officers agree in action, a teacher may be employed without the consent of the other. So, if *both* the Moderator and Assessor agree in the employment of a teacher, and neither of them can unite with the Director in the employment of the teacher of his choice, it then becomes the *duty* of the Director to employ the teacher approved by both of the other officers, and in case he refuses to do so, he is subject to a penalty of ten dollars for such refusal. [See Section 131.] In case a District has four additional Trustees, as provided for in section 92, the concurrence of at least two of these becomes necessary in order to the employment of a teacher. Any other construction of the statutes than that here given might prevent the employment of a teacher who was the choice of the other six members of an enlarged District Board, in case the Director entertained a different view. A case precisely like this has recently come to the knowledge of this Department, in which the Director very properly resigned. He might have employed the teacher, however, without impropriety, after having recorded his vote at a meeting of the District Board as opposed to his employment, as he had done. The teacher would then have been employed on the responsibility of the other six members of the Board, he being only an agent of the Board and District.

In single Districts where it is customary to maintain a summer School three or four months, and a winter School for about the same length of time, and commencing late in October, or early in November, the prevailing usage has been for the District officers elected at each annual meeting to hire the teachers employed in the District during the year next ensuing. And there seems to be much propriety in this arrangement, under such circumstances; and any custom, thus established, should not be departed from, except from urgent necessity, unless under instructions from a District meeting. And especially should not an outgoing Board employ a teacher to commence his School after their term of office expires, unless they do so pursuant to an expressed wish of the District at a regular meeting. In case this rule is disregarded, and a teacher is thus employed by an outgoing Board, contrary to usage, and without instructions, they transcend their authority, and become themselves personally responsible for their acts, while the incoming Board are at liberty to contract with the same or another teacher, as they judge will best promote the interests of the District whose agents they are.

But in larger and more populous Districts in which Schools are maintained throughout the year, with the exception of spring, and summer or fall vacations, the usage is not improperly varied. And especially is this so when it is desirable to commence the winter School before the time of holding the annual meeting, and where the District has previously enlarged its Board by adding thereto four Trustees, as provided for in section 92, three of whom always hold over for the year next ensuing. But even then, unless there is known to be great unanimity of feeling among the inhabitants of the District, the better way is to obtain an expression of their wishes on the subject at a regular District meeting called, if need be, for that purpose.

In many townships of the State, School Inspectors have not been accustomed properly to discharge their duty in the examination of teachers. In some instances a certificate has been given by a single Inspector. In other cases one Inspector has been requested to examine candidates without any meeting of the Board, and in case he approves them, he has, by request of the other members of the Board, signed their names to a certificate; when they themselves, have, perhaps, never so much as seen the candidate! And I might add: In not a few instances that have come to my knowledge, certificates have been granted without any examination!! This is, (at least,) a neglect of duty for which Inspectors are liable to forfeit ten dollars.

It should be understood by School Inspectors, by School Teachers, and by Directors, that Teachers who obtain their certificates in this manner, are not what the statutes of the State recognize as "qualified Teachers." A District cannot draw public money unless it has maintained a School three months at least, taught by "qualified Teachers." Neither is a District authorized to pay public money to a Teacher who has only a certificate obtained as specified above. Moreover, the School Inspectors are liable to be fined for granting such a certificate. The provisions of the Sections referred to at the head of this note, should be strictly complied with. The days specified in the statutes for the examination of Teachers, are "the second Saturday of April, and the first Saturday in November in each year." No Teacher can lawfully demand, or reasonably expect an examination at any other time. Neither can the Inspectors be allowed a compensation from the township for examinations on other days. They may decline examining Teachers on other days, and I can see no impropriety in their doing so, if the candidates might have been in attendance on the days specified in the statutes; or they may examine on other days at their discretion, without charge; or they may receive from the applicant or his employers, a reasonable remuneration for their services. It should be borne in mind, also, that no portion of the public money drawn into a School District, can lawfully be paid to a Teacher who has only a certificate as above. The following particulars cannot be too carefully observed:

1st. The Clerk of the Board of School Inspectors should give the notice required by law of the semi-annual meetings for the examination of Teachers. [See Section 86.]

2d. The examination should be *public*, [See Section 88,] and the entire Board of School Inspectors should be present at the appointed time and place, and ready to enter upon the examination. Every Teacher desiring a certificate should also be present. This will give that prominence and publicity to examinations which their importance requires, and which the statutes of the State contemplate. It would also afford Directors and others an opportunity of attending examinations, and of becoming acquainted with the qualifications of different applicants for Schools. Moreover, Inspectors, Teachers and citizens might enter unitedly upon arrangements for the improvement of the Schools of the township, and for the promotion of the cause of popular education, by means of educational societies, Teachers' associations and School celebrations.

3d. In the examination of Teachers for fractional Districts, the provisions of Sections 81 and 89 should be complied with.

It is the office of the Primary School to offer to all our youth, facilities for obtaining a good common English education, such as is necessary to qualify them to know, enjoy, and discharge their rights, privileges, and obligations, as citizens of a free State. The education which it aims to supply, is an elementary one, merely, but symmetrical in its proportions, and as extended as circumstances will permit, its instructions being conducted, under a Constitutional requirement, in the English language.

In the country, where the sparseness of the population is such that it is impracticable to embrace more than from forty to sixty children, within the legal ages, in a School District, because of the amount of territory that would be required, and the distance to which children in the remote portions of the Districts would be removed from the School-house, the course of study cannot be so extended, nor can the classification of pupils be so perfect, as in villages, and densely populated communities, where from three to five or eight hundred children may be embraced within the limits of a single District. But in both instances, alike, the first, and the prominent object in arranging a course of study, must be the fitting of youth who frequent these Schools for the discharge of the duties of life.

In determining what particular studies shall be embraced in a course of study proper for a Primary School, reference must be had to its design, as here stated, and to the circumstances of particular townships and Districts, the

School Inspectors, and the Districts, or the respective District Boards being the judges.

This subject will be again referred to in Part III. of this volume, which see.

NOTE P.

[See Sections 29, 53, 61, 63 and 64.]

HOW MONEYS BELONGING TO SCHOOL DISTRICTS SHOULD BE DRAWN, APPLIED AND RECORDED.

There is a great irregularity in the manner of drawing moneys belonging to School Districts from the hands of both the Assessor and Township Treasurer, and of paying them out when drawn. The Director, for example, often draws public moneys from the Treasurer for the payment of teachers, without even the knowledge of the Assessor. The Moderator, also, frequently draws and applies moneys in like manner, in meeting expenses incurred in behalf of the District. This promiscuous drawing and applying of moneys belonging to School Districts, is unauthorized by law, and highly improper.

1st. All moneys raised by tax in School Districts, for building School-houses, repairs, etc., and all moneys raised on the scholar for School purposes, are lodged by law in the hands of the Township Treasurer. The mill-tax, also, is collected by him, and the Primary School Interest moneys descend from the State Treasury to the Districts through him. These moneys can be lawfully drawn from the Township Treasury, only on the warrant of the Director countersigned by the Moderator. Such warrants should state the fund from which they are to be paid, so as to enable the Treasurer to charge the Districts accordingly.

2d. While moneys belonging to a School District remain in the hands of the Township Treasurer, warrants may be drawn on him payable to the order of "qualified teachers" for "public moneys" due them from the District; or payable to a contractor for building a School-house, to be paid from a fund raised for that purpose; and in a like manner for other purposes. But there is no provision of law for the drawing of any such moneys by the Moderator or Director, to be paid, by them, or either of them, to third parties.

3d. In the course of procedure as above indicated, the Township Treasurer becomes, practically, the Treasurer of the District, as well as of the township; and to an extent that will often be oppressive and unjust; for each School District is provided with a treasurer in the person of its Assessor, who is required before entering upon duty to give bonds for the faithful application of all moneys that may come into his hands by virtue of his office. To avoid this injustice to the Township Treasurer, as well as for the better preservation of a detailed record of the proceedings of the District Board, it is proper for the Director to draw his warrant on the Township Treasurer, payable to the order of the Assessor, for moneys in his hands belonging to the District, which warrant, when countersigned by the Moderator, will be paid by the Treasurer on presentation.

4th. Any and all moneys received by the Assessor should be charged by him to the several funds to which they belong, in a book provided for that purpose. No moneys should be paid out by the Assessor, except on the order of the Director, countersigned by the Moderator. And whenever moneys are paid, the particular fund from which they are paid should be credited with the amount so paid, after the manner indicated below. Each entry should show, to whom money has been paid, and on what account; and especially should all orders presented and paid, be numbered and referred to by number in entering the account. These orders, thus numbered and placed upon file, constitute the Assessor's vouchers for the proper application and payment of all moneys that have passed through his hands.

5th. An account should be kept with all moneys collected by the Assessor on rate bills, in the same manner as with moneys received from the Treasurer. This account should be charged with the amount collected on the rate bill, and credited with the amounts paid therefrom. The manner of keeping all these accounts is sufficiently illustrated in the example referred to, it is hoped, to make the matter understood even by those who have not been accustomed to keep accounts.

6th. When the accounts of a District are properly kept as here indicated, and the Assessor keeps a file of all orders on which moneys have been paid, as his vouchers

Public Moneys. *Dr.*

1858.			$	Cts.
March	10.	To amount of Mill Tax received of Township Treasurer,..........	56	50
June	1.	To amount of Primary School Interest Money rec'd of Township Treasurer,....................	49	50

Building Fund. *Dr.*

1858.			$	Cts.
March	10.	To amount received of Township Treasurer,....................	450	00

for the proper application of all funds that have passed through his hands, not only are he and his bondsmen protected, but a settlement of his accounts is easily and satisfactorily made, and his account book, and his orders properly numbered and filed, enable the District Board to make the report to the annual District meeting required of them by Section 63, "of all moneys of the District received by them, or any of them, during the preceding year, and of the disbursements made by them, with the items of such receipts and disbursements."

7th. But in case the Assessor fails to give the bond required by Section 66, for double the amount of moneys to come into his hands, with sureties approved by the Moderator and Director, all moneys belonging to the District must remain in the township treasury till required for use, when they may be drawn out on proper warrants made payable to the parties entitled to them. In such case the report of the District Board required by Section 63, may be made from the records of the Director properly kept.

Public Moneys. *Cr.*

			$	Cts.
1858. March	25.	By amount paid John Brown, a "qualified Teacher," on order No. 1,	45	00
Aug.	7.	By amount paid Susan Allen, a "qualified Teacher," on order No. 5,	27	50

Building Fund. *Cr.*

			$	Cts.
1858. March	15.	By amount paid H. Allen, builder, on order No. 2,	160	00
April	1.	By amount paid H. Allen, on order No. 3,	150	00
June	3.	By amount paid M. O. Brown, for painting School-house, on order No. 4,	60	00

NOTE Q.

[See Sections 96, 102 and 103.]

MAP OF SCHOOL DISTRICTS.

The Township Clerk is required to make a map of the Districts and parts of Districts in his township, and file one copy of the same in his office, and one with the Supervisor; and whenever any changes are made in the boundaries of Districts, he is required to file a new map as above, within one month thereafter; but his omission to do so will not affect the validity of any other proceedings. The defect may be supplied by a record of the order of the Inspectors making such alteration.

The omission to make the maps required by the Sections referred to at the head of this Note, and to keep on file a full record of all proceedings of single and joint Boards of School Inspectors, often leads to great embarrassments in School Districts, engendering not unfrequently, vexatious law suits. The duty in question, then, becomes one of the most important ones required of the Board of School Inspectors.

NOTE R.

DIVISION OF COUNTIES AND TOWNSHIPS.

Where a County Clerk shall receive from the Superintendent the notice of the amount of Public Money apportioned to the townships of his county, provided for by Sec. 7 on page 161 of this volume; and where said county shall have been divided after the annual reports were made, and before said notices were received, he should immediately give notice to the clerk of each county into which any portion of said county shall have been incorporated, advising him of the amount of said money apportioned to each township in any such new county, and that said money will be held by the Treasurer of the original county, subject to the order of the Treasurer of such new county.

This rule should also be observed by the clerk of any township that shall have been divided under similar circumstances.

NOTE S.

[See Sections 71, 79, 81, 86, 91 and 92.]

SCHOOL INSPECTORS—THEIR ELECTION AND PAY—MEETINGS OF BOARD, ETC.

Each organized township, on the first Monday of April, annually, elects one School Inspector, and the Township Clerk is School Inspector *ex-officio*. [See Article 11, Section 1, of the Constitution. Compiled Laws, page 66.]

The same provision for the election, annually, of one School Inspector, is found in the statute, under the head "Township Meetings." [Sec. 8, Compiled Laws, page 228.]

On page 229, Compiled Laws, under the above head, is the following:

"Sec. 13. Each School Inspector elected as aforesaid, shall hold his office for two years, and until his successor shall be elected and qualified, except when elected to fill a vacancy, in which case, he shall hold during the unexpired portion of the regular term: *Provided*, That where there shall have been no previous election for School Inspectors in any township, there shall be two such Inspectors elected, one for one year, and one for two years, who shall severally hold their office accordingly."

School Inspectors receive a compensation at the rate of one dollar per day, for the time spent in the duties of their office. [See Compiled Laws, Chap. 12, Sec. 95, page 244.]

The law imposes but three meetings upon the Board of Inspectors each year—two for the purpose of examining Teachers, and one to make the annual report to the County Clerk. The whole number at the expense of the township, cannot exceed six. It is made their duty to divide the township into School Districts; but the time and place of meeting for such purpose, the manner or occasion for such division, all redivisions or changes in Districts, classification of scholars, or meeting with the Inspectors of other townships for the purpose of forming or changing fractional Districts, are matters subject to their discretion. There is no process pointed out in the law, by which any number of citizens of a township may lay the Board of Inspectors under legal obligation to hold a meeting, or by which the Board of one township may make it obligatory on that of another to meet them to transact business that mutually interests both townships. It is presumed that no Board will take advantage of this discretionary power, to the neglect of the educational interests of their township; but should they thus fail in their duty, an adequate remedy may be applied in due time, by the election of more reliable men to fill their places.

FORMS FOR PROCEEDINGS UNDER THE SCHOOL LAW.

No. 1.

Form of Notice to be given by the Clerk of the Board of School Inspectors to a Taxable Inhabitant of a School District at the time of its formation.

(See Sections 1, 2, 3, 4, 7, 15 and 129.)

To A. B. of the Township of

SIR—You are hereby notified that the School Inspectors of the township of , have formed a School District in said township, numbered and bounded as follows: No. , bounded (here insert the boundary.)

The first meeting of said District will be held at on the day of A. D. 18 , at 6 o'clock, P. M., [unless some other hour is designated by the School Inspectors,] and you are hereby instructed to notify every qualified voter of said District, either personally or by leaving a written notice at his place of residence, of the time and place of said meeting, at least five days before the time appointed therefor, as above; and after so notifying every qualified voter within the boundaries above described, you will endorse on this notice a return, showing such notification, with the date or dates thereof, and deliver the same to the Chairman of the meeting, to be held at the time and place above mentioned.

Given under my hand, this day of A. D. 18 .

Signed: C. D.,

Clerk of the Board of School Inspectors.

NO. II.

Form of Notice of first meeting of a School District, to be left at the residence of Taxable Inhabitants thereof, in case the person designated by the Clerk of the Board of School Inspectors does not notify them personally.

[See Sections 1, 2, 15 and 129.]

To A. L.:

SIR—The Board of School Inspectors of the township of have established School District No. , of which you are a resident, and I am instructed by the Clerk of said Board to notify you that the first meeting of said District will be held at , on the day of , A D., 18 , at o'clock in the noon, for the election of officers and the transaction of such other business as may be necessary.

Dated this day of , 18 .

(Signed,) A. B.,

The person appointed to give notice.

NO. III.

Form of Endorsement upon Notice received from Clerk of Board of School Inspectors on the formation of a School District.

[See Sections 3 and 15.]

I do hereby certify that I notified all the qualified voters of the within named School District, on or before the day of , 18 ,

(Signed,) A. B.,

The person appointed to give notice.

NO. IV.

Form of Acceptance of office by District Officers, to be filed with the Director.

[See Sections 5, 130 and 148.]

I do hereby certify my acceptance of the office of in School District No. of the township of

Dated this day of , 18 .

(Signed,) A. B.

—

NO. V.

Form of Notice of Annual Meetings.

[See Sections 11, 13, 50 and 130.]

Notice is hereby given, that the annual meeting of School District No. , of the township of , for the election of School District Officers, and for the transaction of such other business as may lawfully come before it, will be held at , on Monday, the day of September, A. D. 18 , at o'clock in the noon.

Dated this day of September, 18 .

(Signed,) , *Director.*

—

NO. VI.

Form of Request to be made by five Legal Voters of a District to the District Board for the calling of a Special Meeting.

[See Section 12.]

To the District Board of School District No. , [or to A. B., &c., one of the District Board :]

The undersigned, legal voters of School District No. of the township of , request you, in pursuance of

Section 12, of the Primary School Law, to call a special meeting of said District, for the purpose of

Dated this day of , A. D. 18 .

(Signed,)

Form of Notice of Special Meetings.

[See Sections 12, 13 and 50.]

Notice is hereby given to the taxable inhabitants of School District No. , in the township* of , that in pursuance of a written request of five legal voters of said District, a special meeting of said District will be held at , on the day of , A. D., 18 , for [here insert the object or objects of the meeting.]

(Signed,) A. B., *Director.*

NO. VII.

Form of Rate Bill and Warrant.

[See Sections 29, 32, 33, 34, 35, 45, 46 and 58.]

Rate Bill, containing the name of each person liable for Teachers' wages in District No. , in the township of , for the term ending on the day of , A. D. 18 , and the amount for which each person not exempted

---

* Vary for fractional Districts.

from the payment thereof is so liable, with the fees of the Assessor thereon.

Names of inhabitants sending to School.	Whole No. of days sent.	Amount of School bill.	Assess'rs fees thereon.	Amount for fuel.	Whole am't to be raised.
James Emerson,	104	$1 04	$0 05	*	$1 09
John L. Barney,	416	4 16	0 21	$1 25	5 68
William Jones,.	313	3 13	0 16	*	3 29
Peter Parley,.. .	54	0 54	0 03	*	0 57
S. C. Goodrich,	104	1 04	0 05	0 50	1 62
M. Barney,.....	104	1 04	0 05	*	1 09
F. Sawyer,.....	416	4 16	0 21	*	4 37
	1511	$15 11	$0 76	$1 75	$17 71

To the Assessor of School District No. , in the Township of :

You are hereby commanded to collect from each of the persons in the annexed rate bill named, the several sums set opposite their respective names in the last column thereof, and within sixty days after receiving this warrant, to pay over the amount so collected by you, (retaining five per cent. for your fees,) to the order of the Director of said District, countersigned by the Moderator; and in case any person therein named, shall neglect or refuse, on demand, to pay the amount set opposite his name as aforesaid, you are to collect the same by distress and sale of the goods and chattels of such persons wherever found, within the county or counties in which said District is situated, having first published said sale at least ten days, by posting up notices thereof in three public places in the township where such property shall be sold.

At the expiration of this warrant, you will make a return thereof in writing, with the rate bill attached, to the Director; stating the amount collected on said rate bill, the amount uncollected, and the names of persons from whom collections have not been made.

* In the preceding rate bill those persons who are not rated for fuel, furnished the same according to the provisions of Section 40. Those who did not furnish their proportion of fuel, are charged for fuel in the rate bill according to the provisions of the same Section, and five per cent. for collecting the same. (See Section 45.)

Given under our hands this day of , in the year of our Lord, one thousand eight hundred and

A. B., *Director.*
C. D., *Moderator.*

Remark 1. In making out the rate bill for a term of School, the amount of public money to be applied to the term is first deducted from the amount of the Teacher's wages, and any balance remaining to be collected, is apportioned to the several persons having sent to School during the term, in proportion to the number of days sent by each.

Remark 2. Any money received for tuition of children attending School from without the District, under any rule established by the District, or by the District Board, is to be applied like the public money in the reduction of the Teacher's wages; but—

Remark 3. In case children are received into the District to attend School, without any condition having been imposed, the persons sending them should be embraced in the rate bill, and the amount due from them should be collected as in other cases.

Remark 4. In case it becomes necessary to enforce a collection, the Assessor should post the following notice in three public places in the township, at least ten days previous to sale:

Form of Notice of Assessor's Sale.

[See Sections 33, 34 and 46.]

Notice is hereby given, that by virtue of the warrant annexed to a rate bill for School District No. , of the township of , bearing date the day of , 18 , I have levied on the goods and chattels of , and shall expose the same for sale at public auction, at the house of , in the said School District, (or where-ever the property may be,) in the township of and county of , on the day of , 18 , at the hour of o'clock, M.

Given under my hand at , this day of , 18 .

E. O. B.,
Assessor of said District.

Remark 5. The following is a proper form for Assessor's return to accompany the rate bill and warrant:

Assessor's Return of Warrant.

I, , Assessor of School District No. , township of , do hereby make this, my return of the annexed warrant, with rate bill attached, and certify the amount collected on said rate bill to be the sum of dollars and cents; the amount uncollected, dollars and cents; and that the following are the names of persons from whom collections have not been made, and the amounts which are uncollected from each person:

NAMES.	Dollars.	Cents.

Dated this day of , A. D. 18 .
(Signed,) A. B., *Assessor.*

Any sums that *cannot* be collected by the Assessor are to be included in the next report of the District Board to the Supervisor, as provided in Section 57.

For neglect to collect any sum or sums embraced in the rate bill that are *collectable*, the Assessor is subject to a penalty of ten dollars. (See Section 130.)

NO. VIII.

Form of Contract between Director and Teacher.

[See Sections 39, 60 and 85.]

It is agreed between A. B., Director of School District No. , in the township of , on the part of said District, and C. D., a qualified Teacher of the township of , that the said C. D. is to teach the Primary School of said District for the term of , commencing on the day of , A D. 18 , for the sum of per ; and that for such services, properly rendered, the said A. B. is to pay the said C. D. the amount of his wages as ascertained by this memorandum, on or before the day of , A. D. 18 .

In witness whereof the said parties have hereunto set their names this day of , A. D. 18 .

A. B., *Director*,
C. D., *Teacher*.

This contract is approved by
E. F., *Moderator*,
G. H., *Assessor*.

Remark 1. The Teacher should be furnished with a copy of this contract, and a duplicate should be filed with the Director.

Remark 2. The wages should be specified per week or month. The latter is preferable. [See Note C.]

Remark 3. Section 60 expressly provides that no School moneys apportioned to any District, shall be appropriated to any other use than the payment of Teachers' wages, and that no part thereof shall be paid to any Teacher who has not received a certificate from the School Inspectors *before commencing the School*. [See Form No. 17.]

Remark 4. In case of enlarged District Boards, the approval of at least two of the four Trustees is necessary in the employment of Teachers, in addition to the approval of the Moderator or Assessor.

The concurrence essential in the employment of Teachers is stated at length in Note O., which see.

NO. IX.

Form of Endorsement for the Extension of Warrant.

[See Section 47.]

We do hereby extend the time for the collection of the annexed rate bill, thirty days, [any shorter period may be specified,] beyond the time named in the annexed [within] warrant.

Dated this day of , 18 .

A. B., *Director*,
C. D., *Moderator*.

NO. X.

Form of Order upon Assessor for Moneys to be disbursed by School Districts.

[See Sections 29 and 53]

Assessor of School District No. , Township of :

Pay to the order of , the sum of dollars, out of any moneys in your hands belonging to the aforesaid School District.

Dated this day of , A. D. 18 .

A. B., *Director*.

NOTE.—The above order must be countersigned by the Moderator.

NO. XI.

Form of Warrant upon Township Treasurer for Moneys belonging to School Districts.

[See Sections 29, 53 and 109.]

Treasurer of the Township of :

Pay to the order of , the sum of dollars, out of [here insert the particular fund,] in your hands, belonging to School District No. , of said township.

Dated at , this day of , A. D. 18 .

A. B., *Director.*

NOTE.—The above warrant must be countersigned by the Moderator.

NO. XII.

Form of Report by the District Board to the Supervisor.

[See Sections 56, 57, 58, 106 and 108.]

Supervisor of the Township of :

The undersigned, District Board for School District No. , in said township, do hereby certify that the following taxes have been voted in said district, during the School year last closed, viz:

[Here specify the amount of each tax voted, and the purpose to which it is appropriated: Also, the amount of taxes imposed by the District Board, and give the sum total of the whole,] which you will assess upon the taxable property of said District, as the law directs.

Dated at , this day of A. D. 18 .

A. B., *Moderator,*
C. D., *Director,*
E. F., *Assessor.*

NO. XIII.

Form of Assessor's Bond.

[See Sections 61 and 62.]

Know all men by these presents, That we, A. B., [the Assessor of School District No. , in the township of ,] C. D. and E. F., [his sureties,] are held and firmly bound unto the said District, in the sum of [here insert a sum of double the amount to come into the Assessor's hands,] to be paid to the said District; for the payment of which sum well and truly to be made, we bind ourselves, our heirs, executors and administrators, jointly and severally, firmly by these presents.

The condition of this obligation is such, that if A. B., Assessor of said District, shall faithfully apply all moneys that shall come into his hands by virtue of his office, then this obligation shall be void; otherwise of full force and virtue.

Sealed with our Seals, and dated this day of A. D. 18 .

A. B., [L. S.]
C. D., [L. S.]
E. F., [L. S.]

Signed, sealed and delivered in presence of

Remark. This bond should be endorsed as follows:

"We approve the within bond."

[Signed.] G. H., *Moderator*,
I. K., *Director*.

—

NO. XIV.

Form of Bond to be given by the Chairman of the Board of School Inspectors.

[See Sections 68, 69 and 70.]

Know all men by these presents, that we, A. B., [the chairman of the Board of School Inspectors of the township of ,] and C. D. and E. F., [his sureties,] are held and firmly bound unto the said township, in the sum of, [here insert the sum of double the amount to come into said chairman's hands, as nearly as the same can be ascertained,] for the payment of which sum well and truly to be made to the said township, we bind ourselves, our heirs, executors and administrators, jointly and severally, firmly by these presents.

The condition of this obligation is such, that if A. B., chairman of the Board of School Inspectors, shall faithfully appropriate all moneys that may come into his hands by virtue of his office, then this obligation shall be void, otherwise of full force and virtue.

Sealed with our seals, and dated this day of , A. D., 18 .

A. B., [L. S.]
C. D., [L. S.]
E. F., [L. S.]

Signed, sealed and delivered in presence of

Remark. This bond should be given before any moneys come into his hands, and should be endorsed as follows:

"I approve the within bond."

[Signed,] G. H., *Township Clerk.*

NO. XV.

Form of Appointment of District Officers by District Board.

[See Section 66.]

The undersigned, members of the District Board of School District No. , in the township of , do hereby appoint A. B., *Director* of said District, to fill the vacancy created by the removal, [resignation or death, as the case may be,] of C. D., the late incumbent.

Dated this day of , A. D. 18 .

E. F., *Moderator.*
G. H., *Assessor.*

Remark 1. The words in *italics* in the above form should be varied to suit the case.

Remark 2. The Director should record any appointment that may be made, and persons appointed to office should file with the Director a certificate of acceptance, according to the provisions of Section 5. [See Form No. 4.]

NO. XVI.

Form of Appointment of District Officers, by School Inspectors.

[See Section 95.]

The undersigned, School Inspectors for the township of , do hereby appoint O. P., *Assessor* of School District No. , in said township, to fill the vacancy created by the *death* of Q. R., the late incumbent.

Dated this day of , A. D. 18 .

A. B.,
C. D.,
E. F.,
School Inspectors.

☞ See the remarks following the preceding Form.

NO. XVII.

Form of Certificate to be given by School Inspectors to Qualified Teachers.

[See Sections 39, 85, 86, 87, 88, 89 and 90.]

The undersigned, Inspectors of Primary Schools for the township of , in the county of , having personally examined A. B. at a regular meeting of the Board, called for that purpose, and having ascertained his [or her] qualifications in respect to moral character, learning, and ability to instruct a Primary School, DO HEREBY CERTIFY, that he [or she] is duly qualified for that service, and accordingly he [or she] is hereby *licensed* to teach Primary Schools in said township *for two years* from the date hereof, unless this certificate shall, before that time, be annulled according to law.

Given under our hands this day of , A. D. 18 .

C. D.,
E. F.,
G. H.
School Inspectors.

☞ See 3d Remark following Form No. 8.

NO. XVIII.

Form of Notice of Meeting of Inspectors for Examination of School Teachers.

[See Section 86.]

Notice is hereby given, that for the purpose of making an examination of all persons who may offer themselves as candidates for Teachers of the Primary Schools of this township, the Board of School Inspectors thereof will meet [here insert the time and place of meeting.]

Dated this day of , 18 .

A. B., *Township Clerk.*

Remark 1. Whenever the Inspectors deem it necessary to re-examine any Teacher, they shall serve the following notice upon him, according to the provisions of Section 90:

Form of Notice for Re-examination.

To A. B.:

SIR,—You are hereby notified that the undersigned, School Inspectors for the township of , will hold a meeting at on the day of , at o'clock, . M. You will please appear before them at the time and place aforesaid, for re-examination. It is our purpose to annul your certificate if you are found deficient in the qualifications requisite for a Primary School Teacher.

☞ This notice should be dated and signed in the same manner as the above Certificate.

Remark 2. In case it be found necessary to annul the Teacher's certificate, it shall be sufficient for that purpose for the Clerk of the Board of School Inspectors to make the usual record of their proceedings: *Provided*, the Teacher appears before them and gives up his certificate, which it is his duty to do. Otherwise, in addition to said record, the Inspectors shall cause the following notice to be posted up in three public places in the township, or to be inserted in a newspaper of the township, if there be one:

"The undersigned, School Inspectors for the township of , having this day re-examined A. B., a Primary School Teacher in said township, and regarding him incompetent to discharge the duties of his office, we hereby give notice that his certificate is annulled according to the provisions of law."

☞ This notice should be dated and signed in the same manner as the preceding one.

NO. XIX.

Form of Certificate to be given to the Director of a School District by the Board of School Inspectors when they establish the Site.

[See Sections 19 and 20.]

The inhabitants of District No. , in the township of , having failed, at a legal meeting, to establish a site for a School-house, the Board of School Inspectors hereby certify, that they have determined that the said site shall be as follows: [Describe as in the deed.]

Given under our hands this day of , A. D. 18 .

A. B.,
C. D.,
E. F.,
School Inspectors.

NO. XX.

Form of a Deed.

[See Section 59.]

Know all men by these presents, That A. B. and C. D., his wife, of the township of , in the county of , and State of Michigan, party of the first part, for and in consideration of the sum of dollars, to them paid by the District Board of School District No. , of the township, county and State aforesaid, the receipt whereof is hereby acknowledged, do hereby grant, bargain, sell and convey to School District No. , the party of the second part, and their assigns, forever, the following described parcel of land, namely:

[Here insert description.]

Together with all the privileges and appurtenances thereunto belonging, to have and to hold the same to the said party of the second part, and their assigns, forever. And the said party of the first part, for themselves, their heirs, executors and administrators, do covenant, grant, bargain and agree, to and with the said party of the second part, and their assigns, that at the time of the ensealing and delivery of these presents, they were well seized of the premises above conveyed, as of a good, sure, perfect, absolute and indefeasible estate of inheritance in the law, in fee simple, and that the said lands and premises are free from all encumbrances whatever; and that the above bargained premises, in the quiet and peaceable possession of the said party of second part, and their assigns, against all and every person or persons lawfully claiming or to claim the whole or any part thereof, they will forever warrant and defend.

In witness whereof, the said A. B. and C. D., his wife, party of the first part, have hereunto set their hands and seals, this day of A. D. 18 .

A. B., [SEAL.]
C. D., [SEAL.]

Signed, sealed and delivered in presence of H. I., J. K.

Remark. In order to protect the District in its title to a site, the deed thereof must be recorded in the Register's office.

☞ It will readily be seen how the preceding form should be varied, in case the person giving a deed is unmarried.

NO. XXI.

Form of a Lease.

[See Section 59.]

Know all men by these presents, that A. B., of the township of , in the county of , and State of Michigan, of the first part, for the consideration herein mentioned, does hereby lease unto School District No. , in the township, county and State aforesaid, party of the second part, and their assigns, the following parcel of land, to-wit: [here insert description;] with all the privileges and appurtenances thereunto belonging; to have and to hold the same for and during the term of years from the day of , A. D. 18 . And the said party of the second part, for themselves and their assigns, do covenant and agree to pay the said party of the first part, for the said premises, the annual rent of dollars.

In testimony whereof, the said parties have hereunto set their hands and seals, this day of , A. D. 18 .

A. B., [SEAL.]
Lessor.

C. D.,
E. F., [SEAL.]
G. H.

District Board of School District No. of the aforesaid township.

Signed and sealed in the presence of
I. J.,
K. L.

Remark. A Lease, like a Deed, must be recorded in the Register's office, in order to protect the District in its title to a site.

☞ The Lessor will probably want a copy of the lease. If so, a duplicate should be made and signed as above, and placed on file with the Director, to be delivered with other papers of his office to his successor.

NO. XXII.

[See Sections 41, 54 and 130.]

Form of Annual Report of the Director to the School Inspectors.

1	Whole District.	No. of District whose School house is in the township.
2	Fractional District.	
3	Number of Children in the District between the ages of four and eighteen years.	
4	Whole number of Children that have attended School during the year.	
5	Number of months a School has been taught during the year by qualified Teachers.	
6	Name of each Qualified Teacher. (See Note relating to "Qualified Teschers.")	
8	Number of months a School has been taught by each Teacher.	
9	Total amount of wages paid to each Teacher.	
10	Amount of public money received from Township Treasurer.	
11	Whole amount of money raised by tax upon property in the District.	
12	To build School-house.	Purposes for which it was raised, and the amount raised for each particular purpose.
13	To repair School house.	
14	On the Scholar, to pay Teachers' wages- (See Section 140.)	
15	For all other purposes.	
16	Amount raised by rate bill.	

NOTES TO FORM NO. XXII.

Fractional Districts, No. 2.—A FULL REPORT from a FRACTIONAL DISTRICT should be made ONLY to the INSPECTORS OF THE TOWNSHIP IN WHICH THE SCHOOL-HOUSE IS SITUATED. (See Section 81.)

A SEPARATE REPORT should be made to the Clerk of each of the other townships in which the District is IN PART situated, giving merely ☞ the number of children between the ages of four and eighteen years, residing in that part of the District situated within each of said townships.☜ This latter report is required by Section 82, and constitutes the basis upon which books are drawn from the Township Library in accordance with the provisions of Sections 82 and 115, but ceases to be of any practical utility where the operations of the latter Section are suspended in accordance with the provisions of Section 144.

Qualified Teachers, No. 6.—A "Qualified Teacher," within the meaning of the statutes, is one who holds a certificate from the School Inspectors, in accordance with the provisions of Section 85 of the School Law. District Boards should see that all Teachers they employ possess such a certificate BEFORE BEGINNING TO TEACH A SCHOOL. Otherwise, they can neither pay them public money, nor receive any on account of their teaching. (See Sections 60 and 80.)

NO. XXIII.

Form of Annual Report of the School Inspectors to the County Clerk.

[See Sections 79, 131, 132 and 133.]

1	Whole Districts.	No. of each District whose School house is in the township.
2	Fractional Districts.	
3	Number of Children in each District between the ages of four and eighteen years.	
4	Whole number of Children that have attended School during the year.	
5	Number of months a School has been taught in each District by qualified Teachers.	
6	Number of qualified male Teachers that have been employed in each District.	
7	Number of qualified female Teachers that have been employed in each District.	
9	Total amount of wages paid to Teachers in each District.	
10	Amount of Public Money received from Township Trersurer in each District.	
11	Whole amount of money raised by tax upon property in each District.	
12	To build School house.	Purposes for which it was raised, and the amount raised for each particular purpose.
13	To repair School-house.	
14	On the scholar, to pay Teachers' wages.	
15	For all other purposes.	
16	Amount raised by rate bill.	
17	Number of Volumes in the Township Library.	
18	Amount of mill tax raised in the township. [See Sections 107, 142 and 143.]	
19	Amount of fines, penalties, etc., received of County Treasurer for the purchase of books for Township Library. [See Section 116]	

Annual Reports.

Great pains have been taken in the preparation of the preceding forms for the Annual Reports of Directors and School Inspectors. It is made the duty of these officers to make *full returns.* In some instances the reports have hardly shown more than the number of children between the ages of four and eighteen years.

To facilitate the work of making these reports, and to obviate any occasion for mistakes, the corresponding heads in the several forms are designated by the same number. No. 11 should embrace the total amount of taxes upon property, raised by the *districts* for School purposes, excepting that specified in No. 16. The money raised by townships will be reported under head No. 18.

[See notes J. and K.; also notes appended to the tables in the Superintendent's Report.]

NO. XXIV.

Form of Warrant on the Township Treasurer for Library Moneys.

[See Sections 107, 109 and 116.]

To the Treasuer of the Township of County of , Mich.:

Pay to the order of , the sum of dollars, from any Library moneys now in your hands, or to come into your hands, the same being for Library Books purchased for the Library of said township.

Dated at , this day of 18 .

A. B.,
C. D.,
E. F.,
Township Board of School Inspectors.

☞ The form of this warrant may be varied to suit the circumstances of the case.

PART III.

The Primary School System;

School Architecture;

School Furniture;

School Apparatus;

School Arrangements;

Warming and Ventilation;

School and Literary Books.

THE PRIMARY SCHOOL SYSTEM.

ORIGINAL DESIGN.

The original legal provisions for the support and management of the Primary Schools of Michigan were of a general character, and made no distinction between the different circumstances of the most sparsely populated settlements and the growing towns or villages. At the time of the passage of the first Primary School law by the Territorial government, and even when the State Constitution was adopted, and the first State School law enacted, there were very few villages large enough to furnish more scholars than could be accommodated in a single School-house. Had it been otherwise, it is probable that the legislation would have been the same; for the reason that the defects of the system, copied from older States, had not been considered, and no remedy was of course sought. The legislation seemed only to provide for, or to anticipate for the future, single Districts, to include no more territory than would furnish scholars sufficient for a single School-house, and one Teacher. This was probably the only system adapted to the necessities of sparsely settled sections, where to obtain the required number of scholars for a School, some must travel perhaps two miles, with bad roads, to reach a common centre.

The only system thus adapted to the necessities of the case in the country, was given also to the towns; and in many instances, the small villages, with the territory immediately adjacent, furnished no more than enough scholars for a single District. While this state of things continued, it was all that could be done; but in three or four years, perhaps, the increase of population was such, that one Schoolhouse was not large enough; and the first, and probably the only thought was, to divide the District and build another house; naturally leaving the old one badly located, in reference to its new relations. But soon a swarming of both hives was necessary, and another division was made, and a third District created. Thus in many villages there were created, in a very few years, two, three, and four School Districts, with as many enclosures dignified with the name of Schoolhouses, within pistol shot of each other, and most of them badly located.

One section of the village, perhaps, had a School eight months in the year, another six, and another three—or none at all. Each acted independently of the others, as Districts; one may have had what was called a good School, (good by comparison,) and another, a wretchedly poor one—and sometimes the only rivalry seemed to be, to prove which could have the most objectionable School appliances, and the worst management, and acquire the reputation of sustaining the name of a School with the least expense. In some instances it may be, a District might be found, where a few citizens of enlarged and liberal views, were able to infuse a similar spirit into the hearts of their neighbors, and in their District a Schoolhouse was built and furnished in a style that was the delight of the children, and the pride of its patrons; while the children of an adjoining District—the every-day playmates, out of School, of the favored ones—were required to assemble at the miserable hovel, built with less taste, and attended to with less care, than was the horse-barn of many of the fathers of the injured pupils. Two lads might leave home from opposite sides of the street, walk together for a time, and one turn one way to his pleasant School, with joyous associations, while the other went another way to his School, envious of his fellow, and disgusted and disheartened by the prospect before him.

Under such circumstances, the children often felt that they were paying a dear price for their education, inasmuch as it was at the expense of all pleasant enjoyment, and by doing continual penance. Their oppressed hearts told them that their parents were doing them a serious wrong, in thus degrading them, while their friends were provided with an elegant building, a popular Teacher, and everything to make their School pleasant and desirable.

THE MAIN DIFFICULTY.

But the above were not the only, or the greatest evils of the system. The District in which the most enterprise was shown, was yet sadly deficient in the highest means of success. There was a radical defect in the system, which could be but partially removed in a small District School, with a single Teacher.

A man with but one mind, or but two hands, can hardly be expected to do half a dozen things at the same time, and do all well. If half a dozen things must be done at the same time, and in the best possible manner, the first suggestion of any mind would be, that at least three (if not six) persons should be employed. But if the place where the work is to be done is so small that but one person can occupy it, then he alone must do the best he can, and labor with such success as he may. This is the difficulty in the single-District School. There are several things to be accomplished, and there is room for but one laborer.

There are several things to be done, or several grades of labor, in the Primary School. They all relate to the same subject, but comprise a variety in action, scarcely less than will be found in the manufacture of the Teacher's desk, from the time the tree is cut in the forest, till it receives the last application of varnish from the hand of the finisher. Teaching a child his letters is as unlike teaching Algebra, as sawing the lumber for the desk is unlike putting the lock upon the drawer. And if one Teacher is required to do both, including all the intermediate branches, perhaps ten or twelve in number, can he be expected to labor otherwise than under most serious obstacles to success? Difficulties in the government of a School similar to those in teaching, will be found where all ages are brought together. The child of six years not only should be taught by a standard different from the one adapted to the youth of sixteen, but he should be governed by a different rule. And this it is extremely difficult to do, in a School of promiscuous ages. Many a little one has been almost martyrized by rules made for the larger scholars.

Suppose a Director orders three dozen desks for his Schoolhouse and the manufacturer has them in different stages of progress. He divides them into six classes, according to the amount of work that has been done upon each. In the morning he commences his labor by working half an hour upon the class just commenced; then he works half an hour upon a class that was commenced yesterday; then half an hour upon a class ready to be put together—and so on, till the last thirty minutes before noon are spent upon those which are thereby completed. In the afternoon he goes through the same varieties. What would be thought of such a mechanic's judgment? His folly would be as deplorable as is the necessity of an analogous course in the best classification that can be made in a single-District School. In the latter case, however, the Teacher can do no better. He divides the matérial upon which he works—the knowledges which he is manufacturing—into several classes, according to their state of advancement, and appropriates a few minutes to each in rotation; and while he is attending to one class, the others are to a greater or less extent, losing the time. This is a graded School, in the lowest sense; so low that the term is inapplicable; and the divisions are by common consent called "classes." Yet to this necessity is the Teacher in the single-District School shut up.

Under this system every District must secure a Teacher competent in every branch of study to be pursued; and the inevitable result was, that in most Schools, only the common elementary branches could be taught, whatever the number in the District who might wish to take deeper draughts at the fountain of knowledge. Yet this system has until recently, been generally pursued from generation to generation; and the youth who wished for more than the mere elements of an education in School, has been subjected to the expense of leaving the paternal roof to obtain it. The great portion could not do this, and thousands have thus outgrown the Primary School, and gone through life, vainly dreaming of realms of knowledge to which they might never attain.

Thousands of our fellow citizens now in middle life, as well as of more advanced age, obtained what was called "a good Common School education," and yet never studied anything more than Reading, Writing, Grammar, Arithmatic and Geography. Their subsequent education has been only self directed, and though an active mind must progress, with what immense loss has it been! Many a young man in the country has gone through with these studies, and at the age of fifteen he knew all that his instructor could teach him; and thus situated, with a bare foundation laid, and his soul panting for a higher flight, he found no one to point out his course, to direct him to higher studies—much less to instruct him in them!

Many a man it is not doubted, will in these remarks see his history written. With buoyant spirit he took the hand of his guide in the path of knowledge. From the humility and ignorance of childhood, up the base of the hill of science he rose. At every step, new beauties met his eye, new aspirations thrilled his soul, fatigue was forgotten, imagination foretold his triumph, and he dreamed of no barrier that he could not easily surmount, to prevent his standing ere long upon the hill-top, where he could take in the almost boundless view of all knowledge! But alas! in the midst of his high hopes and brilliant anticipations, his guide informed him that he had accompanied him as far as he had ever been—as far as he had strength to go, and he must pause in his journey, or seek another guide. He could neither guide him farther, or direct him what path to pursue, in an effort to go alone. His circumstances did not allow of his finding a competent guide; his prospect was blighted, and he has since been wandering in the wilderness of knowledge, with comparatively slight progress, vainly longing to stand upon the summit of the mount, where he may hold converse with the mysteries of that existence which he dimly sees and strangely feels!

The great portion of Primary Schools in the land could not secure Teachers for any other than the lower branches pursued; and many who were employed, were incompetent even in those. The wages usually paid, were not a sufficient inducement for men to qualify themselves for the work, much less to make it a profession. Poor pay, short terms, and disgusting Schoolhouses, were not peculiarly calculated to inspire a love of teaching, in those who were fitted for it; and the army of Teachers was composed mainly of young men who could not earn a dollar a day by labor, and young women who found it their most genteel means of aiding an indigent family, or of buying their wedding dress. Neither class expected to follow the pursuit for any considerable length of time. Occasionally there might be one who was considered a sort of professional Teacher; but in a majority of such instances, probably, they were those who had failed in other pursuits.

Doubtless those who taught, had some ambition to excel—but what a standard! They could not go to the necessary expense and time for a thorough preparation, and their only model was in the Teachers who had preceded them. Those they strove to excel *by imitating them!** As *their* Teacher "kept the School," so they *kept* it! And required as they were, to do a dozen things at once, it is not strange that the work was poorly done, and that the pupils made no greater progress in the common branches, in two years, than they might have made in one, had they been taught to reason as well as to recite, to think as well as to remember, and to investigate causes as well as effects.

A soldier who excelled in every martial characteristic, except that he was repeatedly intoxicated, was asked by his commander, why he who was a pattern soldier in all other respects, would persist in degrading himself by that one bad habit. Touching his hat with overacted politeness, he replied: "Why, Captain, could you expect to find a man with *all* the cardinal virtues for *seven dollars* a month?" And thus might the Teachers of Common Schools have asked in former days—and perhaps, sometimes yet: Can you expect all knowledge in a School Master, for less wages than he can earn by sawing wood?† Is it a wonder that Common Schools came to be regarded with no small degree of contempt by all—parents, Teachers and scholars? Is it any wonder that so many attended School with little or no interest in its exercises—realizing only the idea of poor Schools for poor scholars?

The whole system was defective, and calculated to perpetuate a race of poor Teachers, half developed scholars, and uninterested parents. With wages so low that few were tempted to engage in teaching, save those who were too young, or too incompetent, or too indolent, to enter

* The writer once making an official visit to a School "kept" by a "qualified teacher," urged upon him that he might derive advantage from the experience of others, and for this purpose invited him to become a subscriber to a School Journal published in the State. But he indignantly rejected the proposition, saying, "his own experience had placed him beyond the reach of improvement!" He excelled only in imitating himself.

† An experienced female Teacher, receiving a visit from a School officer at her School, feeling that an apology was necessary for its appearance, remarked to her visitor: "It ain't much they pays me; and it ain't much I teaches their children."

upon the ordinary pursuits of life, and with Schoolhouses whose location, architecture, furniture and surroundings, were often a disgrace to civilized humanity, there was little to elevate the School to its proper dignity, and make it a place for the children to love. Yet parents thought they felt a deep interest in their Schools—and doubtless they did, in their way. A free people could not be indifferent to the education of their children. The fault was less in them than in the system; which they seemed to regard as susceptible of but little improvement. Had they appreciated what their Schools might be, even with all the inherent evils of the system, great improvements would have ensued. There was no necessity even in the country, for farmers to send their sons and daughters to a Schoolhouse built with less architectural taste than were their granaries, and with scarcely more regard to the decencies of life, in its appendages, than characterize the abodes of the lowest tribes of savages! Some may regard these comparisons as too strong; but we speak only of what most persons must have many, many times witnessed.

Had Districts remedied these evils—so glaring, so obnoxious, that it is strange they were not sooner seen—and adopted the plan of paying male Teachers forty or fifty dollars per month instead of twelve or fifteen, and increased the wages of female Teachers in proportion, a short time would have witnessed a great improvement. But they saw not the evil; or seeing it, could imagine no remedy. And they could hardly be expected to employ the talent that would command those wages in other pursuits, to teach the many children to read, because a few wished to pursue a more advanced course. And had they done so, the vital evils of the single-District system would have remained untouched, so far as the system was concerned.

FOR POPULOUS SETTLEMENTS, A BETTER WAY.

Suppose four Districts, embracing not much more than a mile square each, as is the case in some of our towns, each with its School hovel and Teacher, and each with forty scholars. One has a competent Teacher to instruct the large scholars, and the smaller ones are neglected. Another has a female to teach the small children, and the large ones stay at home, or attend only to make difficulty. Now let these Districts become one, with a commodious Schoolhouse near the centre, and the number of scholars will probably be increased from one hundred and sixty, to two hundred. Let them be divided into three grades, and perhaps eighty would come into the Primary Department. These would be taught by two females, who at whatever wages might be paid them, would probably accomplish more than any Teachers of the other sex. The studies of this Department would be simple, and the Teacher's success would depend more upon the tact, in which females excel, than in the talent of more learned men. The next, or Intermediate Department, might include seventy more of the whole number, and would require one competent Teacher, and the payment of as high wages, perhaps, as is paid to both the female Teachers in the lower Department. The other, or High Department, would take the remaining fifty of the scholars, who would enter it sufficiently advanced to engage in History, Philosophy, Book-keeping, Algebra, Geometry, or Astronomy. This grade will require a Teacher of still higher attainments, and commanding higher wages. He will also be the head of the other Departments. If the single Districts before employed a male Teacher in the winter and a female in the summer, as is usual, we have now two of each for the year—which is practically the same thing, and no portion of the children will be at any time excluded from School for the want of an appropriate Teacher. The wages paid may be increased, but probably not more than equal to the increased number of scholars. To furnish instruction to all, we are no longer required to realize the figure of the poet, when he talks of

"The ocean being into tempest toss'd,
To waft a feather, or to drown a fly!"

In other words, we are no longer required to employ a University scholar to teach a portion of our children their letters, or let the others go untaught. We may thus obtain a full supply of Teachers, by the simple principle of a "division of labor," and each will labor under the most advantageous circumstances.

WHAT EVERY VILLAGE AND CITY SHOULD DO.

From the foregoing—which is but a mere glance at the subject—the remedy, where circumstances will admit of its application, is readily suggested. Wherever the population is sufficiently dense to furnish within a convenient distance from a common centre, more scholars than can be properly instructed by one Teacher, the territory thus included should still comprise but one District, with two or more School rooms, where the small scholars can occupy one apartment, and the larger another; each with a Teacher of qualifications adapted to his or her position. If the number of children within such bounds requires more than two Teachers, they should be divided into three grades. Where the number does not exceed four or five hundred, several considerations would counsel but one central building, with rooms for the several grades; but when the children exceed five hundred, it will be better to use the central house for the Higher Departments alone, and provide for the Primary Department in as many smaller houses variously located, as the demand may require. The congregating of more than five hundred children of all ages in one building, is of doubtful policy; and in a place of five thousand or more inhabitants, it is desirable that the small children be not exposed to the bustle, not to say the danger, and bad moral influences, of the crowded business streets through which they must pass less or more, to attend the central School. These considerations were at first a serious objection in the minds of many, to Union Schools; and it was truly an objection in large villages, if but one house was contemplated.

The small children will comprise not far from two-fifths of the whole. With branch Schoolhouses, they will have a less distance to travel, and will be more directly under their parents' eye. The other three-fifths of the scholars can meet at the central building without inconvenience, where they may be divided into as many grades, or sections of grades, as circumstances may demand. It is still but one School, with a common interest, a common expense, controlled by the same officers, and with teachers responsible to one head.

WHAT IS BEING DONE.

There is perhaps no subject upon which public sentiment has undergone a greater change within the last ten years, than that of Primary Schools. Villages and cities that have hardly doubled in population within that time, have ten to fifteen times the amount of money invested in Schoolhouses that they had, eight or ten years ago. It is doubtful whether, ten years since, there were ten Schoolhouses in all the villages of this State, that would now be pronounced so much as respectable in appearance. In this respect the villages were behind the country in enterprise, taking into account their difference in circumstances. But what a change! Now almost every village of any importance—several of them having become cities in their government—has its Schoolhouse or houses, to attract the traveller's eye with as much prominence as their churches, or other public buildings.

The city of Adrian, eight years since, had not two thousand dollars invested in School property. The value of her Schoolhouses and grounds is now not far from thirty-five thousand dollars. Yet the accommodations are not equal to the wants of her two thousand children, and four or five thousand dollars per annum it is expected will be expended for two or three years to come. Yet no tax-payer doubts that this expenditure has increased the real value of his property more than equal with the tax he has paid.

The city of Ann Arbor, with twelve hundred and thirty-nine children, has within five years, erected a Schoolhouse one hundred feet in length, costing, with the grounds, twenty-eight thousand dollars; and her citizens are not satisfied with that.

The township of Dexter has less than five hundred children; yet the *village* has a Schoolhouse that cost seven thousand dollars. This expense has been incurred for about two hundred and fifty children.

The city of Monroe, with twelve hundred and forty-five children between the legal ages, has recently erected a Schoolhouse at an expense of ten thousand dollars.

The village of Tecumseh has within two years past, completed a Schoolhouse at an expense of fifteen thousand dollars. The Report for the last year states the number of children between the legal ages, to be four hundred and sixty-eight; and the number attending School, four hundred and twenty-two.

Seven years ago, the village of Niles, with about five hundred children, had *one* School, and employed a Teacher at fifteen dollars per month—or it would be as correct to say that a Teacher was paid that sum, and they had no School; for the average number in attendance required but ten and one-half seats! The name of a School was kept up sufficiently to draw their portion of the Interest fund, and that, probably, was all that was expended. It seems almost incredible that a place of business enterprise like Niles, could sink so low in educational affairs. But the citizens of that place resolved to redeem themselves from their reproach, and Niles has now a Schoolhouse one hundred feet it length, standing upon a lot forty by sixteen rods, or four acres in size, beautifully ornamented with native forest trees—the whole costing about thirty thousand dollars!

The city of Ypsilanti contains nine hundred and sixty-four children within the legal ages. A Schoolhouse that cost fifteen thousand dollars was recently burned. Another is already erected, one hundred and twenty feet front, the center ninety-three, and the wings seventy feet deep —the whole costing forty thousand dollars.

These are examples of the educational spirit that now animates the citizens in most cities and villages in the State. Several other places might be named, where an equal or similar enterprize prevails. Every new movement begets new interest, dignifies the Primary School, and stimulates all classes in the noble work of Universal Education.

SCHOOLS IN THE COUNTRY.

As has been remarked, the Schools in the sparsely settled sections of the State cannot avail themselves of the benefits of the graded system to any considerable extent. This is a misfortune inseparably connected with their position; but that they cannot do all that is desirable, is no reason why they should not do the very much that is within their power, for very great improvement. Let Schoolhouse be located, erected, and furnished with taste; let the unsightly, inconvenient hovel with all its repulsive aspects and surroundings, give place to a building and accompaniments which, though on a small scale, the children may love and honor, as to them indeed a *temple* of knowledge—a place where they shall delight to repair—a place more attractive to them than are the homes of a majority—a place truly of poetry and flowers—a place of both natural and artificial beauty—a place inviting rather than repulsive to the unsophisticated child, whose love of the beautiful is pure, and one of the strongest elements of his character. Then, whatever the expense, give them the best Teacher that can be obtained—not necessarily the most learned, but the one with the best faculty of teaching to others what he himself knows—and all your increased expense shall be returned ten-fold in the more rapid development of the minds of the children you love.

The first requisite to success in teaching, is to inspire an *interest in the mind* of the child. And can this be done by an arbitrary command—"be interested?" The farmer can lead his horse to water—but can he *make* him drink? So you may compel a child to attend School where he can evoke not one pleasant association for his mind to rest upon, and command him to be interested in study. It is to him a prison; he sighs to be away among the flowers and fields teeming with beauty and song, or rolling snowballs, and practicing the poetry of motion with his hand-sled. What mother would send her child to learn his Sabbath School lesson in a goose pasture, on the border of a green-coated frog pond? Yet such a course would be as wise as to send him to the Primary School, with such inconveniences and non-attractions as are often provided. Give the children a Schoolhouse which they will love, and the number attending it, will be greatly increased, to lighten the burden of expense. The improvements in the Town Schools—the Normal School—Teachers' Associations, and all the attendant influences, with the general interest in Primary School Education that has been awakened within the few past years, are fast raising up Teachers with a higher standard of qualification than most Districts in the country have formerly been able to obtain. But to secure their services, higher wages must be paid than in former days. The race of twelve-dollars-a-month School Masters, it is hoped, is about to become extinct.

Yet all the increased expense of houses and Teachers will be only real retrenchment, in point of true economy. It is believed that such improvement might thus be made in the country Schools, even without grading, that the children would make greater progress in *two* years than they have formerly done in *three!* while their enjoyment in their duties would be incalculably increased.

A PHILOSOPHICAL VIEW.

The expense of these improvements is unworthy of a thought, if a just view of the importance of the subject is taken. Shall the parent toil, and cheerfully expend large sums, to be often renewed, to clothe his child, so that his *person* may appear well in society for a few brief years, and grudge an equal amount for a permanent endowment of his intellect, which is to exist forever? Education is very far from being for this life alone! If we know anything of the philosophy of the human soul, and its powers, Education does not become valueless, or annihilated, when we step out from this physical prison—when we shake off these chains of flesh—and go forth an enfranchised intellect, to the realities of a higher existence. What we *possess*, is left behind; but what we *know*, is a part of ourselves, inseparable from us, and must inhere in our nature throughout a now mysterious future State. Education is the training of the immortal nature; and a subject really of no less importance while in the flesh, than it will be when the flesh has returned to dust. We train dogs and horses—shall we educate our children with no higher view than he has who learns his dog to carry his basket?

Is it not to be apprehended that some who wish to educate their children, have views of the subject but little higher than this, and are satisfied if they learn barely enough to pass through life respectably and successfully—educating them much as the showman does his monkey, only with reference to his ability to make money? How unworthy of a being made "but a little lower than the angels," are such views!* There are perhaps some who would say—"while we are in the flesh, we must attend to the wants of the flesh; and when we go forth upon another existence, we will prepare for its circumstances as we meet them." But as well might the student in College spend all his time while there, in furnishing his room with extravagance and pernicious luxuries, debasing his mind and ruining his health, and when remonstrated with, reply—"while I occupy this room, I must enjoy it; when I go out to engage in life's responsibilities, there will be time enough to prepare for them!"

If we could take a true view of the subject, we should perceive that our moral and intellectual necessities are primary, and our physical wants secondary. Our moral and intellectual nature is the end, and material appliances are the means. But men often reverse this order, and make their immortal nature the slave of the mortal; they devote all their interest and labor for that which dies, and are regardless only of that which will ever live!

Men live and toil mainly for their children. They seek to hoard up money and lands to leave for their children to use when they have passed to the home for all. But how many see to it with proper care, that their children are rightly educated, and prepared to occupy and enjoy the inheritance which they leave, or hope to leave them? How many appear more anxious to leave their children property and possessions to lose or squander after they die, than, while they live, to fill their minds with moral and intellectual wealth, of which nothing here or hereafter, can rob them!

A wealthy individual left at his death, a princely sum to endow a College. Strangers to him became the managers

---

* A professedly Christian parent being once remonstrated with for not sending his daughter to School, said: "'Cretia ain't very well, and I'm afraid if I send her to school now, she'll die before she gits to be a woman, and then I shall lose all it costs me."

of the fund, and gave the institution a tone according to their own bias, and used the money in quite a different manner from what he intended; and his munificent grant was but little better than thrown away, as he would have regarded the matter, could he have returned to view the results. His son who inherited his vast estate, saw the failure, and profited by his father's error. He founded a College while he lived to superintend its inauguration, and determine its character. His money was thus used as he designed; every dollar produced its intended result; and he saw the benefits he had conferred upon his fellow men. Which was the wiser man? Like the latter, the wise man will use whatever means are necessary for his children while he lives, and make the education of their minds and hearts his great object; so that if he leaves them little or much else, he is sure to give them an inheritance for all the future of their being.

MUTUAL EXCHANGES.

In many cases there might be found a partial remedy for the ungraded School in the rural Districts, by an exchange of scholars between the towns and the country. Such an exchange would be mutually beneficial. Men often send their children—particularly their daughters—away from home, when they know that their own School is in every respect equal to the one to which their children are sent. Education consists not in the knowledge of books alone. The person is educated but partially, who has not studied the world outside of home. Such an one may know much, and the probability is, that he will yet be a narrow-minded bigot in all things. To become a full-grown man, he needs to study men, and learn "the ways of the world" outside of his own little world. The astonishing increase of travel in these days, is probably doing more to overcome the bigotry, and humble the self-conceit of the people of our land, than all other influences combined could do, in a time when thousands did not go a hundred miles from home during their lives. Going abroad shows men that this is a great world—that possibly their house is not the only "centre" of it—that there are thousands of rivers larger than theirs, and thousands of men who after all, know more than they do—truths which perhaps, they would never have learned so as fully to appreciate, from books.

The child of the farmer, cut off by circumstances, from all save a limited intercourse with the world, needs, more than all others, the advantages of going away from home; but this is ordinarially attended with an expense that few are able to bear, to any extent that will produce marked results. The end may be gained in some measure, however, without expense, and the lack of a high department in the country School so far supplied, by sending his more advanced children to the town to attend a graded School, and receiving a child from town to board in exchange, which child will also be benefited in various respects. He is probably more ignorant of the country than the farmer's child is of the town; and he or she will obtain quite as much and as useful information, by associating with the country, as the other will by his intercourse with the town. Both will learn that there are many more things in the world than they ever dreamed of under their parental roof. This need not interfere with the legal exclusiveness of School Districts, as "a fair exchange is no robbery;" and it is believed that no School Board would object to a measure mutually so beneficial. The youth from the country might thus pursue higher branches of study than they could in their own ungraded School, and at the same time have the advantage of observing the habits and customs of other people, of acquiring that ease of manners which comes by association with strangers, and of gaining that self-reliance which they can never possess while ignorant of their fellow man. If the School Board in the towns object that the exchange would not be equal, as probably the scholars they would receive, would be older than those who go into the country, and require more experienced teachers, let them charge a trifling tuition. The difference at most, would be but slight, and by consultations, the Boards of the respective Districts might arrange conditions satisfactory to all. Such an intermingling of families would do much to destroy the petty jealousies, envyings and exclusiveness of feeling that often exists between the town and the country. The young would thereby extend the circle of their acquaintance, and so far increase their opportunities of meeting with the most suitable partner for life. The change would often prove highly conducive to the health of the parties, and all concerned would feel more than before, that all men are their neighbors, and realize more fully the true brotherhood of mankind. The subject is suggested to the reader's consideration.

UNION SCHOOLS.

By a "Union School" is to be understood something more than a mere consolidation of two or more Districts, and the gathering of all the children to be taught under one roof. Twenty Districts might unite, and yet, the union be only united confusion and anarchy. On the other hand, any number of Districts may unite under the provisions of Sections 92 and 93 of the Primary School Law, and continue to use all the old Schoolhouses, with no other, and yet realize the complete design of a Union School. It may be the same thing, whether they do this, or occupy but one great central building; but in the latter case, they must divide into separate rooms; and it matters not whether the several grades are separated by several streets, or only by a brick wall. The important characteristic of a Union School is the gradation of its departments; and this may be done as well with separate houses as with separate rooms. If several houses are made use of, the Primary Department will be in one, to which all the small children will repair. Another house will be for another grade, and so on; and the children from all parts of the same District will meet and pass each other daily on their way to School. In a village of moderate size, it will usually be found expedient to occupy but one house; but experience has shown that in large towns, it is a better policy to have several houses. The law under which our Union Schools are established, had not for its end the mere union of Districts for a consolidation and saving of expense, by making education more a wholesale business; all this was but a means to the end; which end was, to *grade* the School, as it could not be done with limited numbers. The advantages to be derived from thus grading the School according to the studies pursued, has already been alluded to.

In the establishment of our earliest Union Schools, the plan was adopted of erecting one house for all the scholars. Where the population has but slightly increased, the single house generally continues to be used; but in the rapidly growing towns, the one house has soon become filled, and the plan is being changed by the erection of branch houses for the Primary departments. By this division, it becomes no less a Union School. They are controlled by the same Board, and the same Superintendent or Principal has charge of all as before.

Any single District may avail itself of all the advantages of a Union School, if it has scholars enough to require several Teachers. In that case the scholars may be classified under separate Teachers, and the School becomes thereby a *Graded School.* But single Districts seldom contain scholars in sufficient numbers to adopt this course; hence a union of Districts as the remedy.

The Union School proper is no more than a large graded Primary School, with as many grades, or departments, as the number of scholars and variety of studies may require, to furnish in the best manner, a good common education to its pupils, and prepare them morally and intellectually, for the responsibilities of life.

A PREPARATORY DEPARTMENT.

Our State has a University, which after a struggle of years in its early history, almost for its very existence, now stands upon broad and sure foundations, and is preparing many of our young men for a commanding influence in society. But in that struggle, the Branches, which were projected to facilitate the preparation of those who would wish to enter the University, expired; and in all probability, they will never be revived. A more than substitute however, has been found, by connecting with the Union Schools, a department with all the advantages and appliances expected in the Branches. This feature of the Primary School, additional to the advantages it has formerly afforded to the young, is in harmony with its design, and an extension of its benefits. The extent to which the Primary School shall go in its instruction, is decided only by custom; and it will hardly answer in this age of the world, for Custom to declare its laws, like those of the Medes and Persians, unchangeable, whenever an advancing age, new circumstances, and new views, make a modification desirable. One of the main objects of the Union School is to teach successfully, higher branches than could be taught in the single-District School. By what rule then, shall the limit of these additional studies be prescribed? Most evidently, by expediency, and regard to the greatest good of the greatest number.

The State has provided a University where our young men may walk in the highest paths of literature. Its attempt to afford them facilities for reaching its classic halls proved a failure. Thus the State has acknowledged an obligation in this matter. The State cannot endow an

Academy in every county, and private Schools to supply the want, are too expensive for the masses—a great portion of those who wish for their aid, being persons of limited means. It were cruel mockery for the State to proclaim a free University to its youth, and at the same time remind them that they can reach it only by a heavy preliminary expense. The Union School has established one department additional to the highest ordinary advantages of the old system—why not add another, and meet this great want in our otherwise admirable educational system, and give our young men and women all the advantages of the Academy, in their own immediate vicinity?

But one possible objection, it is believed, can be urged against this plan; and that is not valid, because the assumption is not true in fact. That is, that such a department would add to the expense of the Primary School. This is on the supposition that whatever one person gains, some other person must lose; but this is not always true. Two farmers may exchange horses, and both make a good bargain. Much more may this be the case, in business arrangements relating solely to moral and intellectual means.

It is not here proposed or recommended to admit students to this department absolutely free, or subject only to their share in the rate bills. It is probable that a moderate tuition should be charged them. They might, pursuant to the provisions of sections 141 and 142 of the School Law, be charged such tuition as the Boards shall deem just, and those residing within or without the District be received on the same terms. The burden of expense in attendance at a High School, is not in the tuition, but in the payment for board, where the student is required to go from home. But here, where the greater number would board at home, a small tuition, and yet more than sufficient to meet the increased expense of the School, would be a very small consideration with those availing themselves of so great advantages.

By these means, the number of persons who will pursue the higher branches of science, without reference to a University education, will be greatly increased, and thus the blessings of education be more widely extended, and the number of competent School Teachers increased. The Primary School will be dignified in the minds of the young, and their desire for higher advancement stimulated. Thus it would seem to be in every way expedient and beneficial to all parties concerned, to establish such a department wherever it is called for in our Union Schools, under such regulations as the several District Boards may determine.

SCHOOL BUILDINGS, AND THEIR APPENDAGES.

The style and expense of Schoolhouses will of course be in conformity to the taste, ability, and enterprise of the citizens of the District. There are few Districts in the town or country, where the ability of the inhabitants is not sufficient for the fitting up of a building and grounds, on a scale co-extensive with the demand, and in a style equal to the taste they should cultivate, and the interest which they should have in the subject. Wherever the subject of education is properly appreciated, as much regard will be had to the style of the Schoolhouse, as there is to that of the church. Our Creator could be worshipped by the "great congregation" in a rude structure designed for secular use; and our children may bow at the shrine of knowledge in a log hovel; but neither is desirable, if it can be avoided. As a man, in view of towering mountains, the mighty cataract, or an ocean storm, realizes more sensibly, the majesty and power of his Maker, so the child in a beautiful Schoolhouse, surrounded by verdant shade, and blooming flowers, will more fully realize the dignity of his own nature, and the desirableness of its improvement, and be more interested and stimulated in his course.

The Schoolhouse and all its surroundings and furnishing, should be such as at the same time to please and improve the taste of the pupils. Who does not know the immense influence the place he is in, has upon not only the child's mind, but also upon the minds of men? The man whose heart is properly educated to pure and elevated thoughts, may resist the influences of such places as are suggestive of unworthy ideas, while another who perhaps, passes in promiscuous society for a person of ordinary refinement, will break out, as it were, with the most degrading and vulgar thoughts and language—perhaps publish his deep self-degradation upon the walls! A true education should develop not only the intellect of the child, but every good quality of character; so that he may at last stand a perfect man, in all his moral, intellectual, and social being. And to do this, the Imagination requires cultivation no less than the Causality and Comparison. Yet is it not true, that Schools have aimed too exclusively, to store the mind with facts, while the moral nature has been little regarded, and the imagination entirely neglected, and given over, a prey to every influence that debases it, and through it, degrades the whole character! No quality of the mind is more active or powerful, or exerts a greater influence upon character, than the imagination; and thousands of good men have been led to ruin, only because their imagination in early life, was left undirected, uncontrolled, and uneducated.

The School where our children spend years of the most impressible portion of their life, and where their characters are being formed almost as imperceptibly as the gathering of the dew upon the flower, should have attractions inviting to their taste, and elevating to their thoughts. For the same reason, the child should be kept from all places and scenes that tend to degrade the mind. The parent who permits his child to resort to places or scenes thus degrading, is as truly guilty, as he who sends his child to a School of crime. The surest way to ruin a young man, is to corrupt and debase his imagination. That is the traitor within the castle of the heart, that opens the gates to the enemy. Who ever sent his child to a circus, and did not find that there, in a single lesson, he learned more vulgarity and debasement of thought, than he could unlearn by all counteracting influences in many weeks?

The beautiful in nature and art will have a far better influence for the child's moral purity than will the uncomely and repulsive. The child trained to refinement of speech and manners, will be far less subject to the influence of degrading thoughts, and less prone to improper or vile conduct, than if educated a clown in manners at home, and a blackguard in speech in the streets. Purity of heart is doubtless often found in the lowest walks of life, and under the most unfavorable circumstances; but it is in spite of the circumstances, and the purity is less elevated, and the virtue less ennobling than they would have been, in a more favorable position; and there is little doubt that many a man might trace his moral ruin, in no small degree, to the circumstances of his early life, whose unpropitious influences awakened low thoughts, diminished self respect, and spoke to the mind and imagination only of degradation and abasement.

The soul of the child holds constant converse with the material world around him. His heart talks to the birds and flowers, and they speak back to him the language of joy and beauty. The world is ever discoursing to his vivid imagination, of beauty, purity, harmony, love, and all that can awaken and strengthen high and worthy aspirations in his soul; or it is suggesting dark thoughts to his lower nature, and poisoning his imagination, which in turn poisons all the fountains of his moral being. As the images of material things are pictured upon the eye, so their influences are constantly impressing the heart—especially of the young. How desirable then—how essential—that the School room and the School shall speak favorably to their thoughts, cultivate self respect, and whisper ever to the heart, of propriety of speech and conduct, and make study pleasant, (and thus successful,) not only for its intrinsic value, but for its delightful and elevating associations! Make all beautiful. Let the architecture speak to them, thoughts grand and noble. Let the furniture talk to them of refined manners, and social courtesy. Let trees and flowers join their voices in songs of gladness, hope, and beauty. Let the chrystal fountain rise to gurgle forth its admonition to activity, and let everything be fitted to unite in the grand chorus that shall inspire the young hearts with pleasant, ennobling, elevating, energizing thoughts and emotions. He who loves his children with a love worthy of their high nature, will feel that money can hardly be expended in a better investment.

These considerations have of late, come to be better appreciated perhaps, in the towns than in the country. But there is no reason why the country Schoolhouse should not be inaugurated with all the taste that can be displayed in the towns. That the former is comparatively a small building, is no reason why it may not be beautiful. If it is small, it can be adorned with the less expense. The location should be select, the grounds capacious, and attended to with all the care of a flower garden. To say the least, the whole should be equal in appearance, to the best house and grounds in the District. Attention should be given to the roads, in reference to the Schoolhouse, so as to make it as easily accessible as the nature of the case will admit. Who can wonder that in many places, when the children are "dismissed," they feel as though they were released from prison! A man may be excusable for not giving his child a good house to live in—poverty may forbid it. But no such excuse will justify the use of a hovel in the midst of a thistle field, for a School. The Schoolhouse is built by the property in the district; equally for the benefit of the poor, but not by them; and there is perhaps, no District where the aggregate means may not erect and furnish a good one without embarassment.

The Schoolhouse should also be located and constructed with careful reference to health. Before the introduction of stoves, there was little danger of scholars suffering for want of fresh air. The danger then, was entirely in the other direction. In the winter there was too much air; and the children found it necessary to ask permission to "go to the fire," quite as often as they sought aid in their studies. On the introduction of stoves, it was found necessary, in order to make them available, to make the room "tight." Accordingly every crevice was closed, the plastering—if the house could boast the dignity of a plastered wall—was repaired, and the cold air shut out, and the other extreme reached. Instead of freezing the children, the tendency then was to stupify them, by their breathing the air over and over, poisoned both by their lungs, and by the heated iron of the stove. The art of warming the room was attained; but how to warm it without detriment to health, all seemed profoundly ignorant.

A child will make little progress in study, while uncomfortably seated, while suffering with cold, or stupified by breathing bad air. All our efforts therefore, for the education of the young, will lose a great part of their power unless these evils are avoided, in the construction, furnishing, and warming of our Schoolhouses.

It is believed that the citizens of this State are in a measure sensible of the importance of the subject here discussed, and that the suggestions made, will meet the approbation of all who give them due consideration. Under the provisions of law which require the Superintendent of Public Instruction to "prepare and cause to be printed with the Laws relating to Primary Schools, all necessary forms, regulations and instruments for conducting all proceedings under said laws, with such instructions relative to the organization and government of said Schools as he may deem advisable," and believing the work demanded by the importance of the subject, and the increasing public interest in education, he has prepared the following plans for Schoolhouses, furniture, &c., with such suggestions relative to warming, ventilation, location, and kindred considerations, as it is hoped will be of service to those who would adopt all true improvements, and avail themselves of every possible means to make the education of the young a leading interest in the State.

SCHOOL ARCHITECTURE.

In all well directed efforts of an enlightened people for the improvement of their Schools, the location, size, and construction of the Schoolhouse itself, will claim and receive early attention These local habitations of our Schools are themselves important agencies in the work of instruction. And though silent, they often speak more eloquently and persuasively than the living Teacher. Too much attention, then, cannot be given to the pleasantness and healthfulness of their location ; to the comfort and convenience of their arrangements ; to the facilities for rendering the School attractive, both as relates to its internal construction and its outward surroundings ; to the furniture of the house itself, to the apparatus employed to render the instructions of the Teacher more attractive and impressive ; and to the means of securing a genial temperature even during the severity of our winters, and a pure and healthful atmosphere where numbers are congregated. For no proposition can be more apparent than that, if there is one house in the District more pleasantly located, more comfortably constructed, better warmed, and more inviting in its general appearance, and more elevating in its influence than any other, that house should be the Schoolhouse.

LOCATION OF SCHOOLHOUSES.

In looking at the location of Schoolhouses through the country at large, it cannot have escaped the attention of the ordinary observer, that they are usually located with little reference to taste, or the health and comfort of Teacher or children. They are generally on one corner of public roads, and sometimes adjacent to a cooper's shop, or between a blacksmith's shop and a saw-mill. They are not unfrequently placed upon an acute angle, where a road forks, and sometimes in turning that angle the travel is chiefly behind the Schoolhouse, leaving it on a small triangle, bounded on all sides by public roads.

At other times the Schoolhouse is situated on a low and worthless piece of ground, with a sluggish stream of water in its vicinity, which sometimes even passes under the Schoolhouse. The comfort and health, even of innocent and loved children, are thus sacrificed to the parsimony of their parents.

Scholars very generally step from the Schoolhouse directly into the highway. Indeed, Schoolhouses are frequently one-half in the highway, and the other half in the adjacent field, as though they were unfit for either. This is still the case, even in some of our principal villages, though many of them have, within the last few years, nobly redeemed themselves.

Schoolhouses are sometimes situated in the middle of the highway, a portion of the travel being on each side of them. When scholars are engaged in their recreations, they are exposed to bleak winds and the inclemency of the weather one portion of the year, and to the scorching rays of the meridian sun another portion. Moreover, their recreations must be conducted in the street, or they trespass upon their neighbors' premises. Such situations can hardly be expected to exert the most favorable influence upon the habits and character of the rising generation.

We pursue a very different policy in locating a church, a court house, or a dwelling. And should we not pursue an equally wise and liberal policy in locating the *District Schoolhouse?*

In this State six hundred and forty acres of land in every

township are appropriated to the support of Primary Schools. Suppose there are eight School Districts in a township: This would allow eighty acres to every School District. It would seem that when the general government has appropriated *eighty acres* to create a fund for the support of Schools, that each district might set apart *four acres*—which is but one acre in twenty—as a site for a Schoolhouse.

Once more: one School District usually contains not less than twenty-five hundred acres of land. Is it asking too much to set apart *four acres* as a site for a Schoolhouse in which the *minds* of the children of the District shall be cultivated, when *twenty-four hundred and ninety-six* acres are appropriated to clothing and feeding their *bodies?*

I would respectfully suggest, and even *urge* the propriety of locating the Schoolhouse on a piece of firm ground of liberal dimensions, and of inclosing the same with a suitable fence. The inclosure should be set out with shade trees, unless provided with those of nature's own planting, and ornamented with shrubs and flowers. Scholars would then enjoy their pastime in a pleasant and healthful inclosure, where they have a *right* to be, protected alike from the scorching sun and the wintry blast. They need then no longer be hunted as *trespassers* upon their neighbors' premises, as they now too frequently are.

SIZE OF SCHOOLHOUSES CONSIDERED IN CONNECTION WITH THE PHILOSOPHY OF RESPIRATION.

Some of our principal cities and villages can now boast as noble structures for Schoolhouses as can any of the older States of the Union, as will appear from the plans and descriptions of those hereto appended. And the work of improvement, in this respect, is perhaps now going on as rapidly in the State of Michigan, as in any of the older States. But as yet, in view of what remains to be done, it can hardly be regarded as more than well begun.

Within the last fifteen years I have visited half of the States of the Union for the purpose of becoming acquainted with the actual condition of our Common Schools. I have therefore noticed especially the condition of Schoolhouses. Although there is a great variety in their dimensions, yet there are comparatively few Schoolhouses less than sixteen by eighteen feet on the ground, and fewer still, perhaps, larger than twenty-four by thirty feet, exclusive of our principal cities and villages. From a large number of actual measurements, not only in New York and Michigan, but east of the Hudson River, and west of the Great Lakes, I conclude that, exclusive of entry and closets, when they are furnished with these appendages, Schoolhouses are not usually larger than twenty by twenty-four feet on the ground, and seven feet in hight. They are, indeed, more frequently smaller than larger. Schoolhouses of these dimensions have a capacity of three thousand three hundred and sixty cubic feet, and are usually occupied by at least forty-five scholars in the winter season. Not unfrequently sixty or seventy, and occasionally more than a hundred scholars occupy a room of this size.

Now let us proceed to consider what changes are produced upon the vital qualities of air by respiration, and the quantity hence, that is essential to maintain the healthy respiration of forty-five students three hours—the usual length of a single session, and half of the length of the two daily sessions of School; and often there is little ventilation during the customary recess at noon.

The quantity of air that enters the lungs at each inspiration of an adult, has been variously estimated from thirty-two to forty cubic inches. To establish more definitely some data upon which a calculation might safely be based, I some years ago conducted an experiment whereby I ascertained the medium quantity of air that entered the lungs of myself and four young men, was thirty-six cubic inches, and that respiration is repeated once in three seconds, or twenty times a minute. I also ascertained that *respired air will not support combustion.* And it is a principle well established by science, and sustained by experiment, that air which will not support *combustion* will not sustain *animal life.* We hence reach another and a *more important* truth, viz., that AIR ONCE RESPIRED WILL NOT FURTHER SUSTAIN ANIMAL LIFE.

That part of the experiment by which it was ascertained that respired air will not support combustion, is very simple, and I here give it, with the hope that it may be tried at least in every Schoolhouse, if not in every family of the State. It was conducted as follows:

I introduced a lighted taper into an inverted receiver (glass jar) which contained seven quarts of atmospheric air, and placed the mouth of the receiver into a vessel of water. The taper burned with its wonted brilliancy about a minute, and, growing dim gradually, became extinct at the expiration of three minutes. I then filled the receiver with water, and inverting it, placed its mouth beneath the surface of the same fluid in another vessel. I next removed the water from the receiver by *breathing into it.* This was done by filling the lungs with air, which, after being retained a short time in the chest, was exhaled through a siphon (a bent lead tube) into the receiver. I then introduced the lighted taper into the receiver of respired air, by which it was *immediately extinguished.* Several persons present then received a quantity of respired air into their lungs, whereupon the premonitory symptoms of apoplexy ensued. The experiment was conducted with great care, and several times repeated in the presence of respectable members of the medical profession, a professor of chemistry, and several literary gentlemen, to their entire satisfaction.

It may be well to note the changes that are produced in the vital qualities of the air in respiration. The chemical properties of the atmosphere are attributable chiefly to the presence of *oxygen*. Nitrogen, which constitutes about four-fifths of its volume, has been supposed to act as a mere diluent to the oxygen. *Increase* the proportion of oxygen in the atmosphere, and the vital powers will speedily suffer from excess of stimulus; the circulation and respiration become *too rapid;* and the system generally becomes highly excited. *Diminish* the proportion of oxygen, and the circulation and respiration become *too slow;* weakness and lassitude ensue; and a sense of heaviness and uneasiness pervades the entire system. As has been observed, air *loses* during each respiration, a portion of its oxygen, and gains an equal quantity of *carbonic acid*, which is an *active poison*. When mixed with atmospheric air in the ratio of one to four, it extinguishes animal life. It is this gas that is produced by burning charcoal in a confined portion of common air. Its effect upon the system is well known to every reader of our newspapers. It causes dimness of sight, weakness, dullness, a difficulty of breathing, and ultimately *apoplexy* and *death*.

Now a simple arithmetical computation will abundantly satisfy any person who is acquainted with the composition of the atmosphere, the influence of respiration upon its fitness to sustain animal life, and the quantity of air that enters the lungs at each inspiration, that a School-room of the preceding dimensions contains quite too little air to sustain the healthy respiration of even *forty-five* scholars three hours—the usual length of each session; and frequently the Schoolhouse is imperfectly ventilated between the sessions at noon, and sometimes for several days together.

The reader will please note the following particulars: **1.** The quantity of air breathed by forty-five persons in three hours, according to the data just given, is three thousand three hundred and seventy-five cubic feet. **2.** *Air once respired will not sustain animal life.* **3.** The

School room was estimated to possess a capacity of three thousand three hundred and sixty cubic feet—*fifteen feet less than is necessary to sustain healthy respiration.* 4. Were forty-five persons whose lungs possess the estimated capacity, placed in an air-tight room of the preceding dimensions, and could they breathe pure air till it was all once respired, and then enter upon its second respiration, *they would all die of apoplexy before the expiration of a three hours' session.*

These conditions, it is admitted, cannot be fulfilled. But numerous instances of fearful approximation exist. We have no air-tight houses. But in our latitude, comfort requires that rooms which are to be occupied by children in the winter season, be made very close. The dimensions of rooms are, moreover, frequently diminished, in order that the *warm breath*, and animal heat, may lessen the amount of fuel necessary to preserve a comfortable temperature.

It is true, on the other hand, that the quantity of air that children breathe, is somewhat less than I have estimated, but the derangement resulting from breathing impure air, in their case, is greater than in the case of adults, whose constitutions are matured, and who are hence less susceptible of injury. It is also true in many Schools, that the number occupying a room of the dimensions supposed, is considerably greater than I have estimated. Moreover, in many instances, a great proportion of the larger scholars will respire the estimated quantity of air.

And again: all the air in a room is not respired *once* before a portion of it is breathed the second, or even the *third* and *fourth* time. The atmosphere is not suddenly changed from purity to impurity—from a healthful to an infectious state. Were it so, the change, being more perceptible, would be seen and *felt* too, and a *remedy* would be sought and applied. But because the change is gradual, it is not the less fearful in its consequences. In a room occupied by *forty-five persons*, THE FIRST MINUTE, *thirty-two thousand four hundred cubic inches of air impart their entire vitality to sustain animal life, and, mingling with the atmosphere of the room, proportionately deteriorate the whole mass.* Thus are abundantly sown in early life the fruitful seeds of disease and premature death.

This detail shows conclusively sufficient cause for that uneasy, listless state of feeling which is so prevalent in crowded School-rooms. It explains why children that are amiable at home are mischievous in School, and why those that are troublesome at home are frequently well-nigh uncontrollable in School. It discloses the true cause why so many Teachers who are justly considered both pleasant and amiable in the ordinary domestic and social relations, are obnoxious in the School-room, being there habitually sour and fretful. The ever-active children are disqualified for study, and engage in mischief as their only alternative.

On the other hand, the irritable Teacher, who can hardly look with complaisance upon good behavior, is disposed to magnify the most trifling departure from the rules of propriety. The scholars are continually becoming more ungovernable, and the Teacher more unfit to govern them. Week after week they become less and less attached to him, and he, in turn, becomes less interested in them.

This detail explains, also, why so many children are unable to attend School at all, or become unwell so soon after commencing to attend, when their health is sufficient to engage in other pursuits. The number of scholars answering this description is greater than most persons are aware of. In one District I had occasion officially to visit a few years ago in the State of New York, it was acknowledged by competent judges to be emphatically true in the case of not less than *twenty-five scholars.* Indeed, in that same District, the health of more than *one hundred* scholars was materially injured every year in consequence of occupying an old and partially decayed house, of too narrow dimensions, with very limited facilities for ventilation.

The health of scores and hundreds of children in every part of our State, as well as in the older States generally, is suffering from the same and like causes.

From the preceding exposition we are enabled to understand why the business of Teaching has acquired, and *justly too*, the reputation of being unhealthy. There is, however, no reason why the health of either Teacher or pupils should sooner fail in a well regulated School, taught in a house properly constructed, and suitably warmed and ventilated, than in almost any other business. Were it not so, an unanswerable argument might be framed against the very *existence* of Schools; and it might clearly be shown that it is *policy*, nay, DUTY, to close at once and forever, the four thousand Schoolhouses of Michigan, and the hundred thousand of the nation, and leave the rising generation to perish for lack of knowledge. But our condition in this respect is not hopeless. The evil in question may be effectually remedied by enlarging the house, or, which is easier, cheaper, and more effectual, by frequent and thorough ventilation. It would be well, however, to unite the two methods.

I once visited a School in which the magnitude of the evil under consideration was clearly developed. Five of the citizens of the District attended me in my visit to the School. We arrived at the Schoolhouse about the middle of the afternoon. It was a close, new house, eighteen by twenty-four feet on the ground—two feet less in one of its dimensions than the house concerning which the preceding calculation is made. There were present forty-three scholars, the Teacher, five patrons, and myself, making fifty in all. Immediately after entering the Schoolhouse, one of the District officers remarked to me, "I believe our Schoolhouse is too tight to be healthy." I made no reply, but secretly resolved that I would sacrifice my comfort for the remainder of the afternoon, and hazard my health, and my life even, to test the accuracy of the opinions I had entertained on this important subject. I marked the uneasiness and dullness of all present, and especially of the patrons, who had been accustomed to breathe a purer atmosphere.

School continued an hour and a half, at the close of which I was invited to make some remarks. I arose to do so, but was unable to proceed till I opened the outer door, and snuffed a few times the purer air without. When I had partially recovered my wonted vigor, I observed with delight the renovating influence of the current of air that entered the door, mingling with and gradually displacing the fluid poison that filled the room, and was about to do the work of death. It seemed as though I was standing at the mouth of a huge sepulcher, in which the dead were being restored to life. After a short pause, I proceeded with a few remarks, chiefly, however, on the subject of respiration and ventilation. The officers, who had just tested their accuracy and bearing upon their comfort and health, resolved immediately to provide for ventilation in the manner herein recommended.

Before leaving the house on that occasion, I was informed an evening meeting had been attended there the preceding week, which they were obliged to dismiss before the ordinary exercises were concluded, because, as they said, "We all got sick, and the candles went almost out." Little did they realize, probably, that the light of life became just as nearly extinct as did the candles. Had they remained there a little longer, both would have gone out together, and there would have been reacted the memorable tragedy of the *Black Hole* in Calcutta, into which were thrust a garrison of one hundred and forty-six persons, one hundred and twenty-three of whom perished miserably in a few hours, being suffocated by the confined air.*

VENTILATION OF SCHOOLHOUSES.

The preceding disclosure manifests the importance of frequent and thorough ventilation. But the ordinary facilities for ventilating School-rooms, are almost entirely restricted to opening a door, or raising the lower sash of the windows. The prevailing practice with reference to their ventilation, is opening and closing the door, as the scholars enter and pass out of the Schoolhouse, before School, during the recesses, and at noon. Ventilation, *as such*, I may safely say, has been practiced only to a very limited extent, and in a very imperfect manner. It is true, the door has been occasionally set open a few minutes, and the windows have been raised, but the object has been, either to let the *smoke* pass out of the room, or to *cool* it when it has become *too warm*, NOT TO VENTILATE IT. Ventilation, by opening a door or raising the windows, is imperfect, and frequently injurious. A more effectual and safer method of ventilation, where special arrangements have not been provided for the purpose, is to lower the upper sash of the windows; or, in very cold or stormy weather, to open a ventilator in the ceiling, and allow the vitiated air to escape into the attic. In this case, there should be a free communication between the attic and the outer air, by means of a lattice window, or otherwise.

But any such arrangements for ventilation are at best very ill-adapted to the purpose. The subject will therefore be again referred to in connection with warming; for the two should be considered together, and especially as a Schoolhouse may be best ventilated when best warmed, and best warmed when best ventilated.

* For a more extended discussion of this whole subject, see the Author's work on "The Means and Ends of Universal Education."

SIZE AND CONSTRUCTION OF SCHOOLHOUSES.

In determining the size of Schoolhouses, due regard should be had to several particulars. There should be a separate entry or lobby for each sex, which should be furnished with a scraper, mat, hooks and shelves—both are needed—sink, basin, and towels. A separate entry thus furnished will prevent much confusion, rudeness, and impropriety, and promote the health, refinement, and orderly habits of the children.

The principal room of the Schoolhouse—and each such room where there are several departments—should be large enough to allow each occupant a suitable quantity of pure air, which should be at least twice the common amount, or not less than one hundred and fifty cubic feet. But a large space for each pupil is less important where thorough provision is made for ventilation. There should also be one or more rooms for recitation, apparatus, library, etc., according to the size of the School and the number of scholars to be accommodated.

Every School room should be so constructed that each scholar may pass to and from his seat without disturbing or in the least incommoding any other one. A house thus arranged will enable the Teacher to pass at all times to any part of the room, and to approach each scholar in his seat whenever it may be desirable to do so for purposes of instruction or otherwise. Such an arrangement is of the utmost importance; and without the fulfillment of this condition, no Teacher can most advantageously superintend the affairs of a whole School, and especially of a large one.

In determining the details of construction and arrangement for a Schoolhouse, due regard must be had to the varying circumstances of country and city, as well as to the number of scholars that may be expected in attendance, the number of Teachers to be employed, and the different grades of Schools that may be established in a community.

COUNTRY SCHOOLHOUSES.

In country Districts, as they have long been situated, and still generally are, aside from separate entries and clothes-rooms for the sexes, there will only be needed one principal School-room, with a smaller room for recitations, apparatus, and other purposes. In arranging and fitting up this room, reference must be had to the requirements of the District; for this one room will be occupied by children of all ages, for summer and winter Schools, and often for the secular, but more especially for the religious meetings of the neighborhood. But in its construction primary reference should be had to the convenience of the scholars in School; for it will be used by them more, ten to one, than for all other purposes. Every child, then, even the youngest in School, should be furnished with a seat and desk, at which he may sit with ease and comfort. The seats should each be furnished with a back, and their hight should be such as to allow the children to rest their feet comfortably upon the floor. This is as necessary to the *health* of children as to their *comfort*.

From considerations heretofore presented, it is believed no one can fail to see the advantages that would result to a densely settled community from a union of two or more Districts for the purpose of maintaining in each a School for the younger children, and of establishing in the central part of the associated District, a School of a higher grade for the older and more advanced children. If four Districts should be united in this way, they might erect a central house, C, for the larger and more advanced scholars, and four smaller ones, P P P P, for the younger children. The central School might be taught by a male teacher, with female assistants, if needed; but the Primary Schools, with this

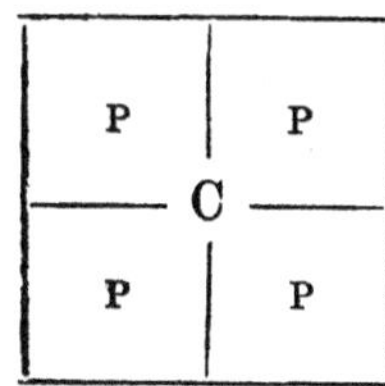

arrangement, could be more economically and successfully instructed by females. Legal provisions are already made in this State for such a consolidation of Districts. This would invite a more perfect classification of scholars, and would allow the central Schoolhouse to be so constructed, and to have the seats and desks of such a hight as to be convenient for the larger grade of scholars, and still be comfortable for other purposes for which it might occasionally be necessary to occupy it. Such an arrangement, while it would obviate the almost insuperable difficulties which stand in the way of proper classification and the thorough government and instruction of Schools, would at the same time offer greater inducements to the erection of more comfortable and attractive Schoolhouses.

SCHOOLHOUSES IN CITIES AND VILLAGES.

The plan suggested in the last paragraph may be perfected in cities and villages. For this purpose, where neither the distance nor the number of scholars is too great, some prefer to have all the Schools of a District or corporation conducted under the same roof. However this may be, as there will be other places for public meetings of various kinds, each room should be appropriated to a particular department, and be fitted up exclusively for the accommodation of the grade of scholars that are to occupy it.

In cities, and even in villages with a population of three or four thousand, it is desirable to establish at least three grades of Schools, viz: the Primary, for the smallest children; the Intermediate department, for those more advanced; and a Central High School, for scholars that have passed through the Primary and Intermediate Schools. While this arrangement is favorable to the better classification of the scholars of a village or city, and holds out an inducement to those of the lowest and middle grade of Schools to perfect themselves in the various branches of study that are pursued in them respectively, as the condition upon which they are permitted to enter a higher grade, it also allows a more perfect adjustment of the seats and desks to the various requirements of the children in their passage through the grades of Schools.

The extent to which the gradation of Schools may advantageously be carried, is well illustrated in the public Schools of the city of New York, two hundred in number, in which six hundred Teachers are employed, and in which one hundred thousand children annually receive instruction. The Free Academy, which stands at the head of the public School system of New York, and which is a School of the highest grade, was established by the Board of Education in 1847. The expense of the building, without the furniture, was $46,000, and the annual expense for the salaries of professors and teachers is about $10,000.

No students are admitted to the Free Academy who have not attended the Public Schools of the city for at least one full year, nor these until they have undergone a thorough examination and proved themselves worthy. Its influence, hence, is not confined to the one hundred or one hundred and fifty scholars who may graduate from it annually, but reaches and stimulates the six hundred Teachers of the city, and the hundred thousand children whom they instruct, and thus elevates the Common Schools of the city, and places them much more favorably before the public than they otherwise could be.

Smaller cities, and especially villages with a population of but a few thousand, can not, of course, maintain so extended a system of public Schools; but they can accomplish essentially the same thing more perfectly, though on a smaller scale. For the benefit of Districts in the country and in villages, a few Plans of Schoolhouses will be here inserted.

Plan No. 1.—Schoolhouse for fifty-six Scholars.

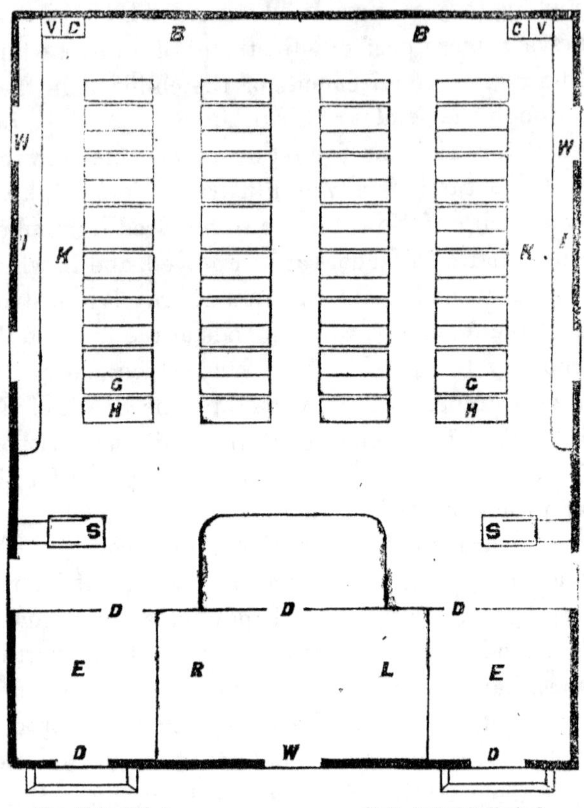

Size, 30 by 40 feet. Scale, 10 feet to the inch.

D D, doors. E E, entries lighted over outer doors, one for the boys and the other for the girls. R L, room for recitation, library, and apparatus, which may be entered by a single door from the Teacher's platform, as represented in the plan, or by two, as in Plan No. 3, p. 457. S S, stoves with air-tubes beneath. K K, aisles four feet wide—the remaining aisles are each two feet wide. C V, chimneys and ventilators. I I, recitation seats. B B, black-board, made by giving the wall a colored hard finish. G H, seats and desks, four feet in length, constructed as represented on the 357th page. Other styles of seats and desks are given on pages 387 to 402 of this volume. This plan is from the author's work on Universal Education.

Plan No. 2, Fig. 1.—Front Elevation

Figures 1, 2 and 3, of Plan No 2, are on a scale of 20 feet to the inch.

Plan No. 2, Fig. 2.

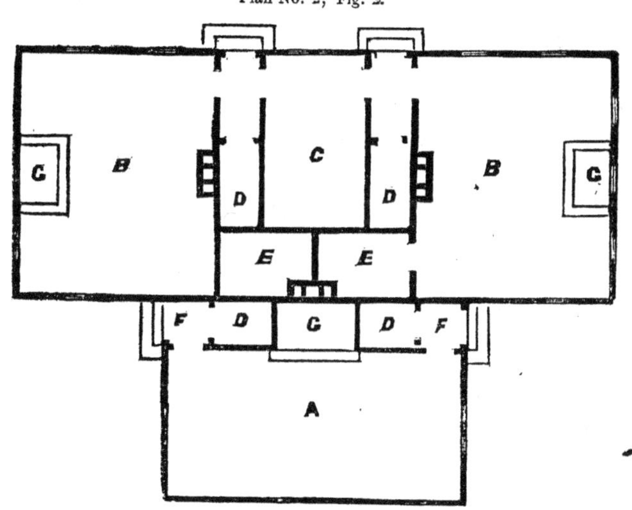

A, School-room for Primary classes, both sexes. B B, School-rooms for second grade, sexes divided. C, Recitation-room, common for both sexes, and repository for books and instruments. D D D D, Clothes-rooms. E E, Wood-closets. F F, Entrance lobbies. G G G, Teachers' platforms. A side elevation is given on the next page.

Plan No. 2, Fig. 3.—Side Elevation

The three Figures of Plan No. 2, are each on a scale of 20 feet to the inch.

The drawings of the three figures represented in Plan No. 2, were furnished by Messrs. Jordan & Anderson, of Detroit. This plan, it will be seen, has separate entrances, on opposite sides of the building, for boys and girls, who meet in the Primary Department, represented at A on the preceding page. Separate entrances for the sexes are also provided on the other front, for students attending the Second Grade, in the rooms represented at B B.

This plan, it will be seen, provides separate entrances for the boys and girls of each of the two departments. As the Schoolhouse has two fronts, it might appropriately occupy a square, or be located between two streets, in a village or city, which would readily admit of separate play yards for the boys and girls of each of the two departments.

Plan No. 3, Figs. 1 and 2, on the two following pages, is from the author's work on Education. It is adapted to the division of a School into three Departments—for Primary, Intermediate and High Schools. The rooms of this plan may be furnished with a simple style of seats and desks, as represented at Fig. 1, or by the improved furniture represented on pages 387 to 402 of this volume.

Plan No. 3, Fig. 1.—First Story.

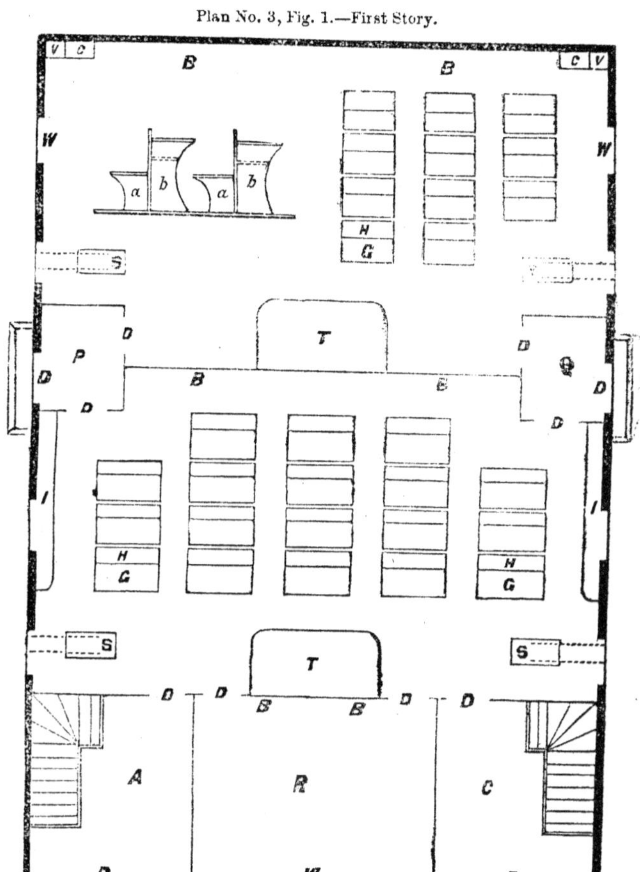

Size, 36 by 54 feet.

Scale, 12 feet to the inch.

A, entrance for boys to the High School. C, entrance for girls to High School. P, entrance for boys to the Primary and Intermediate Departments. Q, entrance for girls to the same. D D, doors. W W, windows. T T, Teacher's platform and desk. G H, desk and seat for two scholars, a section of which is represented at *a b*. I I, recitation seats. B B, blackboards. S S, stoves, with air-tubes beneath. *c v*, chimney and ventilator. R, room for recitation, library, apparatus, and other purposes.

For an explanation of the advantages to be derived from the use of air-tubes, see page 374th of this volume.

Plan No. 3, Fig 2.—Second Story.

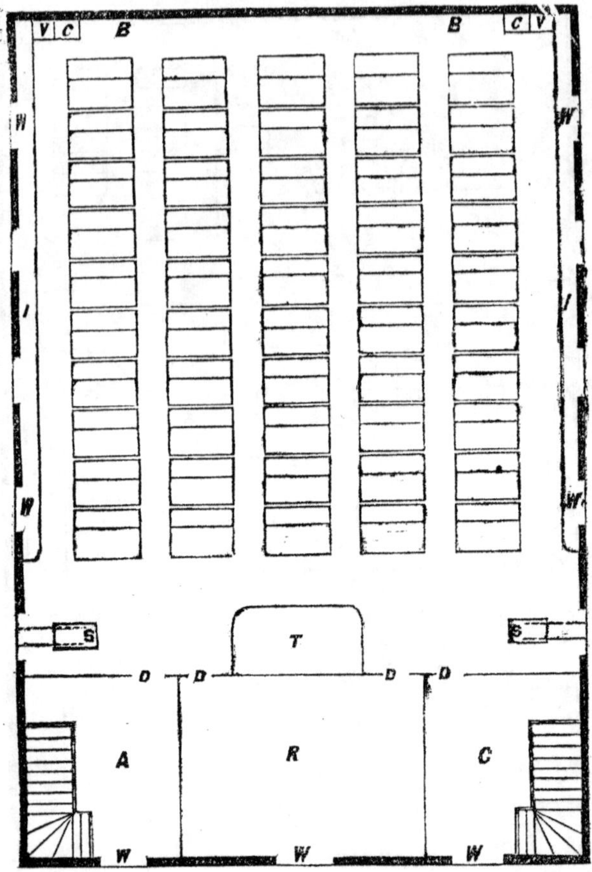

A, entrance for the boys, through the lobby below. C, entrance for the girls. D D, doors. W W, windows. S S, stoves. *c v*, chimney and ventilator. T, Teacher's platform. R, recitation-room. I I, recitation-seats in principal room. B B, blackboard.

The use of the tubes represented by dotted lines beneath the Stoves, is explained on the 374th page of this volume. A description of an admirable style of ventilating School Stove, with an explanation of the advantages to be derived from its use, will be found on the 375th page.

For the different styles of blackboard, see page 418.

Plan No. 4, Fig. 1.—Front Elevation.

Front Elevation of the Monroe Union Schoolhouse.

Figure 1 represents the Front Elevation of the Union Schoolhouse, recently erected in the city of Monroe. A side elevation of this Schoolhouse is given on the next page. The ground plans of the several stories of this building, are represented on the 361st and 362d pages.

This Schoolhouse has been erected by W. H. Beaman, Esq., under contract, for something less than ten thousand dollars. He has kindly furnished the plans from which these engravings have been prepared.

The plans, originated and matured by John L. Stevens, Esq., of Monroe, have been well carried out by the contractor. The Schoolhouse, completed, is a credit to the educational enterprise of the city, and appears in striking contrast with its condition fifteen years ago, when the writer first entered upon the discharge of the duties of Su-

Plan No. 4, Fig. 2.—Side Elevation.

Side Elevation of the Monroe Union Schoolhouse.

perintendent. At that time there was not a public School building of any kind in the city. Now there are three or four other respectable Schoolhouses in the city beside this.

A like improvement has been made within this time, in the Schoolhouses of Ann Arbor, Tecumseh, Jackson and Niles, and in those of other cities and villages of the State.

On pages 363 to 365 are plans of the Bishop Union Schoolhouse of Detroit, which is the last Schoolhouse erected, and the best building occupied by the public Schools of that city. This Schoolhouse has been named in honor of the late President of the Board of Education of that city, as was the Barstow Schoolhouse, erected a few years ago, in honor of the late, lamented President of the Board.

Plan No. 4, Fig. 3.—Basement.

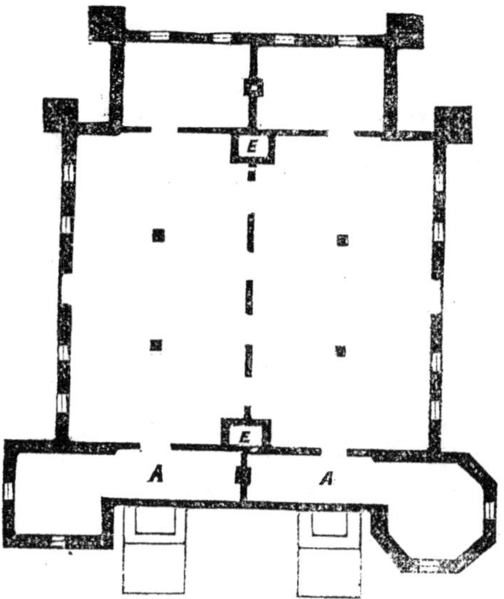

A A—Halls; B B—Furnaces.

Plan No. 4, Fig. 4.—First Story.

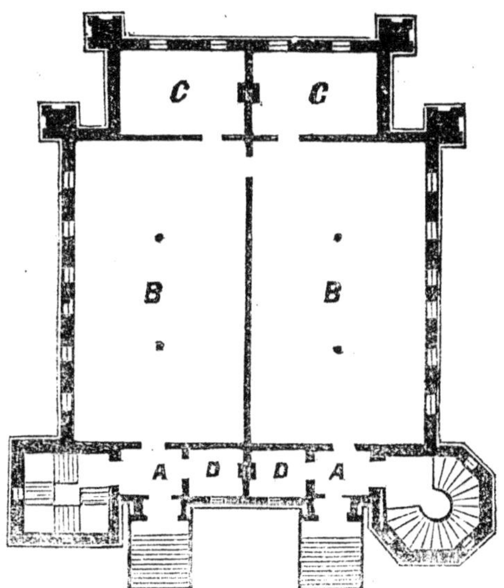

A A—Halls; B B—Class-rooms; C C—Recitation-rocms; D D—Clothes-rooms.

Plan No. 4, Fig. 5.—Second Story.

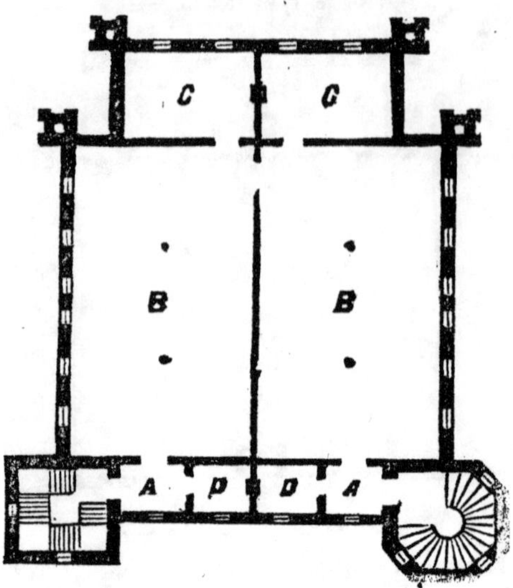

A A—Halls; B B—Class-rooms; C C—Recitation-rooms; D D—Clothes-rooms.

Plan No. 4. Fig. 6.—Third Story.

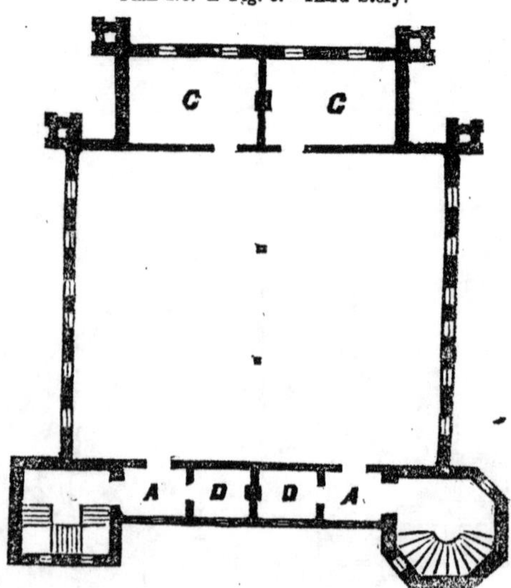

A A—Halls; C C—Recitation-rooms; D D—Clothes-rooms.

Plan No. 5, Fig 1.—Front Elevation.

The several Figures of Plan No. 5, are on a scale of 30 feet to the inch.

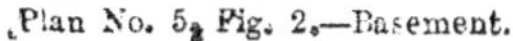

Plan No. 5, Fig. 2.—Basement.

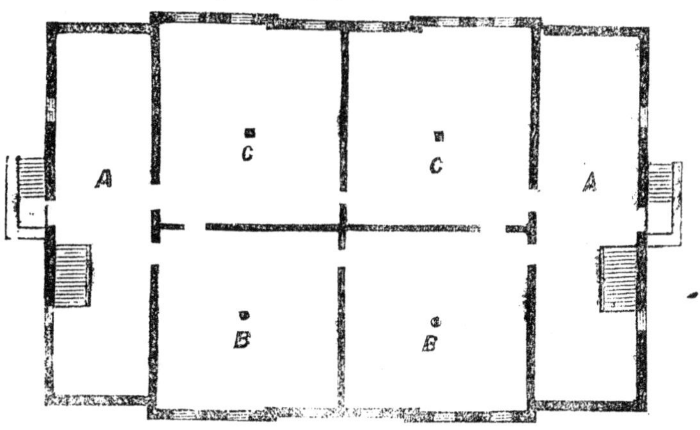

A A—Halls; B B—Class-rooms; C C—Fuel-rooms.

Plan No 5, Fig. 3—First Story.

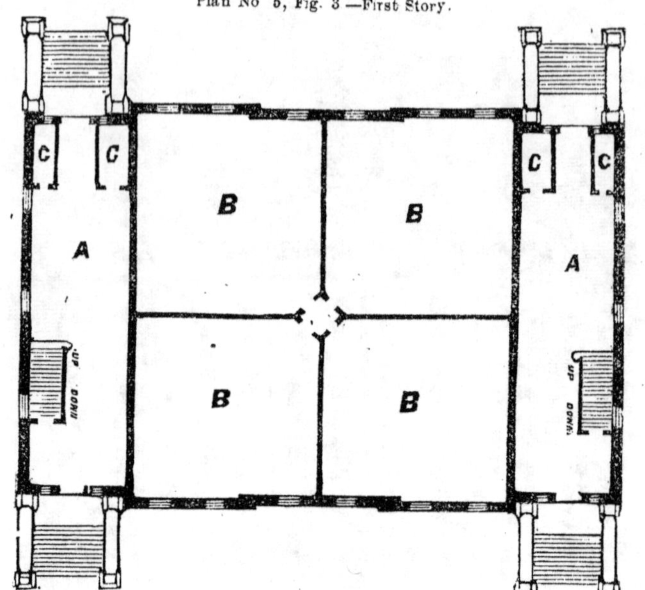

A A—Halls; B B B B—Primary-rooms; C C C C—Clothes-rooms.

Plan No. 5, Fig. 4.—Second Story.

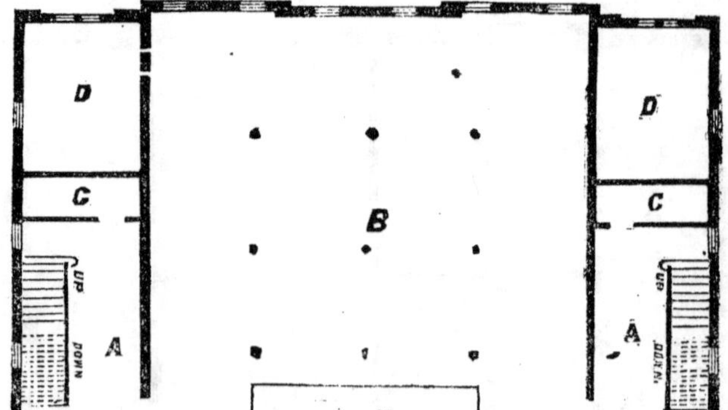

A A—Halls; B—Class-room; D D—Recitation-rooms; C C—Clothes-rooms; E—Teachers' Platform.

Plan No. 5, Fig. 5.—Third Story.

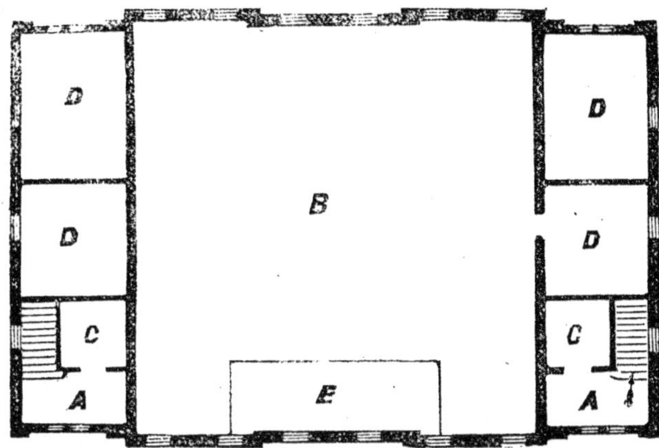

Scale of 30 feet to an inch.

A A, Halls. B, Class-room. D D D D, Recitation-rooms. C C, Clothes-rooms. E, Teachers' platform.

Drawings of the Plans of the Bishop Union Schoolhouse, from which these engravings have been prepared, were furnished me by Messrs. Jordan & Anderson, of Detroit, who originated, matured and carried out the plans, as they likewise did those of the Ypsilanti Union Schoolhouse.

The Front Elevation of the Ypsilanti Union Schoolhouse appears as a Frontispiece to this volume. The Ground Plans of the building are given on pages 366 and 367.

A Front Elevation of Hillsdale College has been furnished by the Officers of that Institution. This noble structure is represented at the 368th page of this volume.

UNION PUBLIC SCHOOL, YPSILANTI, MICHIGAN.

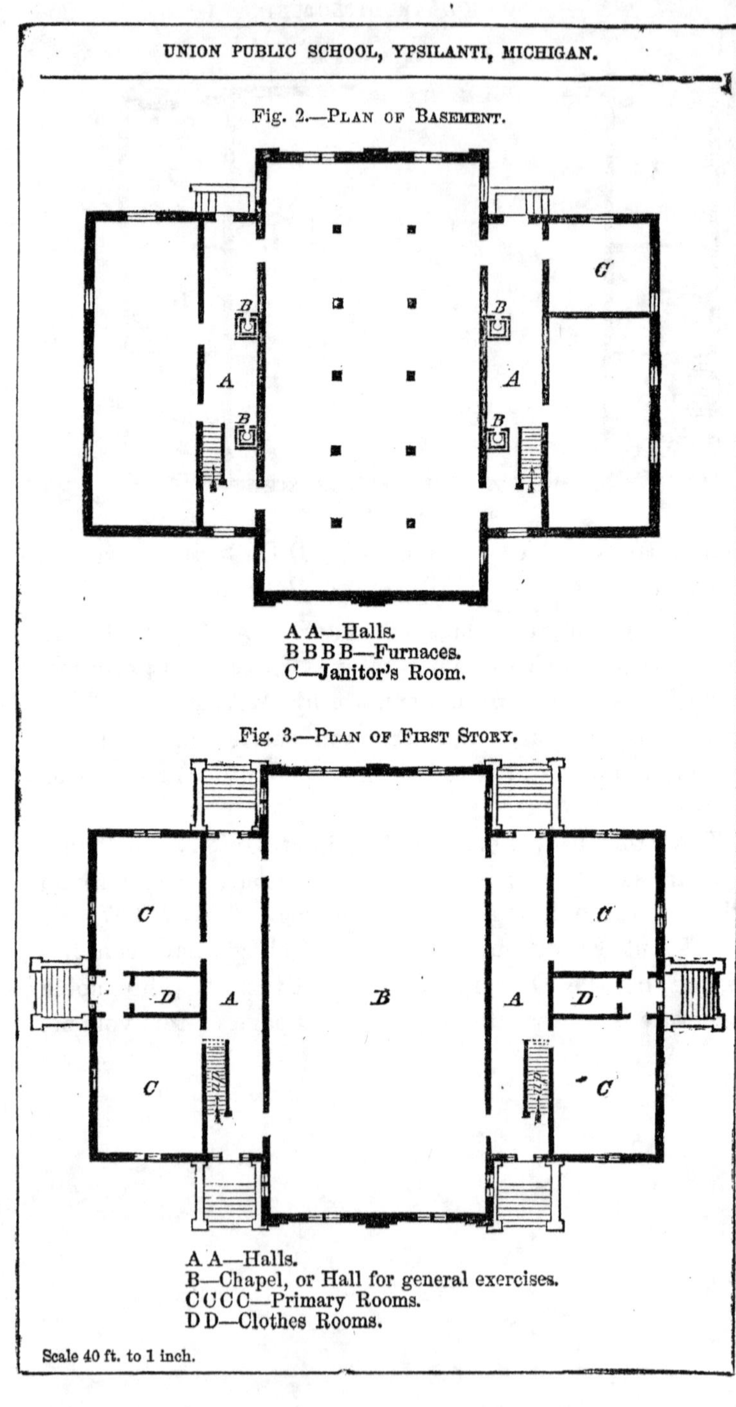

Fig. 2.—PLAN OF BASEMENT.

A A—Halls.
B B B B—Furnaces.
C—Janitor's Room.

Fig. 3.—PLAN OF FIRST STORY.

A A—Halls.
B—Chapel, or Hall for general exercises.
C C C C—Primary Rooms.
D D—Clothes Rooms.

Scale 40 ft. to 1 inch.

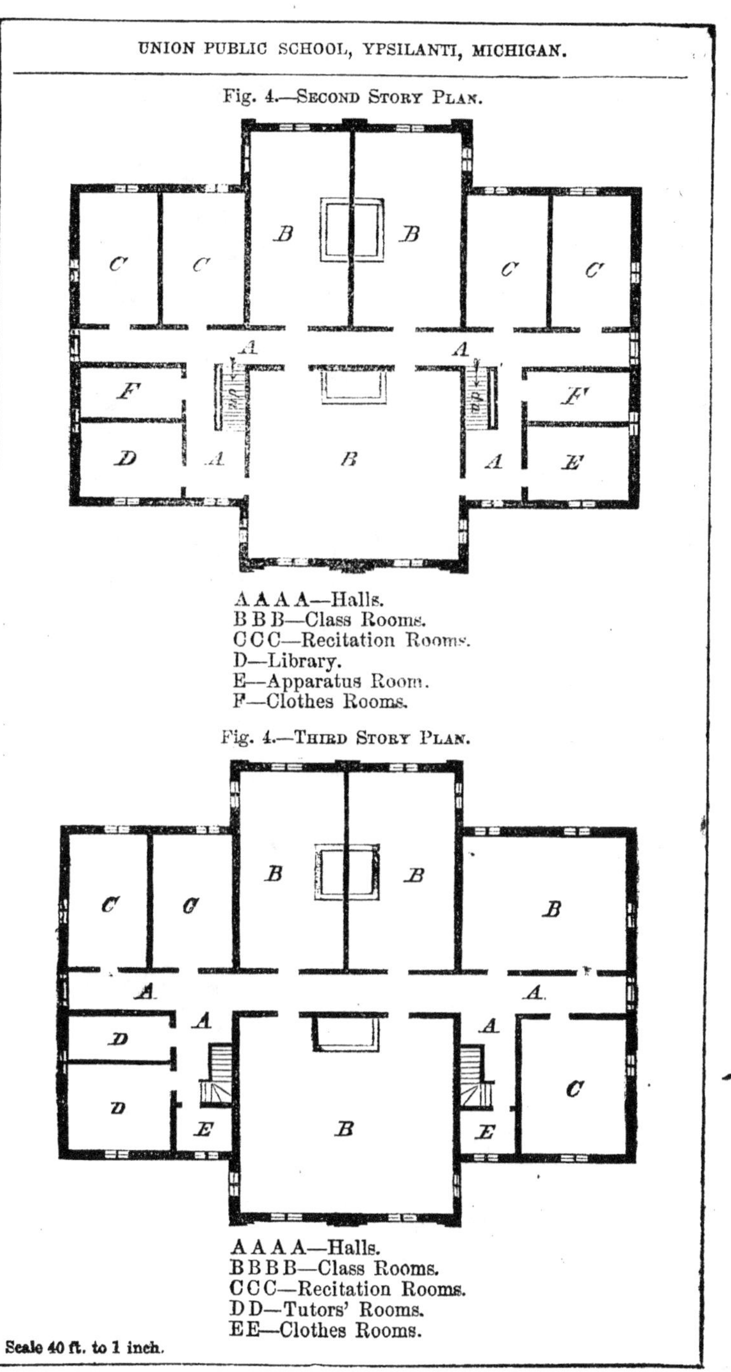

Fig. 4.—Second Story Plan.

Fig. 4.—Third Story Plan.

HILLSDALE COLLEGE.

WARMING AND VENTILATION.

1st. *Warming by Stoves.*—Next in importance to pure air in a School-room is the maintenance of an even temperature. This is an indispensable condition of health, comfort, and successful labor. It is one, however, that is very generally disregarded; or, perhaps I should say, one that is not often enjoyed.

Schoolhouses are generally warmed by means of stoves, some of which are in a good condition, and supplied with dry, seasoned wood. The instances, however, in which such facilities for warming exist, are comparatively few. It is much more common to see cracked and broken stoves, the doors without either hinges or latch, with rusty pipe of various sizes. Green wood, also, and that which is old and partially decayed, either drenched with rain or covered with snow during inclement weather, is much more frequently used for fuel than sound, seasoned wood, protected from the weather by a suitable woodhouse. With this state of things, it is exceedingly difficult to kindle a fire, which burns poorly, at best, when built. Fires, moreover, are frequently built so late, that the house does not become comfortably warm at the time appointed for commencing School. These neglects are the fruitful source of much discomfort and disorder. The temperature is fluctuating; the room is filled with smoke a considerable part of the time, especially in stormy weather; and the School is liable to frequent interruptions, in fastening together and tying up stove-pipe, etc.

This may seem a little like exaggeration. I know full

well there are many noble exceptions. But in a large majority of instances it is believed some of these inconveniences exist; and the most of them coexist much more frequently than persons generally are aware of. I speak more confidently on this subject, having personally visited several thousand Schools in this and other States of the Union. Besides, I have myself many times heard School officers and patrons, who have visited their School with me for the first time in several years, say, "We ought to have some dry wood to kindle with; I didn't know it was so smoky; we must get some new pipe; really, our stove is getting dangerous," etc. And some of the boys have relieved the embarrassment of their parents by saying, "It don't smoke near so bad to-day as it does sometimes!"

The principal reason why the stoves in our Schoolhouses are so cracked and broken, and why the pipes are so rusty and open, lies in the circumstance that green wood, or that which is partially decayed and saturated with moisture, is used for fuel, instead of good seasoned wood, protected from the inclemency of the weather by a suitable wood-house. There are at least three reasons why this is poor policy: 1. It takes double the amount of wood. A considerable portion of the otherwise sensible heat becomes latent, in the conversion of ice, snow, and moisture into steam. 2. The steam thus generated cracks the stove and rusts the pipe, so that they will not last one half as long as though dry wood from a wood-house were used. 3. It is impossible to preserve an even temperature. Sometimes it is too cold, and at other times it is too warm; and this, with such means of warming, is unavoidable. Scores of Teachers have informed me that, in order to keep their fires from going out, it was necessary to have their stoves constantly full of wood, and even to lay wood upon the stove, that a portion of it might be seasoning while the rest was burning! Aside from the inconvenience of a fluctuating temperature, this is an unseemly and filthy practice, and one that generates very offensive and injurious gases.

The subject of warming and ventilation is of late properly engaging an increased share of public attention. I have frequently heard the following and similar remarks: "The use of stoves in our Schoolhouses is a great evil;" "Stoves are unhealthy in our Schoolhouses, or in any other houses." etc. This idea being somewhat prevalent, and stoves being generally used in our Schoolhouses, their influence upon health becomes a proper subject for consideration.

Combustion, whether in a stove or fireplace, consists in a chemical union of the *oxygen gas* of the atmosphere with *carbon*, the combustible part of the wood or coal used for fuel. Carbonic acid, the vitiating product of combustion, does not, however, ordinarily deteriorate the atmosphere of the room, but, mingling with the smoke, escapes through the stove-pipe or chimney.

The Stove, in point of economy, is far superior to the Open Fireplace as ordinarily constructed. When the latter is used, it has been estimated that nine-tenths of the heat evolved ascends the chimney, and only one-tenth, or, according to Rumford and Franklin, only one-fifteenth, is radiated from the front of the fire into the room. Four-fold more fuel is required to warm a room by an Open Fireplace than when a Stove is used. Oxygen is, of course, consumed in a like proportion, and hence, when the Open Fireplace is used, there is necessarily a four-fold greater ingress of cold air to supply combustion than where a Stove is employed.

But what is of still greater importance, when a Fireplace is used, it is impossible to preserve so uniform a temperature throughout the room as when a Stove is employed. When a Fireplace is used, the cold air is constantly rushing through every crevice at one end of the room to supply combustion at the other end. Hence the scholars in one part of the room suffer from cold, while those in the opposite part are oppressed with heat. The Stove may be set in a central part of the room, whence the heat will radiate, not in one direction merely, but in all directions. In addition to this, as we have already seen, only one-fourth as much air is required to sustain combustion, on both of which accounts a much more even and uniform temperature can be maintained throughout a room where a Stove is used than where a Fireplace is employed.

Whence, then, has arisen the prevailing opinion that Stoves are unhealthy? There are two sources of mischief, either of which furnishes a sufficient foundation for this popular fallacy. The first has already been referred to, and consists simply in the almost total neglect of proper ventilation. The other lies in the circumstance that School-rooms are generally kept too warm. In addition to the inconvenience of too high a temperature, the aqueous vapor existing in the atmosphere in its natural and healthful state is dissipated, and the air of the room becomes too dry for healthy respiration.

The evil being seen, the remedy is apparent. Reduce the temperature of the room to its proper point, and supply the deficiency of aqueous vapor by an evaporating dish partially filled with pure water. If this is not done, the dry and over-heated air, which is highly absorbent of moisture in everything with which it comes in contact, not only creates a disagreeable sensation of dryness on the surface of the body, but in passing over the delicate membrane of the throat, creates a tickling, induces a cough, and lays the foundation for pulmonary disease, especially when ventilation is neglected.

The water in the evaporating dish should be frequently changed, and kept free from dirt and other impurities. Care also should be taken not to create more moisture than the air naturally contains, otherwise the effect will be positively injurious. The evil complained of is attributable mainly to the maintenance of too high a temperature. Were a thermometer placed in many of our School-rooms —and a Schoolhouse should never be without one in every occupied apartment—instead of indicating a suitable temperature, say sixty-two or sixty-five degrees, or even a summer temperature, it would not unfrequently rise above blood heat. The system is thus not only enfeebled and deranged by breathing an infectious atmosphere, but the debility thence arising is considerably increased in consequence of too high a temperature. The two causes combined eminently predispose the system to disease.

The change from inhaling a fluid poison at blood heat, to inhaling the purer air without at the freezing point or below, is greater than the system can bear with impunity. A uniform temperature, which is highly important, can be more easily and more effectually maintained where a stove is employed, furnished with a damper, and supplied with dry, hard wood, than where a fireplace is used. In the former case the draft may be regulated, in the latter it cannot be.

A great amount of air enters into combustion even where a stove is used. A still greater quantity enters into the combustion where a fireplace is employed, in proportion to the increased amount of wood consumed. Much of the heated air, also, where an open fireplace is used, mingling with the smoke, passes off through the chimney, and its place is supplied by an ingress of cold air at the more distant portions of the room. There is hence not only a great waste of fuel, but a sacrifice of comfort, health, and life.

Even where a stove is used there is a constant ingress of cold air through cracks and defects in the floor, doors, windows, and walls, which causes it to be colder in the outer portions of the room than in the central portions and about the stove. The evil is the same in kind as that already referred to in speaking of fireplaces, but less in degree. This evil, however, may be almost entirely obviated by a very simple arrangement, which will also do much to render ventilation at once more effectual and safe, especially in very cold and inclement weather. The arrangement is as follows:

Immediately beneath the floor—and in case the School-house is two stories high, between the ceiling and the floor above—insert a tube from four to six inches in diameter, according to the size of the rooms, the outer end communicating with the external air by means of an orifice in the underpinning or wall of the house, and the other, by means of an angle, passing upward through the floor beneath the stove. This part of the tube should be furnished with a register, so as to admit much or little air, as may be desirable.

This simple arrangement will reverse the ordinary currents of air in a School-room. The cold air, instead of entering at the crevices in the outer part of the room, where it is coldest, enters directly beneath the stove, where it is warmest. It thus moderates the heat immediately about the stove, and being warmed as it enters, and mingling with the heated air, establishes currents toward the walls, and gradually finds its way out at the numerous crevices through which the cold air previously entered. If these are not sufficient for the purpose, several ventilators should be provided in distant parts of the room, as already suggested.

This simple arrangement, then, provides for the more even dissemination of heat through all parts of the room, and thus secures a more uniform temperature, and, at the same time, provides a purer air for respiration, contributes greatly to the comfort and health of the scholars, and fulfills several important conditions which are essential to the most successful prosecution of their studies, and to the maintenance and improvement of social and moral, as well as intellectual and physical health.

Ventilating School Stoves.—But the best means of warming by stoves, so far as I am advised, is in the use of "Chilson's Ventilating School Stoves, for wood." I had hoped to be able in this connection to give a cut of this Stove; but its construction may be sufficiently understood from the following concise description. The Stove is formed of double plates, each plate containing a series of half columns which, when put together, form a column through which the hot air passes rapidly. The cold air should be taken into the room under the Stove, by means of tubes communicating with the outer air, as indicated in Plans of Schoolhouses Nos. 1 and 3.

Patented by Ira Mayhew, Albion, Mich.

Great inconvenience often results from Smoke, not only, but from rain and melting snow which enters the open tops of chimneys, and leaches through the accumulating soot of stove pipes upon books, papers, and the furniture of School-rooms. More especially is this true in the case of Stove Chimneys which often do not reach the ground. To obviate these inconveniences, the tops of chimneys should be protected. This is the object of the invention here represented. It excludes storms from chimneys upon which it is placed. It prevents downward currents of air, and its construction is such that all winds acting upon it have a tendency to diminish the windward openings, and by the agency of connecting rods to open the leeward ones. The effect hence is to promote draft and ventilation. It also lessons the liability to fires from the burning out of chimneys, and protects their tops from the wastes of the weather.

2d. *By the Use of Furnaces.*—The preceding method of warming by Stoves has been given, because in small districts the stove has been employed, and will continue to be used. But this means of warming is by no means desirable.

In view of the importance of the subject, I deem it proper here to present the most improved methods of heating known; for no one will question but that the comfort and health of human beings ought always to be regarded; and especially during the periods of growth and study. This requires, among other things, the maintenance of an equable temperature, during the cold and inclement seasons of the year; and, so far as practicable, during the excessive heat of summer. It also requires that the vital qualities of the air remain unchanged, while maintaining this equable temperature, even during the rigors of a severe winter. These are conditions of health, as well as of comfort, which a regard for the latter would lead men generally to observe, but for the difficulties to be overcome.

We have heretofore remarked that the atmospheric air is composed, chiefly, of the two gases, *nitrogen* and *oxygen*, united in the ratio of four to one by volume, with exceedingly small and variable quantities of carbonic acid gas, and aqueous vapor. No other mixture of these, or of any other gases will sustain healthy respiration. Such are its constituents when taken into the lungs in the act of breathing. When expelled from them, however, its composition is found to be greatly changed. While the quantity of nitrogen remains nearly the same, eight and a half per cent. of the oxygen, or vital air, has disappeared, and been replaced by an equal amount of carbonic acid gas, which is an active poison. When this gas is mixed with atmospheric air in the ratio of one to four, it is fatal to animal life, producing almost instant death.

We have seen that about thirty-six cubic inches of air enter the lungs at each inspiration, and that respiration is repeated once every three seconds, or twenty times a minute. We have further stated the vital truth that, AIR ONCE RESPIRED will neither support combustion NOR ANIMAL LIFE. Moreover, in proportion as air once respired is mingled with the atmosphere of a room, the vital qualities of the whole are impaired, and it gradually becomes an active poison.

By making a computation based upon the amount of air respired by one person in a given time, the number of children ordinarily attending School, and the size and capacity of the Schoolhouses they occupy, it will be found that these Schoolhouses are not ordinarily of sufficient capacity to furnish air enough for the respiration of their occupants three hours, or even for the *preservation of their lives for this length of time*, were it so arranged that they could breathe all the air once over, without entering upon its second respiration. But this is not the case. The air in a room is not all respired *once*, before a portion of it is breathed the second, or even the *third* and *fourth* time. The atmosphere is not, hence, suddenly changed from a healthful to an infectious state. Were it so, the change would be so perceptible as to be distinctly *felt*, and a *remedy* would hence be sought. But because the change is gradual, and insidious,—undermining the health of all persons, and especially of children, who, while engaged in study, imperatively require pure air as a condition of the healthy development of either body or mind,—it is not therefore the less fearful in its consequences. In a room occupied by *one hundred persons*, THE FIRST HOUR, *twenty-five hundred cubic feet of air* (which is equivalent to the contents of a room twenty feet square, and six and a fourth feet high) *impart their entire vitality to sustain animal life, and, mingling with the atmosphere of the room, proportionately deteriorate the whole mass.* This affords sufficient cause for the fearful inroads made by disease during the susceptible period of youth.

An All-wise Providence has beneficently provided a remedy for these evils, while we dwell *in the open air;* for the carbonic acid which is exhaled from the lungs, *by its increase of temperature while in the lungs*, is rendered specifically lighter than the surrounding atmosphere, and is hence borne up, and away, to become the food of plants, which, in turn, absorb this gas, and, retaining the carbon, and appropriating it to their own growth, throw off the oxygen, to mingle with the air, and thus again fit it for the respiration of animals. It is in this manner, by a beneficent provision of the Creator, that animals and plants are perpetually interchanging kindly offices.

Situated as we are in civilized life, much study is requisite to enable us to profit by this beneficent law; for by artificial arrangements we dwell quite too much *within doors.* By voluntarily thus incarcerating ourselves we interrupt this provision of Nature, by which the animal and vegetable kingdoms minister to each others health and well being. It is true, by leaving doors open, and raising windows—or, what is better, by lowering windows from the top—we may, in part, facilitate these natural arrangements, while we dwell in houses, and especially during the warm season, when the evil would be least felt. But during cold weather, this arrangement, being incompatible with comfort, if not always with health, is generally disregarded.

A new and a difficult problem is then presented for our solution; which is, *how to maintain a comfortable and equable temperature, during the cold and inclement seasons of the year, without impairing the vital qualities of the atmosphere.*

In order more fully to comprehend the subject in all its bearings, and if possible to reach a result in which all may rest satisfied, we will consider the advantages and the disadvantages of the various methods of warming to which we have been accustomed, and which are still in use.

Years ago, the large Open Fireplace was in common use. It had its advantages, and its disadvantages. So much heated air passed rapidly up the chimney, that it proved an efficient *ventilator*. But as a means of *warming*, it was less effectual; for the place made vacant by the rapid passage of heated air up the chimney, had to be supplied by cold air entering the doors, windows, and crevices around the room. Hence it might be said, without exaggeration, "while one side was scorching hot, the other was freezing cold." Certain it was, that when the heads of children were in an atmosphere above blood heat, that about their feet was below the freezing point.

The Fireplace has generally been superceded, and especially in Schoolhouses, by the Close Stove, which, it was claimed, saved half of the wood. Stoves, likewise, have their advantages, as well as their disadvantages; for, if less warm air is uselessly carried up the chimney, and less cold air is hence admitted through the surrounding crevices to supply this loss, ventilation is at the same time less efficient than where Fireplaces are used.

More recently Hot-Air Furnaces have been considerably employed, not only in dwelling-houses, but more especially in Churches and in our larger Union Schoolhouses. These, too, have their advantages, and their disadvantages. They leave the rooms warmed by them free from the care of a fire *in the rooms*, both as to noise and litter. They also serve as ventilators; for, when a room is full of air, it is evident no more air can be introduced, till that within is allowed to escape through ventilating tubes, or otherwise. While the heating process thus goes on, ventilation continues.

But Hot-Air Furnaces, as heretofore commonly employed, have been very objectionable. They have generally occupied a small brick enclosure in the basement. Cold air is introduced within this brick-work, and, immediately surrounding the often intensely hot furnace, has its vital qualities changed before it enters the apartments to be warmed. The oxygen of the air unites, to some extent, with the often red-hot furnace with which it comes in contact, forming an oxide of iron, and thus the nitrogen is set free. The oxygen of the aqueous vapor in the atmosphere, in like manner combines with the intensely heated furnace, forming again oxide of iron, and setting the hydrogen of the aqueous vapor free. In these and other ways the natural state of the atmosphere is disturbed, and its vital qualities are so impaired as to render it unfit for respiration.

Often, because of the intense heat to which they are subjected, these furnaces become cracked and broken, and hence leak smoke and offensive and hurtful gases, which mingle with the heated air and enter the apartments that are occupied, and thus annoy and injure those they were intended to comfort and benefit.

The truth of these remarks, upon these two methods of heating, I think is fully realized by those who have given the most attention to the subject. We have seen, in many instances, in the eastern cities, as well as in the west, the dry heating air furnace discarded, and a return to the close stove. And we have seen, if not a disposition to return to the large open fireplace, at least a tendency to substitute the grate for the stove and furnace. But the grate possesses the same advantages, and is subject to the same objections that have been mentioned as pertaining to the open fireplace, though neither exists to so great a degree. As an *active ventilator* it may advantageously be used in connection with the *ordinary furnace*.

Of late, Steam Heating Furnaces have been introduced, to some extent. These are of different kinds. The one hitherto most in use, traverses with pipes the apartments to be heated, through which pipes live steam is sent. The heating quality of these is good. The vital proporties of the air remain unimpaired by this process. But these furnaces possess no ventilating power, and they are further objectionable, on account of their leaking, and the crackling noises the pipes emit, while heating and cooling, and with every variation of temperature.

STEAM HEATING FURNACES.

In concluding what I have to say on the subject of Warming and Ventilation, I propose to submit what, after careful study, I believe to be the best method of warming and ventilation known to the civilized world. It consists in the use of Super-heated Steam without sensible pressure, as the agent in warming pure air during its passage through it in tubes, in the manner described below, which is sufficiently illustrated by the following diagram. Two styles of furnace, both involving essentially the same principle, and the same detail of arrangement, have been patented, and are now offered to the public,—the one under the name of the "Perkins Steam Heater," and the other as "Bulkley's House Furnace, by Super-heated Steam without pressure." In my my remarks concerning it I shall employ the term "Steam Heating Furnace."

The illustration on the following page has been furnished by Messrs. Dudley & Holmes, of Detroit, who have, within the past year, put the Perkins Steam Heater into the City Hall in Detroit, and into the new Union Schoolhouse in Kalamazoo. They have also, within that time, put the Perkins Heater into several private residences in the State, all of which, so far as I know, give satisfaction. The one in the writer's residence, in Albion, fully realizes all that is here said in its praise.

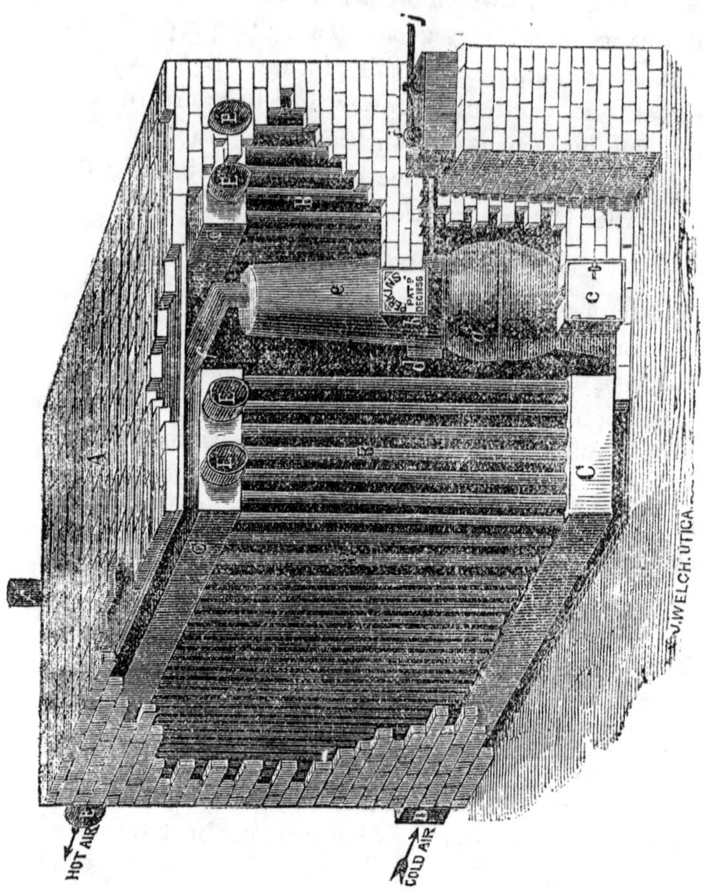

The Perkins Steam Heater.

A. Represents the Furnace wall, broken away.

B. B. B. Air-pipes traversing the steam chamber.

C. C. Air Chambers, *sub* (lower) and *super* (upper.)

D. Cold air entrance. There may be two or more.

E. E. E. E. Hot air pipes, leading to apartments to be warmed.

a. Fire pot; *b.* Feed door; *c.* Ash door; *d.* Water vessel; *e.* Cockle; *f. f.* Smoke pipe; *g.* Water pipe for feeding vessel *d.*; *h.* Outside water reservoir; *i.* Ball cock; *j.* Water pipe to supply reservoir.

In the use of this Steam Heating Furnace *the air is warmed during its passage through pipes that are inserted in a chamber of steam.* These pipes are from one hundred and sixty to two hundred in number, depending upon the size of the building to be warmed, and should be about three inches in diameter, and from five to six feet in length. They thus possess, in the aggregate, a capacity about equal to that of a tube a yard in diameter. The pure cold air from without, is conveyed to a *sub* chamber *below* that in which the furnace, or stove is situated, and traverses these pipes that pass upward through the steam chamber, to a *super* chamber above the steam chamber, from which super chamber the heated air is conveyed by pipes and registers, in the usual way, to the apartments to be warmed. These apartments should be furnished with ample ventilators leading upward, through the roof of the building, to the open air.

Each room warmed should be furnished with two ventilating registers, both communicating with a ventilating tube, one near the ceiling, and the other near the floor. When a room is to be warmed, the heating register should be opened to introduce the warm air, and the *lower* ventilating register should be opened to allow the cold air to pass off, as the warm air enters and displaces, first, that in the upper part of the room, and afterward that below, till the entire room is brought to a uniform temperature. By leaving these two registers open, the room will be kept constantly warm, while an active ventilation will be kept up. The tops of these ventilating tubes should be furnished with caps, for the purpose of excluding storms, and to prevent a downward current which might otherwise interrupt the ventilation, in case of adverse winds.

The intermediate Steam Heating chamber, of which I have spoken, is separated from both the *sub*, and *super* air chambers, by horizontal metallic plates ; but these chambers are connected by the tubes already referred to, which traverse the steam chamber, by means of which the air is heated in its passage from the *sub* to the *super* chamber. The permeating, super-heated steam, surrounding these pipes, presenting a heating surface of more than 600 square feet, warms the air in its passage through them, to a comfortable and genial temperature, without affecting its vital quality, or in any way rendering it unfit for healthy respiration. Persons occupying buildings thus warmed and ventilated, may safely dwell *within doors*, amid the severity and inclemency incident to the winters of this latitude, with all the physical comfort, safety to health, and immunity from disease, that are experienced by persons dwelling in tropical and salubrious climes.

The cost of this mode of heating, which is somewhat greater than that attending the introduction of the ordinary Furnace, will probably prevent its being generally employed in small separate School buildings; but it is commended to villages and cities that are erecting new and improved Union Schoolhouses, Church Edifices, and Public Halls, in which the health and comfort of their occupants are more regarded than the expense of heating. And this, it is believed, will be less, exclusive of the cost of the Furnace itself, where this method of heating is adopted, than in any of the ordinary methods of warming.

The excessive heat of our summers may be mitigated, as is commonly understood and practiced, by sprinkling floors. The water thus evaporating renders large quantities of caloric latent, which would otherwise be active, and by this means the temperature is reduced. In dwelling houses and School-rooms in which carpets are used, the same result may be reached by hanging wet cloths on lines arranged for that purpose. The evaporation from these cloths will produce the same effect upon the temperature that is secured by sprinkling the floors, and for the same reason.

Where the Steam Heater is employed, the temperature of any room that becomes excessively heated in the winter, (should such an event occur,) may be reduced by opening the upper ventilator. Houses thus warmed may be thoroughly ventilated, summer or winter, in the same way.

This arrangement will also mitigate the intensity of the summer heat.

CHILSON'S CONE FURNACE.

Of the dry hot-air Furnaces, which some may choose to employ, I know of none better than Chilson's Cone Furnace, of which a diagram will be hereto appended. This Furnace is designed for coal, and its construction is such as to more thoroughly economize fuel than any other with which I have any knowledge ; while its extensive surface, all of which is heated to nearly the same temperature, without any part of it becoming excessively hot, is less likely to impair the vital qualities of the air exposed to its surface. For the same reason it is less liable to crack and leak poisonous gases, than are most Hot-Air Furnaces.

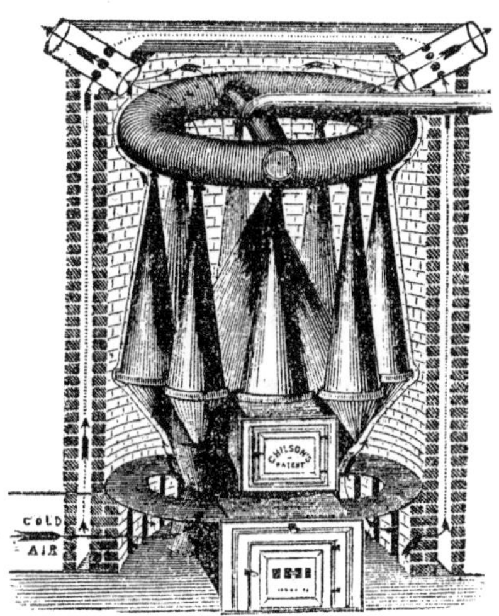

This cut represents an elevation of Chilson's Cone Furnace, and a section of the brick work with which it is surrounded. It shows, also, how the cold air penetrates the brick work below, and how the air, when warmed, is drawn off above.

The large central cone, immediately over the fire pot, retains the gases that are evolved by the burning coal, until they are themselves consumed; and the surrounding cones, leading to the annular chamber, reflect the heat back, so that comparatively little escapes through the smoke pipe.

SCHOOL FURNITURE.

The improvements in School Furniture are all of recent date. But tasteful and commodious furniture, adapted to the comfort and wants of children, attractive in its appearance, and elevating in its influence, is even more important in our Schoolhouses, which are to be occupied by children during the most susceptible period of their lives, than is the furniture in our Dwelling Houses and Churches. The truth of this statement seems but recently to have gained a lodgment in the public mind. The house of Mr. Ross, the pioneer in this department in the country, which was established in 1838, is still manufacturing and sending out improved School Furniture from the city of Boston. More recently, similar establishments have been opened in New York, Buffalo, and other cities.

The cuts which I am enabled here to present, have been furnished me by establishments in the three cities just named, and may be regarded as representing *specimens* of their work. Nos. 1 to 6 are from the house of W. Chase & Son, 198 Seventh Street, Buffalo. Nos. 7 to 17 are from the house of Nathaniel Johnson, 490 Hudson Street, New York. Nos. 18 to 29 are from the house of Joseph L. Ross, corner of Hawkins and Ives Streets, Boston, with branch houses, 413 Broadway, New York, and 194 Lake Street, Chicago, where the Messrs. Chase have also a branch.

A simple style of Seats and Desks, entirely of wood, is represented in Plan No. 3 of Schoolhouses. The styles of furniture here given are so constructed as to admit of being taken apart and snugly packed for transportation.

No. 1.—Chase's Portable Intermediate Single Desk and Chair.

Two sizes of this style of Desk are manufactured, with the hight of the side next the scholar, 22½ and 24 inches. Primary School Desks of the same design, and of varying sizes, are also manufactured.

No. 2.—Chase's Portable Intermediate Double Desk.

Two sizes of the double Desk are also manufactured, with the hight of the side next the scholar the same as No. 1. Primary School Desks of the same design, and of varied sizes, are also manufactured.

These Desks have open spaces beneath the top to receive books and papers. The Chairs have iron backs.

No. 3.—Chase's Portable Grammar Desk.

Three sizes of this Desk are manufactured, 24½, 26 and 27½ inches high. This arrangement gives each pupil the benefit of a single Desk, as does No. 1.

No. 4.—Chase's High School Double Desk and Chairs.

Three sizes, are manufactured, 24, 25½ and 27 inches high. Each cover opens a separate apartment in the desk designed for the exclusive use of one pupil. This arrangement, though less commodious than single seats, allows a separate apartment for each pupil's books.

The new Union Schoolhouse at Kalamazoo, I am advised, is furnished with this style of desks and seats.

No. 5.—Chase's Teachers' Desk with Four Drawers, and Cloth Top.

A good and convenient Desk is of hardly less importance to the Teacher than is a good boarding place. Both, indeed, are essential to his comfort and highest success.

The style of Desk here represented gives the Teacher the benefit of drawer room, which is very important, and while it adds greatly to his convenience, it may often be made to protect valuable books and papers belonging to the District.

No. 6.—Chase's Teachers' Desk with Eight Drawers.

This style of Desk affords an increased amount of drawer room, which will be found convenient where there are not cupboards or closets connected with the School-room.

Should greater hight be required, as in case of standing to read, a portable Desk like that represented by No. 23, may be used on either of these Desks.

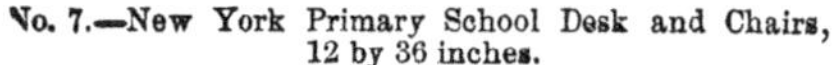
No. 7.—New York Primary School Desk and Chairs, 12 by 36 inches.

No. 8.—Ink Well

No. 9.—Single Grammar Desk and Chair for Public Schools. Desk 15 by 24 inches.

This Desk has an Ink-well like that represented at No. 8, furnished with a cover, and inserted near the back, at the right hand. The Ink is thus more secure than in movable inkstands. These Ink-wells are so arranged as to be taken out, cleaned and refitted as circumstances shall require. Their advantages are hence manifest.

No. 10.—New York Public School Desk and Chairs, 15 by 42 inches.

There is a shelf under the Desk, for the accommodation of books and papers, with an Ink-well for both scholars occupying the Desk.

No. 11.—Double Desk with Falls and Chairs, 19 by 42 and 20 by 48 inches.

This arrangement allows a separate space for the books and papers of each pupil, while both use a common Ink-well. These Chairs, like those represented in Nos. 9 and 10, are furnished with a strong back brace, which adds to their strength, though not to beauty.

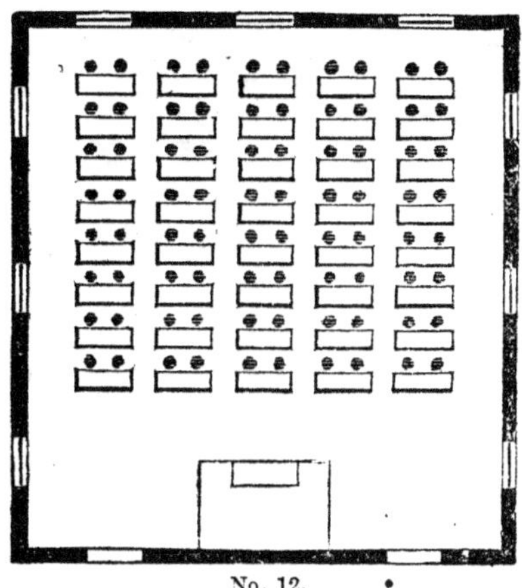

No. 12.

The above plan represents a School-room 32 by 35 feet, with double Desks, 15 by 42 inches; outside aisles 3 feet, and intermediate aisles 1 foot 3 inches wide. A room of this size will seat eighty scholars, two at a Desk. It gives each pupil a seat adjacent to an aisle, with a free passage around the outside of the room.

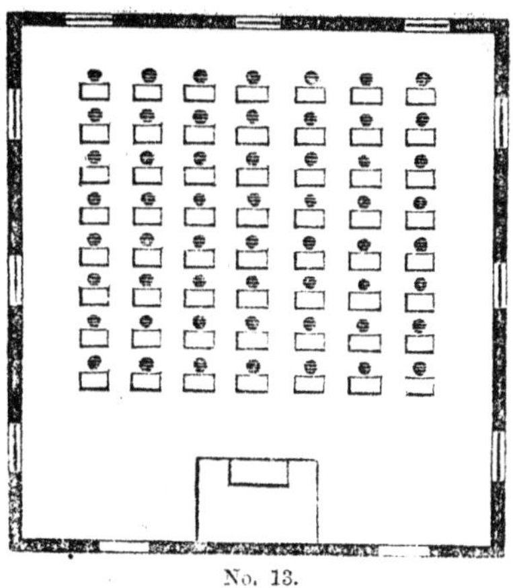

No. 13.

The above plan represents a School-room 32 by 35 feet, with single Desks 15 by 24 inches; outside aisle 3 feet, and inside aisles 1 foot 9 inches wide. This arrangement acommodates fifty-six scholars with single Desks. But this manner of seating is preferable to the preceding, where there is sufficient room to admit of it.

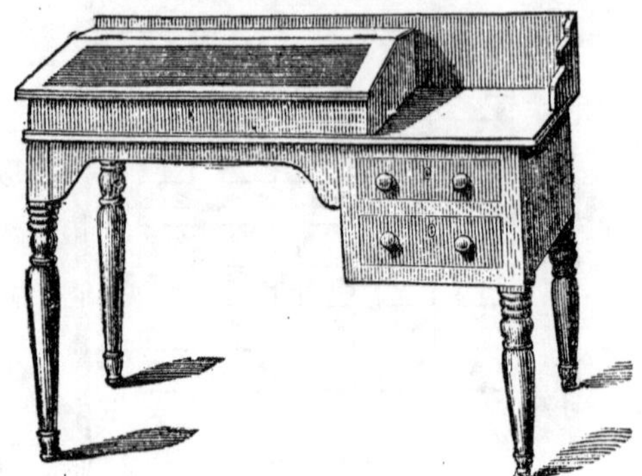

No. 14.—Usher's Desk, with 2 Drawers, 24 by 42 inches.

This style of Desk is arranged for an Assistant Teacher, and might answer a good purpose for the Principal of a small School. It would certainly be much better than a table without drawers.

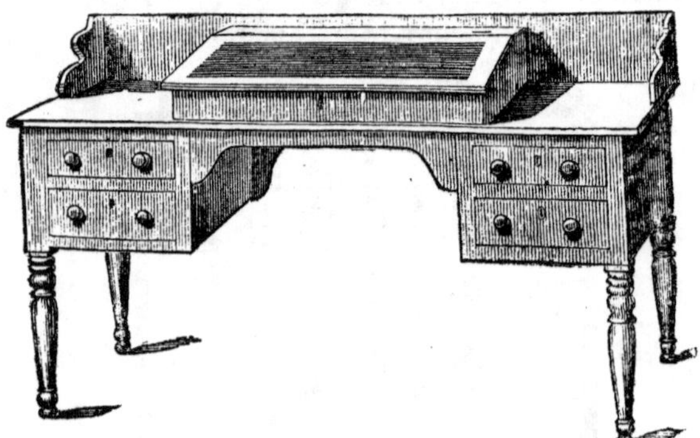

No. 15.—Teacher's Desk, with 4 Drawers, 24 by 60 inches.

Each of these principal Desks has a small portable Desk placed upon it, or made in connection with it, which gives an inclined surface for writing, which some prefer. The tops of these Desks it will be seen are hung with hinges, so as to admit of being opened and shut. When portable, they can be removed when the desk is sufficiently high for the occupant without them, and when a level surface is preferred.

No. 16.—Teacher's Desk, with 9 Drawers and Level Top, 24 by 60 inches.

This Desk has a broad and deep drawer at the top, which will be convenient for keeping Outline Maps, and large papers which should not be rolled or folded.

No. 17.—Excelsior Ladies' College Desk.

This Desk is so arranged as to admit of its being shut up, when not in use, like a piano. It is represented as open, exhibiting the interior construction. This arrangement, it will be seen, has its advantages, and especially when it is desirable to leave papers in security, when they are soon to be consulted again.

No. 18.—Ross' Union (Portable) Primary School Single Desk and Chair.

No. 19.—Ross' Union (Portable) Primary School Double Desk and Chairs.

Nos. 18 and 19 represent Primary School Chairs and Desks. Of these, three sizes are manufactured, the Chairs being 10, 11 and 12 inches in hight, and the front of the Desks being 20, 21 and 22 inches in hight, respectively. These sizes are adapted to the comfort of the smallest children in Primary Schools. No. 18, for one child, is eighteen inches long; and No. 19, for two children, is three feet long.

Children during their earliest years in School, require a comfortable seat, and a good desk, as much as at any later time in their School course. Their otherwise idle hours may be pleasantly occupied in elementary lessons in spelling, writing, drawing, and composition. Composition will thus become as easy and as pleasant to them as conversation.

These Desks and Chairs are made so as to be taken apart and packed in a small space for transportation.

No. 20.—Ross' Union (Portable) Grammar School Single Desk and Chair.

No. 21.—Ross' Union (Portable) Grammar School Double Desks and Chairs.

The Chairs in this grade of furniture vary from 13 to 16 inches in hight. The smallest are adapted to children from 8 to 10 years of age, while the largest will accommodate pupils from 16 to 18 years of age.

The single Desks are two feet long, while the double ones are three feet and ten inches in length.

The Desks, in front, range from 23 to 28 inches in hight; and are thus adapted to the sizes of the children for whose occupancy they are intended.

The Well at the left is open for use, and the one at the right is closed. Both are on the same plane with the top of the Desk, and are hence not subject to be overturned.

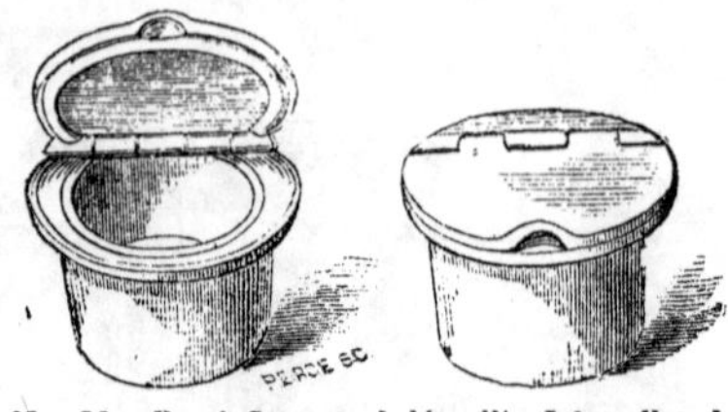

No. 22.—Ross' Improved Metallic Ink well and cover combined, lined with Glass, designed for Public and Private Schools, Seminaries, Academies, &c.

This Desk may be placed upon a horizontal table, when more hight is needed, or an inclined surface is desired; and it may be removed when not required for use.

No. 23.—Ross' Portable Desk, with Cloth Top.

The prices of these several grades and styles of School Furniture are not here given, for they may differ from various causes. Specimens only of the varieties that are manufactured are here represented. On page 387, I have given the names and address of the Houses that have kindly furnished the facilities for these illustrations, and stated which have been furnished by them respectively.

School officers and others desiring any of these styles of furniture, by opening a correspondence with the Houses manufacturing them, will be furnished with prices, and more minute descriptions than can here be given.

If information is desired of any particular style of School Furniture here given, by observing its No., and referring to the 387th page, the reader will see the address of the Manufacturers, from whom the desired information can be obtained; for copies of this volume will be furnished to each of the Houses herein referred to.

No. 24.—Ross' Boston Public School Teachers' Desk, with Two Drawers.

The Desk here represented is of simple construction, but will be found very convenient, and may sometimes be made to answer all the purposes of a more expensive one.

Where articles of the kinds here described cannot well be procured from a regular manufacturer, those of similar construction may be procured near home, though not always of so good a quality, or at so advantageous rates.

No. 25.—Ross' Teachers' Desk, with Three Drawers and Table Top.

This style of Teacher's Desk has drawers at the right of the Teacher, where they are most conveniently reached. The greater part of the surface of the Table is also at the Teacher's right, when sitting to it. This may be used with or without the small portable Desk represented by No. 23.

No. 26.—Ross' Teachers' Desk, with Five Drawers and Top Desk.

This Desk affords good facilities for writing in the middle, with spaces for books of reference at the right and left. The larger central drawer will also accommodate maps, large sheets of drawing-paper, and articles that should neither be broken nor rolled.

No. 27.—Ross' Teachers' Desk, with Nine Drawers and Table Top.

The preceding cuts and illustrations represent the principal styles of improved School-room Furniture; and the reader's attention has been directed to establishments devoted exclusively to manufacturing and furnishing the same. These manufacturing Houses have frequent orders for School Furniture, not only from our Western cities, but from various parts of the Western States, and from both sides of the Mississippi.

No. 28.—Ross' Improved Drawing Desk, supported on Stanchions. Pattern C.

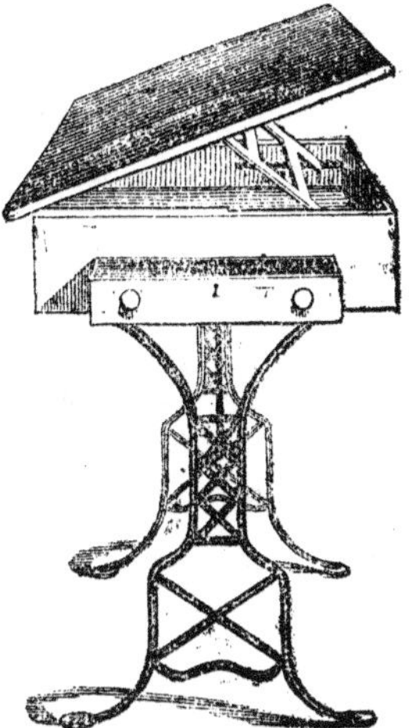

No. 29.—Ross' Improved Drawing Desk. Pattern D.

I conclude these illustrations of improved School Furniture, by inviting the reader's attention to two styles of Drawing Desk. And I am glad to know that the subject of Drawing is attracting, and deservedly too, an increased share of public attention. Too much attention can hardly be given to it, unless to the exclusion of other and equally fundamental branches; nor can attention be directed to it at too early a period of the child's attendance upon School.

"Drawing—whether of maps, the shape of objects, or of landscapes—is admirably adapted to discipline the sense of sight. Children should be encouraged carefully to survey and accurately to describe the prominent points of a landscape, both in nature and in picture. Let them point out the elevations and depressions; the mowing, the pasture, the wood, and the tillage land; the trees, the houses, and the streams. Listen to their accounts of their plays, walks, and journeys, and of any events of which they have been witnesses. In these and all other exercises of the sense of sight, children should be encouraged to be strictly accurate; and whenever it is practicable, the judgment they pronounce, and the descriptions they give, should, if erroneous, be corrected by the truth. Children can not fail to be interested in such exercises; and even where they have been careless and inaccurate observers, they will soon become more watchful and exact.

"It is by the benign influence of education only, that the senses can be improved. And still their culture has been entirely neglected by perhaps the majority of parents and Teachers, who in other respects have manifested a commendable degree of interest in this subject. That by judicious culture the senses may be educated to activity and accuracy, and be made to send larger and purer streams of knowledge to the soul, has been unanswerably proved by an accumulation of unquestionble testimony. Most persons, however, allow the senses to remain uneducated, except as they may be cultivated by fortuitous circumstances. Eyes have they, but they see not; ears have they, but they hear not; neither do they understand. It is not impossible, nor perhaps improbable, that he who has these two senses properly cultivated will derive more unalloyed pleasure in spending a brief hour in gazing upon a beautiful landscape, in examining for the same length of time a simple flower, or in listening to the sweet melody of the linnet as it warbles its song of praise, than those who have neglected the cultivation of the senses experience during their whole lives."—*Mayhew on Education, pp.* 191 *and* 192.

SCHOOL APPARATUS.

A gentleman of large experience, and of close observation, many years ago remarked at a convention of County Superintendents of Common Schools, in the State of New York—*It is singular that children learn so* MANY *things out of School, and so* FEW *things, in School.* The remark impressed me, as I doubt not it did other Superintendents present; and twenty-five years of experience as a Teacher and a School Officer, have convinced me that it is no less singular than *true.*

It then becomes us to inquire *why this is so.* If I mistake not, the reason consists in the fact that a much more natural method of instruction has commonly been pursued *out of School,* than has hitherto been generally practiced *in School.* In School, until within a few years,—and in too many Schools it is still true,—children *say* their A, B, C's three times a day, but do not *learn* them in months. Out of School they *see objects,* become familiar with their *uses,* and learn their *names.* In School, many a child *has said* his A, B, C's *twenty-six times* without learning one of them; while out of School, the same children may have each *learned* the names and uses of *twenty-six things* the first time they have seen them.

In this life, *the senses* constitute the great medium of communicating knowledge to the human mind; and especially is this true of *sight* and *hearing.* While, then, the skillful parent or teacher addresses the minds of his children through the sense of *hearing,* he will greatly increase the interest of his young learners by addressing, also, their sense of *sight*, through which the strongest impression can be made upon the mind. Especially is this important during the first years of a child's instruction, whether at home or in *School*.*

Mr. F. C. Brownell, Secretary of the Holbrook School Apparatus Company, 413 Broadway, New York, has kindly furnished me the following cuts, which represent *samples* of an extensive range of simple and ingenious, though cheap Apparatus for Schools. The various articles here referred to, together with improved Apparatus and School Furniture generally, may be obtained at the office of the Secretary, as above, or of Mr. George Sherwood, President of the Company, at 194 Lake street, Chicago, to whom I have already referred as supplying orders for improved School Furniture.

Several of the articles represented in miniature, in the foregoing cut, I am enabled to illustrate singly in the following pages:

* This subject cannot well be pursued to a greater extent here. In the writer's work on the *Means and Ends of Universal Education*, an entire Chapter of about fifty pages is devoted to "the education of the five senses," to which the reader is referred.

Figure 1.—Numeral Frame.

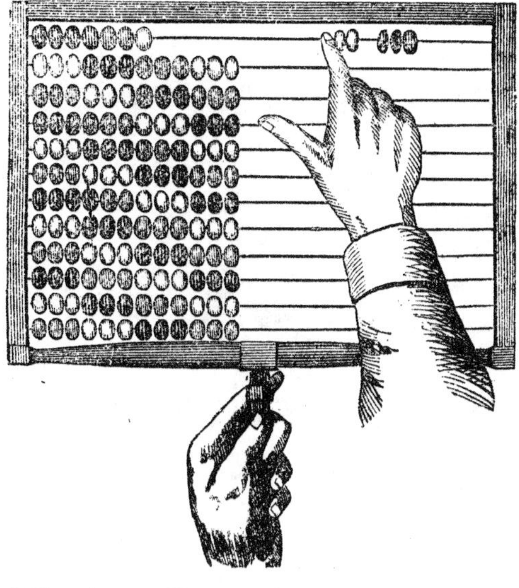

A skillful Teacher will turn the Numeral Frame to good account in teaching many things. It was primarily employed for teaching small children to count. It may, however, with equal advantage be used as a medium of addressing the minds of children through the eye, while we speak to the outer ear, in illustrating all of the simple, and some of the more complex operations upon numbers. By this means the first lessons of children may be rendered more attractive, and impressions thus made upon their minds will be stronger and more permanent. In the use of this simple instrument, addition, subtraction, multiplication, and division, may be well illustrated, as may also many of the principles of fractions.

It may be turned to admirable accouut in illustrating our Decimal Currency and decimal fractions. By its use, also, the square of any single figure may be readily shown. The roots of all perfect powers expressed by not exceeding two figures, may likewise be readily illustrated by it.

Fig. 2.—Holbrook's Drawing Slate.

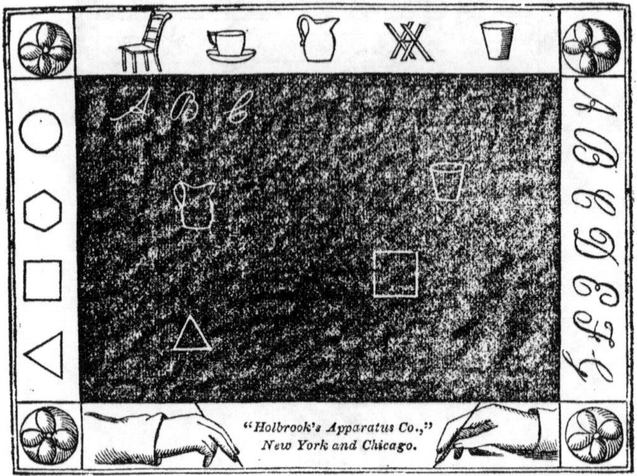

This, or something similar, has already been incidentally referred to, as a means of turning the otherwise idle hours of children to good account, by affording them pleasant employment in writing, drawing, and composition. On the margin of the slate the manner of holding the pen is indicated. There are also copies of letters to be written, and objects to be drawn. Children have sometimes, by the aid of a slate and pencil, made great proficiency in learning to read, entirely without books. This is done by their writing or printing out their own reading lessons, which they are sure to understand, and which they sometimes read with dramatic effect.

The following figures for representing Geometrical Solids, may be rendered more suggestive than is at first apparent.

The light portions of the three cubes represented in Fig. 3, show the *squares* of the numbers 1, 2 and 4, to be 1, 4 and 16; while the cubes themselves as distinctly show that the *cubes* of the numbers 1, 2 and 4, are 1, 8 and 64—facts which, without illustration, are often difficult for children to comprehend.

Fig. 3.—Cubes.

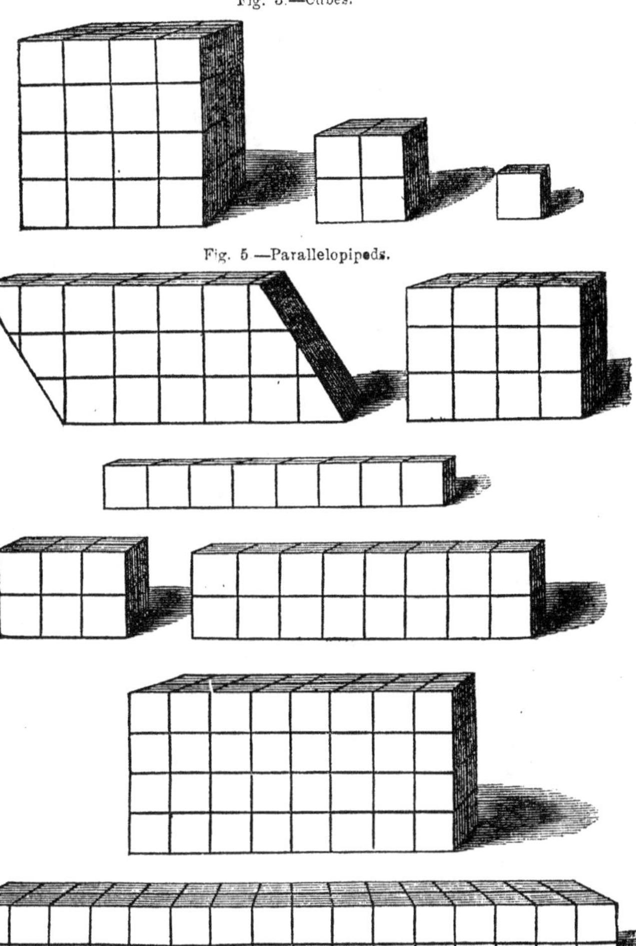

Fig. 5.—Parallelopipeds.

Fig. 6.—Sphere and Spheroids.

Oblate Spheroid. Sphere. Prolate Spheroid.

Fig. 7.—Cone, Pyramid, Frustrum, etc.

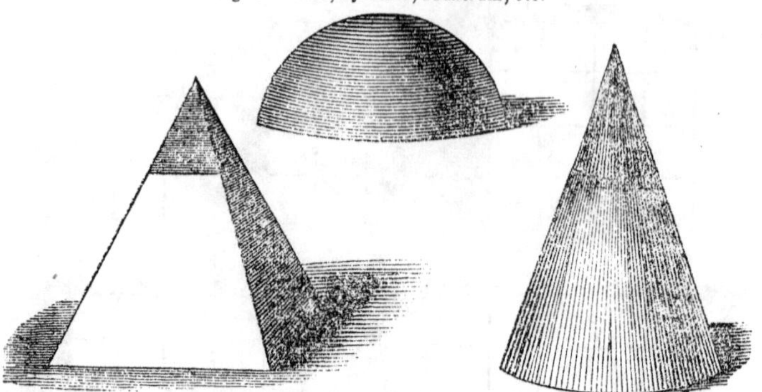

Pyramid and Frustrum. Segment of a Sphere. Cone and Frustrum.

Fig. 8.—Prisms and Cylinder.

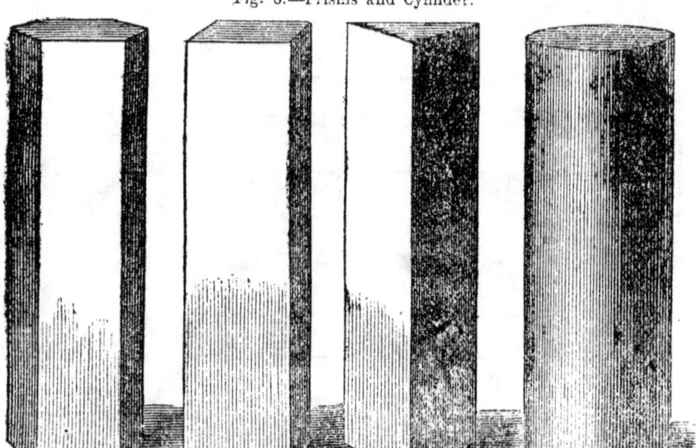

It is often extremely difficult to give a distinct idea of Geometrical Solids here represented, without the solids themselves for illustration. The cuts here introduced, even in the absence of the solids they represent, may be made to illustrate many a practical problem in common life. They suggest the forms of lots into which a farm should be divided in order to economize material for fences. They also suggest the most economical shapes for buildings, boxes, bins, etc., so as to afford the greatest cubical capacity with the least surface.

A most excellent method of disciplining the sense of sight, and in such a way as to interest children, and secure to them great practical advantage, by familiarizing them with distances, while they are learning the definitions of figures in plane geometry, and a method that is adapted to the capacity of children during their first years in school, is given on the 188th and following pages of the writer's work on the "Means and Ends of Universal Education," which was prepared and published eight years ago, pursuant to a Resolution of the Senate and House of Representatives, adopted in February, 1849.

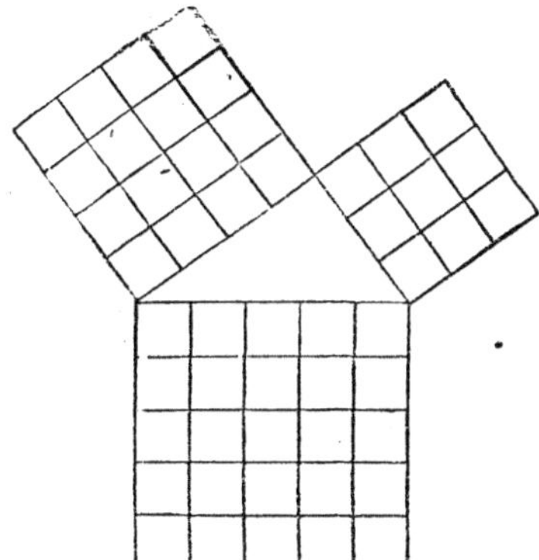

Fig. 9.—Carpenter's Theorem.

This Figure represents to the Eye the truth of what is popularly known as the Carpenter's Theorem, to wit: *The square described upon the hypotenuse of a right-angled triangle is equal to the sum of the squares described upon the other two sides.* Although not a *demonstration*, it will carry with it a clear conviction to many minds, and will be of great service to the student in arithmetic, who is unable to advance to the study of geometry. It may also awaken an interest in some minds that will not rest satisfied without mastering the demonstration.

Fig. 10.—Cube Root Block.

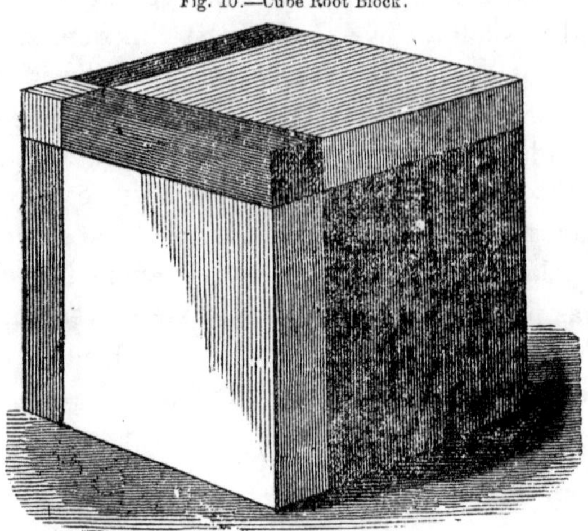

The extraction of the cube root can be more easily and more satisfactorily explained to most persons unacquainted with algebra or geometry, in the use of the block represented by Fig. 10, than in any other way.

Figures 11 and 12, on the next page, represent the Terrestrial Globe, and a Hemisphere Globe, both of which will be found to enhance the interest of the pupil in the study of geography, and to facilitate his easy acquisition of this important branch of study. Pupils now often study geography for months, and even for years, learning definitions, and bounding States and Countries, without *knowing* for themselves the form of the Earth, or possessing any distinct idea of zones, latitude, longitude, etc. A good eight-inch globe, like that represented at Fig. 11, which will cost from $6 00 to $10 00, in the hands of a Teacher who is in any degree competent to instruct, will enable him to impart more instruction in relation to zones, latitude and longitude, day and night, the currents of the ocean, etc., in six days, than has often been acquired in as many months.

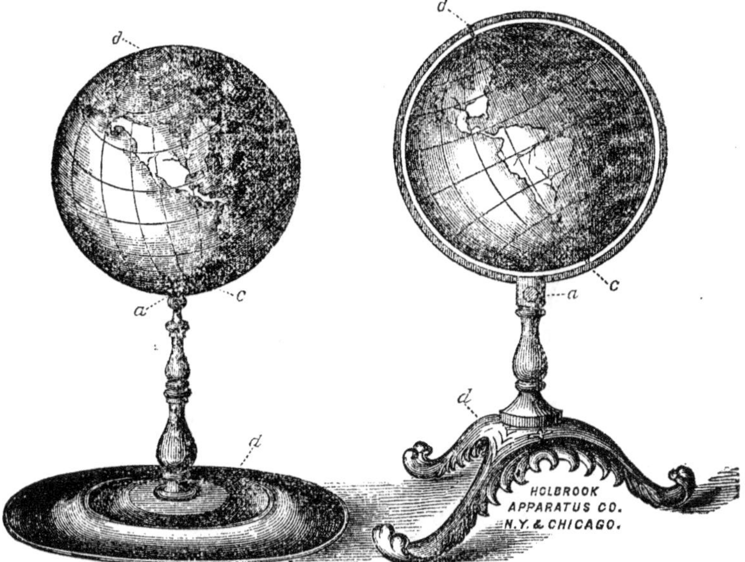

Fig. 11.—Terrestrial Globes.

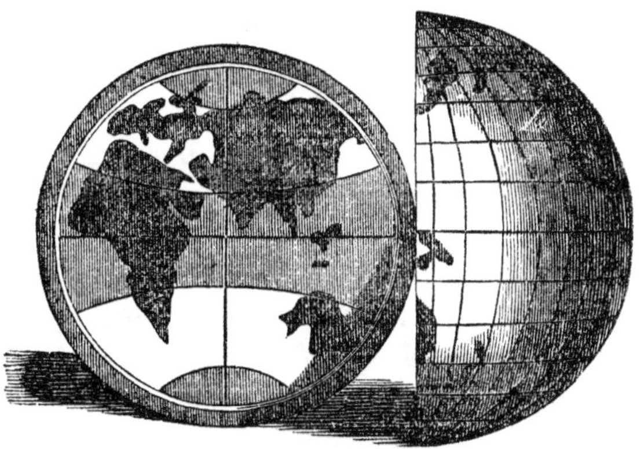

Fig. 12.—Hemisphere Globe.

The Hemisphere Globe, represented at figure 12, is also an important aid in the study of Geography.

The use of Outline Maps, and the practice of Map-drawing, will be found a sure means of rendering the knowledge acquired of geography, distinct, correct, and permanent, without which, time spent in its study is hardly better than thrown away.

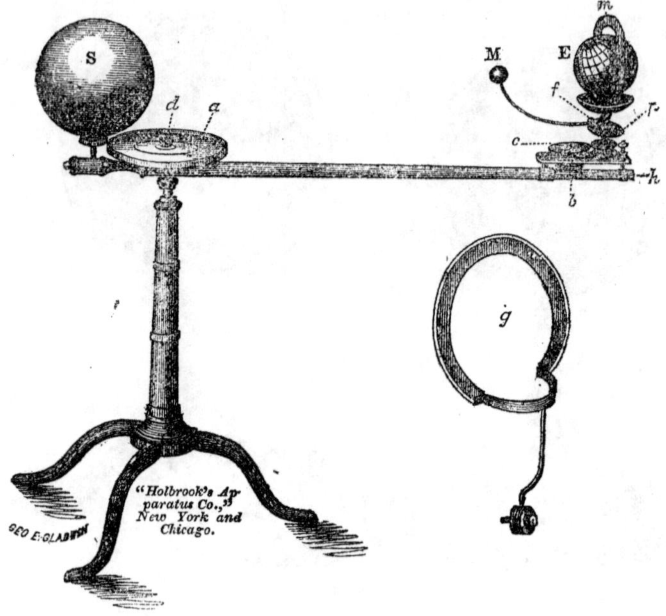

Fig. 13.—The Tellurian.

The Tellurian, which is represented at Fig. 13, furnishes better and clearer illustrations than can otherwise be given of many interesting and important phenomena, among which are the sucession of day and night; the changes of the seasons; the varying length of days and nights at different seasons of the year; the rising of the Sun north of east, and its setting north of west, in the Summer, and its rising and setting south of these points in the Winter; the changes of the Moon; solar and lunar eclipses; spring and neap tides; the later daily recurrence of the tides; the length of days on the Moon; the appearance of the Earth to observers on the Moon; the Harvest Moon; and the difference between a solar and the siderial year. All of these, and other phenomena, may be explained by the use of the Tellurian, or Season Machine, as it is sometimes called, with a clearness and simplicity that bring them within the comprehension of children.

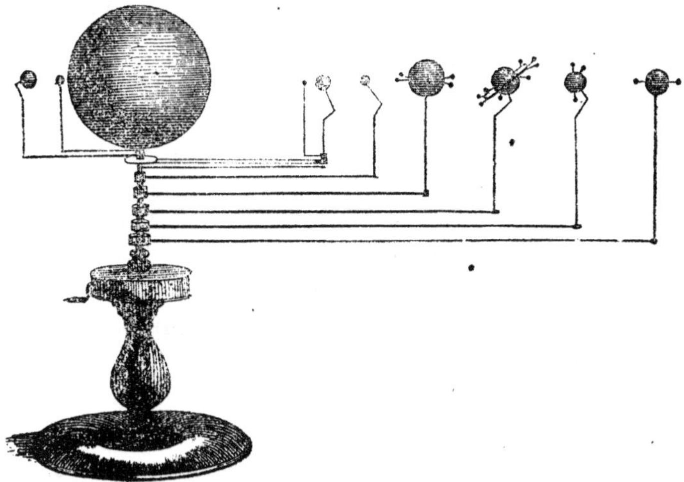

Fig. 14.—The Orrery, or Planetarium.

Some persons may be inclined to regard the suggestions here given as theoretical, and even *visionary*, and may wonder why the Superintendent, in an official document, does not restrict himself to things *practical*. Such persons may regard it the exclusive office of a *practical* education to teach the art of increasing material riches—of gathering *shining dollars*. But I regard that *practical* which awakens *bright thoughts*, which elevates the affections, which entertains the imagination, which widens and hightens the range of reflection, and which renders frail mortals more appreciative and more worthy children of our Father in Heaven. Shall we not, then, regard that *practical* which gives a rational idea of a plurality of worlds; which teaches that many of the stars of heaven are worlds like our own, with days, and nights, and changing seasons, and some of them several hundred times larger than our Earth, and all of them probably inhabited by rational and intelligent beings; which teaches, also, that other stars are, like our Sun, centers to other Systems, like our Solar System; and all, it may be, retained in their position by one common law, which may be taught to children; shall we not, I say, regard such teachings *practical?*

Or shall we suffer our children to become men and women *physically*, though babes *mentally*, holding, as some of their fathers and mothers do, the unworthy opinion that the stars of Heaven are merely tiny lights for no useful purpose, and only occasionally visible; or that, at best, they are *eye holes* through which God looks down to see what naughty children and wicked men do; himself a great spy, secreted behind the thick curtain of night?

I need not say, such thoughts are degrading to humanity, and unworthy of the beneficent Father of us all. We need, then, the Orrery, represented by Fig. 14, which will aid us and our children in comprehending the annual revolutions of the sisterhood of planets, and the magnificent machinery of the Solar System. This instrument, thus becomes one of the most practical inventions of this, or of any age. It costs $12 00 to $15 00, according to the style of manufacture.

Section 23, of the Primary School Law, provides that Districts may raise money by tax for the purchase of globes, outline maps, and apparatus for illustrating the principles of astronomy, natural philosophy, agricultural chemistry, and the mechanic arts.

The Celestial Sphere represents the Earth, (*a*,) surrounded by the heavens, and indicates the Celestial Meridians, (*d*, *d*,) the Equator, (*f*,) and the Zodiac, (*e*.) It also represents the poles of the heavens, which are simply the poles of the Earth extended. The Zodiac is divided into twelve equal parts, representing the twelve signs. Its lower edge is marked with degrees; and on its upper edge months and days are indicated. The axis (*g*,) may be inclined to any angle desired, by loosening the thumb-screw, (*c*,) as represented at 2 and 3.

By means of this instrument, the real horizon of any place on the globe may be shown; also the lengths of the

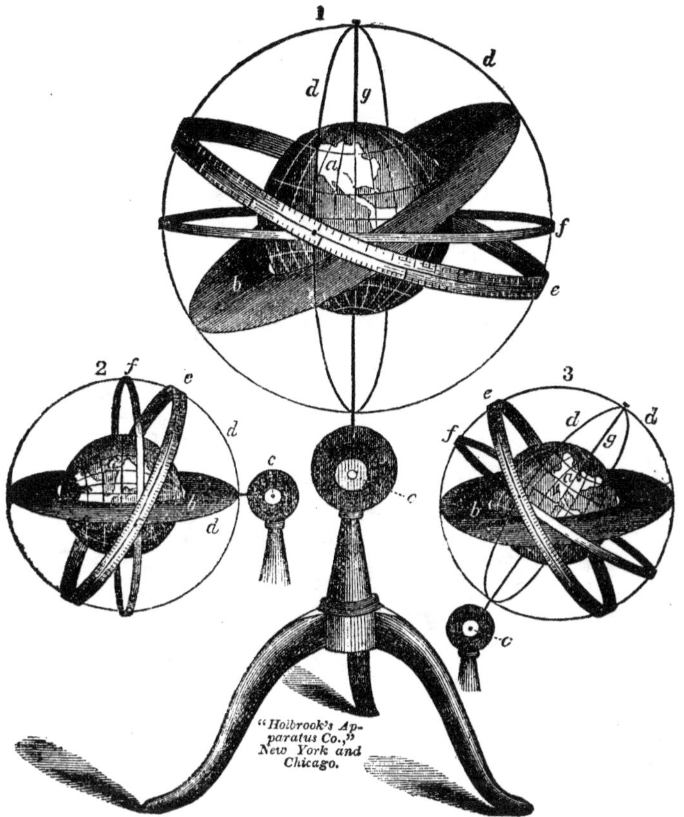

Fig. 15.—The Celestial Sphere.

days and nights on any part of the earth, and at any season. The time of the rising and setting of the sun, and the sun's appearance at the Poles, and his place in the Ecliptic on any day of the year, may likewise be illustrated by it. The Celestial Sphere may be obtained at a cost of $8 00 to $12 00.

School officers and others desirous of procuring any or all of the articles of School Apparatus here illustrated, will find the address of parties through whose agency the same, and improved articles of Apparatus generally, may be obtained, at the 404th page of this volume. They may doubtless be procured at other places; but these are named as they have kindly furnished the means of illustration here used.

Hereto are also appended illustrations of another style of School Desk, and an approved style of Inkstand; also, a cut representing in miniature one of a series of ten Philosophical Charts; all of which may be obtained at either of the establishments last referred to.

HARTFORD SCHOOL DESK.

SATTERLEE'S PATENT INKSTAND.

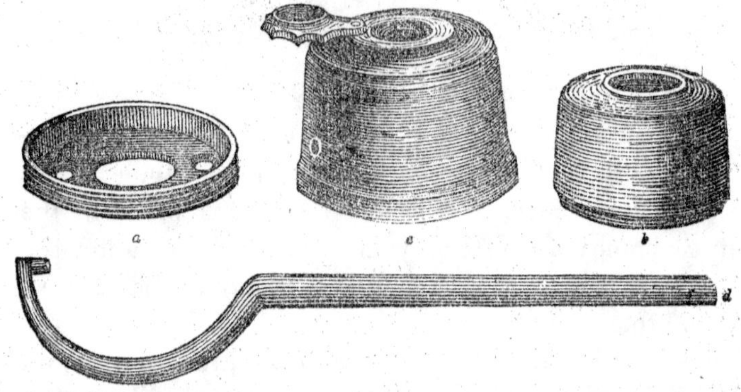

A NEW INVENTION FOR SCHOOLS.

EXPLANATION.—The iron plate (*a*,) with a screw-thread on its rim, is held securely to the desk or table by two common screws. On this is placed the glass font (*b*,) to contain the ink. The cap (*c*,) of Japanned iron, surrounds the glass font, and is screwed on to the base-plate, or removed at pleasure, by the lever (*d*.)

NO. 10.

JOHNSON'S

PHILOSOPHICAL CHARTS,

Ten in the Set,	DESIGNED FOR THE USE OF SCHOOLS AND ACADEMIES.	Price $15, 00

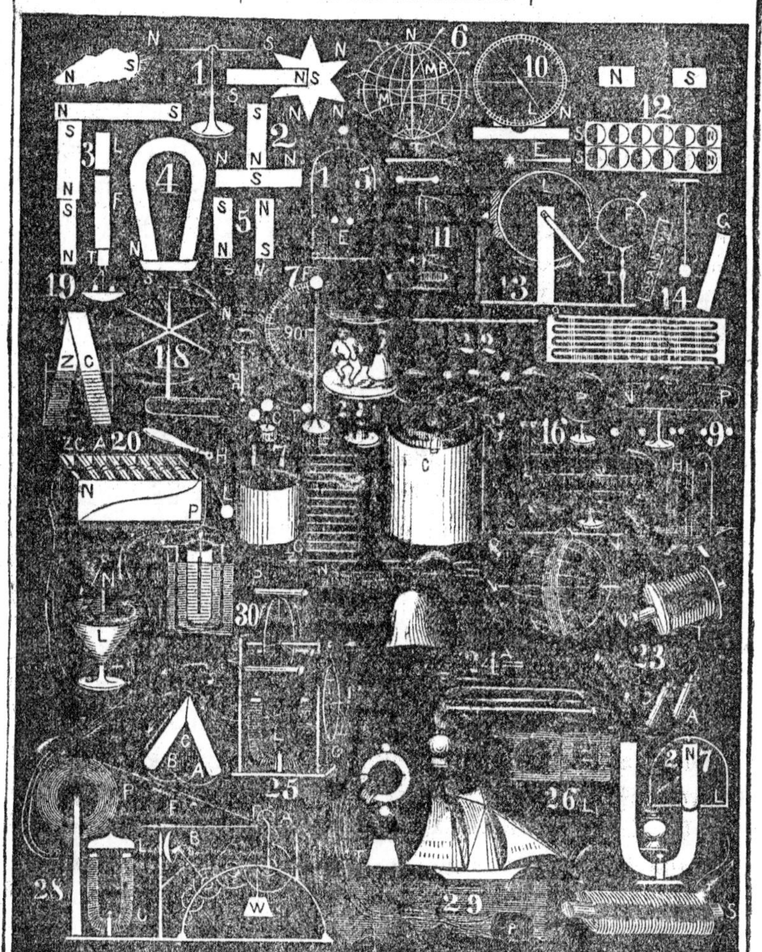

Facsimile of Chart, No. 10, Reduced

Address at 413 Broadway, New York, — F. C. BROWNELL, *Sec'y.*
" " 194 Lake Street, Chicago, Ill., — GEORGE SHERWOOD, *Prest.*

PLASTER BLACKBOARD.

As a substitute for the painted board, paint black a portion of the plastered wall, covered with hard finish, (*i. e.* plaster of Paris and sand ;) or, color the wall by mixing with the hard finish, a sufficient quantity of lamp-black, wet with alcohol, at the time of putting it on. The hard finish, colored in this way, can be put on to an old, as well as to a new surface. Unless the lamp-black is wet with alcohol, or sour beer, it will not mix uniformly with the hard finish ; and when dry, the surface, instead of being a uniform black, will present a spotted appearance. The wall should not be varnished.

The plaster blackboard is pleasanter to work upon than the painted board. It also shows the work better.

SLATE BLACKBOARD.

In the class-rooms of the American Asylum for the Deaf and Dumb, and in all similar Institutions, where most of the instruction is given by writing and drawings on the blackboard, large slates about three feet wide and four feet long, are substituted for the blackboard. They cost from two to three dollars, and are superior to any form of blackboard, and in a series of years prove more economical.

SHEPHERD'S PATENT SLATE GLOBE.

Drawings with the slate pencil can be made on this Globe as perfectly as on any slate. It is mounted like an ordinary globe, and is used by pupils studying Geography, who draw on the Globe the parallels, meridians, and countries, and write on the horizon the names of animals, vegetables, minerals, etc., for each zone or country. The larger sizes are suitable for class use, while the smaller sizes may be used by the pupils at their seats.

This Globe is manufactured by the Holbrook Apparatus Company, in sizes from four to nine inches in diameter, and at prices from one dollar and fifty cents to six dollars.

SCHOOL ARRANGEMENTS.

The Primary Schools of our State should all be made noble Asylums, to which children will cheerfully go, and in which they will remain with pleasure. Then will their uplifting influence upon both children and parents be everywhere felt. Then, and not till then, will the beneficent design of their establishment be fully realized.

The appurtenances to our Schoolhouses should not be restricted to the narrowest limits possible—to a water-pail, a cup, a broom, and a chair for the Teacher—which is more than many Schoolhouses have hitherto been supplied with.

In addition to all of these, every Schoolhouse should be furnished with the following articles:

1. An evaporating dish for the stove, where one is used, which should be supplied with clean pure water;

2. A thermometer, by which the temperature of the room may be regulated;

3. A clock, by which the time of beginning and closing School, and conducting all its exercises, may be governed;

4. A shovel and tongs;

5. An ash-pail and an ash-house. For want of these, much filth is frequently suffered to accumulate in and about the Schoolhouse, and not unfrequently the house itself takes fire and burns down;

6. A wood-house, well supplied with seasoned wood;

7. A well, with provisions not only for drinking, but for the cleanliness of pupils;

8. And last, though not least, the ample School yard, of which we have heretofore spoken, should, in the rear of the building, be divided by a high and close fence. One portion of it, appropriately fitted up, should be assigned exclusively for the use of boys, and the other for girls. Over this entire arrangement the most perfect neatness, seclusion, order and propriety should be enforced, and everything calculated to defile the mind, or wound the delicacy or the modesty of the most sensitive, should receive attention in private, and be made a matter of parental advice and co-operation.

CONFINEMENT OF SMALL CHILDREN.

Small children, whether at home or in the School, should have short lessons assigned them, and they should be encouraged and stimulated by all suitable means to get them well. Among other things they should learn to "sit still." But here, more especially, "their lessons should be short."

Children are young animals as well as immortal beings; and if we would look properly to the promotion of their highest and most enduring good, we must see well to it that we do not overlook or disregard the laws that govern their animal natures.

The lambs of the flock, and the young of animals generally, delight to skip and play, and betimes to rest their weary limbs, and take food and repose.

The same law applies to children, who are but young human animals. They need, however, like the lambs that gambol about the green pasture, both protection and restraint. Proper regard for this organic law requires that the smaller children in School be allowed a recess as often, at least, as once an hour; and that all be allowed and encouraged frequently to change their position.

I fully concur in the opinion expressed by Dr. Caldwell, who says, "It would be infinitely wiser and better to employ suitable persons to superintend the exercises and amusements of children under seven years of age, in the fields, orchards, and meadows, and point out to them the richer beauties of nature, than to have them immured in crowded School-rooms, in a state of inaction, poring over torn books and primers, conning words of whose meaning they are ignorant, and breathing foul air."

A change of position calls into action a different set of muscles, and relieves those that are exhausted. The object of exercise is to employ all the muscles of the body, and especially to strengthen those that are weak. It ought hence to be frequently varied, and always adapted to the peculiarities of individuals. And especially is this true in childhood and early youth.

EXERCISE AND EXPERIMENT ROOM FOR CHILDREN.

A good and substantial room, well fitted up, and properly warmed in cold weather, in which children may conduct their sports, under the supervision of a teacher or monitor, is of the utmost importance; and especially is this true of all Schools for small children. Such a room is, indeed, for these, hardly less important than the School-room. It should be supplied with various kinds of ingenious appliances, and such as are calculated to interest and instruct children, and to promote the development of their physical organizations. Among these should be included See-saws, weights and measures of various kinds, etc., etc. These are important for both boys and girls; but, as they are uncommon, it may be well to suggest the proper mode of using them, and the benefits to be derived therefrom.

The benefits that would result to the health of children, from the introduction and use of the See-saw, under proper regulations, are not all of the advantages it would confer. The See-saw, when employed by children, under proper supervision, is a means of imparting intellectual, social, and moral instruction.

For this purpose a good, smooth, strong plank should be

well hung and properly balanced. The distance from the fulcrum or point of support should be accurately graduated, and marked in feet and inches. Then, knowing the weight of one scholar, the weights of all the others may be ascertained by their relative distances from the fulcrum when they exactly balance.

These interesting experiments may be tried by any child as soon as he understands the ground rules of arithmetic, and the simple fact that, for two children to balance, the product of the weight of one multiplied into his distance from the fulcrum will exactly equal the product of the weight of the other into his distance from the fulcrum.

Such simple experiments, when mingled with sports, and made interesting to young children, serve the double purpose of attaching them to the School, and of fixing in their minds the habit of observation and experiment, and of understanding the why and wherefore, which will be of incalculable service to them all the way through life.

Weights and Measures serve the same general purpose, and may be rendered well-nigh as useful as slates and black-boards. Thousands of children recite every year the table, "Four gills make a pint, two pints make a quart, four quarts make a gallon," etc., month in and month out, without acquiring any distinct idea of what constitutes a gill or a quart; and even without knowing which of the two is the greater. But let these measures be once introduced into the experimental play-room, and let the child, under the supervision of the Teacher or Monitor, actually *see* that four gills make a pint, etc., and he will learn the table with ten-fold greater pleasure than he otherwise would, and in one-tenth the time.

The same general remark will apply to the other tables of weight and measure, to experimental philosophy, and to nearly every branch of study pursued in the Common Schools of our country.

During these exercises, it is apparant that while the

physical and intellectual natures of the child are undergoing appropriate development and growth, its social and moral natures will be best cared for. And especially will this be true, when the Teacher employed is an amiable and accomplished female, whom children will soon learn to regard as, next to their own mothers, the best and most beautiful of Earth.

THE TEACHINGS OF SCHOOLHOUSES.

Cicero somewhere observes that the face of a man will be tinged by the sun, for whatever purpose he walks abroad; so, by daily associations, the minds of all persons are influenced, and their characters permanently affected, by scenes with which they are familiar; and especially is this true during the impressive periods of childhood and youth.

Many persons seem to think that Schoolmasters and Schoolmistresses do all the teaching in our Schools. But it is not so. Fellow-students, neighbors, and citizens teach by precept and by example; and especially do *Schoolhouses teach.* And oh! what lessons of degradation, pollution, and ruin they sometimes impart! as he cannot fail to be convinced who has extensively observed their actual condition through the country.

I remember to have seen the fond parent accompany his lovely child of four summers to the School the first day of its attendance. The child had seen pictures of Schoolhouses in books. Pictures, if not always pretty, usually please children. It was so in this case. The child, anxious to go to School, talked of the Schoolhouse on the way. There arrived, the parent passed his innocent little one into the care of the teacher, with a few remarks, and was about to retire, when the child, clinging to him, said, pathetically and energetically, "Pa! pa!! I don't want to stay in this ugly old house; I am afraid it will fall down on me; I want to go home to our own pretty parlor."

But the parent, breaking away from his child, leaves it in tears, with a sad heart. How cruel to do such violence to the tender feelings of innocent children! And how baneful the influence! The School, instead of being a comfortable, pleasant, and delightful place, as it should be, is to the child positively offensive, and the Schoolhouse a dreary prison. "Just as the twig is bent, the tree's inclined." The child learns to hate School, to hate instruction, and all that is good. He soon becomes the practiced truant. In a few years he arrives at manhood; but, instead of being a blessing to his family and a useful member of society, he too frequently drags out a wretched life, in ignorance and penury, dividing it between the poor-house and jail, and terminating it, peradventure, upon the gallows.

It needs the pen of a ready writer duly to portray the influence of neglected Schoolhouses. Parents seem to have forgotten that, *while men sleep, the enemy comes and sows tares;* that if good Schoolhouses do not *elevate*, neglected ones will *pollute* their children.

SCHOOL AND LIBRARY BOOKS

Recommended by the Superintendent of Public Instruction, as suitable for use in Primary Schools, for Teachers, and for Township Libraries.

The Statutes make it the duty of the Superintendent of Public Instruction, in printing the School Laws, with Forms, Regulations and Instructions for conducting proceedings under them, to append thereto a list of such books as he shall think best adapted to the use of Primary Schools, and a list of books suitable for Township Libraries, with such rules as he may think proper for the government of such Libraries.

The present Superintendent, in printing an edition of the School Laws in 1847, appended thereto such a list of books, and rules for the government of Libraries. A like service was performed by his successor, in 1852. This delicate and important duty is now again undertaken. It is to be borne in mind, however, that this action is only recommendatory. But in order to increase the value of the list of books here given, the Superintendent has conferred freely with many competent Teachers, and, so far as practicable, has aimed to present a list that should reflect their preferences.

There is a great variety of books in use in the Schools of nearly every Township in the State. This variety causes an unnecessary expense to Parents, and is a perplexity to Teachers, preventing, as it too frequently does, a proper classification of Scholars; it is hence an impediment in the improvement of our Schools, which should be removed as early as practicable. It is NOT *necessary* to the removal of the difficulty, that the same series of books should be used throughout the State. This, indeed, would be *impracticable*, if desirable. It might be well, however, for all the Schools of a Township, to use a uniform series of books; and especially is it *essential that a uniform series of books be used in every School District.*

In arranging the following list of books, the Superintendent has embraced none but what, so far as he has been able to examine, he thinks well of; and none but what have received the cordial recommendation of reputable Teachers who have used them. When a special partiality is entertained, it is indicated in the connection. This list may bring to the knowledge of young Teachers, and of inexperienced School officers, books with which they have not been familiar. If, then, those they have been accustomed to use have been unsatisfactory, it will afford them a better opportunity of making a selection with which they may rest satisfied. When any of the books here named are in *general use* in the Schools of a Township, the Superintendent would not recommend a change. But when there is not a uniformity, he would advise that a series be selected and recommended for general use; either,

1. By a County Educational Society, after being first examined and recommended by a committee appointed for that purpose; or, if this is not done,

2. By a Township Educational Society, where one exists, after being examined and recommended as above; or finally, if neither of the preceding methods is adopted,

3. By the several School Districts in district meeting assembled. Districts have, sometimes, at a regular meeting, called for that purpose, appointed a Committee to report a List of Books for use in their Schools. At an adjourned meeting they have heard the report of the committee, and adopted it, with or without modification, and

passed a resolution to continue the use of the books then adopted, until they should be changed by a regular meeting of the District, called for that purpose.

Any committee, by examining the following list of books, and by considering what are in use in their Schools, can arrive at the recommendation of the Superintendent in their particular case.

Rules recommended for the government of Township Libraries, may be found in Note K, of this volume, pp. 266 to 269.

1.—*Spellers and Definers, etc.*

Sanders' Speller, Definer, and Analyzer;
Town's Spelling and Defining Books;
Webster's Elementary Spelling Book;
McGuffey's Eclectic Spelling Book;
Hazen's Speller and Definer;
McElligott's Young Analyzer and Analytical Manual;
Lynd's Class Book of Etymology;
Town's Analysis of the English Language.

2.—*Reading Books.*

Sanders' Series of School Readers;
Town's Series of School Readers;
Webb's Word Method and Normal Readers;
McGuffey's Eclectic Series of School Readers;
Fowle's Dialogues—Sweet's Elocution;
Lovell's Speakers, and School Dialogues;
The National Series of School Readers;
Magathlin's National Speaker;
Porter's Rhetorical Reader;
Comstock's Phonetic Reader, Speaker, and Elocution;
Clagget's Elocution Made Easy;
Howe's Practical Elocutionist;
Russell's and Goldbury's Series of School Readers;
The Child's Guide—Intelligent Reader;
The Village School Reader.

3.—*Arithmetics.*

Thomson's Mental, Practical, and Higher Arithmetics;

[Ten years ago, the writer, after a critical examination of this Series of Arithmetics, expressed the opinion that in point of excellence it was superior to any other Series with which he was acquainted, which opinion he still holds.]

Davies' Elementary and University Arithmetics;

Tracy's Series of Arithmetics;

Perkins's Elementary and Higher Arithmetics;

Greenleaf's Series of Arithmetics;

Robinson's Arithmetical Series;

Stoddard's Intellectual and Written Arithmetics;

Adams's, Emerson's, Ray's, and Smith's Arithmetics.

4.—*Geographies.*

Cornell's Geographical Series;

Colton and Fitch's Geographical Series;

Monteith and McNally's Gegraphical Series;

Mitchell's, Olney's, and Smith's Geographies.

5.—*Grammar and Composition.*

Welch's Analysis of the English Sentence;

Sill's, Goold Brown's, and Tower's Grammars;

Wells's [W. H.] School Grammar;

[Ten years ago, after a careful examination of this work, the writer expressed the opinion that it was the best School Grammar with which he was acquainted, which opinion he has not had occasion to change.]

Kirkham's Grammar—Pierce's Grammar;

Frost's Easy Exercises in English Composition;

Parker's Progressive Exercises in English Composition;

Parker's Aids to English Composition;

Tower and Tweed's Grammar of Composition;

Wilson's Elements of Punctuation;

Knighton's Young Composer;

Brookfield's First Book in Composition;
Composition and Rhetoric, by Quackenbos;
Knighton's Etymological School Grammar.

6.—*Philosophies.*

First Lessons in Natural Philosophy, by Miss Swift;
Silliman's First Principles of Philosophy;
Olmsted's Rudiments of Nat. Philosophy and Astronomy;
Smith and Coffin's Natural Philosophies;
[The last three works named are interspersed with practical questions, involving the fundamental principles of the science, which very much enhances their value.]
Johnston's, Comstock's, and Wells' Philosophies.

7.—*Physical Geographies.*

Fitch's Outlines of Physical Geography;
Somerville's Physical Geography;
Warren's Physical Geography.

8.—*Book-keeping.*

Palmer's, Preston's, Jones', and Fulton & Eastman's;
Winchester's, Northend's, and Crittenden's Book-keeping;
Cochran's Agricultural Book-keeping, with Blanks for keeping Field Accounts;
[A pioneer and valuable work in its department.]
Mayhew's Book-keeping, by Single and Double Entry, with Examples for Practice;
[This work is especially adapted to District Schools. In its use, the pupil improves his knowledge of Arithmetic and Penmanship, while learning Accounts. It has been ten times as extensively used in the Public Schools of the City of New York, as any other book, and has been the only Book-keeping authorized in the Public Schools of Brooklyn, and several other cities.]

9.—*Chemistries.*

Johnston's Catechism of Agricultural Chemistry and Geology;

[This work, by its brevity and simplicity, is admirably adapted to the capacity of children; and when illustrated by cheap and simple experiments, as the author recommends, it cannot fail to make a lasting impression on the juvenile mind.]

Wells's Chemistry—Science of Common Things;

Youmans' Class Book of Chemistry;

Silliman's First Principles of Chemistry;

Beck's, Johnson's, Phelps', and Comstock's Chemistries.

10.—*Physiologies.*

Primary Lessons in Physiology, by Mrs. Jane Taylor;

Griscom's First Lessons in Physiology;

[This work, to which are added brief rules of health, is worthy of a place in every Common School in our land, and should be introduced where a more extensive treatise is not already in use.]

The House I Live in, by Dr. W. A. Alcott;

[This deservedly popular Treatise on Physiology, has already been productive of incalculable good.]

Cutter's Anatomy, Physiology and Hygiene;

Comstock's, Lee's, and Loomis' Physiologies;

Bushnan's Animal and Vegetable Physiology;

Goadby's Vegetable and Animal Physiology;

[This admirable work is by Dr. Goadby, Professor of Vegetable and Animal Physiology, and Entomology, in the Michigan Agricultural College.]

11.—*Algebras.*

Tower's Intellectual Algebra;

Thomson's, Davies', Perkins', Robinson's, Greenleaf's, and Stoddard & Henkle's Algebras.

12.—*Drawing Books.*

Drawing Exercises on Slates for Young Children;

Coe's Drawing Cards, including Lessons in Landscape, Heads, Animals, and Figures;

Easy Lessons in Drawing, by F. W. Otis;
Ruskin's Elements of Drawing;
Chapman's American Drawing Book;
Schuster's Drawing Cards and Books.

13.—*Botanies.*

Phelps's Botany for Beginners;
Comstock's Young Botanist;
Gray's Botanical Series, in six books;
Green & Congdon's Class Book of Botany;
Torry & Gray's Flora of North America;
Botany of the U. S. Exploring Expedition.

14.—*Singing Books.*

Bradbury's Singing Bird, for Schools;
Bascom's School Harp—The Musical A, B, C;
Greene's School Melodies—Musical Boquet;
The School Singer, by Bradbury and Sanders;
The Juvenile Choir, by George Kingsley;
The Primary School Song Book, by Mason & Webb;
The Song Book of the School Room, by Mason & Webb;
The Singer's First and Second Books, by J. & H. Bird;
Edson's Vocal Guide—Pease's Philosophy of Music.

15.—*Astronomies.*

Mattison's Elementary and High School Astronomies accompanied by sixteen colored Maps—one set of Maps for a School;

Abbott's Young Astronomer;
Smith's Astronomy;
Olmsted's School Astronomy;
Norton's Natural Philosophy and Astronomy;
Norton's Astronomy, for Colleges and Seminaries;
Bouvier's Familiar Astronomy;
Burritt's Geography of the Heavens.

16.—*Science of Government.*

Shurtleff's Governmental Instructor;
Sheppard's Constitutional Text-book;

St. Leonard's Book on Property Law;

Montesquieu's Spirit of Laws;

The Constitution of the United States of America, with an Alphabetical Analysis; the Declaration of Independence; the prominent political acts of George Washington; electoral votes for all the Presidents and Vice Presidents; the High Authorities and Civil Officers of Government, from March 4, 1789, to March 3, 1847; Chronological Narrative of the several States; and other interesting matter, with a descriptive account of the State Papers, Public Documents, and other sources of Political and Statistical Information, at the Seat of Government: by W. Hickey, Philadelphia; T. C. & P. G. Collins;

[This work was first prepared and published under a resolution of the Senate of the United States, passed February 18, 1847.]

Wedgwood's Revised Statutes of the United States;

Young's Science of Government;

Story on the Constitution of the United States.

17.—*Natural History.*

Frost's Class Book of Nature, for Schools;

Ruschenberger's First Books of Natural History;

Bigland's Natural History of Animals;

Goldsmith's Natural History, abridged for Schools;

Haskell's and Ackerman's Natural Histories.

18.—*School Histories.*

Willson's Historical Series, 6 Books;

Willard's Historical Series, 3 Books;

Robbins's, Goodrich's, and Bloss's Histories;

Monteith's, and Quackenbos's History of the U. S.;

Whelpley's Compend of Universal History.

19.—*Rhetoric and Belleslettres.*

Mills' Outlines of Rhetoric and Belleslettres;

Shaw's Outlines of English Literature;

Cleveland's Compendium of English Literature;
" English Literature of the 19th Century;
" Compendium of American Literature;
Beauties of Ruskin, by Mrs. L. C. Tuthill;
Harrison on the English Language;
Milton's Paradise Lost;
Young's Night Thoughts;
Pollok's Course of Time;
Thomson's Seasons and Cowper's Poems, with Notes by J. R. Boyd;
Philosophy of Sir William Hamilton, by O. W. Wight;
Boyd's Elements of Rhetoric and Literary Criticism;
Kame's Elements of Criticism;
The Study of Words, by R. C. Trench, B. D.;
The English Language, by R. C. Trench.

20.—*Miscellaneous.*

Dymond's Essays on Morality;
Abercrombie's Intellectual and Moral Science;
True's Elements of Logic;
Winchester's and Root's Penmanship;
Payson's, Dutton's and Scribner's Penmanship.

21.—*Apparatus.*

Cornell's improved Terrestrial Globe, accompanied with a small book showing the manner of using it;

[The price of this ingenious article, secured to the inventor by patent, is $3 00. By it a great variety of interesting and useful problems, relating to the changes of the seasons, the lengthening and shortening of the days and nights, etc., etc., may be readily solved.]

Holbrook's School Apparatus;

[The set embraces a Numerical Frame, a Drawing Slate for children; Geometrical Solids; A Cube Root Block; Terrestrial and Hemisphere Globes; The Tellurian, or Seasons Machine; The Orrery, or Planetarium; The Celestial Sphere; A Slate Globe, etc., all of which, except the last, are illustrated at the 404th to 413th pp. of this volume, where the address of manufacturers is given. Sets, less or more complete, may be had for five dollars to thirty-five dollars. Particulars may be learned of parties whose address is given at the 404th page of this volume.]

Mitchell's Outline Maps, one Set for a School;

[These Maps are an invaluable auxiliary in the study of Geography. There are twenty-four large Maps in the series, varying in surface from six to twenty-four square feet. The entire Set, put up in a portfolio, may be obtained for fifteen dollars.]

Olney's Elementary Geography and Outline Maps;

[This Set contains seven Maps, varying in size from five to ten square feet. The Set, put up in portfolio, may be obtained for five dollars and a half. One Set of Maps is sufficient for a School.]

Bliss's Geography, and Outline Maps;

[The Maps are eight in number, and vary in size from six to twelve square feet.]

Mattison's Astronomy, accompanied by sixteen colored Maps, each thirty-six by forty-two inches, designed to illustrate the Mechanism of the Heavens;

[One Set of the Maps is sufficient for a School. They are an invaluable auxiliary to the study of Astronomy. They are put up in two styles; the *best*, with cloth backs, and mounted on rollers, is sold for $20 00. The second quality, without cloth backs, is sold for $15 00. Every student, pursuing the study, will need a book, the price of which is, I believe, fifty cents.]

The Normal Chart of the Elementary Sounds of the English Language. By David P. Page, late Principal of the New York State Normal School;

[This Chart is about forty-two by fifty inches, and costs about two dollars. Salem Town and C. W. Sanders have each also prepared Charts of Elementary Sounds. One of these Charts would constitute an important article of apparatus in any School where the English Language is spoken.]

Willard's Chronographer of American History;

Willard's Temple of Time;

Henry's Family and School Monitor;

[The the three preceding sheets are mounted on rollers, and contain each, about six square feet. They are adapted to the purposes of instruction in families and Schools.]

Fulton's Chirographic Charts, accompanied by a set of Writing Books and a Key;

[The Charts are eight in number, and each contains about five square feet. They cannot fail to be useful in teaching penmanship to classes.]

One Blackboard, at least, is indispensable. This should extend, when practicable, across the entire end of the School-room.

[For the best mode of manufacturing blackboards, see the 418th page of this volume.]

Every School-room should be furnished with the measure of an inch, foot, yard and rod. If there are not separate measures provided, the distances should at least be marked off on the edge of the blackboard. Where such measures are provided and properly used, even young scholars obtain a better idea of distance, than adults now commonly do.

Every School-room should be furnished with a clock, by which all the exercises of the School should be regulated, and a thermometer to regulate the temperature.

Counters, a numerical frame, drawing tablets, or small slates, real measures of every kind, linear, superficial, cubic and liquid; weights, geometrical diagrams, etc.—articles which the pupil can see, touch, draw upon his slate, and experiment with—will prove invaluable helps in giving children a correct idea of number, form, size, distance, weight and measurement.

The cardinal points should be accurately painted upon

the ceiling, if a clear idea of them cannot be otherwise represented. A correct understanding of them is of the utmost importance in teaching geography.

Apparatus sufficient for conducting some of the simple experiments in natural philosophy and chemistry, would do much toward creating an interest in those important branches of study.

22.—*Books and Periodicals for Teachers.*

The "School Teacher's Library," consisting of seven 12 mo. volumes, published by A. S. Barnes & Co., embraces the following works:

1. *Theory and Practice of Teaching:* By David P. Page, A. M., late Principal of the New York State Normal School.

2. *The Means and Ends of Universal Education:* By Ira Mayhew, A. M., Superintendent of Public Instruction in Michigan.

3. *The Teacher and the Parent:* By Charles Northend A. M., Superintendent of Public Schools, Danvers, Mass.

4. *American Education, its Principles and Elements:* By Edward Mansfield, Author of "Political Grammar," etc.

5. *American Institutions and their Influence:* By Charles DeTocqueville; with Notes, by Hon. John C. Spencer.

6. *Logic and Utility of Mathematics,* with the best methods of Instruction explained and illustrated: By Charles Davis, L. L. D.

7. *Root's School Amusements.*

Webster's Quarto Dictionary; [This contains three times the matter found in any other Dictionary compiled in this country. This invaluable work, published by G. & C. Merriam, Springfield, Mass., has been purchased, under a provision of law, by half of the School Districts of the State, and orders for it are still received almost daily. But it should be in every Township Library, for reference, as well as in every Schoolhouse. No private Library can be complete without it, and especially should every Teacher possess it. It is the best Dictionary, and the most valuable work for reference, in the English language.]

Goold Brown's Grammar of English Grammars; [the most elaborate work on the subject ever published.]

Unconscious Influences, by Rev. H. Vincent;

Mann's Lectures, Addresses and Reports on Education;

Three Hours' School a Day, by Wm. L. Crandal;

Crandal's Report on the Public School Policy of New York, Published by Fowler & Wells;

Dr. R. T. Trall's Family Gymnasium;

Use and Abuse of Alcoholic Liquors, by Dr. Carpenter;

Cowdery's Moral Lessons, for Teachers and Schools;

Locke Amsden, or the Schoolmaster.

Periodicals for Teachers.

Every Teacher will find it to his advantage to read regularly one good periodical devoted to the interests of Education. Of the many published in the country, I note the following:

The Michigan Journal of Education, Ann Arbor, Mich;

The Ohio Journal of Education, Columbus, Ohio;

The New York Teacher, Albany, N. Y.;

The American Journal of Education, Hartford, Conn.

23.—*Books for Township Libraries.*

Township Libraries are intended both for children and adult persons, and their object is not only to form a correct taste in the young, and to aid in their education, but also to please and instruct all classes of persons, and thus to afford facilities for rendering all better and happier who have access to them. They should, therefore, contain "milk for babes," and those of tender years, as well as strong meat for maturer persons, and those who are able to receive and digest it. We therefore deem it advisable to place first on the list of books for Libraries such as seem peculiarly adapted to the capacities of children.

24.—*Juvenile Libraries.*

The Rollo Books, fourteen in number; the Lucy Books, six in number; and the Jonas Books, six in number—twenty-six in all—from the fertile pen of the Rev. Jacob Abbot, who knows well how to write for children, are admirably adapted to a Juvenile Library. They are published, in part, at least, by Clark, Austin & Smith, of New York. Their titles are as follows:

Rollo Books.

1. Rollo learning to Talk;
2. Rollo learning to Read;
3. Rollo at Work;
4. Rollo at Play;
5. Rollo at School;
6. Rollo's Vacation;
7. Rollo's Museum;
8. Rollo's Experiments;
9. Rollo's Travels;
10. Rollo's Correspondence;
11. Rollo's Philosophy, Water;
12. Rollo's Philosophy, Air;
13. Rollo's Philosophy, Fire;
14. Rollo's Philosophy, Sky.

Lucy Books.

1. Cousin Lucy's Stories;
2. Lucy's Conversations;
3. Lucy at Study;
4. Lucy at Play;
5. Lucy on the Mountains;
6. Lucy on the Sea Shore.

Jonas Books.

1. Jonas's Stories;
2. Jonas a Judge;
3. Jonas on a Farm, Winter;
4. Jonas on a Farm, Summer;
5. Caleb in Town;
6. Caleb in the Country.

This list might be very greatly extended. We add to it such as we are able, and such as we think will subserve the purpose for which these Libraries are established.

Sedgwick's Poor Rich Man and Rich Poor Man;
The Swiss Family Robinson, 2 vols.;
Natural History of Insects, 2 vols.;
Son of a Genius;
Uncle Philip's American Forest;
Sedgwick's (Miss C. M.) Live and Let Live;
The Twin Brothers--Lessons of Charity;
Embury's (Mrs. C. E.) Pictures of Early Live;

Taylor's (Jane) Pleasures of Taste, and other Stories;
Sedgwick's (Miss C. M.) Means and Ends;
Barbauld's (Mrs.) Things by their Right Names;
Ellet's (Mrs. E. P.) Rambles about the Country;
The Little Commodore—the Travels of a Boy;
Our Cousins in Ohio, by Mary Howitt;
Gabriel; A Story of Wichnor Wood, by Mary Howitt;
Willard's Morals for the Young;
Cowdery's Moral Lessons, for Families and Schools;
Live and Learn: a Thousand Mistakes Corrected;
Day's History of Sandford and Merton;
One Step: to What It Will Lead;
Slim Jack, the Circus Boy;
Robert Dawson;
Jane Hudson;
Who shall be Greatest? by Mary Howitt;
Sedgwick's (Miss) Love Token;
Praise and Principle, by Miss M. J. McIntosh.

While the preceding works are generally more especially adapted to the tastes and capacities of children, so gradual are the developments from juvenile to adult life that many of them will be found equally interesting and instructive to older persons. So, on the other hand, many of the following will be eagerly sought, and profitably perused, by children, as well as by adults. Indeed, there is a large amount of reading that seems equally adapted to persons of all ages; for while the young should become maturer as they advance in age, the old should always cherish and maintain habits of thought that shall render their associations with the young mutually endearing.

25.—*Historical and Geographical.*

Mrs. Sheldon's History of Michigan;
Heroines of History, by Mary Howitt;
Frost's Pictorial Wonders of History;
History of the Bonaparte Family;

McIntosh's Book of Indians;
Millard's Travels in Egypt, Arabia Petræa, and the Holy Land;
Balfern's Glimpses of Jesus;
Life in Israel; or, Portraitures of Human Character;
Peabody's History of the United States;
Willson's Outlines of History, Ancient and Modern;
Willson's American History, Antiquities, etc.;
Ricord's Empire of Rome;
Knighton's Outlines of History;
Hughes' Scripture Geography and History;
Schmitz's Manual of Ancient History;
Schmitz's Manual of Ancient Geography;
Smyth's Lectures on Modern History, by Jared Sparks;
Incidents in American History, by J. W. Bair;
Tschudi's American Antiquities, from the German;
The Ancient Hebrews, by Abram Mills;
Thirty Years' View, by Thomas H. Benton;
Kohlrausch's History of Germany;
Russid: Translated from the French of M. DeCustine;
The Exiles of Florida, by Hon. J. R. Giddings;
Memoirs of Washington, by Mrs. C. M. Kirkland;
The Queens of England, by Francis Lancelott, 2 vols.;
Thatcher's Tales of the American Revolution;
Lockhart's Life of Napoleon Bonaparte. 2 vols.;
Lanman's History of Michigan;
Robertson's History of America;
Ferguson's History of the Roman Republic;
Allison's History of Europe, 4 vols., 8 vo.;
Spark's Writings of Washington, 12 vols., 8 vo.;
" Life and Writings of Washington, 1 vol.;
" Life and Writings of Franklin, 1 vol.;
" Library of American Biography, 10 vols., 12 mo.;
Russell and Jones's Modern Europe;
Murray's Encyclopedia of Geography, 3 vols., 8 mo.;
McCullock's Universal Gazetteer;
Botta's American Revolution, 2 vols., 12 mo.;

DeTocqueville's Democracy in America, 2 vols., 12 mo.;
Goldsmith's Geographical View of the World;
Gibbon's Decline and Fall of the Roman Empire;
Guizot's History of the English Revolution;
Guizot's History of Civilization in Europe;
Hammond's Political History of New York;
Hallam's History of the Middle Ages;
Burnet's Notes on the Northwestern Territory.

26.—*Biography, Travels and Explorations.*

Life of Dr. E. K. Kane, and other Explorers;
Livingstone's Travels and Explorations in South Africa;
Life and Times of Thomas Jefferson;
Life and Times of Alexander Hamilton;
Sarah B. Judson, by Fanny Forester;
Memoir of Dr. Stoddard, Missionary to the Nestorians;
Lyell's Travels in North America;
Dr. Elder's Life of Dr. E. K. Kane;
Dr. E. K. Kane's Arctic Explorations;
American Biographical Series, including Lives of Capt. John Smith, Gen. Israel Putnam, and Benedict Arnold;
Biography and History of North American Indians;
Life of Benjamin Franklin, by O. L. Holley;
Life of Isaac T. Hopper, by Mrs. L. M. Child;
The Progress of Religious Ideas, by Mrs. L. M. Child;
Silliman's Visit to Europe, 2 vols., 12 mo.;
Tschudi's Travels in Peru, from the German;
History of Peter the Great, by Sarah Bradford;
The Americans in Japan, by Commodore Perry;
From New York to Delhi, by Robert C. Minturn;
Country Rambles in England;
Louis Napoleon and his Times, by H. W. DePuy;
Life of Joseph Brant, by W. L. Stone, 2 vols.;
Rambles in Iceland, by Pliny Miles;
Ethan Allen and the Green Mountain Heroes of '76;
Kossuth and his Generals, by H. W. DePuy;

Memoirs of the Life and Writings of Dr. Chalmers;

Works of Rev. W. E. Channing, D. D., 6 vols.;

Illustrated Biography of all Nations, by C. C. Savage;

Lights and Shades of Missionary Life; or Sketches of nine years spent in the Region of Lake Superior, by Rev. J. H. Pitezel;

Bayard Taylor's Travels, seven 12 mo. volumes;

1. Views A-Foot;
2. Eldorado;
3. Lands of the Saracan;
4. Central Africa;
5. India, China and Japan;
6. Northern Travel;
7. Burton's Journey to Mecca and Medina, with an Introduction by Bayard Taylor;

Irving's Life of Washington, 4 vols., 12 mo.;

Paulding's Life of Washington, 2 vols.;

Life of Washington, by M. DeWitt, with an Introduction by M. Guizot;

Isham's Mud Cabin, travels in England;

Irving's Life of Columbus, 3 vols., 12 mo.

27.—*Agricultural and Horticultural Works.*

Norton's Scientific and Practical Agriculture;

Text-book on Agriculture, by Dr. Davis;

The American Farmer's Encyclopedia, a complete Guide for the Cultivation of every variety of Garden and Field Crops, by Gouveneur Emerson, of Penn.;

Moore's Rural Hand Book, Four Series;

The Young Gardener's Assistant, by T. Bridgeman;

Stephens's Book of the Farm, by J. S. Skinner, 2 vols.;

Sheep Husbandry, by Henry S. Randall;

The Flower Garden, by Joseph Breck;

Allen's Treatise on the Culture of the Grape;

Downing's Fruits and Fruit Trees of America;

Downing's Lindley's Horticulture;

Downing's Ladies' Companion to the Flower Garden;

Liebig's Principles of Agricultural Chemistry;

Liebig's Animal Chemistry; [ology;

Liebig's Chemistry, applied to Agriculture and Physi-

Liebig's Letters on Agriculture;
Parsons on the History, Culture, etc., of the Rose;
Johnston's Elements of Ag'l Chemistry and Geology;
Johnston's Lectures on Ag'l Chemistry and Geology;
Johnston's Lectures on Agriculture;
Johnston's Chemistry of Common Life, 2 vols.;
Griffith's Chemistry—Four Seasons;
Dana's Muck Manual;
Nash's Progressive Farmer;
Buist's Am. Flower Garden Directory;
Buist's Family Kitchen Gardener;
Dadd's Modern Horse Doctor—Cattle Doctor;
Dadd's Anatomy and Physiology of the Horse;
Allen's American Farm Book;
Allen's Domestic Animals--The Stable Book;
Guenon's Treatise on Milch Cows;
Youatt and Martin on Cattle;
Barry's Fruit Garden;
Thaer, Shaw and Johnston's Principles of Agriculture;
Elliott's American Fruit Grower's Guide;
Browne's Field Book of Manures;
History of Morgan Horses;
Reemelins's Vine Dresser's Manual;
Sorgho and Imphee, (Sugar Plants;)
Waring's Elements of Agriculture;
Fessenden's Complete Farmer and Rural Economist;
The Cranberry and its Culture, by Eastwood;
The Strawberry and its Culture, by R. G. Pardee;
Bridgeman's Kitchen Gardner's Instructor;
Fruit, Flower, and Vegetable Gardner's Companion;
Chemical Field Lectures, by Dr. J. A. Stockhardt;
Pear Culture, by Thomas W. Field;
History and Management of Ornamental and Domestic Poultry;
The Food of Animals, by Dr. R. D. Thomson;

Farm Implements, their Construction and Use, by J. J. Thomas;

Rural Architecture, comprising Farm Houses, Cottages and Out Buildings, by L. F. Allen;

Boussingault's Rural Economy, by George Law;

Smith's Landscape Gardening, by L. F. Allen;

Hedges and Evergreens, by Dr. J. A. Warder;

Browne's American Poultry Yard;

Munn's Practical Land Drainer;

Farmer's Cyclopedia of Modern Agriculture, by Dr. Blake;

The American Gardner, by William Cobbett;

The Farmer's Land Measurer, by James Pedder;

Schenck's Gardner's Text Book;

The Fruit Cultivator's Manual, by Thomas Bridgeman;

The Florist's Guide, by Thomas Bridgeman;

The Garden: A manual of Horticulture, Fowler & Wells;

The Farm: A Manual of Agriculture, Fowler & Wells;

Domestic Animals: Cattle, Horse, and Sheep Husbandry;

Fox's Text Book of Agriculture.

28.—*Miscellaneous.*

The Green Mountain Boys, a Historical Tale;

The Rangers; or the Tory's Daughter;

May Martin, and other Tales of the Green Mountains;

Recollections of the Table Talk of Samuel Rogers;

Hypatia; or New Foes with an Old Face;

Wells's, and Peterson's Familiar Science;

Youmans' Hand Book of Household Science;

Peace; or the Stolen Will, by May W. Janbrin;

Four Years on the Pacific Coast, by Mrs. Bates;

The Fireman, by D. P. Dana, of the Boston Fire Dep't;

Locke Amsden, or the Schoolmaster;

Mayhew's Means and Ends of Universal Education;

Dr. Dick's Philosophy of a Future State;

" Christian Philosopher;

" Philosophy of Religion;

Dr. Dick's Improvement of Society;
" Moral Improvement of Mankind;
" Essay on Covetousness;
" Celestial Scenery;
" Siderial Heavens;
" Practical Astronomer;
" Solar System, with Reflections;

[These ten volumes are worthy of a place in the Library of every Family and Teacher.]

Washington Irving's Works—Bracebridge Hall, Tales of a Traveller, Sketch Book, and others;

Theodore Irving's History of the Conquest of Florida;

Dred: A Tale of the Dismal Swamp, by Mrs. Stowe;

The Home Cyclopedia: A Library of Reference, including History and Chronology, Literature and the Fine Arts, the Useful Arts, Universal Biography, Geography, Architecture, &c., &c.;

Illustrated Hydropathic Encyclopedia, by Dr. R. T. Trall;

Encyclopedia Americana: A Dictionary of Arts, Sciences, Literature, History, Politics, and Biography, 14 vols.;

New American Cyclopedia: A Popular Dictionary of General Knowledge, by Charles Ripley and Charles A. Dana;

The Age of Fable, by Thomas Bulfinch;

The Constitution of Man, by Dr. George Combe;

Hand Books for Home Improvement, comprising How to Write, How to Talk, How to Behave, and How to Do Business;

Things Not Generally Known: A Hand Book of Facts in Literature, History and Science, by D. A. Wells;

The Reason Why: Many Hundreds of Reasons for things imperfectly understood;

The Family Gymnasium, by R. T. Trall, M. D.;

The Book of Useful Knowledge: 6000 Practical Receipts;

Milledulcia: A Thousand Pleasant Things;

Men and Times of the Revolution, by W. C. Watson;

The Old Farm and the New Farm: A Political Allegory;

True Riches—What Can Woman do?—The Way to Prosper—Ten Nights in a Bar-room, by T. S. Arthur;

The Three Eras of a Woman's Life, by T. S. Arthur;

Buck's Religious and Entertaining Anecdotes;

Spurgeon's Gems, Brilliant Passages from the author;

Ida Norman; or Trials and their Uses, by Mrs. L. Phelps;

Woman's Life and Mission, by Dr. Monod;

Fuller and Wayland on Domestic Slavery;

Wisdom, Wit and Whims of Ancient Philosophers;

Baldwin's Representative Women of Ancient Times;

Gallery of Portraits, by George Gilfillan;

The Young Ladies' Friend, by Mrs. Farrar;

Parlor Dramas, by William B. Fowle;

Æsop's Fables—Baldwin's Book of Fables;

Reminiscences of Coleridge and Southey, by J. Cottle;

The Imitation of Christ, by Thomas A. Kempis;

German Tales of H. Zschokke, by Parke Godwin;

Thiodolf the Icelander, from the German;

Story of a Pocket Bible, illustrated;

Autocracy in Poland and Russia;

Twins and Heart, by Martin F. Tupper;

Knight's Half Hours with the best Authors, 4 vols;

The Age of Chivalry, by Thomas Bulfinch;

Sears's Pictures of Olden Tme;

Ventilation in American Dwellings, by Dr. Reid;

Hooker's Human Physiology;

Dwight's Grecian and Roman Mythology;

Lippincott's Pronouncing Gazetteer of the World;

Colton's Atlas of the World, 2 vols.;

The British Poets, Library Edition, 50 vols.;

Humboldt's Travels and Researches;

Mackenzie's Life of Commodore Oliver H. Perry;

Bryant's Selections from American Poets;

Halleck's Selections from British Poets;

Lives of Distinguished Men of Modern Times;
Dr. Nott's Counsels to Young Men;
Henry Ward Beecher's Lectures to Young Men;
Reveries of a Bachelor, by Ik Marvel;
The Works of Geo. B. Cheever, and of Mrs. Hemans;
Poems of Longfellow, Bryant, Whittier, Willis, Sigourney;
Dana's Two Years before the Mast, or Life at Sea;
Liebold's Manners and Customs of the Japanese;
Brewster's Lives of Galileo, Kepler, and Tycho Brahe;
Lossing's Outline History of the Fine Arts;
Lossing's Pictorial Battle Fields of the Revolution;
Scott's Letters on Demonology and Witchcraft;
Moore's Power of the Soul over the Body;
Everett on Practical Education;
Potter's Science applied to the Domestic Arts;
Bits of Blarney, by Dr. R. Sheldon Mackenzie;
The Poets and Poetry of Ireland, by Dr. R. S. Mackenzie;
The Poets and Poetry of Scotland;
Wit and Wisdom of the Rev. Sydney Smith;
History of Immígration to the United States;
History of Music, by George Hogarth;
Seaman's Progress of Nations;
Works of Hon. William H. Seward, 3 vols., 8 vo.;
Baker's Life of Seward, with Selections from his Writings;
Macauley's Speeches, 2 vols., 12 mo.;
Nature and the Supernatural, by Horace Bushnell, D, D.;
Peasant Life in Germany, by Anna C. Johnson;
China, Its Recollections and Superstitions, by Rev. M. S. Culbertson;
Literary Attractions of the Bible, by L. J. Halsey, D. D.

INDEX.

A.

U.

V.

www.ingramcontent.com/pod-product-compliance
Lightning Source LLC
LaVergne TN
LVHW020927110826
845150LV00004B/790

* 9 7 8 1 4 2 5 5 5 3 4 4 9 *